For my Leeds people

Race, Nation and Cultural Power in Film Adaptation

Race, Nation and Cultural Power in Film Adaptation

Gillian Roberts

EDINBURGH
University Press

Edinburgh University Press is one of the leading university presses in the UK. We publish academic books and journals in our selected subject areas across the humanities and social sciences, combining cutting-edge scholarship with high editorial and production values to produce academic works of lasting importance. For more information visit our website: edinburghuniversitypress.com

Edinburgh University Press Ltd
The Tun – Holyrood Road
12 (2f) Jackson's Entry
Edinburgh EH8 8PJ

Typeset in Monotype Ehrhardt by
Manila Typesetting Company, and
printed and bound in Great Britain

A CIP record for this book is available from the British Library

ISBN 978 1 4744 8353 7 (hardback)
ISBN 978 1 4744 8355 1 (webready PDF)
ISBN 978 1 4744 8356 8 (epub)

Contents

Figures

Acknowledgements

A person who undertakes two MA degrees, back to back, first in English and then in Film Studies, is probably destined to write a book about film adaptation. It took me a while to get here, however, and I am grateful to so many people for their support along the way. First, I'd like to thank my students at the University of Nottingham on the various incarnations of my North American Film Adaptations course over the years, for thinking through many of these ideas with me and for not minding the smuggling in of some Australian content.

Thanks to my Leeds peers from my PhD days, from whom I learned so much (or indeed, everything) about postcolonialism, to whom this book is dedicated. At Nottingham, various colleagues have kept me going on this project, particularly the members of the School of Cultures, Languages and Area Studies' unofficial Sabbatical Club (2017–18), and the Women and Non-Binary Writing Group. Particular thanks to Katherine Shingler for creating the latter. I benefited greatly from visits to other institutions where I was able to share some of this work and receive feedback. Thanks to Catherine Bates, who invited me to speak at the University of Huddersfield, and to Luke Robinson and Sharif Mowlabocus, who hosted me at the University of Sussex. Thanks to Caroline Herbert and John Richardson for reading some chapters of this book in draft form and to postgraduate students and colleagues who read most of Chapter 6 for a work-in-progress session, especially Andy Duncan, Steve Gallo, Charlotte James, Nathaniel Sikand-Youngs and Dan Watson. I am also grateful to Sinéad Moynihan, whose fellowship at the Harry Ransom Center's papers on Brian Moore unexpectedly benefited me in the form of access to the first draft of the *Black Robe* screenplay.

Thanks to the Faculty of Arts at the University of Nottingham, from whom I received a semester of Pro-Vice Chancellor's Leave to extend my sabbatical in 2017–18. I was also the fortunate recipient of a British Academy/Leverhulme Small Grant, which enabled me to conduct archival visits to the University of Guelph and Victoria University Wellington (VUW). Enormous thanks to Kathryn Harvey at Guelph, where I was able to examine the Tomson Highway Script Collection, and to Chrissy Tetley and Sue Hirst at the J. C. Beaglehole Room at VUW where I read through Witi Ihimaera's papers on *Whale Rider*. I am extremely grateful to the following for allowing me to quote from the archival material: Tomson Highway, Witi Ihimaera, Bruce McDonald, and South Pacific Pictures. Sincere thanks to Duke Redbird for permission to include his image from *Dance Me Outside*. Reasonable attempts have been made to contact the copyright holders of Brian Moore's draft screenplay of *Black Robe*.

Many thanks to Edinburgh University Press, especially Richard Strachan, Sam Johnson, and Gillian Leslie, and the anonymous readers of the proposal and the manuscript, whose suggestions enriched this book. The press's patience during the pandemic has been much appreciated.

Some of the material in this book was published in an earlier form. Part of Chapter 3 was published in 'Discrepant Traumas: Colonial Legacies in *Jindabyne*', in *Postcolonial Traumas*, edited by Abigail Ward (Palgrave, 2015), and part of Chapter 4 was published in 'Cross-Border Film Adaptation and *Life of Pi*', in *Reading between the Borderlines: Cultural Production and Consumption across the 49th Parallel*, edited by Gillian Roberts (McGill-Queen's University Press, 2018).

This book took many years to write, but the final stages occurred amid a global pandemic. I have so many friends and colleagues to thank for getting me through the composition of this book, not least the last stretch. Heartfelt thanks to Susan Anderson, Jennifer Andrews, Catherine Bates, Celeste-Marie Bernier, Susan Billingham, Lee Carruthers, Liz Evans, Katy Fair, Zalfa Feghali, Corinne Fowler, Terri Gilbertson, Andy Green, Anna Greenwood-Lee, Kathryn Harton-Roberts, Caroline Herbert, Nasser Hussain, Emilia Iwanczuk, Pete Kirwan, Kaley Kramer, Mike Lee, Stephanie Lewthwaite, Jon McGregor, Georgina Mak, Ruth Maxey, Vivien Miller, Sinéad Moynihan, Catherine Rottenberg, Maria Ryan, Carli Snowball-Hill, David Stirrup, Charles Tepperman, Robin Vandome, Darrelle Villa, Abi Ward, Ruth Watson and Tara Webster-Deakin.

Writing about how culture moves across borders always makes me think of my family, in far-flung time zones, and now more than ever: thank you to my parents, Delia and Jack; and to my brother, Jonathan. Finally, thanks to the home team: much love and gratitude to John, Esther and Arran, the best companions of the pandemic and beyond, who keep me going every day.

Remapping Adaptation:
Race, Nation and Fidelity

After the astonishing, Booker Prize-fuelled success of Michael Ondaatje's novel *The English Patient* (1992), the first Canadian novel ever to win the prestigious award, filmmakers sought to adapt this 'unfilmable' novel. The resulting film (1996), written and directed by the British Anthony Minghella, produced by Hollywood legend Saul Zaentz, met with its own prize-laden destiny, including nine Academy Awards and five BAFTAs. A lesser-known adaptation story of *The English Patient* is that a Canadian consortium, led by Toronto-based Rhombus Media's Niv Fichman, sought the adaptation rights, with Armenian-Canadian director Atom Egoyan at the helm. Certainly, there was no way their bid could compete financially with Minghella and Zaentz, and the rest, as they say, is history.

When I taught *The English Patient* and its film adaptation, just after the American Russell Banks's novel *The Sweet Hereafter* (adapted by Egoyan), I have often asked my students what they would imagine *The English Patient* directed by Egoyan (at that earlier point in his career in the 1990s) would look like. Generalised declarations that have accompanied discussions of Minghella's adaptation in terms of 'what film can do' or 'what we can expect from a film' fall by the wayside at this point: expectations about chronology and mainstream audience sensibilities evaporate. Suggestions arise about greater fragmentation (closer to Ondaatje's novel and – indeed – to Egoyan's earlier filmmaking aesthetics), and greater attention to the character of Kip – Kirpal Singh – the Sikh sapper whose narrative is minimised in Minghella's film, yet around whom the climax of Ondaatje's novel revolves with a resounding rejection of the West and its imperialist legacies. Other possibilities in this imagined adaptation that was never made include Canadian actors playing the Canadian roles of Hana and Caravaggio (Juliette Binoche and Willem Dafoe, respectively, in Minghella's version). There is also, usually, an acknowledgement that, notwithstanding Egoyan's two Oscar nominations for *The Sweet Hereafter*, this imagined version would never have achieved the same meteoric success as Minghella's.

Why begin this book on film adaptation with a film that doesn't exist, especially when an actual film of *The English Patient* was made, to great acclaim (as well as lampooning, as in the notorious *Seinfeld* episode ['The English Patient' 1997])? Much scholarship on film adaptation emphasises – and rightly so – the differences between the literary and cinematic media, partly although not exclusively a factor in the injunction against using 'fidelity' as an overriding measure of evaluation of the film adaptation. Yet film is a much more plastic medium than many scholars give it credit for, and the medium becomes conflated with particular industrial contexts. What seems impossible in films generally is often unfeasible in mainstream films with commercial considerations that pre-empt a running time much longer than two hours (although Minghella's *English Patient*, despite axing the novel's apocalyptic ending of the bombing of Hiroshima and Nagasaki, still runs to two hours and forty-two minutes).

The purpose of this book is not to ignore these industrial contexts. As Simone Murray (2012) argues, film adaptations are inevitably bound up in industrial priorities, limitations and possibilities, and not just the cinematic half of the adaptation: literature, too – even literary fiction – is subject to a host of industrial factors that govern the publishing industry. Publishing, not just cinema, seeks to maximise its audience. Yet there are authors whose work does not circulate internationally, and presses that continue to publish their work. There are filmmakers whose work does not make its way to the Oscar ballot, and never expect or intend it to. The global cultural marketplace does not treat all cultural products equally, and financial returns are just one, but not the only, marker of success. Literature and cinema in the anglophone world, for instance, that is produced outside the UK/US-dominant axis, may find its way to internationally recognised arbiters of taste such as the Academy Awards or the Booker Prize. Equally, literature and cinema produced elsewhere may not even be published or released beyond the borders of the nation-state where it originates, and still be a cultural and/or financial success 'at home', as it were. Moreover, a text's meaning and resonance 'at home' may alter significantly as it circulates within and is consumed via the global cultural marketplace. Take, for instance, Witi Ihimaera's novel *The Whale Rider* (1987), which most global audiences of Niki Caro's adaptation *Whale Rider* (2002) would never have heard of prior to the film, and who would likely have seen the film without knowing the origins of this international cinematic success.

To study adaptation, however, is precisely to study the relationship between the source text and its incarnation in another medium. The changes are not irrelevant: they are – literally – the adaptation. Deborah Cartmell and Imelda Whelehan acknowledge as much when they 'wonder whether focusing on the "films themselves" is possible or desirable when studying the process of adaptation' (2010, 12). Some changes are greater surprises than others for audiences already familiar with the source text. Some audiences experience the source text after they have seen the adaptation, inverting what 'original' means in their experiences as a viewer and reader. Different audiences have different investments in these changes, depending on their relationship to the culture represented in each version, who is doing the representing, and how.

Audiences come to adaptations through a variety of routes: whether they are already invested in the source text; they've read a review; they've had a word-of-mouth recommendation; they've watched an awards ceremony and the films are still playing or about to play in a local cinema or – increasingly – via a streaming service to which they subscribe. Many, although not all, of the adaptations I write about in this book I first saw in what might loosely be grouped as 'art-house' cinemas. Although these cinemas had – and still have – varying degrees of accommodation of more mainstream fare, on the whole they corroborate Barbara Wilinsky's description of art-house cinemas as 'most often small theaters in urban areas or university towns that scree[n] "offbeat" films such as independent Hollywood, foreign language, and documentary films' (2001, 1): in Canada, at the student-run cinema at my alma mater; a downtown 'art-house' cinema while I was an MA student; in the UK as a PhD student and academic at independent cinemas – in different cities – that belonged to the Europa Cinemas network (prompting an audible lament from the audience immediately after the Brexit referendum). As Murray observes, it is unsurprising that film adaptations, especially of literary fiction, find their way to such cinemas, given that the authors and filmmakers involved in such projects are often 'at some remove from the heart of commercial book publishing and from the Hollywood studio system respectively, . . . [thus] collaboratively broker[ing] an insider–outsider aura' (2012, 160). Each of these cinematic spaces has framed my initial encounter(s) with many of these film adaptations, as has my own position as a white settler Canadian (raised on unceded Algonquin and W̱SÁNEĆ territories). I have now lived at the heart of the former empire, so to speak, for the last two decades, and my consumption of texts from 'home' often features a complicated geographical negotiation, and sometimes indignation at, say, the way a Canadian cultural product is assessed in a British newspaper.

Within the global cultural marketplace, not all cultures circulate, thrive or are celebrated equally. The success of Ondaatje's *English Patient* in 1992

was enormously meaningful for Canadian literature as a moment of accruing cultural power; yet this power would be tempered by descriptions of
Ondaatje outside Canada as a 'Sri Lankan', privileging one half of his
Sri Lankan-Canadian identity, and further tempered still by the adaptation of his Booker-winning novel outside Canada, leading one prominent
Canadian film critic to lament, 'Why can't Canada make its own hit movies?' (B. Johnson 1997). Moreover, the accruing of cultural power through
the Booker Prize reinscribes the UK as the arbiter of taste, to which
Canadian culture (among others) becomes subject (even though many celebrated Canadian texts are never published in the UK). What does it mean
for *The English Patient* to become part of a 'contemporary canon' (Corse
1997, 101) forged by a British literary prize? And what role does the canon
play in contemporary film adaptation?

Several of this book's case studies on adaptations feature canonical
nineteenth-century fiction, which, given that it 'lends itself to cinematic
reworking' (Cartmell 2000, 1), has provided filmmakers with source material for most of cinema's history. The canon confers both cultural and
the possibility of economic value to film adaptation. As Mark Thornton
Burnett writes of late-twentieth- and twenty-first-century adaptations of
Shakespeare, the resurgence of cinematic interest indicates the Renaissance
playwright's position 'as a market asset in the global economy, not least
because his name is associated with forms of value' (2007, 3). Indeed, as
Kamilla Elliott observes of cinematic history, 'British Victorian novels and
novelists have been more frequently adapted to film than any other body
of literature, including Shakespeare (and Shakespeare is the only author
from his period to be so frequently adapted)' (2003, 3). With its primary
focus on adaptations of prose texts, this book does not examine adaptations
of Shakespeare's plays, which are intended to be performed, and therefore
renewed, with each production, whether in the theatre or the cinema, thus
distinguishing them from the nature of adapting prose fiction. But the
canonical power of Shakespeare in terms of both cultural and financial
capital in film adaptation is nonetheless instructive for the other canonical
texts included in this study.

The adaptations of William Makepeace Thackeray's *Vanity Fair*, Jane
Austen's *Mansfield Park* and *Pride and Prejudice*, Emily Brontë's *Wuthering
Heights*, and Henry James's *Portrait of a Lady* examined in this book are
not the first adaptations of these texts, a clear demonstration of the multiple choices that can and have been made in film adaptation as well as the
difference that temporal and industrial contexts make to adaptive deci-
sion-making (for instance, the difference that Hollywood's Production
Code made, or the impact of Bollywood conventions). Focusing on

adaptations mostly produced between the 1990s and 2010s, this book attends to issues of gender, colonialism and gazing back to the empire in its treatment of adaptations of nineteenth-century fiction. Yet these adaptations co-exist alongside adaptations of more contemporary literature emerging from postcolonial and contemporary settler-colonial sites that supplement, in some cases, and counter, in others, the nineteenth-century canon's representation of Indigenous peoples. None of these representations are neutral, in either their literary or their cinematic versions. They are all shot through with implications for cultural power, and demand that we attend to issues of cultural property within the global cultural marketplace.

With such stakes, deciding whether a film is 'faithful' to its source text is far more complicated than the field generally acknowledges. It is not simply a question of the possibilities and limitations of the literary and cinematic media, although these factors should always be considered and embedded in the analysis of adaptation. This book argues, however, that the industrial constraints and preferences that shape cultural production should be examined simultaneously with the texts themselves to assess the work these adaptations do, not only because 'writers and filmmakers can subvert the structure [of the industry] and imbue the adaptation with their own political perspectives' (Hollyfield 2018, 8), but also because, whether politically subversive or not, they circulate culturally specific narratives across the global cultural marketplace.

For the terminology that has long contributed to adaptation studies is loaded in relation to cultural, economic and political power. George Bluestone, who produced the first monograph on film adaptation, *Novels into Film* (1957), describes the source text as 'raw material' (Bluestone 2003, vii). In the context of colonial, postcolonial and settler-colonial narratives, and the parameters of production from which they emerge, 'raw material' is not simply a starting point; indeed, Bluestone even describes fiction to be adapted as 'the ore to be mined by story departments' (2003, 2). From the beginnings of European empires to the present day in Indigenous territories claimed by settler-colonial nation-states, resource extraction fuels – pun intended – the expansion of empire and the rise and consolidation of the nation-state. Cultural property embedded in non-Western epistemology that becomes translated for wider consumption in the global cultural marketplace can be viewed as resource extraction, an absorption of such epistemologies into a Western sign system and worldview. This is not to suggest that adaptations must be as close as possible to their source text, but rather to acknowledge the expropriation of cultural power that resides within some adaptations. Neither is the literary exempt from such

considerations: books, too, draw on raw material in acts that may constitute expropriation and/or appropriation.

This book is interested in the stories that film adaptations tell about
race and nation across the global cultural marketplace, about the contexts in which they are made, and the position of their makers. It does
not posit a singular model of postcolonial, settler-colonial or Indigenous
film adaptation. It draws on nineteenth-century narratives that address
racial and cultural difference and those that hardly articulate those differences, with those textual whispers amplified in late twentieth- and early
twenty-first-century film adaptations. It examines later literary texts that
specifically engage questions of race and nation and their adaptations as
well as texts that do not, only to be transplanted to tell the story of another
place. It investigates literary texts by settler authors attempting to represent Indigenous people and their film adaptations by settler filmmakers. It
attends to literary texts by Indigenous writers and their film adaptations by
settler filmmakers. And it focuses on Indigenous-authored narratives and
their film adaptations by Indigenous filmmakers. Whether or not, and to
what extent, a film is 'faithful' to or challenges its source is not a question
that can be divorced from the authorship of each and the questions of cultural property and cultural power. If, as Robert Stam notes, 'the colonialist
and misogynistic premises of [some] source novel[s] turn "infidelity" into a
kind of political obligation' (2005, 77), what are the obligations of adapting
postcolonial and Indigenous narratives? Notwithstanding Julie Sanders's
argument that 'it is usually at the very point of infidelity that the most
creative acts of adaptation . . . take place' (2006, 20), we must ask: whose
story is this to tell, and to tell again in a different medium? To whom, and
for whom, do they seek to tell it? Who is represented, by whom and to
what effect? How can adaptations intervene in material forged through an
imperial worldview? Can adaptations avoid perpetuating that worldview in
translating the original narrative?

One of the strategies adaptation studies has developed as a workaround
to sidestep questions of fidelity has been the devising of different categories of adaptation (often tripartite 'comparable classification systems'
[McFarlane 1996, 11]): for instance, Geoffrey Wagner's 'analogy', 'commentary', and 'transposition' (1975, 226, 223, 222); Michael Klein's distinctions between 'regard[ing] the source merely as raw material, as simply
the occasion for an original work', 'having a particular perspective on a
literary source, reinterpret[ing] it in order to make a new and significant
statement, one that often in some way relates to the contemporary world',
and adaptations that 'give the impression of being faithful, that is, literal,
translations of the text into the language of film' (1981, 10, 9); and Dudley

Andrew's quasi-equivalents of 'borrowing, intersection, and fidelity of transformation' (1984, 98). While such categories usefully illustrate a wide range of adaptation, they not only 'privileg[e] the notion of "closeness to origin" as the key business of adaptation studies' (Cartmell and Whelehan 2010, 6), but they can also tend to privilege the intention of the director as a means of explicating or justifying the adaptation. Constructive though the acknowledgement of the conception of an adaptation project may be, the insertion of a particular adaptation into one of these categories is insufficient to address the many valences of an adaptation and risks oversimplifying the work that an adaptation (conscious or not on the part of the filmmaker) does. Granted, adaptations that radically resituate the source text geographically and/or temporally can be accounted for by some of these categorisations, but again, the acknowledged and/or intended proximity of the adaptation to the source text does not fully account for the nature of an adaptation. Other scholars have supplemented these tripartite systems of classification, as in Kamilla Elliott's 'unofficial concepts of adaptation' – 'psychic', 'ventriloquist', 'genetic', 'de(re)composing', 'incarnational', and 'trumping' – that she declares 'heretical ways [of] splitting form from content' (2003, 134, 136–81, 4), with *Wuthering Heights* as a case study through its various film adaptations. Here, too, although Elliott invokes critical responses and filmmakers' statements as part of these 'heresies', the proximity between source and adaptation persists.

Adaptation studies abounds in forceful rejection of fidelity criticism, that mode of evaluating a film adaptation on the grounds of its proximity to its source text; indeed, 'fidelity has *always* been robustly challenged in adaptation studies' (Elliott 2013, 24).[1] To name just a few examples of what J. D. Connor calls 'the fidelity reflex' (2007, para. 5), fidelity constitutes 'the most tiresome discussion of adaptation' (1984, 100) for Dudley Andrew; in 'grea[t] need of . . . devaluation' (1996, 8) for Brian McFarlane; and an 'inadequate trope' (2005, 4) for Robert Stam. In her framework for materialising adaptation studies, Murray states that the field's rehearsals of disavowals of fidelity criticism, ongoing for several decades, overstate the issue, arguing that 'few academic critics make any claim for fidelity criticism at all' (2012, 8); yet Nico Dicecco observes that adaptation scholars are most likely to 'deride fidelity as a flawed critical paradigm, or a formal impossibility, while nonetheless maintaining fidelity as an unstated conceptual premise', belying 'the fetishistic disavowal of fidelity' (2015, 165). Moreover, if adaptation scholarship has countered fidelity criticism with intertextuality – as seen in Orr (1984, 72), McFarlane (1996, 10), Stam (2005, 4) and Hutcheon (2013, 21), for instance – Casie Hermansson advocates a 'recuperative view of fidelity . . . which endorse[s] a pluralistic, intertextual vision of adaptation's critical strategies' (2015, 147). Other attempts to recuperate fidelity include Jerod Ra'Del Hollyfield's notion of 'interfidelity', devised for his study of postcolonial adaptations of Victorian literature emerging from Hollywood, that can accommodate industrial concerns as well as 'textual difference, politicised omissions and inclusive rewriting' (2018, 8). In examining film adaptation's relationships to race and nation in the global cultural marketplace, my readings of texts and the industrial contexts from which they emerge are ideological, engaging with what Dicecco refers to as 'the politics of fidelity' and 'the ideological stakes of representation' (2015, 170, 173). Changes between source text and film may make the narrative more, less or differently anticolonial, depending on the adaptation; the 'fidelity' itself is not the point. Less 'faithful' adaptations can produce important critiques of the source text; depending on the source text, they can also introduce devastating distortions, and everything in between these two poles. As Amy S. Fatzinger notes, adapting Indigenous works in particular raises ethical considerations in what often plays out as a tension between 'universal as well as more culturally specific themes' (2016, 309), usually to the detriment of the latter.

It would be a gross overstatement, particularly for me as a settler scholar, to claim to embark on 'decolonising' adaptation studies, given that decolonisation 'is not a metaphor' and using it as such 'domesticates decolonization', that is, the work of 'repatriation of land simultaneous to the recognition of how land and relations to land have always already been differently understood and enacted' (Tuck and Yang 2012, 3, 7). Following Laura De Vos's lead, I suggest we need an 'un-settling' approach to adaptation studies as a means of confronting 'directly . . . settler colonial modes of thought' (2020, 4, n7), for we need to think differently and more carefully about 'fidelity' in relation to Indigenous storytelling and adaptation than we do about critical adaptations of texts from the Western canon, because different epistemologies are at work. Examining the ideological – and epistemological – work that happens in a film adaptation necessitates an examination of textual difference as well as the industrial factors of its production and dissemination across the global cultural marketplace.

In addressing race and nation in film adaptation, I include adaptations where the literary and/or cinematic text emerges from a post- or settler-colonial nation, or where the film adaptation offers a postcolonial, settler-colonial and/or diasporic rereading of the source text. The scope of the book is broadly comparative in its inclusion of literary and cinematic materials from Aotearoa New Zealand, Australian, Canadian, Indian, British and US cultures; however, we must attend to the distinct historical and political distinctions between these cultures and their relationships to postcolonialism, settler-colonialism, Indigeneity and diaspora. For instance, India's 'post-colonized' culture differs markedly from the 'post-colonizing' (During 1985, 371) cultures of Australia, Canada and New Zealand, settler-colonial countries – forged in and continuing to operate through 'a structure of domination that is partly predicated on the ongoing dispossession of Indigenous peoples' lands and the forms of political authority and jurisdiction that govern [their] relationship to these lands' (Coulthard and Simpson 2016, 51) – that also differ from each other in their relationships to Indigeneity, multiculturalism and the metropolitan centres of Britain and the United States. The United States itself is also a settler-colonial, but more powerful, nation-state with a prominent 'neo-colonialist role in establishing a global capitalist economy' (Ashcroft et al. 1998, 163). The UK's and United States' film production industries and their locations within postcolonial diasporas make them important to this study. In focusing on the nations indicated above, the book primarily examines feature films circulating, for the most part, in the global anglophone market.

While acknowledging the national cinemas that many of these films ostensibly 'belong' to, transnational production also features heavily in these case studies. As Hamid Naficy writes, however, 'Within every transnational culture beats the hearts of multiple displaced but situated cultures interacting with one another' (2001, 6); indeed, Will Higbee and Song Hwee Lim point out that 'the national continues to exert the force of its presence even within transnational film-making practices' (2010, 10). This is not to minimise the significance of transnational production, but rather to trace the interrelationships between the national and the transnational. Following Higbee and Lim, we must forge a 'critical transnationalism' that will not 'obscure the question of imbalances of power (political, economic and ideological) in this transnational exchange, most notably by ignoring the issue of migration and diaspora and the politics of difference that emerge within such transnational flows' (2010, 10, 9), but will, rather, amplify them. Where Naficy's notion of accented cinema centres exilic and diasporic filmmakers in 'interstitial' spaces outside the mainstream (2001, 4),[2] this book focuses mostly on cultural production that fits more comfortably within the mainstream, partly due to, as Higbee and Lim note, 'the recent mainstreaming of diasporic or postcolonial filmmakers' (2010, 13), among whom they include Gurinder Chadha. Naficy's later conceptualisation of 'multiplexing' as the 'mainstream kin' (2010: 14) of accented cinema accommodates the larger scale of diasporic filmmakers such as Ang Lee, who, as Lim observes, does not fit into Naficy's original concept of accented cinema given the trajectory of his career leading to 'full citizenship in mainstream filmmaking' (2012, 140). In the works under discussion by diasporic filmmakers such as Chadha, Lee, Nair and Mehta, the 'home' and 'host' cultures are not always or equally visible on screen; and in the context of adaptation, some of these directors adapt works by authors with very different national homes.

Whereas diasporic filmmaking entails displacement, whether or not it is apparent on screen, Indigenous filmmaking offers very different relationships to place, whether that lies explicitly within the context of settler-colonial encroachment, as in Lee Tamahori's *Once Were Warriors*, or an attempt to (re)tell a Traditional Story that precedes the advent of settler-colonialism, as in Zacharias Kunuk's *Atanarjuat: The Fast Runner*. While such productions may be claimed by national cinemas, this claiming of cultural power by the nation-state is at odds with the Indigenous narratives presented, given that, as Māori filmmaker Barry Barclay asserts, 'Indigenous cultures "are outside the national outlook by definition"' (qtd in Murray 2008, 16). Barclay's conceptualisation of Fourth Cinema articulates the ways in which Indigenous filmmaking in this mode diverges sharply from a national cinema that aspires to mainstream attention and works within dominant Western convention and aesthetics. And yet as the contrast between *Once Were Warriors* and *Atanarjuat* will demonstrate, not all Indigenous films sit comfortably within the aims, orientation and aesthetics of Fourth Cinema.

In tracing the phenomenon of film adaptation in postcolonial, settler-colonial and Indigenous contexts in a variety of national locations and a range of transnational relations, this study espouses the notion of 'polycentrism' devised by Ella Shohat and Robert Stam, for '[w]ithin a polycentric vision, the world has many dynamic cultural locations, many possible vantage points' (1994, 48). But where Shohat and Stam's polycentrism focuses 'not on spatial or primary points of origin but on fields of power, energy, and struggle' (1994, 48), *Race, Nation and Cultural Power in Film Adaptation* addresses the spatial alongside those fields. Although some scholars interpret polycentrism to mean that 'everything can be put on the world cinema map on an equal footing, even Hollywood, which instead of a threat becomes a cinema among others' (Nagib 2011, 1), we must distinguish between an individual study's mapping and the asymmetric relations of economic and cultural power that persist beyond the pages of scholarly analysis. To posit equal footing where it does not exist ignores the fact that, in the words of Burnett in *Shakespeare and World Cinema*, 'For the time being, at least, we are in the territory of the not now, not yet', hence his insistence on attending to cinema beyond Hollywood as 'a political obligation' (2012, 3). This is not to oversimplify Hollywood – in its mode of deterritorialised production – as monolithic, but rather to acknowledge that despite the shifts in the spatial locations of Hollywood production, filmmaking in the mainstream Hollywood mode remains dominant. Given that, as Dina Iordanova, David Martin-Jones, and Belén Vidal assert, 'Even in our present age of advanced communications, important alternative efforts can easily remain obscure, due to an absence of international exposure and distribution' (2010, 2), it would be a mistake to overstate a levelling of the playing field in the global cultural marketplace.

Race, Nation and Cultural Power in Film Adaptation examines a range of film industries that have adapted pre-existing narratives: while Hollywood production (very much of the deterritorialised variety) is represented by Ang Lee's *Life of Pi*, national cinemas of Aotearoa New Zealand, Australia, Canada and the UK outnumber Hollywood in this book's case studies. If, as Naficy argues, diasporic films also inform the national cinema of the 'home' nation (2001, 71), Indian cinema is also present through diasporic filmmakers Chadha, Mehta and Nair, although it is essential to acknowledge the transnational relationship configuring production and representation. These films emerging from – or, in the case of Indigenous film, claimed by – national cinemas have received financial support in the form of state funds, implying the nation-state's desire to produce national culture where the market alone cannot be relied upon to generate it. But in some cases, more than one state is involved: the co-production model has generated some of these film adaptations, with films resulting from co-productions between Canada and Australia (*Black Robe*), Canada and the UK (*Midnight's Children*), and Aotearoa New Zealand and Germany (*Whale Rider*). The co-productions have varying degrees of traces of their financial provenance, as the chapters on these adaptations address; but even the Hollywood example of *Life of Pi* renders partly visible the impact of state subsidies that have been harnessed for budgetary considerations.

Thus, this book focuses on no single production model. Rather, it examines a range of models, from a range of locations, in order to assess how race, nation and cultural power circulate via film adaptation within and across the global cultural marketplace. As acknowledged above, adaptation studies has often attempted to forge a taxonomy of adaptation grounded in the degree of proximity between source and adaptation, one that privileges creative intent. In the context of postcolonial film adaptation specifically, Sandra Ponzanesi has produced a list of five categories: 'adaptation of empire or colonial novels with a critical edge'; adaptation of classics with a view to correcting, compensating and including the feminist postcolonial lens'; 'postcolonial [texts] transposed into films by the Western cultural industry'; 'postcolonial novels adapted by postcolonial filmmakers'; and 'Bollywood remakes of Hollywood films' (2014, 125–9). This book examines some adaptations that ostensibly fall into Ponzanesi's categories but offers some different conceptualisations of post- and settler-colonial adaptation.

In addition to including some post- and settler-colonial adaptations of texts that do not overtly thematise race and race relations in the original version, *Race, Nation and Cultural Power in Film Adaptation* also identifies and explores some recurring preoccupations in post- and settler-colonial film adaptation. Moving from adaptations of canonical texts to contemporary settler-colonial and diasporic texts to Indigenous narratives, this book's examination of postcolonial and settler-colonial film adaptation will focus on seven key areas: (1) post- and settler-colonial feminist inflections, where the film adaptation foregrounds a postcolonial or settler-colonial positioning in its framing or selection of elements from the literary text at the same time as it produces a feminist critique of Western canonical fiction; (2) salvaging slavery subtexts, where the adaptation enhances the canonical literary text's subtle invocations of slavery; (3) relocating racism, where the national setting changes from source text to film, enabling an interrogation of race relations and cultural hierarchies; (4) magic realism, where the literary text's blurring of realism and fantasy presents opportunities and challenges for visual representation; (5) cultural appropriation, where Indigenous peoples' cultures are represented by settler-colonial culture; (6) told-to adaptations, where non-Indigenous filmmakers have adapted the literary work of Indigenous writers; and (7) Indigenous self-representation and self-determination, where Indigenous peoples represent their own cultures, producing the original text and its adaptation. Each chapter focuses on either two or three adaptation case studies, thereby enabling a depth of analysis for each case study while retaining a comparative approach.

In examining these modes of adaptation, I explore the implications of 'fidelity' for different adaptations, given the primacy of issues such as race, nation and identity in these texts, asking what kinds of 'infidelity' can be afforded by differently located texts and cultures, especially postcolonial and Indigenous cultures? In the case of films with geographically disparate production and post-production locations within the 'New International Division of Cultural Labour' (Miller et al. 2005: 111), how do such industrial sites interact with diverging formations of postcolonialism, settler-colonialism and Indigeneity? And how does film's circulation in the global cultural marketplace affect interrogations of race, nation and culture in postcolonial film adaptation? My analyses of adaptation case

studies examine the extent to which local and national cultural specificities are translated, disseminated, celebrated or erased. Throughout, I
seek to forge a model of critical adaptation studies that addresses these
questions through close analysis of the literary texts and their film adaptations alongside consideration of the films' production histories, including
(trans)national production contexts and funding structures.

Chapter 1 discusses the effects that foregrounding a settler-colonial or
postcolonial positioning in the framing or selection of elements from the
literary source has on the adaptation of canonical literary texts. It engages
with the transnationalism of filmmaking at the same time as it addresses the
specificities of national film industries and the national and cultural contexts in which individual filmmakers operate. Focusing on Australia-based
New Zealander Jane Campion's 1996 adaptation of Henry James's *Portrait
of a Lady* and Indo-American director Mira Nair's 2004 adaptation of
William Makepeace Thackeray's *Vanity Fair*, the chapter argues that these
films constitute settler- and postcolonial and feminist refractions of these
American and British male-authored canonical novels. While both films
interrogate the figure of the white male collector, they unevenly address
their source texts' representations of race, with Campion privileging white
characters' European experiences and Nair seeking to represent India but
in a manner that aligns with Orientalism. In different ways, however, in
grappling with these canonical novels, Campion's and Nair's films intervene in prevailing representations of the nineteenth century.

Chapter 2 examines Canadian director Patricia Rozema's 1999 adaptation of Jane Austen's *Mansfield Park* and British director Andrea Arnold's
2011 adaptation of *Wuthering Heights*, highlighting the ways in which the
adaptations extrapolate from the suggestions of slavery in the novels in
order to foreground it within the cinematic narrative. Linda Hutcheon
argues that adaptations 'ha[ve] been called both appropriation and salvaging' (2013, 8). Although hostile reviewers suggested these films appropriated their source material, this chapter argues that these films represent
acts of salvage through foregrounding slavery as an essential context,
allowing narratives suggested or buried within the novels to rise to the surface. Problematic associations of white women and enslaved people surface
particularly in the films, requiring scrutiny. The chapter also reads the two
adaptations in relation to hospitality, given the class-inflected and racialised relations within the narratives of accepting 'strangers' into the family
homes whose names double as the novels' and films' titles. Further, the
chapter analyses the films not only in relation to the nineteenth-century
contexts in which the original novels were produced but also in the context
of their moments of cinematic production: namely *Mansfield Park*'s use of

Kirby Hall in Northamptonshire to represent Mansfield Park, implicitly drawing attention to the slavery-based wealth of English country houses; and *Wuthering Heights*'s semiotic invocation of white supremacist political movements in Britain in general and Yorkshire in particular.

Chapter 3 analyses *Bride and Prejudice* (2004), British director Gurinder Chadha's adaptation of Jane Austen's *Pride and Prejudice*, and *Jindabyne* (2006), Australian director Ray Lawrence's adaptation of American author Raymond Carver's short story 'So Much Water So Close to Home' (1988). Both adaptations radically resituate their source material through significant geographical shifts that facilitate an exploration of race relations not found in the original: Chadha's film relocates Austen's English narrative to India, with additional locations in London and Los Angeles; Lawrence's film migrates from the American Pacific Northwest location of Carver's story to New South Wales. Further, *Bride and Prejudice* provides a temporal shift by updating the events to the present day. Transnational production features prominently in both films, through the intersection of Indian, British and Hollywood industries and sensibilities in *Bride and Prejudice* and the international casting of *Jindabyne*, with major implications for the ideological positions of the films. *Bride and Prejudice*'s temporal and geographical relocation and the introduction of racial difference reconfigures 'prejudice' by adding racism and ethnocentrism to the class bias probed by Austen. The film critiques the gap in wealth between India and the West while working to close the aesthetic gap by blending Bollywood and Western cinematic conventions, recalibrating on screen the power discrepancy between India and the imperial and neo-imperial nations of Britain and the US. *Jindabyne*'s updating and relocation of Carver shifts the fallout of a fishing trip amongst four men who discover the dead body of a woman on the first day of their holiday, declining to report it to the police until the end of their trip, to an Australian context in which the dead woman is Indigenous, with racialised implications for the community: one white woman, married to one of the fishermen, attempts to atone in a Sorry Day allegory. That Irish and US stars – retaining their accents and nationalities in the film – play the central couple implicitly restages narratives of settler-colonisation in the midst of the community's crisis. Both films include different translator figures or guides to explain or bridge transcultural gaps, with varying degrees of success.

Chapter 4 examines the working of magic realism in Indo-Canadian director Deepa Mehta's adaptation of Salman Rushdie's *Midnight's Children* (2012) and Taiwanese-American director Ang Lee's adaptation of Yann Martel's *Life of Pi* (2012), both transnational adaptations. Both novels are Booker Prize winners, both have narratives that respond, in varying ways, to the Emergency in India in the 1970s, and both deploy magic realism. If the visualisation of narrative lies at the crux of adapting literature into cinema, these two films raise questions about visibility and veracity in the context of adapting magic realism for the screen. The chapter discusses the elements from the novels that have and have not been visually presented, and the implications of what the audience is made to see. Whereas Meta's film downplays the visual possibilities of the narrative's magic realism, *Life of Pi* largely depends on the opulence of its visuals, but in such a way that suggests a considerable reconfiguration of the narrative. Further, although the radically different production contexts of Canadian cinema and Hollywood impact upon the resources and visual effects offered by these films, questions of transnational production and post-production complicate these films' insertions into national cinemas. For *Midnight's Children*, border crossings feature both in the narrative and in the cinematic production, with this film located within the Indian diaspora (a Canadian adaptation of a British Indian novel) mostly having been filmed in Sri Lanka. *Life of Pi*'s relationship to Hollywood is complicated by its multiple international locations of production and post-production, including its Québécois funding, which has implications for the narrative's present setting and its representation of French language and culture.

Chapter 5 turns to the representation of Indigeneity in cinema, focusing on literary and cinematic texts in which Indigenous peoples have been appropriated by non-Indigenous authors and filmmakers, namely *The Chant of Jimmie Blacksmith* (1978), written by Australian author Thomas Keneally and adapted by Australian director Fred Schepisi; *Black Robe* (1991), written by Northern Irish-Canadian author Brian Moore and adapted by Australian director Bruce Beresford; and *Dance Me Outside* (1994), stories written by Canadian author W. P. Kinsella and adapted by Canadian director Bruce McDonald. The chapter probes the ways in which settler-colonial culture borrows from Indigenous cultures. All of these literary and cinematic texts were produced either prior to or in the midst of debates surrounding the legitimacy of non-Indigenous representations of Indigenous culture in the late 1980s and early 1990s. Fred Schepisi's film adaptation of Thomas Keneally's novel *The Chant of Jimmie Blacksmith* (1972) contains embedded layers of adaptation, given that Keneally based his novel on the historical figure of Jimmy Governor, a mixed-race man who, along with his brother, murdered several white people in early-twentieth-century Australia. The timing of the narrative events coinciding with Australian federation and key developments in the Australian state's relationship to Indigenous peoples in the 1960s and 1970s prior to the publication of the novel and production of the film render this narrative particularly charged in its implications for representing Indigeneity in Australia, especially from a settler perspective. *Black Robe* is also a multiple adaptation insofar as Moore drew on the historical sources of Jesuit writings in New France in the composition of his novel, both appealing to authenticity using historical documents and drawing on a specifically colonial archive, detracting from the novel's occasional attempts to represent Indigenous perspectives. The film's release the year following the so-called 'Oka Crisis' exacerbates the film's neocolonial implications, particularly given the film's construction of the Iroquois. *Dance Me Outside* (1977) was the first of four short story collections published between the late 1970s and late 1980s by the white Canadian W. P. Kinsella about characters living on a Cree reserve, work that presented Indigenous people as unintelligent via its Cree narrator. This chapter examines unused screenplays by the Cree playwright Tomson Highway to illustrate how *Dance Me Outside* may have been adapted differently from an Indigenous perspective; it further examines additional adaptations of *Dance Me Outside*, namely Nick Craine's graphic novel version of the screenplay ultimately used to shoot the film (1994) and CBC television's *The Rez* (1995–7).

Chapter 6 conceptualises the 'told-to adaptation', in which literature written by Indigenous authors is adapted by non-Indigenous filmmakers, as in *Rabbit-Proof Fence* (2002), adapted by Australian director Phillip Noyce from Mardudjara writer Doris Pilkington/Nugi Garimara's memoir of her mother's story, *Follow the Rabbit-Proof Fence*; *Whale Rider* (2002), adapted by Pākehā director Niki Caro from the Māori writer Witi Ihimaera's novel *The Whale Rider*; and *The Lesser Blessed* (2012), adapted by Ukrainian-Canadian director Anita Doron from the novel by Tłįchǫ (Dogrib)[3] author Richard Van Camp. If 'told-to' texts are typically Indigenous authors' narratives that are collected or edited by non-Indigenous people (see McCall 2011), such adaptations can be termed 'told-to adaptations'. *Rabbit-Proof Fence* is a twice-told-to adaptation, insofar as Doris Pilkington Garimara's *Follow the Rabbit-Proof Fence* is the narrative of her mother, aunt and their cousin's abduction by authorities from their community in Jigalong, Western Australia; they were taken to the Moore River Native Settlement to be trained as domestic workers for white society, from whence they escaped, finding their way home along the rabbit-proof fence, the longest fence in the world. Caro's film constitutes an adaptation of an adaptation, for Ihimaera's *Whale Rider* retells the story of a Māori Traditional Story. Caro has invoked the support of the Ngāti Konohi for her making of the film, acknowledging her accountability to them; at the same time, she has stated (Mottesheard 2003) that her film is a more truthful representation of Māori life than that of *Once Were*

Warriors, directed by the Māori filmmaker Lee Tamahori (see Chapter 7). Not only was most of *Whale Rider*'s crew Pākehā, however, but the film is also a New Zealand–Germany co-production, with implications for the narrative. This chapter also examines unused screenplays by Ihimaera to demonstrate the difference having a Māori screenwriter would have made to the adaptation. *The Lesser Blessed* tells the story of a Dogrib teenager growing up in the Northwest Territories in the aftermath of the traumatic death of his abusive father by fire. But whereas the novel contextualises this violence through the legacy of Canada's Indian Residential Schools, this context is omitted in the film, despite its production during the work by the Truth and Reconciliation Commission of Canada (2008–15).

Finally, Chapter 7 focuses on films adapted by Indigenous filmmakers from Indigenous source material, namely *Once Were Warriors* (Tamahori, 1994), adapted by Māori filmmaker Lee Tamahori from Alan Duff's novel, and *Atanarjuat: The Fast Runner* (Kunuk, 2001), adapted by Inuit filmmaker Zacharias Kunuk for the Inuit production company Isuma from an Inuit Traditional Story. This chapter examines the adaptations' relationships to conceptualisations of Indigenous representational sovereignty (Lewis 2006) and Barry Barclay's notion of Fourth Cinema. Both these internationally successful adaptations are 'the embodiment of an insider's perspective, one that is attuned to cultural subtleties in the process of imagemaking [*sic*] as well as in the final image itself' (Lewis 2006, 180) in the countering of non-Indigenous representations of Indigenous cultures; both films were largely made with crew members from the community. However, there is no monolithic version of Indigenous self-representation and self-determination, as these adaptations demonstrate. *Once Were Warriors* and *Atanarjuat* constitute very different examples of Indigenous self-representation, in their geographically disparate locations, their cultural contexts and their temporal settings. Controversial in both its literary and cinematic incarnations, *Once Were Warriors* focuses on late-twentieth-century urban Māori life. Although the novel and film grapple with the legacy of colonialism as it impacts upon the Heke family, Pākehā presence is minimal in the novel and virtually absent from the film. If *Once Were Warriors* minimises Pākehā presence, *Atanarjuat* eschews non-Indigenous presence completely in its temporal setting centuries prior to colonial contact, focusing on the fallout of homicidal discord within a community. Entirely in Inuktitut and an adaptation of an Inuit Traditional Story, *Atanarjuat* derives from a source 'text' that exists in several different versions, with different resolutions to the community's crisis. Both *Once Were Warriors* and Atanarjuat's adaptations alter the resolution of the narratives they translate for the screen, raising questions about how

audiences, Indigenous and non-Indigenous, are addressed and anticipated. Such alterations complicate questions of fidelity with respect to
Indigenous culture.

Thus, this book's case studies begin with adaptations of nineteenth-
century fiction, products of the British empire, and end with examples of
adaptation from within Indigenous cultures. The power relations wrought
by the empire may be scarcely visible in some of these source texts, but
some adaptations seek to bring them to the surface. If imperial legacies
inflect virtually all of these case studies at the level of narrative, cultural
power also impacts upon, and is negotiated through, the production and
circulation of these adaptations within and across the global cultural marketplace as filmmakers seek to retell these stories for local and international audiences.

CHAPTER 1

The Empire Gazes Back?
The Portrait of a Lady and *Vanity Fair*

Both Jane Campion's *Portrait of a Lady* (1996) and Mira Nair's *Vanity Fair* (2004) adapt canonical, male-authored novels of the nineteenth century in ways that address the power dynamic of the male gaze and that reposition the geographical framing of the source text. As such, they furnish examples of Julie Sanders's claim that infidelity to a source text enables 'the most creative acts of adaptation' (2006, 20) through their feminist lenses, forged away from the imperial metropole. Keeping in mind questions of the 'politics of fidelity' (Dicecco 2015, 170), however, Campion's and Nair's departures in their adaptations facilitate degrees of critique of these canonical narratives. Whereas Campion's film frames its source text self-reflexively as a bookend to the narrative presented by the novel, Nair's film, for its part, lends greater weight to colonised spaces and cultures and their interactions with the imperial centre. Both films also rethink their heroine's fate, diverging to various degrees from the narratives of these women's lives as originally conceived by male novelists. Further, both films position a male collector figure as a predator, the downfall of the films' respective heroines, foregrounding the male gaze as ominous.

Campion and Nair made these films when their careers were already established, with their largest budgets to date (McHugh 2009, 140; Muir 2006, 218), enabling their work with high-profile international stars. As late-twentieth- and early-twenty-first-century films, *The Portrait of a Lady* and *Vanity Fair*'s recreations of nineteenth-century society depart from, disrupt and de-familiarise the heritage genre in both narrative and visual terms. Ultimately, *The Portrait of a Lady*'s greater self-reflexiveness announces more assertively its transfiguring relationship to the original text, privileging a gendered perspective, however, over one that engages meaningfully with race. *Vanity Fair*, in contrast, both supplements the novel where the representation of the non-Western Other is concerned and replicates some of its Orientalist assumptions in its more blurred stance on the nineteenth-century original and its own feminist intervention's reliance on exoticist consumption.

The Portrait of a Lady

Jane Campion's film of Henry James's novel *The Portrait of a Lady* (1880–1; 1908) ostensibly constitutes a departure from her previous films – *Sweetie* (1989), *An Angel at My Table* (1990), and *The Piano* (1992) – insofar as her earlier work was set in Australia and her home country, New Zealand. But in adapting James's novel, Campion does not mask her Australasian positioning. Rather, through casting, significant personnel and the framing of the film, Campion transforms James's narrative of an American expatriate woman in Europe in the 1880s into a late-twentieth-century Australasian story. This adaptation retains key features of the novel, including the representation of the male gaze, the transnational identities of American expatriates, and the figure of the collector; however, the film also underscores the female gaze and female sexuality and, through ruptures in realist representation, offers a brief, ironic commentary on the novel's representation of the non-Western Other. The film does display the limits of the settler-colonial gaze, albeit in a self-conscious way, while extending the novel's critique of heterosexual marriage.

In fact, Campion's *Portrait* does not radically overturn James's narrative, although it excises the first hundred pages of the novel (namely Isabel Archer's backstory in the United States), so that the first we see of Isabel is her response to Lord Warburton's proposal at her aunt Mrs Touchett's house – Gardencourt – in England; conversely, the film's ending is slightly premature in relation to the novel, having come full circle to conclude at Gardencourt as well. Nonetheless, in its plot and dialogue, the film could be considered 'fairly faithful to James's original' (Fox 2011, 145), following Isabel's experiences in England with the Touchetts, her rejection of Warburton and Caspar Goodwood in her pursuit for independence, her doomed friendship with the manipulative Madame Merle, her unexpected inheritance, her travels to Italy and beyond and her unhappy marriage to Gilbert Osmond. Despite these proximities to James's novel, the film introduces formal disruptions to foreground a female, settler-colonial point of view while drawing attention to its own artifice.

Indeed, Campion's adaptation replaces a substantial amount of the beginning of James's novel with an unexpected framing of Isabel Archer's narrative. The film begins with the voices of seven late-twentieth-century Australasian young women musing about romantic love while credits, but no other visuals, appear. The women's comments about kissing, lovers 'being entwined with each other', and the reciprocity of love being likened to 'the clearest mirror, and the most loyal mirror' overlap slightly, with one woman's contribution often beginning before the previous woman finishes speaking. After the final woman speaks, the audio track shifts to haunting flute music by the film's composer, Wojciech Kilar, which accompanies shots of (presumably) the women themselves. The first images appear in black and white, beginning with a bird's eye view of the women lying on the ground and forming an oval shape, surrounding the title, 'a film by Jane Campion'. Most of the women, although not all, appear to be white. Subsequently, the women appear individually or in smaller groups, the first in long shot, dancing while listening to a Discman, a dog by her side. The women are clearly marked through their clothing as late-twentieth-century women, a subversion – along with their Australasian accents – of expectations any viewer might have of an adaptation of James's novel. Significantly, many of the shots of these women show them looking back at the camera, meeting its gaze. Two colour shots of women dancing interrupt the black and white sequence, and the dancing women are doubly exposed, a technique that will reappear later in Isabel Archer's narrative. The black and white shots resume, with the women sitting or standing, until a dissolve to the film's title, written in an antique script on one woman's palm.

At this point, the film cuts to a medium close-up colour shot of Nicole Kidman as Isabel Archer, crying, before zooming in on her eyes in an extreme close-up. Isabel Archer is an American character, in both James's novel and Campion's film. But she is connected to the women we first hear and see through the figure of Kidman and the phenomenon of 'the powerfully, inescapably present, always-already-signifying nature of star images' (Dyer 1998, 129): Kidman's name is the first that appears on screen while the women are talking over the credits, and it is she who takes over the film from the women, as it were, as an Australian woman herself.

Thus, the film announces itself from the outset as a late-twentieth-century, Australasian production, one that focuses on how women are gazed at, and how they return that gaze. Although 'most critics disliked this opening' (Polan 2001, 128), Lizzie Francke characterises the 'tangential opening scene' as 'Campion's own preface' (2001, 82). Kathleen A. McHugh expands this correlation with James's own preface to the 1908 edition of his novel, in which James examines 'the worth of a subject for fiction', arguing that Campion's preface and its explicit engagement with female sexuality announces the film's interest in 'things left pointedly unsaid in James, elements that nevertheless have force in his novel' (2009, 147). Despite the fact that Campion's preface may be 'disorienting' for viewers in its 'geographical as well as a temporal anachronism' (Cooper 2008), I would argue that the preface's framing of the narrative that follows reverses the logic of anachronism. The women's voices (and bodies) with which the film begins are not out of place or out of time, but rather a self-reflexive admission of the position from which Isabel Archer's story is represented. In the film, the abrupt shift is from the late twentieth century to the late nineteenth, not the reverse. At the same time, the fact that the film's first images appear in black and white constitutes 'a cinematic time warp in which the present appears with the distance of the past', as Lawrence Kramer argues (2002, 26); alternatively, however, we might argue that through the preface, the past appears with the proximity of the present. Regardless, the film's framing visualises an interpenetration of temporalities.

If the film's 'opening frames emphasize the film's antipodean perspective' (Walton 1997) that is also a late-twentieth-century perspective, it is essential to recognise that the frame is not left open. Critics such as Kramer and Estella Tincknell (2013) have explored the significance of music in the film, particularly the role that Schubert plays, primarily although not solely in the representation of Madame Merle (Barbara Hershey). Her performance of Schubert at Gardencourt initiates Isabel's ill-fated friendship with her, in which Isabel, via Merle's 'interpellation . . . [is] insert[ed] into a script written by others' (Kramer 2002, 29). But while Schubert, in addition to the diegetic music played by Merle, dominates the non-diegetic music of the film, the final credit sequence reprises Kilar's flute composition that accompanied the preface. Aurally, therefore, Isabel's narrative is not simply introduced by the late-twentieth-century preface but is also, in fact, enveloped by it; the music that bookends the film insists upon its late-twentieth-century temporality, into which Isabel's own story – and associations with Schubert – is inserted. With its international cast (American, Australian, British, Italian), film locations (Britain, Italy), source material (authored by an expatriate American), prominent production personnel (New Zealand-Australian director Campion, British-New Zealand cinematographer Stuart Dryburgh, Australian screenwriter Laura Jones, Polish composer Kilar, Australian costume designer Janet Patterson), and production by the French company Polygram, the film might be considered '[a] multinational production on a number of levels' that 'globalizes the plight of James's quintessential American girl' (Walton 1997). However, the Australasian voices that introduce the film and are invoked again at the end through Kilar's score anchor the adaptation's transnationalism in Australasia.

Campion's *Portrait* is also anchored in a settler-colonial culture that, via James's novel, does not engage with Indigenous peoples in Australasia.[1]

On the one hand, the transnational underpinning of Isabel's narrative as an expatriate American in Europe always already invokes cultural difference. On the other hand, the proximity between American and British culture means that, despite the observations of some (usually American) characters, differences between Britain and its former colony appear minor in the narrative, especially because, as J. Hillis Miller observes, the novel's major characters 'are all, with the exception of Lord Warburton, expatriate Americans' (2005, 63). Given the focus on interactions between characters of the same or similar cultures, then, instances in both James's novel and Campion's film where more stark cultural differences appear are all the more conspicuous.

If James's novel 'couches [its] description of Isabel's primary suitors . . . in the terms of colonialism' (Hollyfield 2018, 61), it also invokes indigeneity[2] to exaggerate cultural difference between its white characters, and to separate the imperial metropole from its former colony. Early in Isabel's acquaintance with Lord Warburton, she attempts to exaggerate their differences (given his aristocratic status), namely by pretending to posit that he aligns her, as an American, with Indigenous people who are, in keeping with stereotypical Western representations of the Indigenous Other, uncivilised:

> 'He thinks I'm a barbarian,' she said, 'and that I've never seen forks and spoons' . . .
> 'It's a pity you can't see me in my war-paint and feathers,' she remarked; 'if I had known how kind you are to the poor savages I would have brought over my native costume!' (James 1984, 123)

Moreover, Warburton himself continues this association of US Americanness with a stereotyped indigeneity, in a conversation with Henrietta Stackpole, Isabel's friend from the United States and the novel's character most fond of contrasts between the United States and Britain. Inquiring about the aristocracy, Henrietta asks Warburton,

> 'Are they very ugly? They try to make us believe in America that they're all handsome and magnificent and that they wear wonderful robes and crowns.'
> 'Ah, the robes and crowns are gone out of fashion,' said Lord Warburton, 'like your tomahawks and revolvers.' (182)

In both examples, white characters invoke stereotypes of Indigenous people of the Americas as part of their witty repartee, and their attempts to distinguish the United States from Britain. Isabel is patently not in possession of war-paint, feathers or any 'native costume', given the whiteness integral to her identity. But she performs an act of the imperial gaze upon herself, attempting – in a teasing manner – to describe herself as she imagines – facetiously – that the 'specimen English gentleman' (124) might regard her, all the while clearly knowing next to nothing herself about actual Indigenous cultures in the Americas. Similarly, Warburton both indicates that 'tomahawks' are not, in fact, relevant to Henrietta's national customs, and suggests they are a 'fashionable' feature of her country's past. Indigeneity – and, with it, implicitly, the violence of the colonial encounter – thus appears as a fashion, as well as outdated. At the same time, Warburton's attribution of 'tomahawks' to Henrietta inscribes Americanness through indigeneity while simultaneously marking it as an inappropriate signifier for Henrietta.

Less than two decades after the Civil War, the narrative also gestures, fleetingly, towards slavery, in an exchange between Henrietta and Mrs Touchett, Isabel's aunt. Following Henrietta's declaration that she 'like[s] to be treated as an American lady',

> 'Poor American ladies!' cried Mrs Touchett with a laugh. 'They're the slaves of slaves.'
> 'They're the companions of freemen,' Henrietta retorted.
> 'They're the companions of their servants – the Irish chambermaid and the negro waiter. They share their work.'
> 'Do you call the domestics in an American household "slaves"?' Miss Stackpole enquired. 'If that's the way you desire to treat them, no wonder you don't like America.' (149–50)

Mrs Touchett and Henrietta clash over the meaning of 'slave', with Mrs Touchett attempting to use the word metaphorically, while Henrietta insists upon its literal meaning. The patriotic Henrietta equates Americanness with freedom, despite the relatively short time that has elapsed since emancipation in her country. The expatriate and cosmopolitan Mrs Touchett, in contrast, equates freedom with leisure that can only come with position, means and the luxury of having servants.

Henrietta's future husband, the English Mr Bantling, will visit the United States much later in the novel. James describes Bantling's experience through references to both Indigenous people and African Americans, who together form the means of the characters' dividing Britain's former colony from Europe:

> He appeared never to have heard of any river in America but the Mississippi and was unprepared to recognize the existence of the Hudson, though obliged to confess at last that it was fully equal to the Rhine. They had spent some pleasant hours in the palace-cars; he was always ordering ice-cream from the coloured man. . . . He was now in England, hunting – 'hunting round' Henrietta called it. These amusements were those of the American red men; we had left that behind long ago, the pleasures of the chase. It seemed to be generally believed in England that we wore tomahawks and feathers; but such a costume was more in keeping with English habits. (540)

Using free indirect discourse, James delivers Henrietta's version of Bantling's experiences as an Englishman in the United States, where African Americans are to be remarked upon but are less remarkable than the ability to purchase ice cream on a train. Henrietta describes Bantling as though he has been reverse-colonised, hunting as though he is indigenous and, for Henrietta, backward. The comparison intersects with Henrietta's project of demeaning Britain in order to elevate the United States, which she does here at the expense of Indigenous peoples – or, more precisely, her idea of Indigenous peoples. For Henrietta, only white America can lay claim to progress, leaving behind both the imperial power of Britain and the dispossessed Indigenous peoples of the Americas.

While Henrietta's patriotism is palpable in Campion's film, all references to Indigenous people in the Americas and to African Americans (stereotyped or otherwise) disappear in the adaptation. Of course – and tellingly – no actual Indigenous or African American characters appear in James's novel either, despite their invocation by white American and English characters to serve their own purposes in debate. If Britain is considered suspect by Henrietta because of the power it wields, Isabel herself may be said to possess 'a particularly American vision, one that includes an arrogant naïveté and even an imperialist impulse' (Lamm 2011, 251). Indeed, in the novel, Isabel as good as admits this herself to Osmond prior to their marriage, when she anticipates his opinion about her intention to travel, given the substantial inheritance she has received from her uncle, Mr Touchett:

> You've no respect for my travels – you think them ridiculous . . . You see my ignorance, my blunders, the way I wander about as if the world belonged to me, simply because – because it has been put into my power to do so. (James 1984, 358)

Although in the novel, Isabel posits that Osmond may find her distasteful because she possesses this power as a woman (which, at this stage of their courtship, he denies), she does betray a nervousness about the power she wields and her relationship to the world. But there is (unsurprisingly) no reflection on her position in the settler-colonial nation-state. Given Campion's own Australasian positionings, the absence of such a reflection in the film as well constitutes a missed opportunity.

Instead, the film grapples with cultural Otherness through the representation of Isabel's travels with Madame Merle in a manner that attempts to fuse this Otherness with the sense of impending doom in her relationship to Osmond. For all the grandness of Isabel's plans, her early encounters with Osmond eclipse her travels in terms of the attention given to them by both James's and Campion's narratives. James's description of

Isabel's 'little pilgrimage to the East' (374) with Madame Merle takes up little more than two pages, with most of it dedicated to the alteration in the friendship between the two women. If 'Isabel [finds] much to interest her' (374) in Greece, Turkey and Egypt, it has no interest for the narrator. The pyramids, the Acropolis, and the Strait of Salamis all appear in a single sentence before a statement about Isabel's return to Rome, shortly followed by Osmond's arrival there. 'The East' thus furnishes a background against which Isabel's relationships to Merle and Osmond are staged; the people of Greece, Turkey and Egypt are entirely absent from this abrupt narration of Isabel's travels at the edge of and beyond Europe.

The film addresses Isabel and Merle's travels in a formally disruptive manner. As critics have noted – and, indeed, largely complained – this brief section departs conspicuously from the conventions of realism. A black and white montage entitled 'My Journey 1873', produced using bluescreen (see Gentry 1997, 57), this sequence depicting Isabel and Merle's travel mimics the features of early cinema. The title appears handwritten in an oval frame, underneath a steamship, with a bird's eye view of objects sliding across a surface surrounding the frame, as though tipping back and forth in accordance with ocean waves; the sliding occurs simultaneously with the tilting of the ship in the frame. Piano music plays, in keeping with the exhibition conventions of early, silent cinema. Most of the sequence is devoid of dialogue. Following the title, Isabel and Merle appear on the bow of a ship, holding hands with their arms outstretched. Isabel wears a life preserver around her waist and pirouettes while Merle has her back to the camera, before a jump cut shows both women looking at the camera, Isabel still sporting the life preserver (as though it is a kind of chastity belt, or a sign she is either in danger or anticipates danger). After a cut to a view of the women from behind, with ship's railings in the foreground, a final cut in this part of the sequence gives way to a medium close-up of Isabel, looking forward, with Merle standing behind her shoulder, suggesting her influence over Isabel, the extent to which she is steering the younger woman toward her fate. After a dissolve to a shot of waves, this sense of Merle's steering becomes clear with a superimposition of a close-up on a hand coming around the waist of a white-garmented torso. This motion repeats at a greater distance from the camera, with both arms of a woman in view, and more of her dress visible. The hand's fingers are inserted between the numerous buttons down the front of the dress. The film then cuts to a medium close-up of Isabel, with Osmond (John Malkovich) behind her.

Thus far, the montage has revealed nothing of the geographical component of the travels themselves, only – much like the novel – the two characters occupying Isabel at this point in the narrative. Following Osmond's appearance in the sequence, however, waves superimposed on the image then give way via a cut to an extreme long shot of Isabel and Merle at a harbour, with their luggage, with local people in evidence. The film then cuts to reveal a tent, camels, black parasols and women with their heads covered. Isabel, wearing a white head covering, has only her eyes showing. The disjunction between her present location and where her mind's attention is directed becomes clear through an extreme close-up of Osmond's lips, repeating a line from an earlier scene in Rome, prior to her departure: 'I'm absolutely in love with you', which overlaps with a repetition of 'what I wish to say is . . .'. The montage becomes surrealist with a shot of beans on a metal plate, repeating Osmond's phrase, 'absolutely in love with you', while Isabel prods them with a fork. The film cuts to local women (presumably Egyptian, although none of the film was shot in Egypt) walking in a group, all wearing black, with their heads covered. Isabel is then shown at the foot of pyramids, with children asking her to buy their wares. The voice-over now has Isabel repeating, 'I'm absolutely in love with you', as though hypnotised; her voice then alternates with Osmond's repetition of that phrase. Isabel stares, as though alarmed, into the camera with a pyramid behind her (see Figure 1.1), followed by a superimposition of a medium close-up of Osmond spinning Isabel's striped parasol. Isabel appears as a superimposed figure, tiny and naked, her back to the camera before a cut to her facing the camera, with clouds and the spinning parasol superimposed. Osmond's hand moves across her naked waist while Isabel cries out, as though orgasmically. A cut reveals Isabel in front of a pyramid again, where she faints and the piano music ceases, followed by the title, 'FLORENCE, ONE YEAR LATER'.

Given its departure from realism, the 'My Journey' montage draws attention to itself and has had numerous detractors. It is, however, a key component of 'Campion's densely filmic film' (Stewart 1999, 248) and evidence of Campion 'exploring the full potential of the medium', in the words of her director of photography, Stuart Dryburgh (qtd in Gentry 1997, 51). Garrett Stewart objects to the montage on the grounds of its anachronism: 'This inset footage reads as a technological throwback in the contemporary film's own terms but as a distracting media forecast with the 1870s plot' (1999, 248). Conversely, McHugh reads this anachronism more productively: while the montage may be 'temporally at odds with or too early for the contemporary film in which it is embedded and too late for the time the novel represents', it does, however, 'appropriately simulate the cinema in 1908, the year the revised New York edition of *Portrait* was published' – indeed, the edition of the novel that Campion adapts (2007, 100, 101).

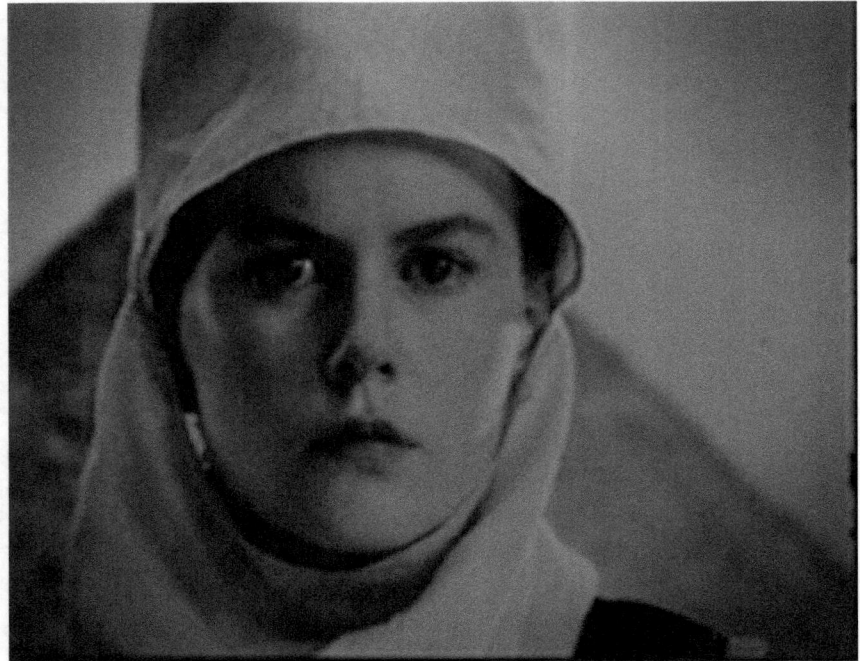

Figure 1.1 Isabel in front of a pyramid in *The Portrait of a Lady*.

Moreover, the disruptive techniques deployed in 'My Journey' appear as cinematic equivalents of the compressed travels of Isabel and Merle in the novel. Isabel, described through free indirect discourse from Merle's point of view, is clearly agitated while travelling: 'Madame Merle continued to remark that even among the most classic sites, the scenes most calculated to suggest repose and reflexion, a certain incoherence prevailed in her. Isabel travelled rapidly and recklessly' (James 1984, 374). The speed and incoherence (as well as jump cuts early in the sequence) of the montage can be easily extrapolated from this passage in the novel; indeed, Alan Nadel writes that in Campion's film, 'Isabel's voyage is represented visually as an extreme fissure in the diegesis, disrupting the coherent cinematic gaze that creates a film's visual world' (1997), without acknowledging the novel's own reference to incoherence. Furthermore, James describes Merle during her travels with Isabel as 'slightly mechanical . . . something of a public performer, condemned to emerge only in character and in costume' (James 1984, 375), for which the staged artificiality of the montage furnishes an appropriate equivalent.

On the one hand, Isabel possesses the privilege of a white, wealthy American; on the other hand, she is a woman, an 'heiress [who] partakes of imperial spoils, but, concomitantly . . . is also a "territory" to be mapped and conquered' (Walton 1997). As Dana Polan argues, Campion's *Portrait*

> fully takes place within the geography of the dominant order and offers little space in which one can break out in new directions. But for the scenes in which Isabel goes on her grand tour – scenes in which her distance from indigenous peoples is suggested by her dismay and by a rear projection that literally separates her off from other cultures – and for a few shots of domestic staff and anonymous passers-by in the film's few shots of public places, *The Portrait of a Lady* moves in a world of Western privilege where little glimpse of alternate experience or of other life options is visible. (2001, 139)

Isabel's travels as depicted in 'My Journey' are 'purposefully Orientalised' (Hollyfield 2018, 70) in their representation of both Isabel and the non-Western Other; local peoples in the places Isabel visits figure as props for her journey (geographical as well as psychological). But the visual and aural superimpositions of Osmond in this sequence suggest her distraction, her lack of engagement with these places and the peoples to whom they belong. The defamiliarisation of the montage, effected by the anachronism and surrealism, underscores Isabel's position of privilege. For all its aesthetic disruption in its representation, her journey with Madame Merle has no impact on her narrative trajectory, just as the brevity of its appearance in the novel testifies to its insignificance to Isabel's fate.

In addition to the ruptures of realism in Campion's adaptation, many critics have also responded negatively to its representation of sexuality, including a fantasy sequence early in the film in which Isabel imagines herself on a bed with Caspar Goodwood (Viggo Mortensen) and Lord Warburton (Richard E. Grant), each caressing her while her cousin, Ralph Touchett (Martin Donovan), observes. As Nancy Bentley argues, however, 'Campion's focus on sexuality [is] the logical result of rendering Isabel's plight in the medium of film, a medium in which female agency is finally inseparable from the questions of the body and its visual image' (2002, 128). Further, James's novel is replete with allusions to the male gaze. Whereas Miciah Hussey argues that Isabel is '[s]urrounded by characters that confine her through objectifying gazes and *mise en scène* that reifies her in aesthetic terms' (2016, 177), Patricia E. Johnson contends that 'James's novel conflate[s] its narrative viewpoint with the monolithic gaze of the male' (1997, 40). Johnson reads James's novel through Laura Mulvey's seminal analysis of the male gaze in classical Hollywood cinema. Although 'Osmond is the ultimate representative of the male gaze, to whom wife and daughter are art objects' (45), even sympathetic male characters are consistently shown to be gazing at Isabel as a means of possessing her. Ralph's voyeurism receives frequent commentary from critics. Indeed,

Alexandra Tankard's analysis of Ralph's position in the novel as a consumptive both declares 'Ralph's desire to identify with Isabel, rather than to possess her as Osmond does' (2008, 70) and acknowledges 'the calculating, almost vengeful, nature of [Ralph's] voyeurism' (75), given his complaint to Isabel, 'What's the use of being ill and disabled and restricted to mere spectatorship at the game of life if I really can't see the show when I've paid so much for my ticket?' (James 1984, 201).

Although Ralph's fascination with his cousin begins as soon as he meets her, his interest in her – in what becomes of her, the life he wishes to live vicariously through her and the financial investment he secretly makes in that life by forfeiting half his inheritance – ultimately fuses together the gaze and a demand for narrative that Mulvey identifies as sadistic: 'Sadism demands a story, depends on making something happen, forcing a change in another person, a battle of will and strength, victory/defeat' (1989, 22). Certainly, Isabel, thanks to Ralph's negotiations with his dying father, becomes 'Ralph's creation', as Peter Donahue argues of the novel (1997, 47), and this literal change in her fortunes is the unwitting cause of her unhappy marriage, dooming her to become an addition to Osmond's collection.

Further, despite his genuine concern for Isabel's welfare as Osmond's wife, Ralph's desire to know, to make Isabel tell of, her troubles bears out Mulvey's correlation between narrative and sadism. In their discussion about whether Warburton truly cares for Isabel's stepdaughter, Ralph's speculation that Warburton is only really interested in Isabel herself prompts Isabel to exclaim, 'Ah, Ralph, you give me no help!' (James 1984, 512). Once Isabel recovers herself, Ralph's response allies his gaze to his demand for the narrative of Isabel's unhappiness:

> Her mask had dropped for an instant, but she had put it on again, to Ralph's infinite disappointment. He had caught a glimpse of her natural face and he wished immensely to look into it. He had an almost savage desire to hear her complain of her husband – hear her say that she should be held accountable for Lord Warburton's defection. . . . [I]t was for his own satisfaction more than for hers that he longed to show her he was not deceived. (514)

At the end of this conversation, Ralph all but challenges Isabel to confess her marital woes. Ralph hypothesises that Osmond will accuse Isabel of being jealous of Pansy, if Isabel does not secure Pansy's marriage to Warburton:

> She blushed red and threw back her head. 'You're not kind,' she said in a voice that he had never heard on her lips.
> 'Be frank with me and you'll see,' he answered.
> But she made no reply; she only pulled her hand out of his own, which he tried still to hold, and rapidly withdrew from the room. (515)

At this point, Ralph attempts to exchange one narrative for another, Isabel's misery for his own response. He tries to bargain with her: her frankness for, presumably, his explicit comfort. In Campion's adaptation, Ralph's attempt to retain Isabel's hand is much more forceful than the novel suggests, and the film emphasises the gendered imbalances of power in the gaze, the coercion embedded in demands for narrative, and the absence of Isabel's consent in multiple scenarios involving men who claim to love her.

In both the novel and Campion's film, Caspar Goodwood illustrates these correlations between the male gaze, coercive demands for narrative and the lack of Isabel's consent most vividly. In the novel, he and Isabel speak frankly about his gaze. Prior to Isabel's first departure for Italy, Goodwood complains to Isabel, '[Y]ou'll be out of my sight indeed!', to which Isabel replies:

> Don't think me unkind if I say it's just *that* – being out of your sight – that I like. If you were in the same place I should feel you were watching me, and I don't like that – I like my liberty too much. (213)[3]

To be subject to Goodwood's gaze, then, is to be captured. One year later, hearing news of her engagement to Osmond, Goodwood immediately travels to Italy to confront Isabel, declaring, 'I came because I wanted to see you once more' (381). His later line in this scene, 'I've done what I wished. I've seen you', appears in the film, underscoring that their meeting is about his desire, not hers. Like Ralph, Goodwood, later guessing at Isabel's unhappy marriage, seeks to force a confession from her:

> 'I do ask one sole satisfaction: – that you tell me – that you tell me – !'
> 'That I tell you what?'
> 'Whether I may pity you.' (559)

That Isabel leaves Goodwood 'unsatisfied' knits together his desire for narrative and sexual desire for Isabel. At Ralph's funeral, Goodwood's gaze appears particularly violent: 'During much of the time Isabel was conscious of Mr Goodwood's gaze; he looked at her somewhat harder than he usually looked in public' (625). Indeed, James often describes Goodwood's ardour for Isabel through violence. Sitting on a bench after the funeral, Isabel stands as Goodwood approaches:

> She had had time only to rise when, with a motion that looked like violence, but felt like – she knew not what, he grasped her by the wrist and made her sink again into the seat. She closed her eyes; he had not hurt her; it was only a touch, which she had obeyed. But there was something in his face that she wished not to see. (631)

Isabel tells Goodwood to leave her alone – 'I beseech you to go away . . . As you love me, as you pity me, leave me alone!' – to which his response is to 'glar[e] at her a moment' (635) before kissing her. During the kiss, Isabel '[feels] each thing in his hard manhood that had least pleased her, each aggressive fact of his face, his figure, his presence, justified of its identity and made one with this act of possession' (636). As Sandra A. Zagarell argues, 'Goodwood's importunity precludes sexual reciprocity' (2014, 29). Miller invokes this lack of reciprocity, the absence of Isabel's consent, in his characterisation of Goodwood's kiss as 'a kind of virtual rape' (2005, 61). In essence, although Goodwood seeks to her free from her abusive husband, he tries to coerce her into his version of that freedom.

Henrietta Stackpole is Goodwood's champion throughout the novel, and the narrative concludes with her telling him, following Isabel's return to Rome, 'just you wait!' (636). The film concludes differently. Whereas the adaptation 'literally skips the first hundred pages of the novel in which Isabel's life in the United States, at Albany, is depicted' (Bessière 2009, 127), it finishes less than a page before the end, with her running from Goodwood after his kiss and reaching Gardencourt. James narrates this moment thus: 'She looked all about her; she listened a little; then she put her hand on the latch. She had not known where to turn; but she knew now. There was a very straight path' (1984, 636). As in the novel, the film's Isabel reaches Gardencourt but does not enter it, looking back, away from the house – at what, or whom, the viewer does not know. This ending diverges from Laura Jones's screenplay, which, in fact, overshoots James's ending, dramatising Isabel's return to Rome and revealing her intention as driven by concern for Osmond's daughter, Pansy:

> **Isabel** steps into the lamplight.
> *Pansy looks at her as if at an apparition. **Pansy**'s voice out of the shadows:*
> PANSY: You've come back.
> *Isabel – eyes dazzled by light – finds it hard to see the girl in the shadows beyond the lamplight.*
> ISABEL: Yes, I've come for you.
> *She holds out her hands towards **Pansy**.*
> *Pansy sees **Isabel**'s hands, held out, in the brightest part of the light.* (Jones 1997, 134)

Thus, the screenplay posits a less masochistic impulse behind Isabel's return, driven as it is by her relationship with her stepdaughter, rather than with her abusive husband. In the film, however, we see no return at all (just as the novel's reader has no access to Isabel following her departure from Gardencourt). Such an ending does not preclude a return to Osmond and/or Pansy in Rome. At the same time, however, it can be read more optimistically as a 'retrospective "gift" to Isabel': 'Campion's

Portrait differs from James's primarily in the openness of Isabel's future' (Cooper 2009, 290). Granted, the film's conclusion does not foreclose the narrative possibility that Isabel *will* return to Rome for Pansy's sake, but neither does the film confirm it.

What is clear, however, is that Isabel does not foresee her liberation through Goodwood. The film certainly accentuates Isabel's sexual desires: the fantasy sequence early in the film; her response even to Osmond during their unhappy marriage, in which Osmond 'humiliat[es] her with her own desire for him' (Boudreau 2000, 49) as he moves as though to kiss her before withdrawing. But it also heightens the threat that Goodwood himself poses to Isabel's liberty. Alistair Fox argues that Goodwood possesses an 'ardent, yet considerate . . . virility' (2011, 149), but in fact, Goodwood is strikingly unresponsive to Isabel's articulated wishes. Prior to the fantasy sequence, Isabel has a confrontation with Goodwood, in which she 'struggles against being his object as he pens her in and touches her face without permission' (Chandler 1997). Henrietta's informing Isabel of Goodwood's presence in England with the statement, 'He's come after you', suggests that Isabel is being hunted. Indeed, in the earlier confrontation scene in London, when Goodwood 'pens in' Isabel, she is backed up against the wall while he holds onto a beam above her, leaning into her space as though cornering prey.

Even Lord Warburton, in the middle of the unwanted marriage proposal with which the film begins, breaches Isabel's space as she sits on a tree branch, enclosed as though in a protective bower. When Warburton, like his literary counterpart, says that when he's 'touched, it's for life', this solemn declaration resembles a prison sentence, a threat (as it is, in legal terms)[4] to Isabel's liberty. Isabel's quitting of Warburton in this scene leads her back to the house, presented in a canted frame, a visual feature 'that directly speaks of the intention to produce a marked effect' (Polan 2001, 132), and that recurs on occasion throughout this film, adding to the ruptures of cinematic realism and defamiliarising the heritage genre.

In its drastic cutting of the narrative beginning, and slightly premature ending (if carrying disproportionally large implications), Campion's adaptation of James's novel, following the film's preface, begins and ends with Isabel in tears. Some critics (e.g. Bauer 1997; Horne 2001, 89) protest that Osmond, as played by John Malkovich, is too hateful, too reminiscent of the actor's earlier role as Valmont in *Dangerous Liaisons* (dir. Stephen Frears, 1988).[5] In the novel, James describes Isabel as '[knowing] of no wrong he had done; he was not violent, he was not cruel: she simply believed he hated her' (1984, 475). Yet this absolution of Osmond from cruelty, even as James writes him, is impossible from a late-twentieth-century perspective. Osmond's 'wish[ing] her to have no freedom of mind' (510) is abusive. And as Rebecca M. Gordon argues of Osmond's character in the novel, 'The very nature of his power over Isabel – his power to quash her ability to resist – is, by definition, violent' (2002, 21). Further, Osmond threatens Isabel when she announces her desire to visit Ralph on his deathbed, as James describes it:

> 'That's why you must go then? Not to see your cousin, but to take a revenge on me.'
> 'I know nothing about revenge.'
> 'I do,' said Osmond. 'Don't give me an occasion.' (582)

Campion's adaptation excises these last two lines, but conveys Osmond's menace in other ways. In the film, Osmond's violence is calculated to be indirect, but that does not detract from the violence itself. Angry about Isabel's failure (or refusal, as Osmond sees it) to secure Lord Warburton as Pansy's husband, Osmond piles cushions on a sofa and then forces Isabel to sit down on them, 'much as a parent might seat a fidgety child, or a collector put a doll on display' (Francke 2001, 84). He slaps her gloves at her, rather than slapping her face with his hands, and stands on her skirt so that she trips on her way out of the room. During their argument about Isabel visiting Ralph on his deathbed, Osmond makes a pretence of trying to protect her by placing his hand between her forehead and the wall against which she attempts to bang her head.

Thus, Osmond wants no evidence of his violence, no mark on his wife, the prized object of his collection. If Campion's film 'visualizes the marital violence James's novel refuses to show' (Sadoff 1998), it does so in ways that maintain the novel's characterisation of Osmond as a collector. For Miller, the novel's Osmond is 'quite exceptionally awful' (2005, 63), despite his being 'of so fine a grain' (James 1984, 312), corroborated by Melissa Valiska Gregory's argument that the novel stages an 'aesthetic refinement [that] merges with sexual power, creating a masculine domination so subtle that it appears nothing more than an extension of good taste' (2004, 149). Thus, Isabel, as the object of Osmond's gaze, and an item in his collection, is always already subject to violence, an argument extended by the film's dramatisation of these relations and elaboration of Osmond's abuse.

Criticism of Campion's film, whether or not it focuses on Osmond's characterisation, reveals a curious misunderstanding of and expectations surrounding adaptation. Dale M. Bauer asserts that 'Campion sheds no light on the Jamesian text, preferring to address her darker vision about women's roles' (1997); Polan claims that the film is 'not so much an adaptation as a reworking of James's novel' (2001, 163), while Gordon infers an 'intention to interpret, rather than adapt, the novel' (2002, 15); Nadel, for his part, views the film as 'not so much an adaptation of James's novel as it is an appropriation of it' (1997). Although these responses to the film in relation to James's work are more circumspect than the *New York Times* review that proclaimed, '[C]alling this Nicole Kidman vehicle an adaptation is like saying that Hitler adapted Poland' (qtd in Verhoeven 2009, 65), each of the critics quoted above ignores the key root of 'adaptation', which is that to adapt is to alter. Similarly, Sadoff's conclusion that Campion and other directors of films adapting James's work function 'to address and resolve current cultural problems' (1998) merely states a fact about the nature of cultural production: it is intimately and inextricably tied to its own context. Rather than attempt to disguise it, Campion's adaptation of *The Portrait of a Lady* self-reflexively announces its own context, positioning itself precisely as a late-twentieth-century, Australasian adaptation of James's novel.

Vanity Fair

If Campion's *Portrait of a Lady* expands the geography of that director's filmmaking beyond Australasia, *Vanity Fair* (2004) is Indian-born, US-educated and now Uganda-based Mira Nair's first film to be shot largely in the UK, at the centre of empire. Where previous feature films of Nair's such as *Salaam Bombay!* (1988), *Kama Sutra* (1997) and *Monsoon Wedding* (2001) have focused on India (and *Mississippi Masala* [1991] on the Indian diaspora in the United States), *Vanity Fair* invokes India even while ostensibly focusing on Britain. In this adaptation of William Makepeace Thackeray's novel *Vanity Fair* (1847–8), a novel whose 'plot . . . covers more than two decades and confronts the reader with dozens of locations . . . and with more than seventy characters from practically all sections of society' (Stratmann 2009, 84), Nair frames Thackeray's novel through the connection between Britain and India, tracing the relationship between imperial metropole and colony through narrative and visual detail. Nair foregrounds – and visualises, where Thackeray does not – India, the country of both her and Thackeray's birth. The film trades in the visual splendour of India and its culture, seeking to infuse its representation of Regency England with the influence of colonised cultures. Although this staging of cultural interpenetration underscores the economic and cultural exchanges of empire and exposes the materiality of imperial wealth, the film struggles to transcend exoticism and the Orientalism of the period it represents. If Hamid Naficy includes Nair in his study of 'accented' filmmakers (those working in 'interstitial' spaces from exilic and diasporic positions), even her late-twentieth-century films have been critiqued for 'elid[ing] power relations and target[ing] foreign audiences, [her] cinematic gaze upon her native home . . . considered touristic, voyeuristic, and superficial' (Naficy 2001, 4, 69);[6] as such, *Vanity Fair* is perhaps consistent with her earlier, smaller-scale work.

Nair's *Vanity Fair* significantly alters the character of the novel's protagonist, Becky Sharp, an orphan we first meet at Pinkerton's school, determined to improve her fortune. The novel traces her fate alongside that of her friend, Amelia Sedley, born into greater (although ultimately precarious) wealth. But whereas Thackeray structures his novel around 'a constant "conversation" between two very different types of women and their corresponding difficulties' (Clarke 2008, 43), Nair devotes more space to Becky's story and presents her in a less mercenary light, celebrating her as a spirited, independent woman more in tune with the temporal context of the film's production than the novel's (including a more pronounced love for her son, to whom she is violent in the novel).[7] Key to the film's recuperation of Becky is her fascination with India, effecting an intersection of the film's postcolonial and feminist approaches. Like *The Portrait of a Lady*, Nair's *Vanity Fair* enhances the source text's representation of the predatory male collector figure (Lord Steyne, in this case), rendering Becky much more obviously the victim of gendered and class-based violence than in the novel. Ultimately, however, Becky's reward in Nair's film – a happy ending that brings her to India – rests on a racist logic of a fear of miscegenation that the film unwittingly replicates.

The extent to which Thackeray's novel focuses on Britain's colonies is the subject of critical debate. For Patrick Brantlinger, 'India remained *background*' for the Calcutta-born Thackeray 'in both biographical and fictional terms', a background that 'seemed at best distant, exotic, and perhaps ominous' (1990, 75, 107). Sandy Morey Norton, conversely, argues that *Vanity Fair* exhibits 'an underlying ambivalence toward domestic and global domination', while conceding that colonised locations 'are conspicuous by their absence in the novel' (1993, 125, 127). For Corri Zoli, *Vanity Fair* 'offer[s] an exemplary instance of British history as imperial, mixed and polycultural' through 'a mass of imperial references which form this novel's most consistent texture' (2007, 418–19). As woven into Thackeray's narrative as Britain's empire may be, however, it occupies a curious position of being simultaneously foregrounded and relegated to the margins. The character of Sambo, the Sedleys' Black servant, offers a case in point. As Andrew Smith emphasises, 'the first character that the reader encounters in *Vanity Fair* is [this] black footman who rings the bell which announces the start of

the novel' (2011, 14). Our introduction to the narrative, Sambo 'is precisely the kind of peripheral figure towards whom postcolonial studies have so effectively directed critical attention', given that, as Smith
points out, '[n]othing in the book happens to him, as it were, in his
own right', and 'his interior life appears largely hidden from the otherwise all-penetrating gaze of the narrator' (2011, 14). In *Vanity Fair*,
minoritised characters are hidden in plain sight, conspicuously present
(in contrast to James's *Portrait of a Lady*) yet incidental to the narrative.

For some scholars, racism forms part of Thackeray's satirical target:
Gerd Stratmann, for instances, summarises Vanity Fair as 'a capitalist
society, status-ridden, obsessed by money and material possessions, characterised by intellectual and spiritual emptiness, by a twisted morality, by
hypocrisy, cruelty and avarice, by racism and discrimination' (2009, 86);
and Micael M. Clarke asserts of the novel that 'Thackeray's critique of
colonialism forms a part of his critique of racism and English jingoism
generally' (2008, 55). Zoli reads Thackeray as satirising 'not racism or
empire *per se*, but its representation' (2007, 425). If some scholars read
Thackeray's representations of colonised peoples as ambivalent (Norton
1993, 126; A. Smith 2011, 14), others more clearly designate Thackeray
as 'an imperial racist' (Parrinder 2006, 236): 'nowhere [in *Vanity Fair*] is
racism the object of satire' (Geracht 2016, 48). This range of responses
to Thackeray's representations of race has implications for Nair's adaptive choices and the way she frames them, although as I argue below,
Thackeray's verbal and visual representations of racialised characters
indicate an alignment of Thackeray with racism, not a critique of it.

Indeed, Thackeray's 'incessant use of racialized details' (Zoli 2007, 419)
replicates the racist assumptions of the society that is otherwise satirised in
the novel. Sambo (his name itself telling about Thackeray's lack of investment in his Black characters) is repeatedly described as 'bandy-leg[ged]'
and 'grinning' (1983, 10, 43). Following the Sedleys' financial ruin, we
are told that 'Black Sambo, with the infatuation of his profession, determined on setting up a public-house' (214), after which he disappears from
the narrative. The character of Rhoda Swartz, first described as 'the rich
woolly-haired mulatto from St. Kitts' (7), has slightly more bearing on
the narrative as a potential, more financially rewarding, wife for George
Osborne, Amelia Sedley's fiancé: 'She was reported to have I don't know
how many plantations in the West Indies; a deal of money in the funds;
and three stars to her name in the East India stockholders' list' (245). The
narrator's own racist descriptions of Miss Swartz intensify in George's
speculations about her: 'Her jet-black hair is as curly as Sambo's. I dare
say she wore a nose-ring when she went to Court' (245). When Amelia's

family is financially ruined, Mr Osborne insists that George break off his engagement with Amelia and marry Miss Swartz instead. If the Sedleys have had concerns about their son, Jos, working in India as the Collector of Boggley-Wollah, marrying a woman who is not white – 'It's a mercy he did not bring us over a black daughter-in-law' (36) – Mr Osborne, in contrast, is more concerned with capital than with race: 'There shall be no beggar-marriages in my family' (259); '*I* ain't particular about a shade or so of tawny' (279). George, having had dalliances with other women in the Caribbean – in Demerara, 'a judge's daughter went almost mad about him; then there was that beautiful quadroon girl, Miss Pye, at St Vincent's' (140) – rejects Miss Swartz in explicitly racist terms: 'Marry that mulatto woman? . . . I don't like the colour, sir. Ask the black that sweeps opposite Fleet Market, sir. *I'm* not going to marry a Hottentot Venus' (259). Thus, Amelia's happiness (however fleeting, given how her marriage to George turns out) arrives at the expense of Miss Swartz, in thoroughly racist terms.

Although Mr Osborne positions Amelia Sedley and Rhoda Swartz as rivals, the latter character, as critics have noted, professes only affection for Amelia, her classmate at Pinkerton's school. Indeed, Thackeray first introduces us to Miss Swartz at the school, when Amelia is about to depart: 'on the day Amelia went away, she was in such a passion of tears, that they were obliged to send for Dr. Floss, and half tipsify her with sal volatile' (7). If Miss Swartz is 'impetuous and woolly-headed', she is also 'generous and affectionate' (8). For Zoli, 'Thackeray uses Miss Swartz's excessive feeling to highlight the serious *lack of feeling* – his most scathing critique – in the race and class hypocrisies of those around her' (2007, 424). In the contrast between Miss Swartz and white characters such as Amelia, George and his sisters, Miss Swartz is not necessarily presented as inferior: 'The idiocy of her behavior and appearance works narratively to highlight the more subtle and malevolent, but equally ridiculous, behaviour and appearance of the Osborne sisters and women like them' (Norton 1993, 127). If '[t]he novel critiques George and Amelia, and more importantly their relationship, through the vehicle of creole Miss Swartz' (Zoli 2007, 423), however, such a function reduces Miss Swartz to a narrative prop. And while Zoli reads Thackeray as satirising but 'not interven[ing] into Victorian discourses of "race" or empire' (2007, 425), Thackeray's own illustrations for his novel replicate grotesque racist caricature. In 'Miss Swartz Rehearsing for the Drawing-Room' (253), she takes up most of the frame, despite the presence of four (smaller) white women, her facial features large and exaggerated, if obscured by the shading of her face. The text adjacent to the illustration describes Miss Swartz 'as elegantly decorated as a she chimney-sweep on May-Day' (252). Her features are less obscured in a subsequent illus-tration (256), but, as Nancy Marck Cantwell observes, their caricatured exaggeration in this image, too, serves to 'contras[t] her elegant figure and dress with her facial features' in a manner that 'raises the troubling aspects of imperialism as it creates increasing social mobility and flexibility' (2015, para. 7), a logic that George Osborne rejects on racist grounds.

Nair reads Thackeray as critiquing the racism and Orientalism of the society he depicts, but the novel's representation of racialised characters suggests endorsement, rather than criticism, of the values espoused by Vanity Fair. Nair's statements about Thackeray's novel indicate, on the one hand, an agreement with those scholars who argue that Thackeray satirised the racism of the English society he portrays. Given Nair's adap-tation's privileging of the margins of empire, the treatment of Thackeray's racialised characters is crucial to assessing the film's position and the kind of postcolonial adaptation it effects. Indeed, the lack of consensus in scholarship about Thackeray's racism prefigures a contradiction in the film's own representations of race and cultural difference, often at odds with Nair's declarations about the critique she considers *Vanity Fair* to offer. In her film, the character of Sambo becomes Biju (Paul Bazely), instead, an Indian servant in the Sedleys' house who has no lines of dia-logue.[8] The similarity between the servant's name and the French word for jewel (*bijou*) suggests that this character functions as 'an exotic com-modity' (Machalias 2011, 49) himself. Bereft of dialogue in the film, Biju appears only to be looked at, particularly because his 'costume . . . empha-sizes his foreignness' (Machalias 2011, 49), with his Indian rather than English clothing, and his painted face. Biju is a silent observer, a reminder of Britain's empire and the patterns of migration it sets in motion. He also appears as a conduit for Indian culture (especially culinary culture) as he serves Becky (Reese Witherspoon) the Indian dishes she requests while dining at the Sedleys, in an attempt to impress Jos (Tony Maudsley) and win him for a husband in order to escape her governess fate; she claims to be 'enraptured with every scent and flavour of the East'. Much as Biju serves as evidence of empire, however, his absolute silence in the film sug-gests his character has not evolved much beyond that of Sambo in the novel; like Sambo, according to Smith's critique, Biju does not exist in his own right, and the audience has no access to his interiority.

A contrast with the 1998 BBC adaptation of *Vanity Fair* is instructive. In this six-part serial, written by Andrew Davies and directed by Marc Munden, Sambo is Samuel, according to the credits, and only 'Sambo' to his employers, who complain in the second episode of his having become 'strange and uppity'. Like the novel's Sambo, Samuel intends to open a pub following the Sedleys' bankruptcy. But Samuel is dignified and well spoken, and has an antagonistic relationship with Becky, whom he considers 'riff-raff' due to her position as a governess. Just like his novel counterpart, however, he disappears from the narrative once he is no longer attached to the Sedley household.

Nair's depiction of Rhoda Swartz constitutes an even greater departure from the novel than the translation of Sambo as Biju. In her DVD commentary on the adaptation, Nair claims,

> The scene where George Osborne is introduced to the Jamaican heiress to marry her was such a fantastic example of how Thackeray clear-sightedly viewed society's old hypocrisy about race and money. It was very important for me to have this scene, and in a perverse way I wanted Rhoda Swartz, played here by Kathryn Drysdale, to be the most beautiful woman in this film. (2005)

Thus, Nair's contradictory glossing of the scene in the film attributes a critique of racism to Thackeray while acknowledging her intention to depart drastically from his representation of Miss Swartz; Nair's description of Miss Swartz's casting as 'perverse' encapsulates the contradiction. The character in the film diverges from the source text because of both her beauty and her intelligence. She is no longer a former classmate of Amelia, but instead a friend of George's sister, Maria. As such, Miss Swartz has no sentimental attachment to Amelia as she does in the novel. Further, she speaks coolly and explicitly to George (Jonathan Rhys Meyers) about the prospect of their marriage, and the financial and social stakes of such a match:

> MISS SWARTZ: Let us speak frankly. My fortune is great; my birth is not. So I must choose between a poor nobleman or a rich bourgeois like you.
> GEORGE: Upon my word. You've a very precise grasp of the matter.
> MISS SWARTZ: I would have liked a title. But my guardian says if you and I combine our fortunes we may buy one whenever we wish.

The Miss Swartz of the film is therefore more mercenary than her literary counterpart. Indeed, whereas Zoli argues of the novel's Miss Swartz that she throws into relief the other characters' lack of feeling, in the film it is she who most characterises this lack.

George's protests to his father invoke this lack of feeling when he says, 'I cannot believe you are seriously suggesting Miss Swartz as the companion of my heart and hearth'. Ultimately, however, George's rejection of her invokes the racism of his character in the novel, if in more veiled terms: 'To begin with, she's not English.' The fact that Miss Swartz clarifies in the film that she left Jamaica when she was three (and speaks with a perfect English accent) underscores George's racism and his resistance to any expansion of what 'English' means. But his appeal to 'honour', to the promises made between his family and Amelia's, complicates the viewer's sympathies. If we side with George in his continued loyalty to Amelia (Romola Garai), then we become complicit in his suggestion that interracial relationships are dishonourable. The film ultimately makes it impossible to identify with George, of course, given his treatment of Amelia after their marriage. The novel may criticise Amelia for her lack of feeling for the devoted Miss Swartz and her failure to reciprocate the friendship of 'her only ally' (Zoli 2007, 424), but Nair's film encourages us to identify with the white woman in this scenario, as we are primarily guided to be emotionally invested in Amelia's happiness. Miss Swartz may be the most beautiful woman in the film, but she will disappear following the shot of her, on her own, overhearing the row between George and his father. At the same time, Nair's decision in casting Miss Swartz does implicitly – if perhaps unwittingly – critique Thackeray's representation of this character, however much Nair claims Thackeray's satirical target is the Osborne family.

If our encouraged sympathies for Amelia complicate our reception of Miss Swartz in the film, Nair's adaptation is most interested in the character of Becky Sharp. Changes to Becky's character to make her more palatable to the audience include a greater tenderness for Amelia and for her son. Further, two key shifts in narrative and characterisation centre her fully in the audience's sympathy and the film's framing: her naïveté, rather than her guilt, in her relationship with Lord Steyne (Gabriel Byrne), who is presented as a predator in the film; and her interest in India, enhancing her status and weaving her into the adaptation's 'celebratory Indianness' (Stratmann 2009, 88). However, the nature of Becky's fascination with India, and indeed the film's own representation of India and empire, often draw on exotic and Orientalist discourses, complicating the nature of the film's celebration.

Miss Swartz may appear mercenary in the film, but the novel's most mercenary character is Becky Sharp, whose attempts to transcend her humble origins lead her, in Norton's view, 'to represent a monstrous and devouring capitalism that grows out of empire' (1993, 126). The film's Becky reveals her, from the outset, both to participate in and challenge the commodification of people, while her own downfall will result from her self-commodification. The film's beginning adapts Thackeray's preface's conceit of his characters as puppets (1993, 2) by having Becky, as a child, perform a puppet show in which a daughter protests to her mother that she does not want to be sold off to a lord. At this point, a lord enters the scene in the form of Steyne, who has come to buy a portrait of Becky's dead mother, entitled *Virtue Betrayed*, from her father, whose work he collects. The young Becky insists that the price of four guineas is not high enough, and extracts ten from Steyne instead. When Steyne asks if she would be happy to sell for the portrait for ten guineas, Becky replies, 'No. But it will be too much to refuse', as she struggles with a clash of moral, sentimental and economic values.

Becky becomes reacquainted with Lord Steyne following her return to England with her husband, Rawdon Crawley (James Purefoy), and Steyne becomes her patron in her attempt to climb the social ladder (Rawdon having been disinherited by his wealthy aunt for having eloped with Becky). A collector of Francis Sharp's work, Steyne, 'the embodiment of brute imperial force' (Hollyfield 2018, 85), is determined to add Becky to his collection as well; as far as his logic is concerned, he purchases rights to Becky's body through his financial support. Following the party at Steyne's house where the king has been in attendance, watching Becky perform a 'slave dance' with other aristocratic women, Becky gazes at her mother's portrait, insisting the price she demanded for it as a child was 'not high enough'. Steyne's response, 'The trouble is, Mrs Crawley, you've taken the goods. It's too late to query the price', indicates that he intends for Becky to 'pay up' by awarding him sexual favours.

The film underscores the status of Becky's body as currency when she reads a letter from Rawdon, ambushed by Steyne's men and taken to debtor's prison, while Steyne stands behind her, aggressively stroking her chest. Unlike previous adaptations such as the BBC serial, and unlike the novel's ambiguity surrounding Becky's relationship with Steyne, Nair's film portrays Becky as a victim of Steyne's aristocratic misogyny. Steyne is figured in the film as 'a menace' (Moya 2010, 82), and although Becky encourages his attentions, her limits are clear. In Rawdon's absence, Steyne grabs at her necklace. To Becky's protest, 'Suppose my wish is to finish now, if I ask no other favour?', he lunges at her, insisting, 'You've had your wishes, Mrs Crawley.' We see Becky's resistance to Steyne and her groaning in anguish as Rawdon opens the door, assuming Becky's consent, and casting her out of his life as a result.

This version of the scene diverges from both the novel and the BBC serial, both of which privilege Rawdon's perspective as he interrupts his wife and Steyne. Thackeray describes the scene thus:

> Rawdon heard laughter within – laughter and singing. Becky was singing a snatch of the song of the night before; a hoarse voice shouted, 'Brava! Brava!' – it was Lord Steyne's.

> Rawdon opened the door and went in. A little table with a dinner was laid out –
> and wine and plate. Steyne was hanging over the sofa on which Becky sat. The
> wretched woman was in a brilliant full toilette, her arms and all her fingers sparkling
> with bracelets and rings; and the brilliants on her breast which Steyne had given her.
> He had her hand in his, and was bowing over to it to kiss it, when Becky started up
> with a faint scream as she caught sight of Rawdon's white face. (675)

After Rawdon throws out Steyne and discovers the money Steyne has given Becky in his wife's desk, the novel's narrator muses,

> What *had* happened? Was she guilty or not? She said not; but who could tell what was
> truth which came from those lips; or if that corrupt heart was in this case pure? All
> her lies and her schemes, all her selfishness and her wiles, all her wit and genius had
> come to this bankruptcy. (677)

The BBC adaptation resembles the novel insofar as it follows Rawdon's perspective. We hear Becky and Steyne laughing together, then see them only as Rawdon sees them, in long shot, reclined on a sofa, once he opens the door. The beginning of the next episode shows Becky sitting on the floor, whispering to herself, 'I am innocent'. Thus, the viewer witnesses two interpretations of the event: Rawdon's (the only one dramatised for the viewer), and Becky's insistence (to herself) upon her innocence. In contrast, Nair's version gives the viewer access to Becky and Steyne before Rawdon's interruption. Becky's cry is not in response to Rawdon's arrival but in response to Steyne's aggression, her realisation that she can no longer manage the transaction of 'taking favours from a tiger', about which Rawdon has warned her.

All three versions of this scene, however, lead to the same conclusion: Rawdon's rejection of Becky. Only Nair's version leaves viewers in no doubt that Becky, though naïve, is innocent. Thus, her fate appears doubly unjust, given Steyne's predatory nature and her husband's refusal to forgive her. As a result, Nair's film must offer a narrative compensation in order to 'rewar[d] her at the end of the film' (Moya 2010, 85). The happy ending in India with Jos Sedley (see Figure 1.2) fuses the film's recuperation of Becky with its visual and narrative privileging of the colonial periphery, one announced through the shorthand of a cut to a shot of adorned elephant feet.

If Thackeray's *Vanity Fair* invokes the colonies (not only India but also other sites such as the Caribbean, Canada, and China) without dramatising any of the narrative there, Nair's film both brings the colonies to the metropole and stages some scenes in the colonies themselves. As previously indicated, the servant Biju is one means of interpolating Britain's relationship to India into the narrative. Other means of foregrounding

Figure 1.2 Becky's happy ending in India with Jos.

the relations of empire include references to Rawdon's elder brother, Pitt's pamphlets 'on the Chickasaw tribes' and 'the Emancipation issue',[9] the costuming of Jos Sedley, in particular, in 'fantastically festooned waistcoats' in 'great Indian colours' (Nair 2005), and the inclusion of racialised extras, such as a group of Chinese men in an early scene of London's streets, and two Black servants standing guard at the gates to Lord Steyne's house, foregrounding London's 'burgeoning multi-culturalism' (Muir 2006, 228). The film's sets deliberately mix a variety of colonial inflections, as production designer Maria Djurkovic acknowledges: 'It's a mixture of everything – Chinese gongs, Moroccan lanterns, and Indian "mushroo" fabrics that we had shipped from India' (qtd in Universal Studios 2004, 60). However, Nair's film omits the Crawleys' financial connections to slavery through the parliament seat 'filled by Mr. Quadroon' (101), and indeed the fact that 'both the London traders Sedley and Osborn [*sic*] have made their fortune in the West Indies triangle trade' (Geracht 2016, 46). Thus, this adaptation privileges a visual opulence of empire, rather than its reliance on enslavement.

In fact, the film problematically displaces enslavement onto an exoticised and eroticised entertainment, the so-called 'slave dance' sequence at Lord

Steyne's house, with which the adaptation replaces the charades scene from the novel (643–52). The charades in the novel are deeply Orientalist, featuring Turkish and Egyptian characters, 'Eastern voyagers' (645), and merchants involved in the trafficking of enslaved people, as well as explicit anti-Muslim sentiment in the reference to an 'odious Mahometan' (645). Where Becky shocks her audience in the novel with her impersonation of Clytemnestra killing Agamemnon, the film's adaptation of this scene via the dance is intended to entice both Steyne and the king through Becky's prominent performance (dressed in black while the other women dance in red and brown costumes), and repel her husband and his brother and sister-in-law. But their repulsion comes from Becky's public eroticism, not from any objection to the construction of, in Nair's words, '[t]he opulence of Eastern splendor. A kind of Orientalist view, like a British view of what they thought the Indian harems, or the Middle Eastern harems, were like' (qtd in Universal Studios 2004, 69). Although Nair evinces a familiarity with the discourse of Orientalism – indeed, the final credits of the film thank Edward Said 'for continuing to inspire' – the film does not distinguish between the Orientalism of the period it represents and its own aesthetics (and their ideological implications). In the absence of self-reflexive contextualising of Regency Orientalism, '[the] film simply reveals Orientalist and colonialist agendas without critiquing the discursive and representative structures that underpin them' (Machalias 2011, 54). The film's dedication to visual splendour in its representation of India and Indian cultural influences as its most privileged currency frustrates what appears to be the director's intention, collapsing the film's visual politics into those of the society it represents.

Scenes in colonial locations fill in the gaps of Thackeray's geographical representation, to an extent. We witness Rawdon's arrival at Coventry Island, where Steyne's machinations have sent him to be governor. This short scene, shot on 'a scrub of land . . . outside the desert in Jodhpur' (Nair 2005), primarily serves to underscore Rawdon's sense of having been banished to a 'graveyard' (where he will die of 'tropical fever'), where his military regalia contrasts sharply with the slight clothing of the 'natives' who carry his belongings for him.[10] Brief scenes set in India feature the character of Dobbin, George Osborne's friend who has long suffered from his unrequired love for Amelia. Dobbin's Indian exile reveal his character, in Nair's words, to have 'gone savage, gone native' (2005), as his hair gets progressively longer, and his dress shifts from English to Indian clothes; further, 'in one scene he seems to be sitting in a stupor in some kind of opium den' (Clarke 2008, 52). Dobbin's masculinity is both recuperated and becomes too dangerous. In a wrestling match with another Englishman, he overpowers his opponent too forcefully: 'Good Lord, Dobbs. Have you lost your mind altogether?' Dobbin replies, 'It's time I returned to England.' Thus, for Rawdon and Dobbin, both disappointed in their relationships with women, the colonies present locations of both besting masculinity (in Rawdon's case) and recuperating it, but too aggressively (in Dobbin's). Dobbin must return to England to recalibrate his masculinity in order to make him worthy of Amelia: assertive enough to force a discussion of their relationship (eventually), but adequately re-Anglicised after his Indian exile.

The film presents a mixed relationship between India and masculinity, for it is Jos Sedley who is most associated with India at the same time as he is the film's least masculine character. Although the film does not place him, as the novel does, in Brussels, where his cowardice leads him to flee the city during the Battle of Waterloo, other male characters do laugh at him when he claims he would go to Belgium were it not for his commitments in India. The film's resolution in India, after Jos has happened upon Becky in Germany, brings together the two characters who, as in the novel, are the most 'nationally hybrid characters' (Zoli 2007, 420), given Jos's dual national positioning and Becky's French mother. They are also the two characters who most disturb gender conventions, with Jos 'oscillating between masculinity and femininity' (Cantwell 2015, para. 20) and Becky's agency and desire rupturing the gender conventions of the period.

Thus, their happy ending is to be found outside Europe, and the film's concluding with Becky and Jos on the back of an elephant 'in a sort-of imperial-style procession of that time' in Rajasthan visually privileges India in its contrasting of 'the heat and light of India with the wintery cold of England' (Nair 2005). While a triumph for Becky (who presumably does not murder Jos for his insurance policy, as the novel hints [877]), it is not clear that the film's version of Jos has transcended 'his fetishized love for all things Indian' (Zoli 2007, 419), as exhibited in the novel. Not only does the film trade in exoticism, therefore (see Machalias 2011, 53), but in reuniting Jos and Becky thus, it also resolves Jos's romantic fate in a way that would soothe his father's racist anxieties. In the film, Becky's first attempt to secure Jos as a husband, when she has only just left Pinkerton's, arouses Mrs Sedley's suspicions, prompting her husband to declare, 'Let Jos marry whom he likes. She has no fortune, but nor had you. Better her than a black Mrs Sedley from Boggley-Wollah and a dozen mahogany grandchildren.' Just as Dobbin must recover from his 'going native' before he is suitable for Amelia, so too Jos, apparently, only gets *his* reward of a happy ending by bringing 'his memsahib home' (Nair 2005) to India.

For Nair, the altered ending returns the novel to its creator's origins: 'we needed Becky to go back to the origins from whence her creator, Thackeray himself, had been born. Because Becky Sharp was entranced with India, from the romance of the chilli peppers to reading the *Arabian Nights'* (Nair 2005). The location shooting in Jodhpur, with which the film ends, allows India to close out the narrative. As Nair acknowledges (2005), earlier scenes in the film set in England were in fact shot in India, namely interiors at Pinkerton's and the dressing room where Rawdon, cinching his wife into her corset, warns Becky about Lord Steyne; conversely, scenes featuring Dobbin in India were filmed in Colchester and Elveden (Universal Studios 2004, 35). This 'trick' of 'Empire . . . on a grand scale' (35) illustrates, at the level of production, the interpenetration of metropole and colony. Similarly, Bollywood influences, both acknowledged by Nair and inferred by critics, juxtapose Western and Indian modes of representation. Nair speaks of the transition between Rawdon and Becky's toddler son walking for the first time to an older version of Rawdy skipping in the park, as 'show[ing] in a slightly Bollywood way the passage of time' (2005), while Clarke attributes the 'slave dance' scene to Bollywood influence (2008, 50). Stratmann invokes Bollywood as though blaming its influence for Nair's choices at the same time as he elevates *Vanity Fair* above Bollywood: the novel's ending 'is obviously not an acceptable ending by the standards of Bollywood', but *Vanity Fair* is 'a far better Bollywood film than most of the others' (2009, 90). Clearly, there is some critical uncertainty about how to position *Vanity Fair* in relation to 'the lenses of Bollywood' (89), and it is perhaps too easy (and lazy) to conflate the prominence of India in Nair's film with Hindi cinema. Nonetheless, as Richard Alleva argues, the film's invocations of India have a tendency towards 'eye candy' (2004, 23), suggesting an ultimately superficial response to the source text.

If, through Jos, 'Thackeray suggests the consequences of unregulated imperial desire' (Cantwell 2015, para. 20), Nair's film valorises imperial desire. Indeed, it is Becky's desire for India that recuperates her and wins her a happy ending through her 'triumphant acquisition of the "beauty" that is India' (Heffelfinger and Wright 2011, 140). The film illustrates the relationship between metropole and colony, but largely through aesthetically pleasing detail. In its representation of Regency Orientalism, the film replicates, rather than critiques or even comments on, that exoticist discourse of the non-European Other. Although the film convincingly presents Lord Steyne as a figure of predatory masculine violence to which Becky falls victim, Becky's salvation through 'the heat and light of India' does little to unsettle, or even question, the imperial imbalance of power.

Both Campion and Nair dislodge the geographical frame of their respective source texts, Campion self-reflexively through her film preface and Nair by showing the colonies only invoked from the metropole but not represented in Thackeray's novel. Whereas Campion's film dramatises transnational relations almost solely between Western nations coded as white, Nair disrupts the whitewashing of British history, insisting visually upon the mutual interpenetration of imperial and colonised cultures. Yet *Vanity Fair* does not acknowledge the politicised implications of this interpenetration, rendering Indian culture beautiful but decontextualised; indeed, as Graham Huggan writes, exoticism is an 'aesthetics of decontextualisation' (2001, 17). Where *The Portrait of a Lady* defamiliarises Orientalism through non-realistic modes of cinema, *Vanity Fair* ends up replicating it. At the same time, Campion's film, while jettisoning James's characters' ignorant comments about Indigenous peoples and African Americans, includes almost no racialised people, apart from a few women in the cinematic preface and the glimpses of local people in the montage of Isabel and Merle's travels. Beyond this surrealist representation, however, the nineteenth-century world Campion depicts, in sharp contrast to Nair's film, is exclusively white.

They are also worlds in which male power is always in the foreground. Both Isabel Archer and Becky Sharp, as emphasised in these two films, are subject to the violence of a male collector figure who seeks to absorb them into his collection. Both films offer a more promising ending for their female protagonists (or at least, a potentially promising one in Isabel's case), fitting for adaptations of the late twentieth and early twenty-first centuries that gaze back, as it were, to their canonical male-authored nineteenth-century source texts. If film adaptations of nineteenth-century literature are often associated with heritage cinema, *The Portrait of a Lady* and *Vanity Fair*, 'post-heritage'[11] films that offer distinctive translations of the novels they adapt in terms of both visual and narrative components, disrupt these expectations in their own ways. Indeed, both films were considered box office failures, perhaps proving too controversial for the tastes of mainstream audiences. But with its more positive (and certain) resolution, despite its interest in non-Western culture, *Vanity Fair* sidesteps troubling questions about nation, race and representation that almost arise but recede from view, while in *The Portrait of a Lady*, those questions of race and representation are never really in view in the first place.

CHAPTER 2

Salvaging Slavery Subtexts
in *Mansfield Park* and *Wuthering Heights*

Published in the early and mid-nineteenth century, respectively, Jane Austen's *Mansfield Park* (1814) and Emily Brontë's *Wuthering Heights* (1847) each contain a slavery subtext: the eponymous country house Mansfield Park in Austen's novel, the site of protagonist Fanny Price's upbringing and development from the age of ten onwards, is owned by her aunt's husband, Sir Thomas Bertram, who also owns an estate in Antigua; the character of Heathcliff in Brontë's novel is brought to Wuthering Heights from the major slave port of Liverpool by Mr Earnshaw, and despite varied descriptions of his appearance is consistently racially Othered. Austen's and Brontë's novels are more oblique in their references to racial difference and empire than Thackeray's *Vanity Fair* and James's *Portrait of a Lady*, but they are products of empire nonetheless. If Austen only alludes briefly to Sir Thomas's ownership and experiences of the Antiguan estate, and Brontë never explicitly specifies Heathcliff's racialised identity, the novels' historical contexts of the late eighteenth to early nineteenth century encompass Britain's involvement in the slave trade as well as significant ownership of slave-holding properties on the imperial periphery. Critical debates surrounding the nature of the Bertrams' wealth and Austen's and/or her novel's position on it and the representation of Heathcliff have reached no real consensus.

Film adaptations of *Mansfield Park*, directed by Patricia Rozema (1999), and *Wuthering Heights*, directed by Andrea Arnold (2011), offer their own versions of these narratives' implication in questions of empire and race, extrapolating from the novels' gestures towards slavery and salvaging this context for their screen versions of these two novels. They thus intervene in critical discourse by visualising the filmmakers' readings of these texts. Further, the construction of domestic spaces and their environs in both these films underscores issues of power as they reside in questions of hospitality in both narratives. Rozema's version of *Mansfield Park* carefully positions Fanny in relation to domestic spaces in order to articulate her relationship to power in ways that many critics of the novel have often failed to do in their political sloppiness where questions of gender and race are concerned. Similarly, Arnold's *Wuthering Heights* uses both interior and exterior settings to trace racialised power in Yorkshire. Linda Hutcheon observes that 'the act of adaptation always involves both (re-)interpretation and then (re)creation; this has been called both appropriation and salvaging, depending on your perspective' (2013, 8). Although both films have attracted criticism for privileging politicised readings of their source texts, as though imposing concerns of the late twentieth and early twenty-first centuries onto nineteenth-century novels, these adaptations simultaneously deliver readings of the novels grounded in historical context and address concerns of the present in their acts of salvage.

Mansfield Park

Sir Thomas's Antiguan estate and the issue of slavery occupy the margins of *Mansfield Park*'s narrative, but they are nevertheless insistently present in Austen's 'colonially alert novel' (Landry 2000, 57). As Katie Trumpener asks, '[W]hat if the effects of slavery and colonialism are not so easily visible, either on the faces of the beneficiaries or on the surface of British social life'? (1997, 176). The Antiguan estate provides the premise for Sir Thomas's long absence (more than a year and a half) from Mansfield Park when he attends to matters on his Caribbean property, given 'recent losses on his West India estate' (24) mentioned, incidentally, early in the novel. Upon Sir Thomas's return from Antigua, Fanny herself introduces the subject of the slave trade, but Austen presents the conversation indirectly, when Fanny says to her cousin Edmund,

> 'I do talk to him [Sir Thomas] more than I used. I am sure I do. Did not you hear me ask him about the slave trade last night?'
> 'I did – and was in hopes the question would be followed up by others. It would have pleased your uncle to be inquired of farther.'
> 'And I longed to do it – but there was such dead silence!' (2003, 184)

Thus, the subject of slavery surfaces in the text only to be submerged, both in the conversation being recounted and in Fanny and Edmund's recollection afterwards, which swiftly shifts to Edmund's praise of Mary Crawford, with whom Edmund is in love for much of the novel.

Critics taking up the references to Antigua and slavery in the novel have, unsurprisingly, focused on this scene, attempting to discern the meaning behind the 'dead silence' that follows Fanny's voicing the issue of the slave trade with which the Mansfield Park household, twinned as it is with

Sir Thomas's Antiguan estate, must be inescapably complicit. As George Boulukos notes, many analyses of *Mansfield Park* consider 'this discussion symbolic of the family's, and the broader society's, desire to avoid or marginalize the colonial violence upon which their economic status depends' (2006, 368). Boulukos argues that Sir Thomas is not offended by Fanny's question, given Edmund's encouragement of Fanny on his father's behalf, and that the novel upholds Sir Thomas 'as a morally exemplary slave-owner' (362), primarily interested in the amelioration of conditions in which enslaved people lived and worked. The fact that Fanny 'love[s] to hear [her] uncle talk of the West Indies' (Austen 2003, 183) suggests she may not be critical of his position as an owner of enslaved people (Boulukos 2006, 369). As Moira Ferguson notes, however, given the news reported in the British press in the years between the abolition of the slave trade in 1807 and the publication of *Mansfield Park* in 1814 'of increasing atrocities' (1991, 119) in Caribbean plantations, the argument in favour of amelioration rather than emancipation would seem to have been undermined by the time of Austen's writing of the novel. Capitani writes of the 'dead silence' following Fanny's invocation of the slave trade that '[o]ne conjectures that it is not just the cousins who are silent, but Sir Thomas as well' (2002, 3); indeed, he does not provide a response to fill that silence, which 'Fanny problematizes' (Tuite 2000, 104). For Edward Said – whose postcolonial analysis of *Mansfield Park* was not the first despite its prompting numerous responses – the dead silence in Mansfield Park's drawing room 'suggest[s] that one world could not be connected with the other since there simply is no common language for both' (1994, 115). Given that Austen provides us reported silence, critics have often sought to fill it with, as Capitani owns, conjecture. Regardless, as Carl Plasa argues, Fanny 'breach[es] social decorum' (2000, 33) by raising the issue of the slave trade, as she speaks it to an unreceptive room.

Mansfield Park invokes slavery in the linguistic sense at three points in novel: Fanny's question about the slave trade; Mrs Norris's claim to 'have been slaving myself till I can hardly stand' (154) in making Rushworth's cloak for the aborted plays;[1] and the narrator's description of Mary Crawford, following Henry's proposal of marriage to Fanny, as being 'not the slave of opportunity' (331). Only Fanny's invocation relates to actual enslaved people, with Mrs Norris's invocation predictably overstating her labour and the description of Mary evincing her jettisoning of social conformity. Much of the critical literature about *Mansfield Park* and the submerged slavery subtext relies on an analogy – and indeed, at times, a fusion – between racialised and gendered oppression, often with an accompanying contention that Fanny herself constitutes a slave at Mansfield Park.

Maggie Malone claims that Fanny 'is the slave at the centre of patriar-chy, and Mansfield Park is the plantation' (1993, 33). Like many critics, Malone vacillates between metaphor and simile in describing Fanny's sta-tus, with the former quotation substituting Fanny for an enslaved woman and a later argument stating that 'Fanny, like a slave, is torn from her home and family at an early age and transported to Mansfield Park, "the planta-tion"' (1993, 33). For Said, Fanny figures 'as a kind of indentured servant or, to put the case in extreme terms, as a kind of transported commodity' (1994, 106). Ferguson describes Fanny's connection to Sir Thomas as a 'master–slave relationship' (1991, 123); and Claudia L. Johnson contends that 'Sir Thomas exacts compliance from Fanny in the same way' (1988, 107) that he does from his slaves.

If 'slave subjectivity has to be effaced' (133) in Austen's novel, Ferguson argues, 'Fanny Price signifies a bartered slave and the sign of the absent female slave' (135). In this analysis, Fanny is both enslaved and not, like the vacillation between metaphor and simile in Malone's reading. For Ferguson,

> [a]s the oppressed daughter of an exigent family, Fanny Price becomes the appro-priate mediator or representative of slaves' silenced existence and constant insur-rectionary potential. In her role as a marginalized other (though in a vastly different cultural context), Fanny Price can project and displace personal-political anxieties and mimic her servile subject position. (133)

What is parenthetical for Ferguson, the 'vastly different cultural context' is, in fact, crucial. If the notion of Fanny-as-slave echoes early feminist analyses of gendered disempowerment (such as those of Mary Astell and Mary Wollstonecraft),[2] the notion that '[t]he 'slave trade' is a trope for the marriage market and for the tyranny of marriage' (Perry 1994, 101) must not paper over the fact that slavery is *not* just a trope, not even in *Mansfield Park*, and not even if Austen's energies were largely devoted to represent-ing 'the condition of white gentlewomen over any concern about black slaves' (Mee 2000, 85).

Whether or not the novel ironises the connection between Fanny's position and slavery, 'even as Fanny . . . occupies the moral center of a Mansfield Park that continues to depend for all its material comforts on the colonized and enslaved inhabitants of Antigua' (Kuwahara 1995, 110), is an urgent question. John Wiltshire criticises Fanny-as-slave readings of the novel on the grounds 'that there is any but the loosest relation between the state of slavery and the condition of a genteel young English woman as depicted in the novel' (2003, 308), although unfortunately, and rather outrageously, he also equates postcolonial criticism of Austen's novel with imperialism's 'ignor[ing] or pervert[ing] the cultural life of indigenous peoples' (317). It is possible – indeed, essential – to acknowledge the fault lines in equating Fanny's position with that of enslaved people without doing away with postcolonial critique. As Plasa cautions, we must not 'pre-suppos[e] the comparability of orders of oppression which, in the end, are radically distinct from one another' (2000, 34), though he, too, likens Fanny en route to Mansfield for the first time to 'the dislocated slave-child who is her historical counterpart' (35). If Fanny's gender allocates her an 'incompletely realized citizenship' (Fraiman 1995, 821), this structure of disempowerment must not be confused with slavery.

Examining *Mansfield Park* through the lens of hospitality enables us to trace relations of gendered, class-based and racialised power that inter-sect at Mansfield Park without collapsing them. Sir Thomas is 'master at Mansfield Park' (343) and at his Antiguan plantation; he is master in terms of patriarchy, class hierarchy and ownership of enslaved people. As Ruth Bernard Yeazell argues of *Mansfield Park*, 'no other novel of Jane Austen's calls such attention to its boundaries, emphasizes so strenuously the line between the in and the out' (1984, 147), boundaries that are clearly articulated in relation to Fanny. We know from the outset of the narra-tive that as far as Sir Thomas is concerned, Fanny 'is not a *Miss Bertram*' (12). Given the difference in 'rank, fortune, rights, and expectations' (12), Fanny can never be the equal of her cousins Maria and Julia. Her welcome at Mansfield is unconvincing: 'Nobody meant to be unkind, but nobody put themselves out of their way to secure her comfort' (15). Indeed, even prior to Fanny's arrival the Bertrams' hospitality is suspect: Sir Thomas declares to his wife and sister-in-law, 'We shall probably see much to wish altered in her, and must prepare ourselves for gross ignorance, some meanness of opinions and very distressing vulgarity of manner; but these are not incurable faults' (11). This expectation of Fanny is a far cry from Derrida's exhortation to hospitality, 'Let us say yes *to who or what turns up*, before any anticipation, before any *identification*, whether or not it has to do with a foreigner, an immigrant, an invited guest, or an unexpected visitor' (Derrida 2000, 77). The anticipation of Fanny is hardly articulated posi-tively. After her arrival, the house itself appears inhospitable in its 'gran-deur': 'The rooms were too large for her to move in with ease; whatever she touched she expected to injure, and she crept about in constant terror of something or other; often retreating towards her own chamber to cry' (15). Indeed, the location of Fanny's chamber, 'the little white Attic, near the old Nurseries' (11), accentuates Fanny's marginal position. Although she is 'not far from the girls' – i.e. Maria and Julia – the fact that Fanny is 'so near Miss Lee . . . and close by the housemaids' clearly displaces her, in both literal and class terms, from the family. For Nicholas Preus, 'the house seems only barely to accept her, and even to reject or eject her' (1995, 169–70). Although Fanny gradually adjusts to Mansfield, as '[t]he place [becomes] less strange, and the people less formidable' (Austen 2003, 17), due to both her class and gender she can never occupy the host position.

Patricia Rozema's adaptation of *Mansfield Park*, like Austen's novel, suggests connections between gendered and class-based oppression and enslavement. It also visualises relations of hospitality, particularly although not exclusively as they relate to Fanny. The scene of young Fanny's (Hannah Taylor Gordon) arrival at Mansfield Park deviates from the novel's insofar as in Austen's version, Mrs Norris travels to Northampton to meet her, whereas in Rozema's film, Fanny arrives at Mansfield Park itself by coach in darkness, at five o'clock in the morning. The film demonstrates the failure of hospitality through canted framing as the coach approaches the house. Her cousin, Tom Bertram (James Purefoy), is on the balcony above the entrance, drunk, his back turned to Fanny and the coachman. In reply to the coachman's protest, 'I was told most definitely to drop her at the entrance of Mansfield Park', Tom insists, 'Then drop her.' Rather than welcome his young cousin into the house, Tom leaves her there, where she stands, shivering and alone, until Mrs Norris (Sheila Gish) arrives in daylight, full of irritation: 'He brought you two hours too early.'

Mrs Norris, although she does not live at Mansfield at this point (she does after the death of her husband, a change from the novel), assumes the rights and privileges of the host at Mansfield Park. She walks ahead of Fanny before turning back and saying curtly, 'Come in', delivered as an exasperated order rather than an invitation. The ruptured hospitality and Fanny's disorientation appear through stylised camera movement, with a rotating shot of the ceiling and tilt downward to a low-angle shot of Fanny that diminishes her in relation to the space. Mrs Norris figures Fanny as always already a disappointment: not only did Fanny's mother 'clearly marr[y] to disoblige her family', as Mrs Norris says to Fanny directly (this line taken from the narrator in the novel), but also, having seized Fanny's shoulders with the imperative, 'Now, let us have a look at you', she delivers the verdict of 'Well . . . I'm sure you have other qualities.' Upon the entrance of Sir Thomas (Harold Pinter), Mrs Norris and he debate where Fanny is to live, either the parsonage or Mansfield proper (a conversation that takes place in the novel prior to Fanny's arrival). Sir Thomas's arrival also ushers in a shift in camera angles, with a high-angle shot of Fanny diminishing her in relation to Sir Thomas's power. Mrs Norris marches Fanny out of the room so that she can continue her negotiations with

Sir Thomas, leaving her in the hallway (still diminished by the high-angle shot), and pointing at her as though telling her to 'stay', like a dog, before shutting the door behind her. Fanny's positioning in liminal spaces between rooms recurs throughout the film, emphasising the extent to which she is not granted the right of free access. The novel articulates this lack of entitlement later in the narrative, following Sir Thomas's return from Antigua, when Fanny 'find[s] herself at the drawing-room door, and after pausing a moment for what she knew would not come, for a courage which the outside of no door had ever supplied to her' (165). In the film, upon Fanny's arrival, the difference between her and her cousins is made evident in the film. Maria (Elizabeth Eaton) and Julia (Elizabeth Earl), giggling at their cousin, introduce themselves to Fanny in the hallway and then enter the room from which Fanny has been barred, where her fate is being decided by her aunt and uncle. Despite Fanny's positioning outside the room, she can hear nevertheless Sir Thomas's advice to his daughters: 'She is not your equal. But that must never be apparent to her. It is a point of great delicacy.' Of course, even without Fanny's overhearing this remark, it is always made clear to Fanny that she is not the social equal of her wealthier cousins, and that her claim to Mansfield Park as home is far less secure than the Bertram sisters'; her role, Mrs Norris indicates to her, is to be her aunt's assistant.

The film includes a scene in which Mrs Norris gives Fanny a tour of Mansfield Park at breakneck speed: at this pace, the tour, intended to introduce Fanny to the house, has the effect of defamiliarising it instead, as it also does for the viewer in conjunction with the stylisation of camera angles and movements. Mrs Norris indicates the gendering of space within the house, pointing out '[t]he billiard room, for the men, of course' and Sir Thomas's study, 'his personal sanctuary' where Fanny is ordered '[n]ever [to] disturb him'. Following the location of the maids' and manservants' rooms – away from the Bertrams' rooms, as in the novel – Fanny is told, 'up here, what was formerly the nursery and then the governess's room, is now your very own room.' The room, full of upturned furniture and dust sheets, hardly appears to be Fanny's 'very own', and the sound of the wind blowing suggests it is an inhospitable space (made more so by the fact that, as in the novel, Mrs Norris refuses to allow Fanny a fire). That Fanny does not wield the power of host even in her 'very own room' is made consistently clear in the film by the several instances where other characters – chiefly Edmund (Jonny Lee Miller), Mary Crawford (Embeth Davidtz), and Sir Thomas, all above her in the social hierarchy – assume the right to enter it.

Sir Thomas's visit to Fanny's (Frances O'Connor's) room, precipitated by Henry Crawford's (Alessandro Nivola's) marriage proposal, prompts the moment of Fanny's rebellion, discussed by many critics (e.g. Jordan 2000, 41), given her refusal to obey her uncle/master in his desire for her to accept the proposal. The scene both rearticulates Fanny's claim to the host position and denies it. On the one hand, Sir Thomas, noting the empty grate, declares that she will have a fire from now on, and that Fanny 'may make [him] more proud . . . than [his] own daughters'. He regrets the 'misplaced distinction' between Fanny and her cousins, despite his being the author of said distinction. But the initiation of Fanny into the host position depends upon her acceptance of Crawford's proposal. When she refuses, he effectively banishes her (much more explicitly than 'the semipunitive scheme' [Johnson 2012, 168] in the novel), sending her to Portsmouth where '[a] little abstinence from the luxuries and elegances of Mansfield Park might bring [her] mind into a more sober state'. Between the scene in Fanny's room and her departure, the film depicts Fanny as the recipient of several lectures by Sir Thomas in different rooms of the house, with extreme close-up shots on her uncle's lips as he attacks her character. The framing of Sir Thomas acts as a counterpart to the canted framing and pronounced camera angles through which Fanny's arrival at Mansfield is conveyed, underscoring the fracture of hospitality and Fanny's precarious status. As Claudia L. Johnson observes of the novel, 'Fanny is slow to grasp that her very presence at Mansfield Park is a gift and that a return is compulsory' (2012, 169). When the film's Sir Thomas asks if a return to Portsmouth, rather than marriage to Crawford, is more palatable to Fanny, she assents, desiring '[t]o be at home again, to be loved by my family, to feel affection without fear or restraint and to feel myself the equal of those that surround me', a clear recognition of both her inability to return the 'gift' of her upbringing and her exclusion from the host position at Mansfield Park.

In the novel, as critics note (see Fraiman 1995, 809–10), Fanny romanticises Mansfield Park once she has returned to Portsmouth:

> At Mansfield, no sounds of contention, no raised voice, no abrupt bursts, no tread of violence was ever heard; all proceeded in a regular course of cheerful orderliness; every body had their due importance; every body's feelings were consulted. If tenderness could be ever supposed wanting, good sense, and good breeding supplied its place; and as to the little irritations, sometimes introduced by aunt Norris, they were short, they were trifling, they were as a drop of water to the ocean, compared with the ceaseless tumult of her present abode. (Austen 2003, 363)

In the film, Fanny tells Henry Crawford that 'Portsmouth is Portsmouth, and Mansfield is home'. Further, she articulates her preference in terms of financial security – 'Poverty frightens me, and a woman's poverty is a slavery more harsh than a man's' – rather than offer the rose-tinted fiction of Mansfield from the novel, which suggests a class-based self-loathing.

If the novel's Fanny misreads Mansfield once she returns to Portsmouth, the film's Fanny collapses poverty, especially gendered poverty, with slavery. (And as she utters this line about slavery and poverty, a ship appears in the background – possibly, although not necessarily, a slave ship.) Neither is it the first time in the film that Fanny makes an equation between gendered oppression and slavery, much as many of the novel's critics do. Unlike the novel, the return of Sir Thomas from Antigua does not constitute the first mention of slavery in the film. As a child, Fanny becomes aware of enslaved people off the coast of England when first travelling to Mansfield Park from Portsmouth (itself a slave port [Aragay 2003, 177]), hearing human cries from a ship in a bay that the coach passes by. The coachman explains that the ship is carrying 'black cargo. . . . Slaves. Probably some captain or heroic ship doctor brought home some darkies as gifts for the wife.' The Bertrams' own relationship to slavery becomes apparent in a conversation between Fanny and Edmund. Speculating that Sir Thomas 'regrets taking [her] in', Fanny is told, '[I]t's problems with the slaves on the plantation. The abolitionists are making inroads.' When Fanny responds, 'That's a good thing, isn't it?' Edmund reminds her, 'Well, we all live off the profits, Fanny. Including you.'

The film's recognition of the Bertrams' – and Fanny's – complicity with slavery prefigures Fanny's likening of herself to a slave. This moment follows the scene in which Fanny asks Sir Thomas a question about the status of enslaved people in England. But unlike the novel, Fanny does not introduce the topic. Rather, Sir Thomas speaks of people he enslaves in response to Lady Bertram's (Lindsay Duncan's) request, 'Do tell us about the Negroes, dear', at the point where Fanny enters the room carrying a tray. Sir Thomas replies by describing 'mulattos' who are 'well-shaped, and the women especially well-featured. I have one so easy and graceful in her movements and intelligent as well.'

He likens 'mulattos' to mules, claiming they 'can never have children', appealing to Edward Long's notoriously racist *History of Jamaica*, when Edmund protests. When Sir Thomas declares his desire 'to bring one of them back with me next trip, to work here as a domestic', Fanny replies,

> Correct me if I am in error, Sir Thomas, but I've read, sir, that if you were to bring one of the slaves back to England, there would be some argument as to whether or not they should be freed here.

Fanny thereby invokes Lord Justice Mansfield's decision in *Somerset v. Stewart* (1772), which critics have noted Austen gestures towards in the naming of both the novel's country house and its title (Kirkham 2000,

117–18; Mee 2000, 84). Fanny's observation leads to the dead silence indicated in the novel; indeed, Rozema's screenplay specifies that a 'dead silence' (2000, 60) ensues. This silence is broken by Sir Thomas's evaluation of her physical appearance and his declaration that they will host a ball in her honour where, according to her uncle, '[s]urely some young man of good standing will sit up and take notice.' Fleeing the room, Fanny is followed by Edmund, to whom she says, 'I'll not be sold off like one of your father's slaves', the film thereby both putting slavery and marriage in contiguous relation to each other and suggesting the possibility that Fanny's later refusal of Crawford's proposal signifies a kind of slave rebellion.

The invocation of Laurence Sterne's *A Sentimental Journey* in the film also blurs the boundaries between slavery and marriage. In the novel, Maria invokes Sterne at Sotherton, Rushworth's estate, prior to Maria's marriage to him: 'that iron gate, that ha-ha, give me a feeling of restraint and hardship. I cannot get out, as the starling said' (93). Sterne's text invokes slavery through the starling's cage,[3] to which Maria compares her imminent (unhappy, as well as doomed) marriage. In the film, Crawford interrupts Fanny in the library (assuming his entitlement to enter without invitation) where she is reading Sterne's novel. Taking the book from her, he reads the starling passage aloud, with Maria (Victoria Hamilton) observing from outside the room. In the film, Maria and Crawford's affair begins during Tom's illness at Mansfield, where they are discovered *in flagrante delicto* by Fanny. When Edmund enters Maria's room, Maria implores him, 'Don't look at me like that, Edmund. Rushworth is a fool, and you know it, and I can't get out. Edmund – I can't get out'. In this way, the film maintains the possibility of marriage, especially in this historical period, operating like slavery in terms of women's lack of rights.

But despite these gestures towards earlier feminist arguments about marriage that deploy slavery as a comparison, the film ultimately undermines them. Sir Thomas's trip to Antigua facilitates the misbehaviour of his children at Mansfield Park during his absence, but the 'offstage action' (Fleishman 1970, 36) that constitutes his experiences there goes unnarrated in the novel and undramatised in the film. Tom, the eldest son, who accompanies his father to the Caribbean, provides a window into Sir Thomas's actions in Antigua. The film characterises Tom as resisting his father's involvement in slavery, as demonstrated in a brief clash between them prior to their departure. In response to Sir Thomas shouting, 'You will do as I say!' Tom replies, 'What, and do as you do? Even I have principles, sir.' At this point, Fanny brings laudanum to Lady Bertram, who can clearly overhear the argument between her husband and son, but only says, 'Ah, you are an angel', before drinking two doses. The film suggests therefore that Lady Bertram's indolence may be a result of coping with her husband's estate's participation in slavery, and its concomitant tensions within her family. Likewise, Tom's own drunkenness implicitly figures as a response to turmoil over his family's slave-dependent fortunes. When Fanny arrives at Mansfield Park, she and Mrs Norris pass by a tortured self-portrait of Tom's, deemed 'very modern' by Mrs Norris, but suggestive again of his resistance to his father's ownership of enslaved people and the expectation that he will carry on his father's work as the eldest (see Rozema 2004, 259) while 'all the lovely people [in Antigua are] paying for this party.' Yet Tom's resistance has its political limitations: in the rehearsal of *Lover's Vows*, interrupted by Sir Thomas, Tom appears in blackface. Although Tom may do so 'as if in sympathy with the slaves', as Jocelyn Harris posits (2003, 60), his claiming the subaltern status of an enslaved person is totally incommensurable with his position as a white, English baronet's heir.

In her analysis of Austen's novel, Ferguson observes that 'the most egregiously and invisibly repressed of the text [are] African-Caribbeans themselves' (1991, 118). Sir Thomas's Antiguan estate remains 'ominously off-stage' (Mee 2000, 90) in Rozema's adaptation, in which enslaved people do not directly appear, either; instead, the film visualises them through the sketches in Tom's notebook, found by Fanny while tending her cousin during his illness. The presence of Sir Thomas at Mansfield Park, accompanied by Tom's sketches of his father brutalising slaves and engaging in sexual relations with enslaved women – common associations with West Indian planters at the time of the novel's publication (see Stewart 1993, 109; Mee 2000, 89) – fuses Sir Thomas as patriarchal master and slave master at his English and Antiguan estates. These images – albeit drawn by the slave master's heir – contradict previous equations of the upper-class English marriage market with the slave trade by depicting the violence of slavery, directly implicated in Mansfield Park's own maintenance. Although Suzanne R. Pucci argues that the film's 'world of early nineteenth-century domestic England remains intact as a smooth visual filmic surface' (2003, 150), Fanny reacts with horror as she flicks through the images (thereby exposing the viewer to them), and continues to do so even after Sir Thomas interrupts her. He angrily claims, 'My son is mad!' and sends her to her room (policing the boundaries of Mansfield Park's space and Fanny's entitlement to them), then tears the notebook before throwing it into the fire.

The film's happy ending in the form of Edmund's declaration of love for and proposal to Fanny is accompanied by an ambivalent development in

Mansfield Park's business: one the one hand, Fanny's voice-over narration tells us, 'Sir Thomas eventually abandoned his pursuits in Antigua'. At the end of the film, Lady Bertram walks around the Mansfield grounds, no longer indolent, and suddenly perceptive about the relationship between Fanny and Edmund: 'Looks like they're finally getting somewhere', she says approvingly. But Fanny informs us that the Antiguan business has been supplanted by 'some exciting new opportunities in . . . tobacco'. The pregnant pause sets up an ironic awareness of the fact that tobacco is hardly an innocent alternative to sugar, given its own imbrication in the labour of enslaved people. Thus, if Mansfield has been ostensibly purified through Tom's recovery from illness, the expulsion of the Crawfords, Maria and Mrs Norris, and the jettisoning of the Antiguan plantation, the film suggests that the Bertrams (indeed, any family in Britain at that time) cannot fully escape complicity with imperialism and the practice of slavery.[4]

Rozema's *Mansfield Park* attempts to redress a gap in representation that Raymond Williams diagnosed in Austen's work, namely that 'money . . . from the colonial plantations . . . has no visual equivalent' (1975, 144). Indeed, the Mansfield Park house itself (furnished with a statue of a Black servant holding a tray and bottle [see Figure 2.1]) is played in Rozema's film by Kirby Hall in Northamptonshire (the county where the fictional Mansfield Park is located). If some critics have protested that this 'oppressive and menacing semi-ruin' (Monaghan 2007, 92) is too old to fit the description of the 'spacious modern-built house' (Austen 2003, 45) that is Mansfield Park in Austen's novel, it nevertheless provides a visual reminder of Britain's role in the slave trade. A somewhat dilapidated building, 'abandoned in 1810 because (it is thought) of massive gambling debts' (Johnson 2000, 3–4) and now run by English Heritage, Kirby Hall has been considered by some critics to be too Gothic to stand in for Mansfield. As Rozema acknowledges in an interview, however, Mansfield Park's appearance as 'Gothic' was intended 'to contribute to its dark and mysterious side' as well as to invoke 'the tradition of the novel in Austen's time' (qtd in Rozema 2004, 259). Further, the emptiness of Kirby Hall/ Mansfield Park was supposed to convey Austen's 'historical period, for the interiors of Regency manor houses were in fact far less crowded and plush than their Victorian counterparts' (Johnson 2000, 3). Thus, as Johnson notes, Mansfield Park, in Rozema's film, 'looks cold, drafty, and in manifest disrepair' (2000, 4). In this respect (as in others), this adaptation departs from other Austen adaptations in the 1990s (referred to be some critics as 'Austenmania' [Sales 2004, 177]), including (although not limited to) Ang Lee's *Sense and Sensibility* and the BBC adaptation of *Pride and Prejudice*.

Figure 2.1 Statue of a Black servant at Mansfield Park.

Rozema's *Mansfield Park*, as Tim Watson argues, 'positions itself in explicit opposition to the nostalgic cult of the English country house', and through the house's representation in particular 'forcefully disrupt[s] and den[ies] the cozy image of elegant, prettified Jane Austen as a refuge from politics' (2005, 62, 63). Indeed, David Monaghan argues that Austen novels 'have too often been reduced to amusing and romantic stories played out within a *mise en scène* made up of nostalgic images of Regency England' (2007, 85); similarly, Deborah Cartmell observes that Austen adaptations tend to offer 'escapist representations of an idyllic past' (2000, 3). Critics have pointed to Rozema's film's divergence from heritage discourses more generally (as Belén Vidal argues, it 'represents the definitive internationalism of the Austen franchise beyond the British heritage aesthetics' [2006, 271]) and particularly heritage cinema. Like Jane Campion's adaptation of *The Portrait of a Lady*, Rozema's adaptation of *Mansfield Park* departs from the conventions and expectations of heritage cinema, but with far more interest in race and Britain's reliance on enslavement, even if it is out of sight. If the more traditional (and financially successful) Austen adaptations of the 1990s 'offer a sentimental view of the English estate and landscape' and 'an idyllic view of the English past' (Groenendyk 2004), Rozema's film counteracts heritage cinema's 'nostalgic and conservative celebration of the values and lifestyles of the privileged class' (Higson 2003, 12).

The Bertrams are hardly unique: 'most gentry families during the period had some connection with slavery' (Johnson 2000, 4).[5] The choice of Kirby Hall as the location for Mansfield Park illustrates this point, given that Kirby Hall was owned in the sixteenth century by Sir Christopher Hatton, who invested in voyages by Francis Drake, whose own Caribbean exploits included participation in the slave trade. Thus, Kirby Hall's own history resonates with the economic foundations of the fictional Mansfield Park estate. 'Heritage', according to Penny Gay, 'is not something [Rozema's adaptation] values but something that it uses: with nice irony' (2004, 387), given Kirby Hall's maintenance by English Heritage. Rozema's film, therefore, might be said to underscore the slavery underpinnings of both the fictional Mansfield Park and the historical (and actual) Kirby Hall. It is not simply heritage cinema, of course, that appeals to a nostalgia for an allegedly 'simpler' English society, structured around vastly unequal economic relations both within and outside the country, but also the heritage industry itself, major players in which include the English Heritage and National Trust organisations. If Julian Barnes accused the 1983 television adaptation of *Mansfield Park* of being a 'National Trust approach to literature: lots of raked gravel, background music, mob-capped actors vaguely familiar from previous classic serials and a deceptive deference to the surface of the text' (qtd in Fergus 2003, 69), Rozema's film represents a sharp divergence from this 'National Trust [or English Heritage] approach to literature', even as it thanks both organisations in the credits, as it surely must do, having used their properties.

In the decades since Rozema's film, however, both organisations have worked to uncover their properties' connections to slavery: coinciding with the bicentenary of the abolition of the slave trade in 2007, English Heritage 'commissioned . . . research . . . into links with transatlantic slavery or its abolition among families who owned properties now in its care' (Andrews 2013, vi); and, more recently, in 2020, the National Trust published their *Interim Report on the Connections between Colonialism and Properties now in the Care of the National Trust, Including Links with Historic Slavery*, which met with pronounced disapproval in conservative (and Conservative) political quarters. Thus, the connections made in Rozema's *Mansfield Park*, itself drawing on postcolonial criticism of Austen's novel, belong to a larger trajectory of scholarship and public discourse on the intersections between English heritage and empire.

If the film has suggested, at times, an equation between marriage and slavery, the personal plight of members of the gentry and their relations and those of enslaved people, it ultimately undermines this comparison, most clearly in the music that accompanies the final credits. The song 'Djonga' ('Slavery'), written and performed by Malian artist Salif Keita, undermines attempts to substitute those incommensurate orders of oppression, in Plasa's terms (2000, 34), for each other: it invokes the enslavement of Africans after much of the film has focused on gendered oppression in upper-class Britain. The wailing sounds of the song not only connect to the cries of people from a slave ship that the young Fanny, in the film, hears on her way to Mansfield Park for the first time (and imagines them later, on her return trip to Portsmouth), but also refuse to let the audience off the hook in confronting the material truths behind the lifestyle of the characters we have been watching. The film's direction by a Canadian woman, starring Australian (O'Connor), American (Nivola), and British actors, knits together in its production the reach of British colonialism. The film might have gone further in depicting Antigua itself, rather than leaving that task to Tom Bertram. But it is nonetheless an anti-heritage film that disrupts the usually 'positively connoted' (Bangert et al. 2016, xxvii) representation of the grandeur of country houses, given their status as 'very physical symbol[s]' of the wealth that the Empire could generate' (Barczewski 2014, 15), by persistently reminding viewers of how their grandeur came to be.

Wuthering Heights

Whereas Rozema's *Mansfield Park* emphasises the Caribbean slavery economy underpinning the fortunes of the English gentry all the while maintaining the geographical displacement of the site of the generation of the Bertrams' wealth, Andrea Arnold's *Wuthering Heights* (2011) visualises the operation of slavery and the plantation economy on English soil itself through the casting of Black actors in the role of Heathcliff as both a child and an adult. The racialised but non-specifically Othered Heathcliff of Emily Brontë's novel becomes firmly contextualised within the operations of the slave trade and Britain's activities within it, collected as he is by Mr Earnshaw in Liverpool, 'the premier slaving port' that would become 'responsible for more than eighty-four percent of the British transatlantic slave trade' (von Sneidern 1995, 172).[6] Relations of hospitality – particularly ruptured hospitality – pervade Brontë's novel through rights of access to both the eponymous Wuthering Heights and the Lintons' Thrushcross Grange and constant depiction of the abuses of power afforded by masters, especially Catherine's brother, Hindley, and later Heathcliff himself. Arnold's film inserts the workings of slavery into these hospitality ruptures and abuses of power.

If *Mansfield Park* suggests an analogy between class-based and gendered oppression and slavery, Arnold's *Wuthering Heights*, through its Yorkshire characters' vicious enunciations of racism and the position of the young Heathcliff, brings slavery itself to the English countryside. The film's aesthetics, obsessively cataloguing the natural world through extreme close-ups, both emphasises the Yorkshire setting and, in opposition to the rendering of Heathcliff as alien, embeds him within the landscape. Through semiotic gestures to late twentieth- and early twenty-first-century far-right politics in Britain in general and Yorkshire in particular, the film's representation of Heathcliff and his relationship to the Yorkshire landscape implicitly comments on present-day racism. At the same time, the famous intersubjectivity of Catherine's claim in the novel, 'I *am* Heathcliff' (Brontë 2003, 82), framed in the film as an interracial intersubjectivity, signals an incomplete understanding of the limits of different modes of oppression – gendered and racialised – as metaphors for each other.

Hospitality, and its failure, begins Brontë's novel through the treatment of the narrator, Lockwood, by Heathcliff, the owner of both Wuthering Heights and Thrushcross Grange, and Lockwood's landlord, as he has rented Thrushcross Grange to him. Instructed by Heathcliff to 'walk in', Lockwood reports, 'The "walk in" was uttered with closed teeth and expressed the sentiment, "Go to the Deuce!" Even the gate over which he leant manifested no sympathizing movement to the words' (3). Lockwood complains of Wuthering Heights's 'churlish inhospitality' (9), both the property's, with its borders traversed with difficulty, and its owner's. In fact, the novel is littered with examples of failed hospitality, from Heathcliff's treatment by the Earnshaws when he first arrives at Wuthering Heights ('Mrs Earnshaw was ready to fling it [i.e. Heathcliff] out of doors' [37]); to the Lintons refusing to welcome Heathcliff at Thrushcross Grange when Cathy is invited in to convalesce after being bitten by one of their dogs; to Edgar Linton's behaviour as a bad guest at Wuthering Heights by insulting Heathcliff; to the adult Heathcliff's lack of respect for boundaries, assuming the right to enter Thrushcross Grange at will when he returns to Yorkshire after Catherine and Edgar's marriage. Just as '[n]o spatial boundary remains intact' (Armstrong 1992, 249) in *Wuthering Heights*, so too relations of hospitality are always already failing throughout the narrative, part of the outsider Lockwood's horror at life 'so completely removed from the stir of society' (Brontë 2003, 3).

In many respects, ruptured hospitality sets the entire plot in motion, given the reception of Heathcliff at Wuthering Heights. Although young Catherine Earnshaw ultimately develops an extremely close relationship with Heathcliff, her first response upon his arrival is to 'gri[n] and spi[t] at the stupid little thing' (37). Again, Derrida's conception of hospitality as saying yes to whatever turns up deviates sharply from the Earnshaws' response to Heathcliff's arrival. Heathcliff is immediately – as he is throughout the rest of the novel – described in non-human terms, both as an object or animal (as the repeated use of the word 'it' to refer to him suggests) and as the spawn of the devil (36). Earnshaw takes Heathcliff in as ostensible act of charity, of hospitable kindness, having seen Heathcliff

> starving, and houseless, and as good as dumb in the streets of Liverpool where he picked it up and inquired after its owner – Not a soul knew to whom it belonged, he said, and his money and time, being both limited, he thought it better to take it home with him, at once, than run into vain expenses there; because he was determined he would not leave it as he found it. (37)

Thus, Earnshaw's charitable act is also the most cost-effective response to Heathcliff's poverty and homelessness. His wife, for her part, 'did fly up – asking how he could fashion to bring that gipsy brat into the house, when they had their own bairns to feed, and fend for?' (37). Mrs Earnshaw's economy diverges from her husband's, as she discerns an impending competition for resources between her children and her uninvited (by her) guest. If Mrs Earnshaw (who dies two years later, as the novel's next page reports) resents Heathcliff's presence, so does her son, Hindley, who 'persecut[es]' Heathcliff while viewing him 'as a usurper of his [father's] affections' (38), an indication that Hindley perceives Heathcliff to have wrongfully claimed the position of host at Wuthering Heights.

This discourse of failed hospitality is inextricable from the racialisation of Heathcliff, as Mrs Earnshaw's horror at 'that gipsy brat' indicates. Yet she is not the first to frame Heathcliff through racialisation. Earnshaw himself, upon his return from Liverpool, reveals Heathcliff with the description, 'it's as dark almost as if it came from the evil'; Nelly Dean's recollection of Heathcliff's arrival depicts him as 'a dirty, ragged, black-haired child' (36). The designation of Heathcliff as 'gipsy' will recur, as in Hindley's response to Heathcliff's demand that Hindley give him his horse, in compensation for Heathcliff's own which has fallen lame. Heathcliff effectively blackmails Hindley, threatening to inform Mr Earnshaw of the beatings he has received from Hindley. Hindley's response collapses Heathcliff's racialisation as 'gipsy', his (for Hindley, perpetual) outsider status, and his associations with both evil and the non-human: '"Take my colt, gipsy, then!" said young Earnshaw, "And I pray that he may break your neck; take him, and be damned, you beggarly interloper! and wheedle my father out of all he has: only, afterwards, show him what you are, imp of Satan'" (39). Thus, Hindley relentlessly Others Heathcliff according to a host of different categories.

Heathcliff's racialised identity is, as critics have noted, uncertain and unstable throughout the novel; as Corinne Fowler notes, 'we have to accept that Emily Brontë chose to be unspecific about his past or his ethnicity' (2020, 199). In addition to the designation of 'gipsy', 'the generic designation for a dark-complexioned alien in England' (Meyer 1996, 97), Heathcliff becomes associated, through his description by other characters, with a range of different identities and origins. Mr Linton, upon the discovery of the adolescent Cathy and Heathcliff at Thrushcross Grange, 'declare[s] [Heathcliff] is that strange acquisition [his] late neighbour made in his journey to Liverpool – a little Lascar, or an American or Spanish castaway' (50). Nelly, trying to improve Heathcliff's appearance prior to Edgar's visit to Wuthering Heights, muses,

> Who knows, but your father was Emperor of China, and your mother an Indian queen, each of them able to buy up, with one week's income, Wuthering Heights and Thrushcross Grange together? And you were kidnapped by wicked sailors, and brought to England. (58)

As Pauline Nestor writes of Emily Brontë's novel, 'It is the mystery surrounding Heathcliff – his lack of a personal history, his sullen uncommunicativeness, his almost magical capacity to remake himself during his absence from Wuthering Heights – which makes him such a suitable focus for others' projections'; indeed, Nestor asserts, 'Heathcliff becomes the receptacle of other people's fantasies' (Brontë 2003, xiii).

Just as other characters in the novel project identities onto Heathcliff, so too do literary critics. Mr Linton's hypotheses about Heathcliff's origins suggest either that 'the boy is of a race subject to European imperialism: Heathcliff may be the child of one of the Indian seamen, termed lascars, recruited by the East India Company to replace members of the British crews who died' or that Heathcliff 'is the cast-off offspring of one of those slaves' (98) trafficked through Liverpool. Regardless, as Cassandra Pybus notes, Mr Linton 'is definite about the boy's status as property' (2011, 16); indeed, so is Earnshaw himself, having 'inquired for [Heathcliff's] owner' (Brontë 2003, 37). Although Elsie Michie reads Heathcliff as Irish,[7] and his representation by Brontë as corresponding to 'the English tendency to caricature the Irish and represent them as an alien people' but 'screen[ing]' those representations through 'references to China, India, Turkey and the West Indies' (1992, 126, 125), the presence of slavery in Britain, a 'submerged social history' (Pybus 2011, 17), suggests Heathcliff's characterisation is not simply a deflection of 'local colonialism' (Michie 1992, 125). Michie contends that the novel's attention to Cathy's whiteness following her return from Thrushcross Grange – her 'fingers wonderfully whitened' (54) in contrast to Heathcliff's 'dusky fingers' (55) – 'suddenly fixe[s Heathcliff] as non-white' (133), but even though 'Heathcliff's racial identity remains ambiguous throughout the narrative' (Mardorossian 2006, 45), the novel, in fact, consistently codes Heathcliff as non-white.[8]

If the Yorkshire Sill family, as studied by Christopher Heywood, and their implication in 'the plantation economy in the region' reveal the possibility of the Earnshaws as an allegorised version of the Sills, who 'practised slaveholding in Dentdale' (1987, 186, 192, 193), the Sills were by no means exceptional, given the estimated 15,000 enslaved Black people in Britain in the late eighteenth century (Beaumont 2004, 143). Further, the novel's 'secret but self-evident theme of slavery' (Heywood 1987, 194) irrupts in dialogue. Nelly uses simile to compare her position to that of a slave following Cathy's return from Thrushcross Grange, claiming Hindley to be 'rather *too* indulgent in humouring [his sister's] caprices . . . [A]s long as she let him alone, she might trample us like slaves for ought he cared!' (89). Following Heathcliff's return to Yorkshire after Cathy and Edgar's marriage, Heathcliff declares himself intent on revenge, but not on Cathy herself: 'I seek no revenge on you . . . That's not the plan – The tyrant grinds down his slaves and they don't turn against him, they crush those beneath him' (112). At this point of the narrative, Edgar refers to Heathcliff as 'a runaway servant' whom Cathy, according to Edgar, mistakenly welcomes 'as a brother' (96). As such, Edgar's view of Heathcliff intersects with Hindley's in rejecting Heathcliff as part of the Earnshaw family and inserting him into the position of servant, where, as an adolescent, he has been subject to being flogged by Hindley (59), his 'master' following the death of Mr Earnshaw.

It may be that, in Brontë's novel, 'evidence that Heathcliff is black is expressed indirectly' (Fermi 2015, 340), but in Andrea Arnold's film adaptation Heathcliff's realisation as a Black man is direct through the casting of Black British actors Solomon Glave and James Howson as the child and adult Heathcliff, respectively.[9] Such casting recalls the appearance of Djimon Hounsou as Caliban in Julie Taymor's 2010 film *Tempest*, given prior postcolonial scholarship on Shakespeare's play, which Taymor has acknowledged. *Tempest*'s featuring Hounsou, from Benin, as an enslaved man, 'brings to the forefront the obvious themes of colonialization and usurpation' (qtd in Friedman 2013, 431) in Shakespeare's play and the lengthy history of the transatlantic slave trade that far exceeded its composition.[10] If Brontë wrote *Wuthering Heights* more than two hundred years after *The Tempest*, Arnold's film followed Taymor's just four years later. What may be '[c]onsidered in the interpretive context of imperialist history' to be Heathcliff's 'collective' status in terms of racialised Othering, as he 'accru[es] associations with India, China, Africa, and the West Indies' (Meyer 1996, 102) throughout the novel, is gestured towards in dialogue but is countered through casting and the inflection of the narrative through the salvaging of the novel's slavery subtext. The inhospitality and abuses of power to which Heathcliff is subject in the novel are forcefully circumscribed by racism in the film. As in the novel, Cathy (Shannon Beer) responds to Heathcliff's arrival by spitting at him. But the embodied experiences and structures of slavery are more explicit. When Nelly (Simone Jackson) takes Heathcliff's clothes from him in order to burn them, we see several scars on his back, semiotically tying him to representations of brutalised enslaved people. Nelly's speculations about Heathcliff's parentage resemble those in the novel, but she posits his mother as an African, rather than an Indian, queen. The film retains Nelly's musing that Heathcliff may have been kidnapped. When the film version of Nelly utters these speculations to a young, Black Heathcliff, the embedded, unarticulated subtext of slavery becomes visible.

Further, Hindley's (Lee Shaw) dislike of Heathcliff, thrown into relief by Cathy's rapid development of affection for him, figures as starkly racist behaviour in the film. Although Hindley refers to Heathcliff as 'dog' in both novel (39) and film, following the scene with the horses in the film, and Earnshaw's (Paul Hilton) castigation of his eldest child, Hindley's hatred for Heathcliff explicitly escalates into racism: in response to Earnshaw's claiming, 'I'd hoped you'd have treated him like he was your brother,' Hindley replies, 'He's not my brother. He's a n—r', prompting Earnshaw to whip his son's hand. Hindley invests in the racialised difference between himself and Heathcliff, as is also made clear when Cathy, following her father's death, protests Hindley's treatment of Heathcliff: 'Hindley, he's our brother!' to which Hindley replies, 'Don't be stupid. Look at him.'

Hindley's treatment of Heathcliff after Earnshaw's death is framed as slavery. Whereas, in the novel, Hindley returns to Wuthering Heights to assume the position of master and 'dr[ives Heathcliff] from their company to the servants' (46), in the film, Hindley banishes Heathcliff from human company, ordering him to 'move in with the animals where you belong.' Joseph (Steve Evets) begins to function as a kind of overseer, maintaining Hindley's denial of Heathcliff's humanity: 'Even the animals work round here. You're here to work! You'll work!' he shouts before whipping Heathcliff. An earlier adaptation of *Wuthering Heights*, ITV's 2009 production, invokes slavery in the relationship between Heathcliff and Hindley, particularly following Heathcliff's return to Yorkshire and his plan to take ownership of Wuthering Heights. Heathcliff offers to Hindley 'my cash, against the skin on your back', which 'suggests a legacy of oppression that is akin to slavery' (Shachar 2012, 165). Yet in this adaptation, Heathcliff is played by the white actor Tom Hardy, making the gesture to slavery more metaphorical. In contrast, in Arnold's film, when Cathy is attacked by the dog at Thrushcross Grange, Mr Linton (Oliver Milburn), as in the novel, identifies Heathcliff as 'the little Lascar. The stowaway.' Although Linton does not repeat his literary counterpart's identification of Heathcliff as an 'acquisition', he does raise the spectre of lynching. There is no question of any possibility of hospitality towards Heathcliff at Thrushcross Grange in either the film or the novel: 'they had not the manners to ask me to stay' (47). But in a gross violation of hospitality, upon first seeing Heathcliff, Mr Linton suggests, 'We should hang you now, boy, before you get any older. Do the county a favour.' The novel's version articulates the duality with which Heathcliff is often described: 'Don't be afraid, it is but a boy – Yet the villain scowls so plainly in his face, would it not be a kindness to the country to hang him at once, before he shows his nature in acts, as well as features?' (50), as Linton attempts to account for both Heathcliff's youth and the danger that he feels Heathcliff poses as a '"savag[e]" who appear[s] to threaten property' (Eagleton 2005, 107).

In the context of the film and Solomon Glave playing Heathcliff, the suggestion of hanging, more briefly and brutally articulated, is recast as a lynching. Linton's racism finds an echo in his son's treatment of Heathcliff when Edgar (Jonathan Powell) visits Wuthering Heights. Nelly, in both novel and film, helps Heathcliff wash, 'evidently believ[ing] that washing will turn the gypsy white, and that such a transformation is to be desired' (Meyer 1996, 118), an example of 'the imperial civilizing mission [of] 'washing and clothing the savage' (McClintock 1995, 208).[11] Although the film's Heathcliff insists 'I like being dirty', he later accepts Nelly's offer to help him 'look smart' in advance of the Lintons' social visit to Wuthering Heights. Whereas, in the novel, Edgar responds to the cleaned-up Heathcliff with mockery of his hair – 'It's like a colt's mane over his eyes!' (59) – in the film, the animal simile is more evidently racist: 'Look at him, he's all dress up like a little circus monkey.' In both novel and film, Heathcliff's angry response to Edgar results in his being locked up by Hindley; in the film, this imprisonment is exacerbated by the confiscation of Heathcliff's clothing.

Like *Mansfield Park*, Arnold's *Wuthering Heights* shows its protagonist denied the power of host through the occupation of interstitial spaces. Heathcliff often appears watching and listening in hallways and outside doors. When Cathy returns from Thrushcross Grange, Hindley warns Heathcliff, 'If I see you talking to her without my permission, you will be told to leave.' Once Nelly has helped him wash, Heathcliff looks in through the window on the Earnshaw siblings and the Lintons. When he enters that room to join them, even prior to Edgar's racist insult, Hindley shouts, 'Get out!' in a refusal, along with all his other punishments, of Heathcliff's claim as host.

If Heathcliff is denied the host position at Wuthering Heights, the film's representation of the Lintons positions them as newcomers to the region. Cathy and Heathcliff first run to Thrushcross Grange in order to investigate 'where the new people live'. Although they are powerful in economic, class and racialised terms, therefore, their belonging to the locality appears less secure. The film focuses intensely on the Yorkshire landscape. Critics have observed previous *Wuthering Heights* adaptations' use of the landscape, such as Amy Martin's claim that Arnold's film merely illustrates 'the continuing importance placed on this outside world that the Hollywood Golden Age created' (2012, 83) in William Wyler's 1939 version. But Arnold's adaptation's 'inordinate interest in the natural environment' (Lawrence 2016, 178) exceeds the previous films by including numerous extreme close-ups on vegetation and animal life, to the point where the 'countryside changes from being the background where the story takes places to being one of the objects of the story' (Rocha Antunes 2015, 5); indeed, the close-ups of natural objects and insects 'disrupt the narrative frame with their visceral presence' (Thornham 2016, 222). Further, the constantly unsettled weather and the excesses of rain and mud turn the Yorkshire setting into 'a relentless physical environment where wind and rain replace dialogue' (Stoneman 2012, 212); even the film's 'soundscape', as Jenny Bavidge notes, 'is immersed in the non-human world' (2016, 118). The film's 'rich and intense sensory and perceptual exploration of the material story world' (Rocha Antunes 2015, 6) suggests a rootedness of the protagonists Cathy and Heathcliff in the region that is not shared by the Lintons.

Neither is this rootedness mitigated by Heathcliff's origins outside of Yorkshire: if Cathy 'acclimatises Heathcliff to his new home' (Lawrence 2016, 178) early on, 'transmitting her familial and cultural lore by sharing . . . her knowledge of the birds that live on the moor' (Hazette 2015, 301), Heathcliff's representation outdoors suggests his belonging in the region. The use of a handheld camera, 'a novelty in 19th-century costume dramas' (Thomson 2012, 42), creates an effect of authenticity in the representation of the landscape (Bangert et al. 2016, xxiv) that is particularly associated with Catherine and Heathcliff in their engagement with the natural world. When Heathcliff returns as an adult to Yorkshire, Cathy (Kaya Scodelario), on the moors away from Thrushcross Grange, demands of Heathcliff, 'How could you have left this? How could you have left me?' Although previous adaptations of Brontë's novel have accentuated a fusion between the protagonists and the Yorkshire landscape (see Shachar 2012, 169), Arnold's film's inflection of this equation more radically embeds Blackness in the region. The film makes this connection even though, as Fowler observes, Arnold herself does not appear to be aware of 'Yorkshire's slavery connections', and 'does not herself challenge the idea that Heathcliff [in the novel] is not really Black' (2020, 205). Nonetheless, the casting of Glave and Howson in the film renders Heathcliff Black and interpolates him into the landscape. If the Lintons are accorded the status of 'new', the film suggests their whiteness does not give them greater access to belonging in Yorkshire. In contrast, Heathcliff's relationship to the land suggests his entitlement – even when unrecognised – to claim the host position from the film's point of view.

Granted, in both novel and film there is a significant shift in Heathcliff's fortunes, and he returns, as an adult, from his unrepresented exile with considerable economic power. In Arnold's film, this shift in fortune is gradually accompanied by a change in his relationship to spaces: whereas when he first arrives at Thrushcross Grange to visit Cathy, Heathcliff stands at the threshold between hallway and room, until Cathy pulls him inside, later he jumps the fence of that property, walks into the house with no knocking or invitation, and ultimately, after Cathy's death, he enters through a window (which Nelly has opened for him) to access Cathy's corpse in a necrophilic scene. His return to Yorkshire has doubled as a return to Wuthering Heights. His former 'master', Hindley, now alcoholic and ill, suddenly offers him hospitality at a (low) price: 'I've got a room for cheap.' After his marriage to Isabella Linton (Nichola Burley) and the death of Cathy, Heathcliff returns to Wuthering Heights, where he discovers the door locked and Isabella refusing to let him in. He smashes the window, fights Hindley and slams Isabella against the wall. Shortly afterwards, a lawyer examines a ledger of Heathcliff's finances, saying, 'Looks like you're the legal owner of the farm, Mr Heathcliff.' This announcement features as the last plot point of the film, Heathcliff's installation as host (and master) at Wuthering Heights. If his return to this location provides a circular narrative trajectory, his economic ascent provides the means for him to claim the position denied to him by Hindley in his childhood.

Thus, Arnold's film concludes before the narrative focusing on the second generation of Heathcliffs and Lintons (like other, but not all, adaptations of *Wuthering Heights*).[12] Indeed, there is no notion in this film of Isabella even being pregnant. Although the film does represent Heathcliff's cruelty and violence towards Isabella, the omission of the second-generation narrative has the effect of somewhat muting Heathcliff's status as 'one of the novel's most horrific oppressors of women' (Meyer 1996, 107) that the novel's more extended narrative of Heathcliff's relationship to both Isabella and Catherine Linton explores in greater depth. Cutting this narrative short, the film minimises the 'spectre of slave rebellion' (von Sneidern 1995, 180), invoked through Heathcliff's abuse of power over the Earnshaw and Linton descendants. If the novel's version of Nelly twins her speculation about Heathcliff's ancestry with the possibility of his parents being 'able to buy up, with one week's income, Wuthering Heights and Thrushcross Grange together', the film does not include his acquisition of the Linton family home, rendering him less powerful as 'master'.

Increasingly, towards the end of Arnold's adaptation, shots of the adult Heathcliff are intercut with flashbacks to the younger Heathcliff, with and without Cathy, acting as reminders both of his long connection to the landscape almost microscopically represented in the film and of the abuse from Hindley that he endured as a child. If previous adaptations of the novel have struggled with how to 'dramatize Heathcliff's violence' (Elliott 2003, 168), Arnold's visual pairing of young and adult Heathcliff suggests a sense of justice at his ownership of Wuthering Heights and a context for his cruelty towards others, especially his wife. The film is framed through articulations of Heathcliff's pain at Cathy's death, opening with the adult Heathcliff alone at Wuthering Heights, throwing himself against a wall and banging his head on the floor while sobbing. The last shots prior to the final credits show the adult Heathcliff walking across the moor, followed by a flashback to the young Heathcliff and Cathy walking. To a certain extent, Arnold's film bears out Shachar's observation that throughout the adaptations of Brontë's novel, '[t]he screen Heathcliff is . . . constructed through parades of masculine pain, in which masculine identity and authority are formed through the evocation of the suffering male body'; however, in earlier adaptations, Shachar argues, this suffering acts 'as a symbol of transcendence of context and circumstances' (2012, 189). In Arnold's adaptation, the combination of the intense focus on the Yorkshire landscape and the salvaging of the novel's slavery subtext counteracts the earlier adaptations' 'transcendence of context and circumstances'. Further, Heathcliff's self-harm following Cathy's death, which appears both at the beginning of the film and again at that point in the chronology later, appears at such length that it mirrors the camera's obsessive detailing of the landscape.

If the last shot prior to the final credits delivers a flashback of the young protagonists wrestling in the mud, the final shot of the film altogether fuses visual representation of the young Heathcliff with verbal representation of the young Cathy. It is young Heathcliff who appears at the end of the credits, with a voice-over from Cathy asserting, 'I am Heathcliff.' Cathy has not uttered this line during the main body of the film (although she does state to Nelly, as she does in the novel [81], 'he's more myself than I am'). Thus, the narrative's most radical claim to intersubjectivity appears beyond the bounds of the narrative, and yet it is the last thing the film's viewer sees and hears. On the one hand, such a positioning of this moment resembles *Mansfield Park*'s shift in attention to actual, historical – rather than metaphorical – slavery through the sounds of 'Djonga' over that film's final credits. On the other hand, if *Mansfield Park*'s trajectory is one of increasing accountability for the lack of representing actual enslaved people, *Wuthering Heights*' final shot raises questions about the ethical limits of such an intersubjective claim: Catherine's gendered oppression cannot be substituted for Heathcliff's racialised oppression.

Indeed, Cathy's affiliation with Heathcliff in both the novel and Arnold's film requires further scrutiny. Despite the viciousness with which Cathy first greets Heathcliff upon his arrival from Liverpool (disappointed as she is that her father has not brought her a whip [36], as requested), her conversation with Nelly following Edgar's marriage proposal demonstrates that she 'resists the biologism implicit in most mid-nineteenth-century conceptions of race', namely by identifying 'Heathcliff's degradation' as the product of Hindley's treatment of him, rather than any intrinsic, racialised attributes (von Sneidern 1995, 177). At the same time, Maja-Lisa von Sneidern argues, 'Heathcliff is [Cathy's] ultimate possession', and Heathcliff 'explicitly characterizes [their relationship] as slavery' (178); similarly, Sandra M. Gilbert and Susan Gubar identify 'Heathcliff's [as] the body that does her will' (1980, 265).[13] Susan Meyer contends that in the first half of the novel, 'Brontë explores the rationale for the association of white women with colonized races by suggesting that white women and races subject to imperialism both experience an oppressive disempowerment' (1996, 108). Although Meyer qualifies this statement by adding, 'Brontë even subtly suggests that the situation is harsher for colonized peoples' (108), the near conflation of oppression suffered by white women and 'races subject to imperialism' resembles the political and ethical problems of positioning Fanny Price as a slave at Mansfield Park. Heathcliff's accrual of mobility and wealth as he becomes 'an atomic capitalist' (Eagleton 2005, 111) may reverse the fortunes of his childhood in ways that Cathy, as a woman, cannot access, but the complicity of white women in the project of imperialism and indeed, enslavement, forecloses any possibility of their being equated to colonised and enslaved peoples.[14]

Given that Arnold's film presents Heathcliff as a Black man, what does it mean for us to see his image as a child at the end of the film, accompanied by the voice of the white Cathy declaring herself to be him? How do we read Cathy's 'utopian expression of a Romantic longing for total identification with the other' (Beaumont 2004, 157–8) in this context? Even the novel's version of this statement has been viewed with suspicion by scholars who doubt whether 'we should accept Catherine's description of her relationship with Heathcliff uncritically' (Stevenson 1988, 61). The radical intersubjectivity of this claim that collapses distinctions of gender – and does so in a historical context of stark, politically legitimated imbalances of power – resonates rather differently in the film's explicitly interracial context that makes the novel's Catherine's 'find[ing] in the powerless Heathcliff a figure of her own dispossession' (Vine 1994, 345) untenable. Cathy's claim to be the Black Heathcliff resembles Fanny Price's likening of herself, in Rozema's film, to a slave, although in *Wuthering Heights*, Cathy eschews simile. It is possible to interpret Cathy's claim in Arnold's film, given the combination of visual representation of Heathcliff with the audio claim of Cathy, as an undermining of Cathy's assertion. Had the claim been included in the scene with Nelly, as it is in the novel, we might have witnessed Cathy's articulation of her *being* Heathcliff with a focus on her (white) physicality. Instead, we are made to look at Heathcliff, his head bowed before the camera, object of the claim rather than its enunciator (see Figure 2.2). Alternatively, the film, ending as it does with Heathcliff's grief for Cathy and his new ownership of Wuthering Heights, problematically collapses the two characters together in accordance with Cathy's declaration. Yet crucially, it is one that leaves Heathcliff silent; and with his head down, he does not return the viewer's gaze.

Prior to this final shot of Heathcliff, the film offers an additional voicing of Heathcliff's perspective through the song 'The Enemy', '[s]pecifically written for the film' (Bavidge 2016, 130) and performed by the British band Mumford & Sons, the only non-diegetic sound in the film. On the one hand, the singer's assertion that he is not 'the enemy' could refer to Heathcliff's racialised position, the fact that he was 'nothing' upon his arrival at Wuthering Heights; on the other hand, the 'you' of the song is clearly Cathy, given references by the singer to being buried beside 'you', as Heathcliff is, ultimately, in the novel. Although the song presents another performance of Heathcliff's subjectivity, it does so through the white

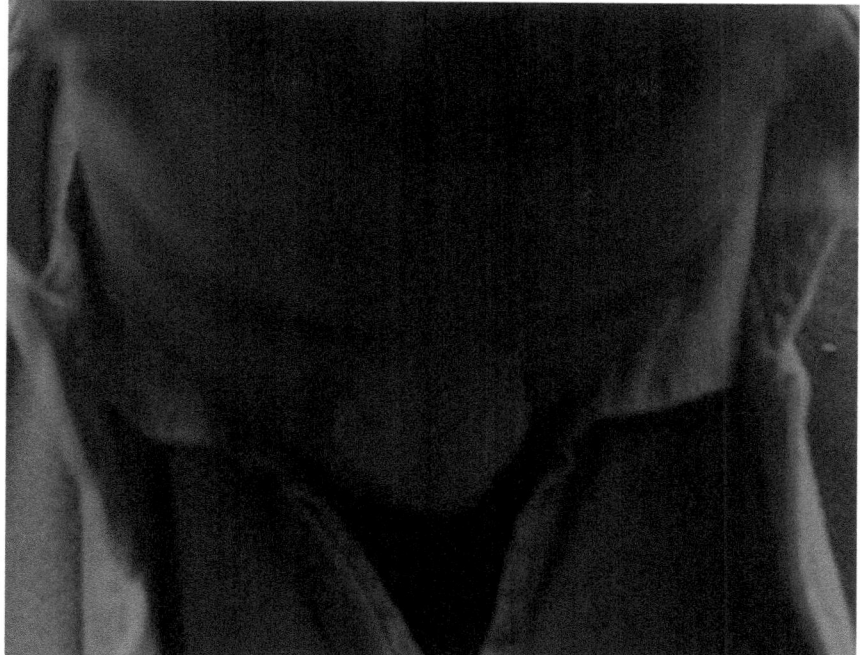

Figure 2.2 Heathcliff in the final shot of *Wuthering Heights*.

singer Marcus Mumford,[15] suggesting the 'enemy' invokes not the spectre of slave rebellion that Heathcliff presents in the latter half of the narrative but, rather, in conjunction with the references to Cathy, protesting against Cathy's insistence to Heathcliff on her deathbed, 'You killed me.'

However, the intrusion not just of the first instance of non–diegetic sound into the film but also its clear twenty–first–century provenance may help encourage a reading of the racism portrayed in the film as pertinent to the present day. Further, Hindley's characterisation in Arnold's film invites us to ally the representation of Hindley's late–eighteenth–century racism with far–right politics in Britain in general and Yorkshire, particularly in the late twentieth and early twenty–first centuries. Hindley's closely cropped hair – which prompts *Sight & Sound* to claim the character 'wouldn't' look out of place in *This is England* (Raphael 2011, 36), Shane Meadows's TV series about 1980s skinheads and racist violence – allies him semiotically with Britain's far-right National Front and its successors such as the British National Party (BNP). Nick Griffin, a leading BNP figure from 1999 to 2014 (and former National Front member), was a Member of the European Parliament (MEP) for North West England between 2009 and 2014. More relevant for Yorkshire, and indeed *Wuthering*

Heights, he stood in the 2005 general election in the Keighley constituency, which threatened to become 'the centre of the BNP's electoral base' (Bunting 2005), and where the BNP had two local councillors; Griffin ultimately came fourth in his constituency with 9.16 per cent of the vote (BBC 2005). The Keighley constituency includes Haworth, home of the Brontë family. Although Greg M. Colón Semenza and Bob Hasenfratz view Arnold's film's representation of Heathcliff's status as 'a crystal-clear analog for the brutal classism of late eighteenth-century English society' (2015, 376), in its semiotic gestures to contemporary British politics, in which the Brontës' own locale has been a particular flashpoint of far-right organisation, Arnold's film not only salvages Brontë's *Wuthering Heights*' slavery subtext for its own sake (and not merely as an analogue for class oppression), but also foregrounds the white supremacist politics of the present day. In invoking the material presence and horrifying viability of the far right in Yorkshire, however, the film falters in its attempt to include Cathy's claim to interracial intersubjectivity, given the currency of her whiteness juxtaposed to Heathcliff's racialisation, of which the film's final post-credit shot of Solomon Glave reminds us so powerfully.

Examining the trajectory of *Wuthering Heights* adaptations, Shachar notes that '[i]f Catherine has become increasingly contained and marginalised, Heathcliff has become increasingly dominant' (2012, 188). Similarly, Arnold's film makes Heathcliff's perspective its central point of view, even at the level of cinematography: as Robbie Ryan, the film's cinematographer, explains, 'The goal was just to follow the action with the rule of staying with Heathcliff's POV – wherever he went, we went with him', with shots 'always over his shoulder, not someone else's' (qtd in Thomson 2012, 46). The audience is made to look with Heathcliff through windows and cracks in doors to access the activities of the white characters. But while Arnold's adaptation shares many of the tendencies of its predecessors, its presentation of Heathcliff as Black marks a strong departure in cinematic readings and renderings of Brontë's novel, invoking 'histories that are at once international and colonial, lying well beyond the village verge and the borders of England's green and pleasant land' (Loh 2013, 1). The film's meticulous focus on Yorkshire plant and animal life, in combination with its salvaging of the novel's slavery subtext, suggests that both Blackness and white supremacy are embedded in both the region's history and its present.

Both *Mansfield Park* and *Wuthering Heights* are named for the properties that feature in their narratives, not only as settings for the action that unfolds but also as focuses in their own right, particularly through the resonance of questions surrounding wealth, property and hospitality. Deploying different representational methods, both films work to counteract the fact that '[s]lave-ownership is virtually invisible in British history' (Hall et al. 2014, 1); indeed, some responses to the National Trust's recent report suggest that certain members of the British public and political classes would prefer to keep it that way. Both white female directors, Rozema and Arnold, and their adaptations of canonical nineteenth-century novels grapple, in implicit and explicit ways, with the relationship between white women and enslaved people. Both adaptations come up against the limits of equating one form of oppression with another. Rozema's *Mansfield Park* perhaps retains empire's 'spectral presence' (Mee 2000, 90) from Austen's novel insofar as it does not directly represent enslaved people, but its trajectory works to unravel politically and ethically problematic analogies between the gendered oppression of white women and the enslavement of African peoples and their descendants. In contrast, Arnold's *Wuthering Heights* directly inserts Blackness and enslavement into the Yorkshire landscape, thus 'reminding the spectator of the colonial legacy that underpins so much of British heritage culture' (Bangert et al. 2016, xxiii), but risks undermining the contextualisation of Heathcliff by reinstalling Cathy's claim to a now explicitly interracial intersubjectivity. Despite their limitations, and the more radically postcolonial choices that might have been made,[16] both films intervene in dominant trends of film adaptation, rupturing many of the complacencies of heritage culture and dominant historiography and, in Arnold's case, using the salvaged subtext of slavery to confront racism in both the past and the present.

CHAPTER 3

Relocating Racism
in *Bride and Prejudice* and *Jindabyne*

Gurinder Chadha's *Bride and Prejudice* (2004) and Ray Lawrence's *Jindabyne* (2006) present radical relocations of their source narratives, Jane Austen's novel *Pride and Prejudice* (1813) and Raymond Carver's short story 'So Much Water So Close to Home' (1988),[1] respectively. In shifting the narrative setting from Regency England to twenty-first-century India, primarily, and from the American Pacific Northwest to Australia, these two adaptations foreground race relations that are not thematised in the source texts but are facilitated by the geographical relocation. A comparison of these two films highlights the very different postcoloniality of India and settler-coloniality of Australia: as emphasised in *Bride and Prejudice*'s dialogue, India had been independent from Britain for nearly sixty years at the point of the film's narrative (and production); as a settler-colonial nation-state, however, Australia, although independent from Britain, has yet to decolonise, a fact central to the film's narrative in its grappling with Indigenous/non-Indigenous relations. Where *Bride and Prejudice* explores the relationships between a postcolonial India and the US and the UK in the context of globalisation, neoliberalism and neo-imperialism, *Jindabyne* grafts Carver's narrative onto the politics of apology in a settler-colonial context amid attempts to reconcile with Indigenous peoples.

Despite the films' shared strategy of narrative relocation effecting an exploration of racism, their genres diverge widely: whereas *Bride and Prejudice*, inspired and inflected by the conventions of Bollywood cinema, is fundamentally a romantic comedy, *Jindabyne*'s drama hinges on trauma, both for individual characters and in terms of the fallout of the colonial encounter. Both films feature an American character out of their depth in a culture to which they do not belong, but whereas *Bride and Prejudice*'s comedy necessitates a forging of this belonging, the settler-colonial context of *Jindabyne* suggests that belonging is always already impossible. Translation, part of the 'constellation of terms and tropes' (Stam 2005, 4) deployed to discuss film adaptation, is particularly apt for examining the relocations of *Bride and Prejudice* and *Jindabyne*: 'Literally "carrying across", translation is itself a form of migration between languages, places, and cultures' (Orr 2013, 286); further, both films include translator figures. But whereas translators are more incidental to *Bride and Prejudice*, and function to guide Western characters and audiences through the film, in *Jindabyne*, the figure of the translator is contested, with the white American character attempting unsuccessfully to operate as an 'embodied translator' (Kaplan 2004, 49), to the detriment of Indigenous/non-Indigenous relations.

Bride and Prejudice

Gurinder Chadha's *Bride and Prejudice*'s dual geographical and temporal relocation of its source material inflects the nature of the prejudice exposed in the narrative: whereas Austen's novel scrutinises class-based prejudice, the 'cultural conflict' (Wilson 2006, 323) engendered by Chadha's characters' prejudice is based on neo-imperial relations of nation and race. As Kobena Mercer argues, 'the diaspora perspective has the potential to expose and illuminate the sheer heterogeneity of the diverse social forces always repressed into the margin by the monologism of dominant discourses – discourses of domination' (1994, 66). Grappling with *Pride and Prejudice* – and, implicitly its recent popular, and very white, adaptations – Chadha's film insists upon the UK's heterogeneity while updating and repositioning Austen's canonical novel in a film that forges dialogue between disparate cinematic traditions. Framed by neoliberal economics, arguments between the characters of Darcy (Martin Henderson) and Lalita (Aishwarya Rai, the film's Elizabeth figure) largely stem from the former's Eurocentrism and stereotypes of India, combining in a casual racism. As *Bride and Prejudice* is both a romantic comedy and transnational film inspired by Bollywood, the conventions within which the film operates demand a recuperation of Darcy (as, indeed, the novel does). The film's refusal to disclose the destination of Lalita and Darcy after their marriage holds the critique of neo-imperialism and neoliberalism in abeyance while, momentarily, valorising India above the competing settings of the UK and the US at the same time as it upholds a possible model for the figure of the NRI (Non-resident Indian). On the one hand, the film's interrogation of race relations via Austen's narrative might be seen to correct Austen's own sense of her novel, that it is 'rather too light, and bright, and sparkling' (qtd in Johnson 1988, 73). If, on the other hand, the relocation of the source material's narrative enables an interrogation of race relations, *Bride and Prejudice*'s status as a romantic comedy provides a very different generic framework as the film both addresses and fails to address the underlying racism of the contemporary neo-imperial and neoliberal order.

Bride and Prejudice operates at the intersection of multiple film cultures. Although some critics locate the film between binary poles of Hollywood and Bollywood (e.g. Wilson 2006, 323), this diasporic film moves between three sites in its narrative and production: India, the US and the UK. Born in Kenya as part of the Punjabi diaspora, Chadha moved to the UK as a child and grew up in Southall, West London, the location of the Bakshi (Bennet) family's UK relatives in *Bride and Prejudice*. Scholars hypothesise that *Bride and Prejudice* was 'targeted . . . to increasingly hybridized audiences' (Karan and Schaefer 2012, 245), but the film might equally be considered the result of its own transnational production and the diasporic position of Chadha, its director and co-writer.

Bride and Prejudice both 'is and is not Bollywood' (Wilson 2006, 324).[2] Some conventions associated with Bollywood appear in the film, such as 'social dance encounters stand[ing] in for the more overt expressions of sexuality that are prohibited by the [Indian film] industry' (Wilson 2006, 326): indeed, none of the couples kiss in *Bride and Prejudice*. The film also makes use of 'visual excess' (Griffin 2014, 533) and features Aishwarya Rai, the former Miss World (1994)[3] turned 'Bollywood superstar who is undoubtedly the central focus of Chadha's film' (Mathur 2007, para. 7). Although *Bride and Prejudice* capitalises on 'the ubiquity of her star image in India and its Diaspora' (Griffin 2014, 538–9), however, it also presents Rai 'as a modern (read Westernised) Indian heroine, which is pretty much an oxymoron within Bollywood conventions' (Mathur 2007, para. 10). If Indian films 'include elements of comedy, (melo)drama, action, romance, and music that do not fit Western aesthetic expectations; in particular, the elaborate and often extradiegetic song and dance numbers' (Desai 2004, 41–2), *Bride and Prejudice* both deploys this combination of elements and inflects them in ways that facilitate a Western viewership. Not only are the songs part of the narrative, but the film's inclusion of locations from outside India (namely England and the US) also departs from Indian cinema's conventional use of international settings: whereas Indian films often contain abrupt introductions of 'incongruous locations' (Dwyer and Patel 2002, 7) – from the point of view of Westerners for whom such sequences constitute a perplexing departure from the narrative – these shifts in setting form part of *Bride and Prejudice*'s plot, minimising 'break[s] in continuity regarding location' (38) as the narrative itself moves between three continents.[4] As a whole, therefore, *Bride and Prejudice* constitutes a kind of translation not just of *Pride and Prejudice* but also of Bollywood convention, one that can be legible to a Western audience.

If, in deploying some Bollywood conventions and drawing on Bollywood references in adapting *Pride and Prejudice*, the film offers an example of 'the colony "talking back" to the metropolis' (Mathur 2007, para. 6) or 'writing back to the canon' (Ashcroft 2012, 14), it is crucial that it does so from within the UK itself as far as production is concerned: UK funding underpinning the production stipulated that 70 per cent of the film be shot in the UK, with many scenes set in India – such as the first wedding in the film, the *garbha* dance, the interior scenes at the Bakshis' house, and some of the exterior scenes at Darcy's family's hotel in Los Angeles – filmed in the UK, either in studio or on location (Chadha and Mayeda Berges 2005). Thus, it is not the case that Chadha's film 'completely dislocated the story in spatial terms' (Oliete Aldea 2012, 172): rather, the film is simultaneously diasporic, transnational and British.

Nevertheless, even as a British film, *Bride and Prejudice* presents a considerable departure for adaptations of *Pride and Prejudice*, 'one of the most adapted of all novels' (Cartmell 2010, 3). If the novel's Darcy reveals his distaste for Hertfordshire society, in Chadha's film, Darcy expresses his horror at India upon arrival: he even hesitates before getting off the plane, holding up other passengers behind him; and from the taxi in Amritsar, he exclaims, 'This is mayhem. This is like Bedlam. What do you mean it's like New York?' Seeing livestock on the road, Darcy asks of his friend, the film's Bingley figure (Naveen Andrews), 'Jesus, Balraj, where the hell have you brought me?' India is monstrous and Other for the newly arrived Darcy, who responds to the offer of food at the party that precedes the first wedding, 'Are you sure this is safe to eat? I don't want to be getting Delhi belly on my first day.' In India to investigate a hotel in Goa his family is considering acquiring, Darcy fears the consumption of anything else. Like the novel's Darcy, he refuses to dance with Lalita when implored to do so (despite a brief dance between them when Balraj throws them together, without introduction). Darcy protests he has work to do instead, rejecting Lalita's initial offer to teach him: 'It's easier than you think. I can show you.' Lalita appears as a potential translator or guide for Darcy, an offer he dismisses as less important than his financial concerns. Lalita's family immediately reads his refusal as an expression of his own white, wealthy, American sense of superiority: 'Rich American. What does he think – we are not good enough for him?' Mrs Bakshi (Nadira Babbar) comments.

This sense of Darcy's self-importance echoes a racialised reference made by Austen's Darcy in the novel, at the party at Lucas Lodge, after Sir William encourages Darcy to dance. To Sir William's comment, 'There is nothing like dancing after all. – I consider it as one of the first refinements of polished societies,' Darcy replies, 'Certainly, Sir; – and it has the advantage also of being in vogue amongst the less polished societies of the world. – Every savage can dance' (Austen 2004, 18).

The 1995 BBC adaptation of *Pride and Prejudice*, directed by Simon Langton, retains this comment by Darcy (Colin Firth), although it also inserts a scene between Darcy and Bingley (Crispin Bonham Carter) at the beginning of the mini-series, in which Darcy tells Bingley, looking at Netherfield from a distance, 'You'll find the society something savage', thereby suggesting an equation between savagery, class and geographical location within Britain. In the 1940 MGM adaptation, directed by Robert Z. Leonard, Darcy's (Laurence Olivier) response to Sir William includes the line, 'Every Hottentot can dance'. The yoking of savagery to class rather than race arises later in the film via Elizabeth's (Greer Garson) irony, when she says to Colonel Fitzwilliam (Gerald Oliver Smith), Darcy's cousin, that Darcy 'liked the landscape [in Hertfordshire] well enough, but the natives, Colonel Fitzwilliam, the natives: what boors! What savages!' But presumably, Darcy's implied racist view through his reference to 'Hottentots' remains unchanged.

In Chadha's film, Darcy makes no reference himself to 'savages'. As Cheryl Wilson notes, however, this line from the novel is adapted in Lalita's dialogue (2006, 327). In the second dance scene, following the first of the film's weddings, Darcy, having refused Lalita's earlier offer to learn how to dance on their first meeting, now concedes, 'I'm a hopeless dancer, but, well, this looks like you just screw in a light bulb with one hand, and pet the dog with the other. Will you teach me?' (see Figure 3.1). His request, however, follows an argument with Lalita about 'standards' for hotels (his own chain charging 400–500 dollars a night for a 'good room', which Lalita points out is 'more than what most people make here in a year') and arranged marriage (deemed 'a little backward' by Darcy, despite his own mother's attempts to marry him off to Anne, the daughter of wealthy friends in what Wickham [Daniel Gillies] describes as 'the ultimate business merger'). Lalita rescinds her earlier offer to teach Darcy to dance, replying, 'I think you should find someone simple and traditional to teach you to dance like the natives.' Lisa Hopkins contends that Lalita 'puts words like "natives" into Darcy's mouth, ascribing

Figure 3.1 Darcy's impression of Indian dancing.

to him racist attitudes he never actually manifests himself' (2009, 128). But I would argue that Lalita holds a mirror up to Darcy, exposing the logic of his dismissal of India on both economic and cultural grounds. After all, Darcy, complaining of the conditions of the Amritsar hotel in which he is staying – 'the best hotel in town', Lalita informs him – says, 'I don't know how business functions here', revealing that he is 'insensitive to (or perhaps just ignorant of) the problem of poverty in India' (Resnick 2005, 91); his attempt to 'translate' Indian dance is also insensitive and belittling, reminding the audience of his poor decision earlier to refuse Lalita's own offer to teach him.

Instead of the novel's scenario in which Jane becomes better acquainted with Bingley and his sisters through a visit to Netherfield, prolonged by an illness she catches by travelling through the rain (according to Mrs Bennet's machinations), *Bride and Prejudice* substitutes the Netherfield visit with a trip to Goa to see the hotel the Darcys might purchase, with Balraj inviting Jaya (Namrata Shirodkar, the film's Jane figure) to accompany them; at Mr Bakshi's (Anupam Kher) insistence, Lalita goes as well (albeit reluctantly) as a kind of chaperone for her sister. At the opulent hotel, Lalita and Darcy argue about India and the ethics and economics of tourism:

LALITA: You said yourself you're used to the best. I'm sure you think India's beneath you.

DARCY: If I really thought that, then why would I be thinking about buying this hotel?
LALITA: You think this is India?
DARCY: Well don't you wanna see more investment, more jobs?
LALITA: Yes, but who does it really benefit? You want people to come to India without having to deal with Indians.
DARCY: That's good. Remind me to add that to the tourist brochure.
LALITA: Well, isn't that all tourists want here? 5-star comfort with a bit of culture thrown in? Well, I don't want you turning India into a theme park. I thought we got rid of imperialists like you.[5]
DARCY: I'm not British. I'm American.
LALITA: Exactly.

Darcy assumes that his desire for consumption testifies to his valorising of India, as though his intention to purchase the hotel is evidence of a better opinion of India than what he has displayed thus far in the narrative. But Lalita calls him on his superficial, financially driven engagement with India in a neoliberal and neo-imperial context that leaves India open to foreign investment unlikely to enrich the lives of local people (with whom she plays cricket on the beach).

As Sohinee Roy writes, this intersection of neoliberalism and neo-imperialism stems from that fact that, 'under the guise of free trade, resources are thrown open to exploitation, repeating earlier imperial practices' (2016, 987). Whereas the novel's Mr Bennet's own financial misman-agement is to blame for his family's insecurity in the event of his death, in *Bride and Prejudice*, 'the Bakshi family's financial situation is a function of the global economy' (Seeber 2007, 3). Lalita's work managing her father's struggling farm puts her in a position to appreciate keenly how 'India experiences the effects of this global neoliberal economy in the rise of tourism and the decrease in agriculture' (Roy 2016, 988). The fact that the hotel used in the Goa shooting location is called the 'Taj Exotica' (Chadha and Mayeda Berges 2005) itself bears out Lalita's fears of exoticist tourism at the expense of the local economy. It is in this context that Lalita is prepared to be won over by Johnny Wickham, whom she meets in Goa, given his professed desire to engage with 'the real India' where 'you don't have to have money to enjoy this place' and 'people . . . have got their priorities sorted.' Wickham also expresses a wish to visit Amritsar, where, Lalita notes, 'not many tourists go', but which Wickham, unprompted, associates with the Golden Temple.

Unbeknownst to Lalita at this stage of the narrative, Wickham will ultimately be revealed as villainous (having impregnated Darcy's then-fifteen-year-old sister, Georgie (Alexis Bledel), and later preying on Lalita's youngest sister, Lakhi (Peeya Rai Choudhuri) – the film's Lydia figure), whereas Darcy's views on India and his economic interest there will shift as a result of his argument with Lalita. In California for the wedding of Kholi (Nitin Ganatra) and Chandra (Sonali Kulkarni) – the film's Mr Collins and Charlotte Lucas figures – Lalita learns, in conversation with Darcy's mother (Marsha Mason), that Darcy refused to buy the Goan hotel, persuaded by her arguments, much to the displeasure of his mother, who accuses him of making 'a decision that lost us a fortune.' Fully interpellated by neoliberal economics, Mrs Darcy insists that 'everybody has their hand on India these days', implying that India is not just a location of foreign investment but also a body to be molested. She refuses to visit India without owning a hotel there, indicating ownership is a prerequisite for her engagement with the country. Otherwise, she is content to consume an exoticist, essentialist simulacrum of India without leaving the United States: 'With yoga, and spices, and Deepak Chopra, and wonderful Eastern things here, I suppose there's no point in travelling there anymore.' Whereas Kholi nods in agreement with Mrs Darcy, Lalita likens such sentiments to equating Pizza Hut with Italy. Meanwhile, Darcy, having been 'comically uncomfortable in his Indian clothes' (Gruß 2009, 51) in Amritsar, has begun to look 'more comfortable' in them, Lalita says, at Kholi and Chandra's Californian wedding.

A shift in Darcy's trajectory in engaging with Indian culture has also already been in evidence at the *garbha*. Whereas at their initial meeting Darcy rejects Lalita's offer of help with dancing, followed by an ignorant and insulting attempt to ask her to teach him on the second occasion, by the time of the *garbha*, when he does successfully ask Lalita to dance (if briefly, before being interrupted by Wickham), Darcy discloses he has been studying *garbha* in preparation and is willing to give it a try despite it being 'a little out of [his] league', a departure from his earlier reductive description of *bhangra* after the film's first wedding.

Although the film's version of the novel's proposal scene – here Darcy's profession of love for Lalita, despite the presence at the wedding of Anne, his white American girlfriend whom his mother wants him to marry – has Lalita angrily recalling her first impression of Darcy as a 'rude, arrogant, intolerant, and insensitive' man, the film's conclusion in India with the double wedding of the eldest Bakshi sisters to Balraj and Darcy reveals Darcy drumming alongside local musicians in Amritsar. From his rejection of Lalita as translator and guide (as well as dance partner) on their first meeting, then, Darcy has undertaken his own study of and engagement with Indian culture. Thus, Darcy is recuperated, having listened to and learned from Lalita, and rejected the corporate values of his mother.

It is not just Darcy's views of India that are under scrutiny in the film, however. The figure of the NRI, in multiple manifestations, appears throughout *Bride and Prejudice*, through anecdotes, characters, and both discarded and possible futures. In Hindi films prior to the release of *Dilwale Dulhaniya Le Jayenge* (*DDLJ*; *The True of Heart Will Win the Bride*, Chopra 1995), as Rini Bhattacharya Mehta notes, the figure of the NRI featured 'as the marginal outsider' (2010, 1), but *DDLJ* heralded a shift in which 'the NRI was not required to return to India and stay there . . . the NRI could remain NR and be the "I"' (Mehta 2010, 2). *Bride and Prejudice*, released just shy of a decade later, is peppered with test cases of NRIs, actual and potential, charting diverging possible pathways of transnational trajectories for the Bakshis' two eldest daughters especially. Early in the film, Mrs Bakshi chastises her husband for their not having relocated to the United States, despite her brother's offered sponsorship of the family and his financial status as the owner of three Subway franchises in New Jersey. Mr Bakshi tells an anecdote of an Indian emigrant who accrued so much wealth in the US that he had three swimming pools: one with hot water for when he was cold, one with cold water for when he was hot, and one empty for when he did not 'feel like swimming at all'. Thus, the film establishes early on an association of the United States with wasteful, conspicuous consumption.

The anecdote returns in dialogue with the arrival of Kholi, who works as an accountant in California (the Darcys among his clients) and returns to India in search of a wife. Kholi boasts of his 'dream home', providing photos of it on his phone: 'Colonial style. Five bedrooms, three and a half bathrooms, $850,000. That's four crores, 25 lakhs. . . . I bought it six months ago. It's already worth $900,000.' Lalita replies, 'I bet it has three swimming pools', puncturing Kholi's self-congratulation for the viewer. In Kholi, we see the view of NRIs as 'largely . . . upwardly mobile' (Mishra 2002, 236), and in his proposal to Lalita, Kholi focuses on his economic capital, astonished that she would turn down the chance to live in America and his 'savings and bonds and stocks' that mean Lalita 'wouldn't even have to work'. Kholi is unprepared for Lalita's insistence that she likes to work, responding with an astonished 'Okay!' that seems anything but; however, he finds in Chandra a willing partner, who is clearly attracted to the lifestyle Kholi offers her.

The UK constitutes the other major location of NRIs in the film through the Bakshis' Southall relatives and, more prominently in terms of the narrative, Balraj and his sister Kiran (Indira Varma, the film's Caroline Bingley figure). Whereas Balraj engages more readily with Indian culture, Kiran, 'easily recognisable as the stereotypical Indian diasporic woman' for those 'familiar with Bollywood stock characters' (Gruß 2009, 52), displays considerable loathing. Balraj admonishes his sister in Amritsar, 'Stop being such a coconut. This is our dear, dear motherland. Enjoy it', suggesting that Kiran has internalised white Western values. She refuses to participate in dancing and cautions Darcy, 'Brace yourself . . . He's about to transform into the Indian M.C. Hammer', as Balraj assumes a prominent position on the dance floor. Kiran explains various parts of the song to Darcy, making comparisons between Indian and Western culture as though she is Darcy's (and, by extension, the Western audience's) translator: for instance, she declares the song to be 'the Indian version of American Idol'. Yet Kiran's contempt for India is so clear that, unlike Lalita with her genuine offer to help teach Darcy to dance at their first meeting, Kiran clearly cannot be a trusted translator for the audience; rather, she demonstrates to a Western audience how *not* to behave. She follows her comparison to American Idol with the phrase, 'I hope you've brought your earplugs', signalling a refusal to listen to or engage in Indian culture. She also asserts, 'The only thing India's good for is losing weight' (while her brother readily eats the food that causes Darcy concern) and implies that Indians are lazy when she says they have 'a lot more free time' than she does.[6]

Clearly, Kiran assesses India's worth to her, even in the context of her UK context, for she and Balraj have a servant in Windsor: 'We brought her over from India. Don't know how we'd manage without her.' Attentive to both class and national hierarchies, Kiran, like her counterpart in Austen's novel, displays great distaste for the Bakshi family for most of the film. However, although Hopkins contends that 'the plot and logic of *Pride and Prejudice* are both left far behind when Kiran . . . actually tells Lalita where Darcy is in the final sequence, as if she were giving her blessing to the relationship' (2009, 116), it is easy to read this conclusion as an adaptation of the novel's coda in which Caroline, following the marriage of Darcy and Elizabeth, 'dropt all her resentment . . . and paid off every arrear of civility to Elizabeth' (Austen 2004, 297). Crucially for the trajectory of Kiran's relationship to India, and the film's valorisation of India over the other national settings, Kiran, having only previously danced at the beach party in Goa – suggesting that she has fulfilled Lalita's suspicions about Westerners in India who want 'India without . . . Indians' – clearly participates in dancing in the final scene, a considerable shift from her attitude earlier in the film.

The double wedding in Amritsar at the end of *Bride and Prejudice*, reprising an early song in the film, 'A Marriage Has Come to Town', centres India as the location of the celebrations and the focus of the narrative conclusion. Yet whereas Austen's novel finishes by revealing the destinations of all major characters – most prominently, Elizabeth moving to Pemberley, of course, in Derbyshire, and Bingley and Jane leaving Netherfield after a year of marriage before purchasing 'an estate in a neighbouring county to Derbyshire' (Austen 2004, 295) to be closer to the Darcys than to the Bennets – *Bride and Prejudice* does not reveal where the two couples will live. Certainly, Mrs Bakshi, early in the film, assumes Jaya will marry Balraj and move to the UK, where the Bakshis can visit her; and although we do not see Balraj in his own home in Windsor, Jaya does pay Kiran a visit there with Lalita and their mother on the way to Kholi and Chandra's wedding in LA. But there are fewer clues to Lalita and Darcy's ultimate destination, not only because 'it is equally hard to imagine Lalita permanently installed in LA as Darcy in Amritsar' (Heinen 2009, 64), but also because Darcy, as he himself admits, has no 'family home'. An American who was raised in England (by Wickham's mother, his nanny), where his family owned two country hotels and where he attended university (Oxford) with Balraj and Kiran, Darcy has no obvious base; indeed, as he discloses to Lalita on the flight to LA, his parents 'lived in separate countries'.

Whereas Pemberley is a central location in the novel, both as Darcy's estate (and Elizabeth's future residence) and as the site where Elizabeth begins to realise her feelings for Darcy, in *Bride and Prejudice*, the Darcys' Beverly Hills hotel both does and does not stand in for Pemberley. On the one hand, 'the establishing shot of Darcy's luxurious hotel . . . replicates the impressive façade of Pemberley as shown in the 1995 version of *Pride and Prejudice*' (Oliete Aldea 2012, 174), and as Lalita begins to warm to Darcy, Chandra teases her (as Elizabeth does Jane following her engagement to Darcy) that seeing his Beverly Hills hotel has contributed to Lalita's shifting regard.[7] On the other hand, the fact that it is a hotel, not a home, and not the site of Darcy's upbringing creates a considerable divergence between the family hotel of *Bride and Prejudice* and the family home of Austen's novel. With luxury hotels 'all over the world', the Darcys might be said to have bases everywhere (apart from India, of course, to Mrs Darcy's chagrin); yet a hotel is a marker of transience, an *absence* of home. Whereas the novel's conclusion has Elizabeth and Jane living within thirty miles of each other, indicating the UK as a possible destination for Lalita and Darcy if Jaya will join Balraj there, *Bride and Prejudice*'s Hindi version's title, *Balle Balle: Amritsar to LA*, suggests California as the endpoint of Lalita's trajectory. But at the beginning of the film, on being told by her friend who is the film's first bride (Shivani Ghai) 'You need to get out of this town', Lalita responds, 'Papa needs me. I couldn't leave.'

The very beginning of the film cross-cuts shots of Balraj, Kiran and Darcy's plane landing in Amritsar with shots of Lalita at her family's farm, the editing juxtaposing the passing over of luggage upon the visitors' arrival to Mr Bakshi's handing Lalita some work-related documents. If Balraj, Kiran and Darcy are immediately contextualised through transnational travel, Lalita has been introduced to us through her rootedness to place.

Thus, the unresolved question of where Lalita and Darcy will live after their marriage is an important one. All four couples who get married over the course of the film are transnational, and the figure of the NRI has been explored through multiple versions in order to heighten the possibility of Lalita herself becoming an NRI. Certainly, her initial dislike of Kholi has much to do with his self-positioning as staunchly American and the internalised racism through which he dismisses 'these Indians' who 'don't know how to treat tourists. There's no sophistication.' Lalita's 'project of cultural nationalism' (Mathur 2007, para. 12) distinguishes her sharply from Kholi and Kiran. But the film itself also largely privileges India through visual splendour. Both the US and the UK appear through some glamorous shots: Darcy takes Lalita to the Walt Disney Concert Hall and on a helicopter tour of the Grand Canyon; and the Bakshis' arrival in London is preceded by shots of recognisable landmarks such as Big Ben, Tower Bridge, St Paul's, and, to 'subver[t]' (Chadha and Mayeda Berges 2005) these more conventional associations with London, a Sikh temple in Southall. Indeed, suburban locations in both the US and the UK feature more heavily in the film, such as Kholi's large, expensive house in a new subdivision that still lacks landscaping, or the older, but still unglamorous London suburb of Southall. After returning from Goa, Lalita dreams about marrying Wickham as 'an overseas bride dressed in white' in a country church (filmed in Turville, Buckinghamshire), part of a 'cultural bricolage of national clichés seemingly derived from heritage film' (Gruß 2009, 53) that includes a maypole and Morris dancing in 'the land of her Majesty'. This dream becomes a nightmare when Wickham turns into Darcy, yet Wickham himself will turn into a nightmare when Lakhi runs off with him in London, and Lalita's real wedding to Darcy will bear little resemblance to the earlier dream in its location and cultural context.

Lakhi's indiscretion, however, does invoke the economic implications of marriage. She asks her distracted mother whether she can go shopping, the cover story she uses to meet Wickham instead, to which Mrs Bakshi replies, 'If we are not bringing back any husbands, and she goes shopping, at least we won't be going back empty-handed.' The economic situation of the Bakshis differs from that of the Bennets, but in *Bride and Prejudice* the family's financial insecurity operates in the context of India's under neoliberalism. If Jane and Elizabeth's marriages to wealthy men provide assistance and financial relief to their family, what are the financial implications of Jaya marrying Balraj and Lalita marrying Darcy? As Wilson observes, 'Chadha's Darcy is not in a powerful position from which he can "rescue" Lalita, and she does not need to be rescued anyway' (2006, 329). Early in the film, Mrs Bakshi points out that her daughters would have more earning power if they lived abroad, indicating a presupposition (one not shared by Kholi) that '[a] career is a given in this world, even if one has a husband' (Troost and Greenfield 2008, 5). At the same time, for (potentially) all of *Bride and Prejudice*'s brides, 'transnational migration may occur through the institution of marriage rather than through incorporation into the feminized industrial economy or international domestic service. In other words, they may be inserted into the global economy through the heterosexual household' (Desai 2004, 229). Yet within the global economy, 'the Non-Resident Indian [has been reimagined to be] central to India's fortunes' alongside 'a reworking of the symbolic boundaries of the nation to include the diaspora' (Punathambekar 2013, 178).

We do not know for certain whether Jaya and Lalita will both join the diaspora or the details of how they might contribute to the nation's fortunes as NRIs. But the film's song, 'A Marriage Has Come to Town', marking the first Amritsar wedding at the beginning of the narrative and returning at the end in celebration of Jaya and Lalita's double wedding, explicitly ties marriage to the local economy in 'a visual conjoining of marriage and the marketplace' (Mathur 2007, para. 12). Although Lalita expresses a sadness that her friend, the bride, will be leaving to join her husband in the UK, she also reflects on how 'the city has gone mad', not just in the celebration that is the wedding, but also the celebration of the *fact* of the wedding, and the selling of wares (food, flowers, jewellery) in the market that contribute to the event. Not only do the people in the streets celebrate by partaking in the singing and dancing, but the camera also tilts down to reveal people within buildings above the dancing before returning its attention to the street itself. Such a comprehensive local celebration, expressed in the vendors' line, 'You got a marriage into town', marks the wedding itself as a community achievement, even one that will result in 'giv[ing] a daughter away', as Lalita ruefully notes.

The song follows a scene between Darcy and Balraj, in which Darcy refers to Amritsar as 'Hicksville, India'. The focus on consumer goods in the market, accompanied by the 'laughter, colour, light, and sound' of the song's chorus, works to counteract Darcy's negative response to Amritsar as it valorises the location for the audience through appeals to the senses.[8] The celebration of Amritsar acts as a rejoinder both to Darcy and to notions of the Punjab in other parts of India, given that, '[d]espite its importance to national development and modernity, Punjab is often imagined by the nation at large as being populated by rubes and bumpkins living in various states of rural retrogression and backwardness' (Mooney 2012, 89). In *Bride and Prejudice*, the final shot that accompanies the song is a bird's-eye view of the crowd, grouped together according to colour of clothing, emphasising a diversity of experiences (consumer experiences, in this context) that Amritsar has to offer. The return of this song at the end of the film suggests, in the absence of further information about Jaya and Lalita's futures, that their weddings in and of themselves constitute significant investment in the local economy, and that, potentially, their first act of economic relevance to India as NRIs is to get married, in Amritsar, in the first place. That the film makes this economic point while showcasing consumer goods indicates a deployment of exoticism to appeal to the Western viewer, in similar ways to Nair's *Vanity Fair*, by contradicting Darcy's initial resistance to India and valorising India over the Western locations with which Darcy and Balraj are primarily associated. But if India, for *Vanity Fair*'s Becky Sharp, allows her to reap the benefits of empire through her financial rescue by Jos Sedley, *Bride and Prejudice* returns to a local focus in Jaya and Lalita's double wedding, with India as a valorised site of origin rather than a realised escape fantasy for a white character.

As a postcolonial adaptation of Austen's Regency text, *Bride and Prejudice* renders both the US and the UK less spectacular than India, minimising their aesthetic power in a film that gestures to the imperial power of both. If the United States is largely associated with materialism and inauthenticity in the film, the UK becomes reduced to 'nothing more than a stop-over on the way from Amritsar to LA' (Mathur 2007, para. 9) at the level of narrative. Hopkins argues that the film demonstrates 'the waning cultural influence of Britain' through the representation of Balraj and Darcy, with the American character being more dominant (2009, 20). Within the film itself, Kholi's privileging of the US as a destination rests partly on the fact that he believes 'UK's finished'. The film clearly allies neoliberalism and neo-imperialism with the United States, through the Darcys' hotel empire, while India has 'got rid of' British imperial and colonial power, according to Lalita. Balraj and Kiran's proximity to Windsor Castle is both a source of excitement for Mrs Bakshi and treated as banal by a nonchalant Kiran: 'Flag's up. Queen's at home.' The film projects a somewhat defused Britain, but one that an NRI might over-valorise at the expense of India, as in Kiran's case. Certainly, Windsor Castle appears far less impressive than the Golden Temple, around which the film's opening establishing shot is framed, with a later shot of Rai singing on a balcony overlooking the Golden Temple. However, if the film minimises British economic and cultural power, it does so, ironically, as itself a product of British culture in both its source text and its own production.

Bride and Prejudice's romantic comedy offers a happy ending that accords not only with its source material but also with generic convention. That we don't know what happens to Lalita and Jaya after their marriages is certainly in keeping with other films in the genre (and indeed, other *Pride and Prejudice* adaptations). In the 'No Life without Wife' song that she sings with her sisters, Lalita longs for a man who will 'walk the world with me', a gesture to cosmopolitan mobility that Darcy certainly possesses. The fact that we do not know which part of the world she will be living in forces us to linger instead on the celebration of the marriage, the successful recuperation of Darcy as 'a reformed American capitalist' (Roy 2016, 994), and the celebration of India in general and particularly Amritsar over more powerful, wealthier Western locations.

In portraying India more sympathetically (as well as more spectacularly) than either the US or the UK, *Bride and Prejudice* also effects, at the level of nation, what Lalita sings of: 'I just want a man with real soul / Who wants equality and not control'; their marriage ultimately suggests, therefore, a levelling out of the imbalances of power between her country and Darcy's. The concluding wedding scene, the film implies, makes a statement about aesthetic, cultural and national values to which Lalita ascribes and Darcy has been won over. The critique Lalita poses to neo-liberalism and neo-imperialism can only be absorbed by the character of Darcy himself; further, just as 'the marriage between Darcy and Lalita . . . does not guarantee social transformation' (Roy 2016, 998), so too Lalita cannot single-handedly reconfigure the world economic order. Thus, the film can only offer the transformation of the individual as a narrative remedy – and, presumably, make its point to other Westerners in the form of its audience, who might also view 'India as technically and culturally backward, because [they] expec[t] it to be so' (Heinen 2009, 64). The film teaches us how *not* to be a tourist and indeed, how not to be an NRI, while at the same time it must take for granted, amid its happy conclusion, the structure of the global economy within which both tourists and NRIs operate.

Jindabyne

If *Bride and Prejudice* focuses on tourists and NRIs in their relationship to India, Ray Lawrence's *Jindabyne*, in resituating Raymond Carver's short story 'So Much Water So Close to Home' by transplanting the narrative from the US Pacific Northwest to Australia – from one settler-colonial nation-state to another, in contrast to *Bride and Prejudice* – foregrounds the experiences of white migrants as settlers on Indigenous territory. Like Carver's short story, the film focuses on a group of men who embark on a fishing trip and discover the dead body of a woman lying in the river but choose to continue their holiday rather than curtail it by reporting the body immediately to the police. In adapting 'So Much Water So Close to Home', *Jindabyne* invokes the trauma of the colonial encounter primarily through the fact that, in the film, Susan O'Connor (Tatea Reilly), the dead woman discovered by Stewart (Gabriel Byrne), Carl (John Howard), Rocco (Stelios Yiakmis) and Billy (Simon Stone), is Indigenous. *Jindabyne* thereby offers an example of what Felicity Collins and Therese Davis call a post-*Mabo* cinema, in which 'Australian cinema [acts] as a public sphere for reprising or going back over established themes of national history, as a site for the politics of recognition, and as a traumatised space of public memory' (2004, 9–10).[9] As part of the film's exploration of the re-enacted trauma of the colonial encounter, the character of Claire (Laura Linney), Stewart's wife, attempts to fulfil the role of an 'embodied translato[r]' who might be 'capable of mediating between communities' (Kaplan 2004, 49), as she strives to bridge the gap between white and Indigenous communities through an always already insufficient apology.

Carver's story is told entirely from the point of view of Claire, and begins after the fishing trip, amidst the negative public attention her husband and his friends have attracted because of their delay in contacting the police about the dead body. We only have Claire's second-hand perspective on the event, which is bound up in the physical revulsion she feels for her husband, the fleshy descriptions of his male body, and the violence of their relationship: she comments on 'his heavy arms around [her]' and his 'thick, sleeping fingers' and recalls him 'tell[ing] her that someday this affair . . . will end in violence' (1993, 73, 78, 79). At one point, Claire imagines herself to be the dead woman:

> I imagine her journey down the river, the nude body hitting the rocks, caught at by branches, the body floating and turning, her hair streaming in the water. Then the hands and hair catching in the overhanging branches, holding, until four men come along to stare at her. I can see a man who is drunk (Stuart?) take her by the wrist. (89)[10]

In this moment of intersubjectivity, Claire tries to replicate the body's point of view.

In *Short Cuts* (1993), Robert Altman's film adaptation of 'So Much Water So Close to Home' (and other Carver stories), we follow the men and witness their discovery of the body, while one of them unknowingly urinates onto the woman where the body floats in the river. The reaction in this film is one of surprise by the men, but also of a distasteful humour, including comments about her naked breasts. Altman's film adapts Claire's perspective upon the return of her husband through the camerawork that slowly zooms in on Claire's shocked face while her husband, obscured, relates the discovery of the body with little emotion. Whereas in Carver's story, Claire's perspective is clear through the first-person narration from her point of view, in *Short Cuts*, Altman privileges Claire's response to her husband's narrative of finding the dead woman by focusing on Claire's face, rather than her husband's, while he recounts the experience. The movement of the camera growing increasingly closer to Claire indicates an alignment of the film (and an encouraged alignment of the viewer) with Claire's view of the events, rather than Stuart's.

Jindabyne diverges from both the Carver original and the Altman adaptation insofar as the discovery of the body by the men is represented as a traumatic moment. We watch Stewart on his own, making his way along the rocky riverbank before catching a glimpse of something in the river. He enters the river cautiously, the movement of a handheld camera's focus on the body replicating Stewart's awkward movement through the water. The body is face down in the river, and once Stewart has arrived close enough to confirm that it is a dead body, he mutters, 'Oh Jesus' and 'Fuck' several times; after turning the body over and becoming more agitated, Stewart screams for his friends for help, shouting again a few moments later when they have not yet arrived. Stewart's traumatic discovery of the body is signalled not only by his personal response to the body, but also through the camerawork and editing. As he shouts a second time for his friends, jump cuts illustrate the trauma of the scene and enhance his isolation (which is also signalled by the echoing of Stewart's cries across the landscape) from those whom he calls for help. The ruptures presented by the jump cuts gesture towards Stewart's discovery of the body as an 'even[t] . . . so overwhelming that [it] cannot be cognitively processed' (Kaplan 2004, 46). Thus, the film's editing both represents Stewart's trauma in discovering the body and creates cognitive ruptures for the viewer.

All four of the men will react significantly differently from those in Altman's film, as the *Jindabyne* quartet is shocked and upset. The fishermen in *Short Cuts* are distinctly *un*traumatised: they carry on their conversation, scarcely missing a beat, discussing whether the woman is dead and what to do about it before deciding to leave her in the water and to begin drinking, their voices audible on the soundtrack even as their bodies are not visible, the camera having cut to the body and remained there. The camera's staying with the body rather than the fishermen forces the audience – if not the men who have found her – to maintain their focus on her. In contrast, most of *Jindabyne*'s scene of the body's discovery is silent, apart from Stewart's cries for help and his shouts to his friends to 'take her' from him, with just a brief reaction from Billy – 'Ah fuck', and 'Fuck this', he says, about to leave – and a counter-response from Carl, which causes Billy to stay with the others. Both the camera and the men retain their focus on the body in *Jindabyne*, with only the sound of birds audible, before the scene cuts to the men standing on the bank, away from the river, solemnly discussing how to proceed. Yet as in both Carver's story and Altman's film, they decide not to report the body to the police immediately, not to remove her body, but to tie her up to a tree branch to preserve her body better for when they do inform the authorities. The men get the holiday they want, as signalled by the brilliant sunshine of the following day, and the enormous fish they catch, photographing each other holding up their bounty. Ultimately, then, their ability to suppress their initial shock and terror at the dead body makes them essentially appear as callous as their counterparts in Altman's film.

Just as *Short Cuts* signals its subversion of the men's position, so too *Jindabyne* presents several high-angle shots of the dead fish on the ground, as though the dead body of the woman is no more important (indeed, quite possibly less) than those of the fish, signalling a gap between the four men and the film's perspective on the dead woman's body. When the men of *Jindabyne* ultimately pack up and leave at the end of their trip, the camera cuts to the body still in the water, with extreme close-ups on the victim's skin and hair as insects crawl over her, emphasising that the men have abandoned her, particularly given the camera's pan to her foot tied to the branch and the focus on the violence the fishing line has done to her flesh. Billy calls his girlfriend as soon as they reach mobile phone reception range to say, 'We found a body. I caught the most amazing fish, though!' As Jonathan Rayner notes, through 'the white male group's apparent indifference to her body' (2009, 303), they become aligned with the white killer who caused Susan's death, who we saw dumping her body into the river in the first place.

The scene that deploys jump cuts to portray Stewart's distress, ultimately showing him as a tiny figure in extreme long shot, has the most intrusive editing in the film, but it is also in keeping with *Jindabyne*'s tendency to use extreme long shots to represent a daunting landscape, one that dwarfs the markers of white settler presence. Throughout the film, such extreme long shots are often accompanied by the sounds of human voices – in particular, Indigenous voices, it is suggested – wailing on the soundtrack, perhaps a representation of 'Australianness as a kind of haunted subjectivity' (Hateley 2009, 141). *Jindabyne* therefore perpetuates Australian films' historic tendency to emphasise 'an unknowable, untamable landscape' (Collins and Davis 2004, 75) at the same time as it gives the impression of a landscape watching the white characters, witnessing their actions – or lack of actions – in relation to the murder victim; indeed, there are several point-of-view shots of the men on their fishing trip in shaky, handheld camera shots through trees, that suggest they are being watched.

Although, in the words of one policeman, 'the whole town's ashamed of [the men]' for 'step[ping] over bodies to enjoy [their] leisure activities', the film, like its source story, largely focuses on Claire's response, making Claire and Stewart the central couple in the film. Significantly, Stewart and Claire are both immigrants to Australia: Stewart is Irish, and Claire is American, reflecting the nationalities of the actors who play them (Byrne and Linney). The director, Ray Lawrence, has commented that this casting reflected 'a certain foreignness with the multi-culturalism [*sic*] of the film' (qtd in Stratton 2009, 22). On the one hand, the casting of Byrne and Linney also allows *Jindabyne* to 'bridge the talents and markets of American and Australian cinema' (Rayner 2009, 301). On the other hand, the casting might also function 'to remind us that all Australians, with the exception of the indigenous peoples, are immigrants' (Buchanan 2012, 52). In this way, *Jindabyne* participates in what Collins and Davis have identified as the 'backtracking' tendencies of post-*Mabo* cinema, 'the way in which history . . . speaks to the dilemmas of the present' (Collins and Davis 2004, 11), for Stewart and Claire's foreignness in Australia is highlighted throughout the film.

Stewart's and Claire's national origins resonate differently: Stewart's Irishness gestures towards longstanding (and contested) notions of 'Australianness as synonymous with Anglo-Celticism' (Gunew 2004, 20), whereas Claire's Americanness inserts her into a similar position in both her home and adopted countries as a white settler. But the positioning of Claire particularly as a new arrival is also suggestive in terms of the film's representation of, in Kaplan's adoption of Mary Louise Pratt's phrase, a 'traumatic contact zone' (Kaplan 2004, 45). In the fallout of the men's return from the fishing trip, and both white and Indigenous disgusted responses to them, Claire seeks to identify and redress 'what *prevents harmonious relations* in colonial encounters' (Kaplan 2004, 46) – or in other words, why she is unable to apologise successfully to Susan O'Connor's family and to offer them redress, insofar as neither the apology nor the redress is accepted.

As Kaplan writes,

> When one's lands have been invaded and snatched away, one's culture destroyed (or nearly so), it is as if a deep wound has been made in the social body. Transmitted from generation to generation, the wound remains open even if split-off from daily consciousness. It means that contact between indigenous peoples and the groups who invaded in the past is inevitably haunted by this past. The traumatic past, that is to say, shapes the nature of contact. (2004, 46–7)

Claire attempts to engage with the O'Connor family as though this traumatic past has not happened, only to be rebuffed. Asked whether *Jindabyne* is 'intended as an allegory for reconciliation', Ray Lawrence, the film's director, replied,

> Not in that sense . . . It's more complex than that. When you do something wrong it is very, very hard to say sorry. While it's something that should happen, because it's happening to human beings, it's not as simple as saying sorry and expecting forgiveness. (qtd in Schembri 2006, Entertainment Guide 8)

In the context of a country that instituted a National Sorry Day for what was done to the Stolen Generations – Indigenous children taken from their families ostensibly to ease their assimilation into the white settler society in a culturally genocidal policy – even if Lawrence shies away from the possibility of allegory, it is clear that Claire's need for forgiveness attempts to sidestep the more fundamental need for decolonisation.

Sorry Day was instituted in 1998, the year following the Bringing Them Home report, which concluded 'that child removal fitted the United Nations definition of genocide' (McGrath 2010, 54). *Jindabyne* predates by two years Prime Minister Kevin Rudd's official apology to the Stolen Generations, which was given on 18 February 2008. In the intervening years between the report and the official apology, as Amanda LeCouteur observes,

> [t]alk and text about the appropriateness of this apology . . . have constituted an ongoing national debate in Australia in forums as diverse as State and Federal parliaments, national and local print and broadcast media, organized community meetings, as well as everyday discussions between people. (2001, 147)

Given that 'it is hard to imagine that any Australian could have remained untouched by this issue, or would not have been involved in the debate at some level' (LeCouteur 2001, 147), *Jindabyne*'s 'resonance . . . with Australia's response to the national apology to the indigenous people is unmistakable' (Buchanan 2012, 47). Just as, 'despite the long history of the "sorry" campaign, there is not nor can ever be a simple solution to

Australia's racial problems' (Hateley 2009, 145), so too it is clear that Claire's attempts at reconciliation cannot achieve the community healing she seeks.

Indeed, the complexity of the ethical and political implications of the official apology has counterparts of sorts in the film. As Diana Brydon notes, 'public acts of apology and remembrance . . . are quickly coming to seem not only routine but also substitutes for more substantive forms of restitution' (2013, 6). On the one hand, as Ann McGrath writes, Rudd's apology to Indigenous peoples in Australia 'was a moment of national inclusion brought about by the much-awaited recognition of past suffering', with 'thousands of Aboriginal and other Australians converging on Parliament House' (McGrath 2010, 47). Former Prime Minister John Howard had refused to offer a national apology, arguing 'that the present generation cannot be expected to take responsibility for the actions of previous generations' (Buchanan 2012, 53), hence the decade elapsing between the beginning of Sorry Day, and the 'hundreds of thousands of ordinary Australians . . . sign[ing] "sorry books" . . . in an act of ceremoniously, if modestly, inscribing personal and collective apology' (Jones 2004, 164), and Rudd's apology on just 'the second day of the new Parliament' (McGrath 2010, 47).

On the other hand, however, as Buchanan argues, although the Stolen Generations

> were owed an apology, at the very least, they were not the only ones owed an apology, nor were their experiences the only experiences suffered by the indigenous peoples for which an apology might conceivably be owed (the loss of their land, forced displacement from their land, genocide, and so on; the list of crimes is long). (2012, 54)

For this reason, Rudd's apology 'was hollow and without an accompanying apology for the act of dispossession that created the conditions under which the wrong could have occurred' (Buchanan 2012, 54). As McGrath notes, an apology for the Stolen Generations was a relatively safe act for non-Indigenous Australians: 'While non-Indigenous Australians often opposed land rights as a threat to their property, the recognition of child theft did not threaten white people's backyards' (McGrath 2010, 62); in other words, the failure to address dispossession of Indigenous Australians soothed non-Indigenous Australians' own anxieties about dispossession. In addition to the limitations of the apology in material terms, the apology was 'worthless, irrespective of its supposed symbolic value, because it did not acknowledge the founding violence' (Buchanan 2012, 58) of the nation, which continues to play out in the twenty-first century: 'Colonisation is not over, and with each new solution, the nation–state adds a new layer of often-painful legacies' (McGrath 2010, 63), as the state's ensuing actions such as the 2007 'Emergency Intervention' in the Northern Territory have demonstrated.

A national apology 'can nobly redeem the nation's reputation' (McGrath 2010, 61) without material redistribution. In *Jindabyne*, Claire's determination to apologise – and, crucially, to get her husband to apologise – resembles the ethical ambiguity of the national apology insofar as she may not seek to achieve anything beyond salvaging her family's reputation, and it is unclear what fundamental change might be effected. Buchanan argues that Claire's status as an immigrant in the film suggests that 'only someone from outside the frame of Australian cultural and political life is capable of seeing the truth and feeling the shame of it' (2012, 52). Yet Claire's ignorance with respect to Indigenous culture, and her determination to operate outside Australian historical context, compromises the extent to which she is capable of 'seeing the truth' or indeed 'feeling the shame' of her own white privilege. Unlike her counterpart in Carver's story, who, albeit briefly, intersubjectively merges with the murder victim, and in Altman's film, where the zoom in to close-up on her face makes clear her identification with the dead woman, *Jindabyne*'s Claire clearly cannot be aligned with Susan O'Connor in the same way. Claire encounters the murderer on the road, but he does not attempt any violence towards her, and, unlike the film's audience, she is unaware that he is responsible for Susan's death.

Rather than identify with Susan O'Connor, then, Claire appears to view herself as an 'embodied translator' as she moves between white and Indigenous communities. If an embodied translator can 'function to bridge the gaps produced by crimes of white Australians in the past, and continuing into the present' (Kaplan 2004, 62), Claire fails to occupy this position for many reasons. First, it becomes clear that she is largely invested in reconciliation between the communities in order to rescue her marriage. As she says to the priest whose help she attempts to enlist, 'I don't understand why this is so hard. I just want to stay connected to people; I just want the man I love to be a good man.' Whether Claire seeks any genuine connection with the Indigenous community – the O'Connor family in particular – is not stated, nor how that connection would be forged, and on whose terms. Ultimately, Claire's priority is her own nuclear family, the desire for her husband to live up to her expectations (and salvage his own reputation). Second, as Hateley notes, 'her failures are a logical product of Claire's White assumptions about universality, the right to know, and the right to act' (2009, 144). For instance, she goes to the mortuary to look at Susan's body, prompting outrage from her friend, Carmel (Leah Purcell), who is Indigenous and the girlfriend of Rocco. Despite Carmel's insistence that Claire has behaved appallingly – 'Spirit hasn't gone anywhere. Dead doesn't mean dead' – Claire privileges her own Western epistemology by emphasising, 'I needed to see her for myself . . . I need to know what happened out there.' Claire is convinced that she acts on behalf of the larger community – 'It's about all of us. Isn't it, Carmel? Who are we?' – but she finds few allies in her mission.

What Claire assumes to be a benevolent intervention on her part in the community ('I'm not the one who's done anything wrong', she tells her husband) is read radically differently by Carmel as an unwelcome intrusion. Carmel exclaims, 'I can't believe you'd behave so disrespectfully – to her and to her family', and compares Claire's viewing of Susan's dead body to 'walk[ing] into a stranger's house while they were asleep and have a good old perve at them.' Carmel's accusation resonates with Stewart's fascination with Susan O'Connor's body, returning to where she is tied up in the river alone one night of the trip, turning her over onto her front and stroking her hair. Further, on more than one occasion, Claire turns up uninvited at the O'Connor family home, the first time having the door slammed in her face, while her young son, Tom, stares in through the window at Susan's father. Although not as potentially 'pervy' as Stewart's actions, certainly, or even Claire's, as Carmel suggests, Tom is nonetheless presented as an unwelcome young voyeur.

The second time Claire arrives at the O'Connors' home, bearing money she has collected from the town to pay for Susan's funeral, Claire receives no answer when she knocks at the door, so walks around to the side of the house, where some of Susan's female relatives are sat; despite her statement, 'I don't want to intrude', Claire does exactly that, walking through the archway to the garden into their space, only superficially acknowledging that they are hosts, that this space is theirs, and she is an unwanted guest. Claire offers the money, claiming that 'the whole town wanted to help', but the film has only shown Claire's request being rebuffed by the white people of Jindabyne. When Claire implores one white woman with the assertion, 'They're our neighbours', the woman responds, 'These people look after their own.' Thus, the film demonstrates explicitly that Claire lies to Susan's family about the town's generosity and implicitly suggests that she may have contributed all the money herself. Claire's claim of the town's desire to offer the O'Connor family financial assistance for Susan's funeral (and implicitly compensation for her death) therefore also functions as an attempt to redeem the town of Jindabyne's reputation, especially that of its white citizens. But not only is this attempt punctured for the audience – 'I don't need you begging all over town on my behalf', Jude (Deborra-Lee Furness) tells Claire – but the O'Connor family also refuses to participate in such a transaction. When Claire claims to Susan's family that 'it's not charity', Susan's sister (Ursula Yovich) asks, 'You buying something, then?' If anything, Claire seeks absolution – for herself, her husband and the white community – but absolution is clearly not for sale.

Claire presents a contrast to more violent encounters in the film, largely involving men, for instance the brick thrown through the camper van window of Billy (the youngest of the four fishermen) and his girlfriend Elissa (Alice Garner), one of many acts of revenge for the men's failure to report immediately their discovery of Susan's body. Indeed, as Susan's sister declares on the newscast, 'I really wonder how differently they would have acted if she were white.' The Carver and Altman antecedents of Lawrence's film suggest that they might not have acted any differently at all, but in the cultural context of *Jindabyne*, the men are doubly powerful – as both male and white – in ways that make them and their failure to act even more significantly complicit with injustice.

At a gathering following the fishing trip that Claire hopes will provide an opportunity to 'finally all sit down and talk', Billy and Elissa describe what they understand to be Indigenous beliefs about place and spirituality:

> Elissa: Yeah, well, I was told that the spirits of the dead cross those mountains. They travel from all over up to the high country.
> Stewart: Oh yeah.
> Billy: Yeah, I think we broke her journey by tying her up.
> Stewart: Bullshit. You know, I thought Catholics were superstitious, but [this takes] the biscuit, really. . . . I mean, think about it, it's just a superstition, you know, 'journey,' 'spirit' –

Stewart's diatribe is cut short when Rocco punches him in the face. His invocation of Catholic superstition recalls earlier scenes in the film, such as that in which Stewart's mother asks St Brigid to protect Stewart's and Claire's house for another year, with their son Tom replacing an old cross on the wall with a new one, and Stewart joining in with a prayer in Irish; further, Stewart's first instinct upon discovering Susan's dead body is to cross himself. At the gathering following the fishing trip, however, in the company of his friends, he not only dismisses his mother's and, presumably, his own beliefs, but also uses his Catholicism as an opportunity to counter Billy and Elissa's claims, which themselves are problematic insofar as they only raise these objections to the men's fishing trip after the fact. Moreover, as Graeme Turner notes of Indigenous people in Australian cinema, 'to be seen as the possessors of an ancient but passé mysticism is not necessarily to the Aboriginals' advantage since it renders them even more unfit for white society, places them at an even greater remove from white rationality' (1988, 140–1). Most importantly in this scene, Carmel is present, glancing up at Elissa when she speaks of the spirits of the dead, though she says nothing about Billy and Elissa's statements. During Stewart's rant about superstition, Carmel remains silent, looking away. Rocco's attacking of Stewart, breaking his nose, ostensibly functions as his (unsolicited) attempt to offer protection to Carmel and her community. But Carmel drives off after saying, 'What was all that, huh? I can take care of myself', clearly unimpressed.

At the white priest's suggestion, Claire attends Susan's smoke ceremony, and implores the other men on the trip and their partners to attend as well. Whereas in Carver's story and the Altman adaptation Claire attends the victim's funeral anonymously, in *Jindabyne*, as Hateley observes, 'It is deeply problematic that Claire and the other non-Indigenous couples assume the right to attend Susan's smoke ceremony' (2009, 144), as some of the Indigenous characters present let them know. One of Susan's male cousins (Jie Pittman) shouts at Claire, undermining her claim that she is there to pay her respects by indicating she has no respect for their family ('She's married to one of the bastards who found Susan'), only to be subverted by a female family member who tells him to 'leave her alone'. When Stewart and the others arrive, Stewart attempts to apologise to Susan's father (Kevin Smith), who hits him on the arm and spits on the ground (see Figure 3.2). 'You don't belong here', Susan's cousin tells Claire, potentially encompassing not just Claire's presence at the ceremony but also the settler-colonial presence in Australia.

Despite these reminders of the extent to which these white onlookers are not welcome, however, '[t]here is something badly wrong with this scene' (Juchau 2006, para. 8); for as Stewart tells Claire that he wants her to come home (to which she does not reply, her return gaze more

Figure 3.2 Susan's father spits in response to Stewart's apology.

ambiguous, I think, than some critics seem to allow),[11] it seems that the ceremony becomes a stage for the film's resolution. In Mireille Juchau's words, 'these [white] suffering characters hijack the Aboriginal ritual, which conveniently functions as the required "profound" event to propel their catharses' (2006, para. 7). Given that '[a]t no point are we invited to understand the particular significance and meaning of this ritual for its black participants because we're given little insight into the texture of their lives, or the particularity of their suffering' (para. 7), it seems that the film may not have transcended white Australian cinema culture's tendency to privilege 'the way Aboriginal and Islanders are meaningful to non-Aboriginals, rather than how Aboriginal and Islanders are meaningful to themselves' (O'Regan 1996, 277). The scene's shooting and editing perhaps function to distance the (white) viewer from the proceedings, with brief shots, repeated dissolves, and camera tilts and constant shifts in the scene's distance from the camera while the Indigenous men are chanting, allowing the viewer just fragments or glimpses rather than full access to the ceremony; in this sense, we might see the film's presentation of the ceremony as partly conscious of the fact that its inclusion is problematic. Conversely, we might read the trajectory of the dissolves and the partial presentation of the ceremony as positing an exoticism and a mysticism of the ceremony for a white audience looking in on 'the world's most anthropologized people' (O'Regan 1996, 93).

However, to return to Kaplan's search for embodied translators who might facilitate the devising of a means of 'transfer[ring] difference into something other than trauma', so that 'communities of both the oppressed and their oppressors can come to terms with, mourn, repent, and repair crimes committed' (2004, 62, 63), I suggest that the smoke ceremony scene of *Jindabyne* does gesture towards a possible embodied translator, but in the form of Carmel, rather than Claire. She leads Tom, the son of Claire and Stewart and her own pupil at school, by the hand, away from the tension of his parents, explaining, 'Come on, we walk through the smoke so the spirits don't latch onto us.' It is a brief moment, but one that indicates the necessity of 'intercultural exchange . . . initiated by' (Kaplan 2004, 60) members of the Indigenous community, not the white community, and underscores how Claire's unwillingness to listen to any Indigenous people – not even her friend Carmel – has made it impossible for Claire to be the one to effect cross-cultural healing.

If *Jindabyne*'s smoke ceremony scene 'seems a superficial display of Indigenous mysticism for the purpose of driving a formulaic white catharsis' (Juchau 2006, para. 9), it is perhaps also a symptom of a film that is primarily concerned with self-reflexively situating white settler Australia in relation to Indigenous peoples, with Claire's necessary, but always already flawed, attempt to apologise figuring as a means of reconciling the trauma of the colonial encounter.[12] In this sense, the film is both 'a memorial of pre-apology Australia' (Hateley 2009, 145), and a proleptic reckoning with the inadequacy of the apology, as Claire's personal failures of apology resonate with the larger failures of the official national apology to the Stolen Generations. But if this film largely concludes in an implausible, unsatisfactory manner through the appropriation of the smoke scene for the possible reconciliation of white characters to each other, it is important that it also identifies an embodied translator who is not the white woman who appoints herself to this role, but an Indigenous woman who engages on her own terms. Whereas Claire is chiefly concerned with reconciliation for the sake of her marriage, it is Carmel who offers a potential facilitation of a 'move[ment] from trauma to witnessing, mourning and reconciliation' (Kaplan and Wang 2004b, 18) for the sake of the community.

The cultural clashes presented in *Bride and Prejudice* and *Jindabyne* certainly differ in scale, given the casual racism and internalised racism in *Bride and Prejudice* and the genocidal context of Susan O'Connor's murder in *Jindabyne*. Released just two years apart, these films also illustrate a divergence in the postcolonial and settler-colonial statuses of India and Australia, respectively, with the latter's failure to decolonise underpinning Carver's transplanted narrative in adapted form. The conclusions of these two films signal their considerable generic differences, with *Bride and Prejudice* ending with a double wedding and *Jindabyne* with Susan's smoke ceremony. In both cases, however, cultural conflict is staged via the nuclear family and the rituals attached to it. We know Darcy is recuperated because he is marrying Lalita, in India, and inserting himself into Indian culture as he drums. Whatever the resolution for Stewart and Claire, his presence at Susan's smoke ceremony is certainly necessary, from Claire's point of view, if they are to reconcile. But whereas the wedding is Darcy's own (and Lalita's), Susan's smoke ceremony is not about Claire or her family – or at least, it should not be. Both *Bride and Prejudice* and *Jindabyne* depict a blundering American character insensitive to the harm they do to a culture they do not know. While Darcy appears to have learned enough, from the film's point of view, to be endorsed as Lalita's partner, whether Claire ultimately becomes aware of the epistemological and cultural violence of her response to Susan's death and attempts to make amends is unclear. What is clear is that Claire cannot fulfil the role of embodied translator, and that the film points us to Carmel instead, at the same time as it is less interested, however, in her story than it is in Claire's family drama.

Bride and Prejudice ends with a wedding; *Jindabyne* begins many years after Claire and Stewart have married: both films focus on transnational couples in their transnational adaptations that relocate their source material. These films take international migration for granted; it is, indeed, the premise on which they are both based, and out of which their narratives unfold. In inserting the figure of the translator into their transplanted narratives that now attend to race relations where the source materials did not, the films implicitly raise the question of whether they themselves adequately translate their cultural contexts, and clashes, for viewers.

Visibility and Veracity: Magic Realism in *Midnight's Children* and *Life of Pi*

The year 2012 saw the release of two films adapted from Booker Prize-winning novels: *Midnight's Children* by the British Indian writer Salman Rushdie, published in 1981, the film version of which was directed by Deepa Mehta; and *Life of Pi* by the Québécois writer Yann Martel, published in 2001, the adaptation directed by Ang Lee. In addition to their place in internationally celebrated literature as Booker Prize winners and their focus on Indian characters and Indian history in the twentieth century, including the Emergency as a key event, the two novels also share an engagement with magic realism. This chapter examines how these two films adapt the magic realist elements of their source texts, discussing the elements from the novels that have and have not been visually presented, and the implications of what the audience is made to see. The visual content of the films conceals the locations of production: both films are transnational, with *Life of Pi* having been made all over the world. Indeed, Lee's film (and its source text) itself gestures to the economics of transnational cultural production. In different ways, both films incorporate the figure of the author: *Life of Pi* as part of its fictional narrative; and *Midnight's Children* via Rushdie's voice-over narration. Although both films engage in the representation of India, only *Life of Pi*, whose Indian setting constitutes a far briefer proportion of the narrative, was (partly) filmed in that country, a representation complicated by a transnational production that configures what is visible to the audience. Given the elements of magic realism, then, both films engage questions of visibility and veracity at the level of production as well as narrative. That production should be transnational, with Mehta (like Rushdie) and Lee part of the Indian and Taiwanese diasporas, respectively, inflects what is visible in particular ways.

Midnight's Children

Given the status of *Midnight's Children*, particularly in the postcolonial literary canon and the late twentieth-century literary canon more generally (the novel not just winning the Booker Prize, in fact, but also the 'Booker of Bookers' in 1993), it is perhaps unavoidable that there would be a considerable weight of expectation accompanying the film adaptation. Indeed, as Rushdie has noted, *Midnight's Children*'s Booker success immediately prompted proposals to adapt the novel, first for television, then as a film; these plans not materialising, more proposals ensued once the novel won the Booker of Bookers.[1] The failure of the intended BBC series to get off the ground meant that more than thirty years would pass between the novel's publication and the film version that the novel's success anticipated (see Rushdie 2002). Just as the novel's profile contributed to such anticipation, so too may have its content: as critics writing about the novel have noted, *Midnight's Children* engages explicitly with film – from the 'cinematic quality of [*Midnight's Children*'s] opening scene' (Almond 2003, 1137) to the borrowed plots from Hindi cinema (Syed 1999, 158) – which generates formal expectations for the viewer who is familiar with the original literary text.

Rushdie's *Midnight's Children* has also frequently been upheld as an example of magic realism by literary critics. As Jean-Pierre Durix writes,

> the magic realist aims at a basis of mimetic illusion while destroying it regularly with a strange treatment of time, space, characters, or what many people (in the Western world, at least) take as the basic rules of the physical world. (1998, 146)

Midnight's Children's slotting into the category of magic realism has been complicated by those who acknowledge that such a label depends upon Western literature's positioning of '[r]ealism [as its] degree zero of representation' (Bassi 1999, 49). Shaul Bassi points out that the West's conventions of realism cannot be mapped onto Indian cultural tradition. Indeed, Rushdie claimed two years after his novel's publication that while

> many people, especially in the West, who read *Midnight's Children*, talked about it as a fantasy novel[, b]y and large, nobody in India talks about it as a fantasy novel; they talk about it as a novel of history and politics. (qtd in Stadtler 2012, 115)

Nonetheless, this chapter discusses *Midnight's Children* in relation to magic realism, examining its adaptation to screen in order to assess what Bassi refers to as Rushdie's 'special effects' in their cinematic incarnation, or lack thereof.[2]

The novel *Midnight's Children* explicitly fuses the fantastic with the historical and the political. Focusing on the development of a newly independent India through its protagonist and narrator, Saleem Sinai, born at the very second of independence on 15 August 1947, the novel projects the nation as 'a mass fantasy', with Saleem 'the living proof of the fabulous nature of this collective dream' (1995, 112). Saleem's fate is aligned with that of the nation, given the simultaneity of his birth and India's, and the fact that a map of India can be discerned from his facial features, as one sadistic schoolteacher points out to him (231–2). Positioned as India's twin, Saleem discovers, at the age of ten, that he has a telepathic connection to 580 other Indian children born between midnight and 1 a.m., 15 August 1947 (those who remain of an original 1,001) – all of whom have special powers. Together, they are the Midnight's Children, the children whose births coincided with India's. The 'exotic multiplicity of [the children's] gifts' (198) includes the ability to walk through reflective surfaces, to cause physical wounds through words, to eat metal, to heal others, to remember everything, to fly, etc. Crucially, the Midnight's Children also include Shiva, the boy born at the same second in the same hospital as Saleem, with whom he was switched at birth by Mary Pereira, the Christian nurse who will become Saleem's ayah: Saleem, born to a poor Hindu street singer and his wife, gets a life of privilege with the Muslim Sinais, while Shiva, the Sinais' biological son, grows up impoverished. In addition to the Midnight's Children, the novel's fantastic elements also include the ability of Saleem's grandmother to dream her daughters' dreams as a mode of surveillance (55); the boatman, Tai, whose refusal to wash has consequences so toxic that his stench kills flowers (27); Saleem's sister's ability to speak to animals (151); the skin of India's capitalists turning white (179); and a 'six-hundred-and-thirty-five-day-long midnight' (443) during the period of the Emergency under Indira Gandhi, just to name a few examples.

Saleem appeals to veracity by stating, 'Reality can have metaphorical content; that does not make it less real' (200). His audience within the text, Padma, Saleem's companion and fiancée, reads his claims about the Midnight's Children through a conventional lens, challenging the veracity of Saleem's story: 'Plenty of children invent imaginary friends; but one thousand and one! That's just crazy!' But although 'the midnight [sic] children [shake] Padma's faith in [Saleem's] narrative' (211), ultimately, Saleem tells us, she is won over. Both Padma and the novel's reader only have Saleem's (and Rushdie's) word to go on. As Ursula Kluwick writes, 'magic realism relies heavily on verbal effects, and its magic arises out of wordplay' (2011, 3). Many of the 'special effects' of Rushdie's writing in *Midnight's Children* exceed the fantastical content of his narrative and structure its form: his occasional eschewing of punctuation; intertextuality (not only of literary texts but also, and especially, cinematic texts, with frequent references to Bombay films and an adoption of film vocabulary);

flashing back and forward in the narrative; and admitting to either lying or making mistakes about both historical and fictional events, metafictional devices that disrupt the stability of the text and readers' ability to 'forget' they are reading a construction – or, in other words, that confound the 'realism' of the text's magic realism.

If the novel's version of Saleem tries to convince Padma, his audience, that his story is true, a different relationship with the film audience is inevitable, as we see the events unfold. Furthermore, Padma, considered by Nancy E. Batty as 'co-creator of [Saleem's] narrative' (1999, 100) does not exist in the adaptation, so the internal challenge to Saleem has not been transferred from novel to film. Predictably, there are several differences between the novel and film versions of *Midnight's Children*, mostly in the form of excisions (particularly of some of the more minor characters and subplots). Rushdie's own involvement in the making of the film suggests an attempt to appeal to fidelity, or at least to forestall critiques of a lack of fidelity while emphasising 'the extent to which Rushdie is playing what Michel Foucault calls "the author function"' (de Zwaan 2015, 256): Rushdie wrote the screenplay and provides the voice-over narration for the film, and is thus largely responsible for the film's verbal elements. At the same time as the film appeals to Rushdie's authority, he also becomes fused with the character of Saleem, speaking in the past tense in the narrator's voice as the events of Saleem's life are recounted visually and aurally.

Given its lively source text, Mehta's adaptation of *Midnight's Children*, surprisingly, offers a rather sedate visual signification. Robert Stam suggests that '[c]inema[,...] associated from the beginning both with realism *and* with the magical' may be always already 'potentially "magical realist"' (2005, 13), yet for a film derived from an arguably magic realist novel, *Midnight's Children* minimises, at best, the magic realism in a formal capacity. If film can produce meaning verbally, aurally and visually, for a narrative that is so bound up in magic realism, the *Midnight's Children* adaptation curiously eschews the opportunity to enhance the visual delivery of the narrative in key aspects. Rushdie's involvement in the film perhaps attempts to signal a continuity between versions of the narrative, yet a sharp diversion emerges: whereas language both conveys the novel's plot and constitutes the novel's magic realism, no visual equivalents of 'the heteroglossic novel' emerge in the film (Aldama 2003, 102). Given that Brian McFarlane advises adaptation scholars to distinguish between modes of 'transfer' and 'adaptation proper' in film adaptation, where transfer 'denote[s] the process whereby certain narrative elements of novels are revealed as amenable to display in film' and adaptation proper 'refer[s] to the processes by which other novelistic elements must find quite different equivalences in the film medium' (1996, 13), 'adaptation proper' in the case of *Midnight's Children* seems peculiarly absent.

A case in point features the Midnight's Children themselves, the focus of the novel and its most spectacularly fantastical element. Although Saleem's family refuses to believe him when he claims he has begun to hear voices in his head, we witness the Midnight's Children both aurally (hearing what Saleem hears) and visually when they appear onscreen. The film's litany of special powers of the Midnight's Children is more or less faithful to that of the novel. In fact, the presentation of these powers is virtually shackled to the novel's version: with the exceptions of a visual rendering of Parvati's powers (as she conjures a bird out of thin air; see Figure 4.1) and one boy, whom Saleem identifies as 'a werewolf from Nilgiri Hills', who appears to have semi-transparent legs, the children's supernatural abilities are simply rendered verbally, with no visual demonstration, shouted out by Saleem as he points out which gift is associated with which child he can see before him. In this case, the film prioritises the verbal, rather than the visual. The film may well be 'faithful' in relating the powers the other children possess, but in this case, it largely fails to *adapt* (in McFarlane's terms) this material for the cinema.

In the novel, as Kluwick notes, Saleem is 'deeply conscious of the improbability of his tale', but 'attempts to convince his audience … of the veracity of the magic events he describes' (2011, 21). Perhaps the reliance on verbal rather than visual signification where some of the more

Figure 4.1 Saleem catches the bird that Parvati conjures.

fantastic elements of the narrative are concerned allows the film's audience to suspend their disbelief more readily. And yet the magic realism becomes less magical for having been portrayed in a more realist mode. Moreover, if magic realism depends upon 'mimesis-as-play' (Stam 2005, 102), the film has not produced 'cinematic images as potent and fantastical as those [Rushdie] produced in prose' (Stables 2013, 103). This is not to accuse the film of being unfaithful to the original novel, but rather to note that, curiously, it has not made the narrative more visual, or adapted (in the true sense of 'changed') the novel's verbal elements into visual analogies.

Despite the retention of key narrative elements, inevitably, numerous other aspects of the novel are not transferred to the film. These include (but are not limited to): the absence of Saleem's uncles – who simply do not exist in the film – meaning that subplots involving his uncle Hanif, the filmmaker, and Mustapha, the civil servant, are not carried over; the neighbours of the Sinais on Methwold's Estate are similarly excised from the narrative, meaning there is no philandering Homi Catrack and no childhood friends for Saleem beyond the Midnight's Children with whom he congregates in his head; the prophecy surrounding Saleem's birth, and its component of nose and knees, knees and nose (a reference to Saleem's overly large nose and Shiva's overly large, indeed, 'superhuman, merciless knees' [443]) is absent; and young Saleem (Darsheel Safary), who is sent to Pakistan (rather than to his uncle Hanif's) following the discovery that his blood type does not match that of his parents, can hear the Midnight's Children in Pakistan, whereas in the novel, Saleem's 'perceptions were, while they lasted, bounded by the Arabian Sea, the Bay of Bengal, the Himalaya mountains, but also by the artificial frontiers which pierced Punjab and Bengal' (196). Further, in the film, the adult Saleem (Satya Bhabha) is much older when he is subject to the operation on his nose that deprives him of his telepathic contact with the other Midnight's Children. Finally, the unsavoury plot elements of Saleem's (semi-)incestuous love for the woman raised as his sister and his obsessive visiting of prostitutes in Pakistan also disappear from the narrative.

Some of these differences (particularly the removal of characters) clearly work to simplify the story for the purposes of producing a mainstream running time for the film. Others function to make Saleem more of a sympathetic character, and these changes find a counterpart in the film's visuals, as well. Not surprisingly, Saleem appears nowhere near as grotesque in the film as the novel describes him. The actor, Satya Bhabha, wears a prosthetic nose, but it is hardly of the gargantuan proportions suggested in the novel (and there is no reference, in the film, to the adult Saleem physically falling apart, with a 'crumbling, over-used body' [9]).[3]

The absence of the character of Hanif means that Saleem must reside elsewhere during his exile from his family; in the film, he stays with his aunt Emerald (Anita Majumdar) and her husband, General Zulfikar (Rahul Bose), in Rawalpindi, for seven years (rather than the five weeks he stays at Hanif's Bombay flat in the novel). The fact that Saleem can still hear the other Midnight's Children in Pakistan constitutes a substantial ideological departure from the novel and its emphasis on the unnatural severing of Partition by the 'soldier's knife that could cut subcontinents in three' (65). Although *Midnight's Children*, as Ananya Jahanara Kabir argues, exhibits a '"light-touch" depiction of the violence of Partition' (2002, 262), the novel underscores the arbitrariness and artificiality of Partition through the fact that Saleem's thoughts stop at the border. Saleem's Muslim family's relocation to Pakistan, eleven years after the event of Partition itself, is described in the novel as 'an exile from which I was incapable of contacting my more-than-five-hundred colleagues: I was flung across the Partition-created frontier in Pakistan' (282–3). In the film, this reduced significance of Partition is perhaps surprising, given Mehta's direction of *Earth*, her 1999 adaptation of Bapsi Sidhwa's novel *Cracking India* (1991),[4] a narrative almost exclusively focused on the trauma of Partition.

Mehta's *Midnight's Children* is a border-crossing, transnational production that produces a diasporic portrait of India with scant representation of India itself: the film was primarily shot in Sri Lanka,[5] 'with additional shoots in Kashmir (Dal Lake), Agra (Taj Mahal), Mumbai, and Karachi' (Mendes and Kuortti 2017, 506). Further, the novel's own representation of borders – namely its multiple narratives of Partition – *is* significantly altered, perhaps due to the time lag of three decades between the novel's publication and the making of the film. The temporal proximity of the novel's publication to key political events of the 1970s contrasts sharply with the distance between the production of the novel and the film. Mehta's adaptation, despite its changes to the narrative of the novel, appeals to fidelity by involving Rushdie in the film (as both screenwriter and narrator). In doing so, it implicitly attempts to compensate both for the gap in political urgency between novel and film and for the absence of the novel's postmodern and magic realist elements.

It is perhaps inevitable that adapting the work of a living author will affect the adaptation process, regardless of whether they are involved as closely in the film adaptation as Rushdie was for *Midnight's Children*. The significant gap in time between the novel's publication and the film's release impacts upon the representation of not only Pakistan and Partition but also the Emergency. Published in 1981, *Midnight's Children* appeared relatively soon after the Emergency; Indira Gandhi was still alive. Saleem's own suffering during the Emergency is muted in the film. In the novel, he is forcibly subjected to a vasectomy as well as a testectomy, and the horror surrounding what is being done to him individually, to the Midnight's Children in general and, indeed, to anyone victimised by the Emergency, constitutes a major focus of the narrative climax. In the film, in contrast, although Shiva (Siddharth) threatens Saleem – 'I'm going to take your life away – bit by bit, like you took mine' – we only see Saleem struggling against the anaesthetic, then coming to in his cell, reaching for his groin, and uttering, 'Vasectomy.' This is not to say that the vasectomy is insignificant – it is still involuntary, and a violation, with immense political objectives and consequences during the Emergency – but the film scales back Saleem's personal horror to a striking extent.

In addition to the narrative differences between the novel of *Midnight's Children* and its film adaptation, there are aesthetic distinctions between the two texts as well. For instance, Rushdie's frequent eschewing of punctuation, usually to signify excess – as in the example: 'Aadam Aziz floated with Tai in his shikara, again and again, amid goats hay flowers furniture lotus-roots' (17) – has no analogy in the film version. There are also distinctions between the literary and cinematic versions where the aesthetic – or the formal – and the narrative are fused. As a consequence of the departure from the production of the actor cast to play her (see Mendes and Kuortti 2017, 510), Padma's absence from the film marks an important structural and narrative distinction. In the novel, Padma – Saleem's immediate audience – continually interjects her responses, often undermining Saleem's 'writing-shiting' (24).

But Padma is not the only means through which the narrative is interrupted in the novel. Saleem constantly interrupts himself, an example of which occurs at the very beginning: 'I was born in the city of Bombay ... once upon a time. No, that won't do' (9). He consistently rushes forwards in his narration, as in the example from early in the novel:

> (... And already I can see the repetitions beginning; because didn't my grandmother also find enormous ... and the stroke, too, was not the only ... and the Brass Monkey had her birds ... the curse begins already, and we haven't even got to the noses yet!) (12)

Further, Saleem makes historical errors that he admits to but refuses to correct:

> Re-reading my work, I have discovered an error in chronology. The assassination of Mahatma Gandhi occurs, in these pages, on the wrong date. But I cannot say, now, what the actual sequence of events might have been; in my India, Gandhi will continue to die at the wrong time. (166)

He also lies about Shiva's fate: following the Emergency and Indira Gandhi's election defeat, we are initially told that 'Major Shiva was placed under military detention by the new régime' (441) and that he was murdered in his cell by a former lover; the following – and final – chapter begins with the confession, 'To tell the truth. I lied about Shiva's death. ... Padma, try and understand: I'm still terrified of him' (443). Following his construction of the period of the Emergency as a perpetual midnight (which is replicated in the film), in the novel, but not in the film, Saleem reflects, 'my presentation of the Emergency in the guise of a six-hundred-and-thirty-five-day-long midnight was perhaps excessively romantic, and certainly contradicted by the available meteorological data' (443). Saleem utters no such confession in the film; therefore, his critique of his own narration does not carry over into the adaptation.

Instead, Mehta's *Midnight's Children* includes no self-reflexive gestures. Given that Hanif is a filmmaker, his absence contributes to the loss of references to cinema. The novel's invocation of cinema is not exclusive to this character, however. Florian Stadtler notes that *Midnight's Children* as a whole 'draws on the conventions of Indian popular cinema' (2014, 37). As Deepa P. Chordiya observes, 'Rushdie uses the vocabulary and techniques of cinema to allow Saleem to splice together fragments and achieve cinematographic effects within a prose narrative' (2007, 107); these include the construction of images as though they were on camera ('long shot', 'close-up', etc), the use of montage and Saleem's tendency to 'rel[y] heavily on flash-forwards and flashbacks to unify the fragments of his narrative' (108). In the novel, references to cinema have a different effect, given the contrast in media; the film takes no opportunity to engage with cinema self-reflexively. Further, in the film there is no internal audience to whom Saleem is held account; and there is no flashing forward in the narrative. If Saleem asks in the novel, 'How to dispense with Padma?' the answer lies in Mehta's film, which appears to be 'reconciled to the narrow one-dimensionality of a straight line' (Rushdie 1995: 150) – Padma's narrative preference, after all. In contrast to the mere streamlining of narrative elements that has occurred in the adaptation of the novel into film, I would argue that these formal distinctions are more significant. Some of the novel's aesthetic elements simply cannot be transferred from novel to screen (the moments where Rushdie omits punctuation, for instance); however, there are no signs of McFarlane's 'adaptation proper' in these instances, that is, cinematic versions of the literary that might convey an analogous meaning.

Moreover, as McFarlane notes of film adaptation generally, 'The novel draws on a wholly *verbal* sign system, the film variously, and sometimes simultaneously, on *visual*, *aural*, and *verbal* signifiers' (1996, 26). At times, the film of *Midnight's Children* visually portrays, with effective economy, what is explained verbally in the novel, such as the reaction of Saleem's aunt, Alia (Shikha Talsania), when his mother (Shahana Goswami), following her divorce from her first husband, becomes better acquainted with Ahmed Sinai (Ronit Roy), who has previously been Alia's suitor. Mehta cuts to Alia's upset facial expression, with no narration of how she is feeling required (cf. Rushdie 1995, 63–4). Other plot elements have been changed in order to stage events that otherwise occur within Saleem's head, or indeed, that do not occur at all: in the novel, when Saleem's mother reconnects with her first husband, Nadir, Saleem witnesses them together in a café, but then proceeds to follow her telepathically on her excursions. In the film, after the first re-encounter with Nadir (Zaib Shaikh), Saleem confronts his mother, and she immediately refuses to see Nadir again. Later in the novel, we are told that Shiva presides over the incarceration of the remaining Midnight's Children during the Emergency; the film, in contrast, stages a fight in the Delhi slum where Saleem has been living between Shiva and Saleem. Once in prison, Saleem tells Shiva, 'I stole your life', Shiva's gun shoved in Saleem's mouth. This dramatic confrontation has no counterpart in the novel, in which Shiva never discovers his true parentage. In the novel, Saleem's fear of Shiva exists within his own head, his fear that Shiva will seek retribution if he discovers the truth (and as such Saleem works to exclude Shiva telepathically from the Midnight's Children conference), but the film substitutes these internal struggles with verbalised, and sometimes physical, confrontation.

If the film makes these changes via Rushdie's own screenplay, Mehta's earlier work has also invoked the Author figure, implicitly appealing to the authority of the original text: in *Earth*, Bapsi Sidhwa herself appears in a cameo role at the end of the film adaptation of *Cracking India*, as the adult Lenny. It is not a speaking role, but Sidhwa's appearance on screen closes out the film. In the case of *Midnight's Children*, Rushdie was intrinsically bound up in the filmmaking process in multiple ways. Although film authorship popularly (and problematically) tends to be conflated with a film's director, Rushdie's having written the screenplay adaptation of his own novel (although Mehta is listed, much further down in the credits, as 'co-writer') reinscribes him as the Author. If Rushdie's voice-over was introduced to 'compensat[e]' for the absent Padma (Mendes and Kuortti 2017, 511), this measure amplifies Rushdie's re-inscription, as he stands in for, and gives voice to, the perspective of the protagonist (and the novel's narrator), Saleem Sinai. As Stadtler notes, the 'distinctive speaking voice' (2014, 81) of Rushdie – 'quintessential celebrity author' (Murray 2012, 44) – prevents the audience from dissociating the original author from the film version.

Finally, Rushdie acted as one of the executive producers for the film; although he occupied this position alongside seven others, Simone Murray argues that 'hiring the [source material's] author as an executive producer' is 'a ploy which can in production terms ensure a useful source of on-hand knowledge about the narrative world conveyed in the book' at the same time as 'it serves to forestall aggrieved fans' predictable complaints that their favourite author's work has been debased by a ham-fisted, faithless adaptation' (2012, 119). In the case of *Midnight's Children*, however, Rushdie's executive producer role sits alongside his screenwriting and voice-over credits. Rushdie's involvement in the filmmaking, therefore, encompassed various roles, some visible (or audible) and others not, in terms of how the audience receives and perceives the film version.

Rushdie has commented on the process of making the film adaptation, observing, 'We set ourselves a task of finding the spine of the narrative' (qtd in Han 2012); thus, narrative, despite excisions from the novel to the film, is paramount in this film adaptation, rather than form and its cinematic possibilities. 'We stuck to the narrative,' Deepa Mehta confirms (qtd in Han 2012), and although this narrative adherence suggests fidelity on the filmmakers' part, to suggest that the novel *Midnight's Children* can be boiled down to its plot takes a very narrow view of this text. Reflecting on the writing of the novel, Rushdie claims, 'The secret of writing the book was finding Saleem's voice' (qtd in Han 2012). As the film's narrator, Rushdie in fact produces Saleem's voice; Rushdie's narratorial voice and Saleem's are one and the same. And unlike in the novel, there are no voices to compete with the narrator's: if '[w]hat ... saves the novel from merely repeating the past is its own self-criticism' (Brennan 1989, 108), the film offers no self-reflexive undermining to complicate, fracture or compromise our understanding. Rushdie claims, '*Midnight's Children* is this idea of India being this home of plenty, this inexhaustible wellspring of stories. And I think the film tries to do that non-verbally' (qtd in Han 2012). Yet everything in the film points to a unity of perspective, a singular, linear and authoritative version of events.

Finally, the tone of the end of the film diverges dramatically from that of the novel. Rushdie writes in the novel, 'Love does not conquer all, except in the Bombay talkies' (444). Yet in rendering *Midnight's Children* as a film, the Bombay talkies' message would appear to speak for the narrative in its new incarnation. The final paragraph of the novel reads:

Yes, they will trample me underfoot, the numbers marching one two three, four hundred million five hundred six, reducing me to specks of voiceless dust, just as, all in good time, they will trample my son who is not my son, and his son who will not be his, and his who will not be his, until the thousand and first generation, until a thousand and one midnights have bestowed their terrible gifts and a thousand and one children have died, because it is the privilege and the curse of midnight's children to be both masters and victims of their times, to forsake privacy and be sucked into the annihilating whirlpool of the multitudes, and to be unable to live or die in peace. (463)

In contrast, the film ends with the following voice-over:

A child and a country were born at midnight, once upon a time. Great things were expected of us both. The truth has been less glorious than the dream. We have survived and made our way. And our lives have been, in spite of everything, acts of love.

As Stadtler argues, this ending for the film is 'rather too upbeat' (2014, 83). The fact that Rushdie himself utters the narration that diverges so widely from the novel might well fend off criticisms of a lack of fidelity, suggesting that Rushdie's 'licence is … used to uplift, while serving the need for resolution in a film intended for popular spectatorship' (Mendes and Kuortti 2017, 508), as he presides as Author, author*ising* the changes that have been made. Indeed, Rushdie, long before the film, commented on the novel's 'pessimism': 'The book has been criticised in India for its allegedly despairing tone. … But I do not see the book as despairing or nihilistic' (2010b: 16). Five years later, however, Rushdie noted that

nobody finds the novel's ending pessimistic any more, because what has happened in India since 1981 is so much darker than I had imagined. If anything, the book's last pages, with their suggestion of a new, more pragmatic generation rising up to take over from the midnight children, now seem absurdly, romantically optimistic. (2010c, 33)

If Rushdie, looking back on the novel's production and publication after the assassination of Indira Gandhi and the ensuing anti-Sikh violence, retroactively read optimism for India in his novel, the next generation, as represented in Aadam Sinai, biological son of Shiva and Pavarti, raised by Saleem, 'on whom Saleem pinned his hopes for India's future', would ultimately be written in Rushdie's 1995 novel *The Moor's Last Sigh* as 'not just a failure but a crook' (Trousdale 2004, 107–8). Thus, Rushdie's optimism for India, as manifested in his fiction through *Midnight's Children*'s characters and their futures, has shifted in the years since 1981, and not just in the film adaptation.

In contrast to the historical and national specificity of the production of the novel, Mehta has claimed a universality for *Midnight's Children*, describing it as 'a quest for home, a quest for family. As we increasingly migrate, national and geographical boundaries are being blurred; we're all looking for home' (qtd in Han 2012). Such an approach to the text's material no doubt attempts to render it more amenable to international representation and circulation, those national and geographical borders having blurred, after all. The film of *Midnight's Children*, a Canada–UK co-production filmed mostly in Sri Lanka, based on a novel written by a British Indian writer, and directed by an Indo-Canadian, cannot help but be a product of displacement, just as Mehta perhaps cannot escape the blurring (if not collapsing) of boundaries. Yet the film offers the comfort of home and family at its conclusion (with fireworks going off over Bombay); the 'apocalyptic explosion' (Stadtler 2014, 48) of Rushdie's novel simply becomes celebratory pyrotechnics to entertain Saleem's newly configured family unit. Yet with Rushdie narrating the film's ending, Mehta's ending becomes Rushdie's as well in a *Midnight's Children* of the twenty-first century, which appears to have recovered from the political realities of the time of the novel's production. If, indeed, as Rushdie's voice-over asserts, 'The truth has been less glorious than the dream', he might well have been describing the film adaptation itself and its emphasis on narrative and on verbal signification, rather than the cinematic possibilities that adaptation might have fulfilled.

Life of Pi

In its portrait of India through Saleem and his family, focusing mainly (in accordance with Saleem's own lifetime) on the period between Partition and the Emergency, *Midnight's Children* presents an 'eclectic hybridity' (Syed 1999, 151) of multiple traditions; indeed, Saleem's own upbringing, as Meenakshi Mukherjee notes, demonstrates 'the co-existence of diversity in the land of his birth through the varieties of mothers [he] has – biological, adoptive and nurturing – Vanita, Amina and Mary Pareira [*sic*], who happen to be Hindu, Muslim and Christian' (1999b, 24). In *Life of Pi*, the eponymous protagonist subscribes to all three of these religions, despite his upbringing as a Hindu. But whereas *Midnight's Children* engages more with the social and political fallout of religious difference, *Life of Pi* focuses more on faith: not only that of Pi himself in all its multiplicity, but also that of the reader. The novel frames the narrative of Pi's experiences as a teenager, his zoo-keeping family dying in a storm en route from India to Canada, and leaving Pi stranded on a lifeboat with a Bengal tiger, as, in the words of Francis Adirubasamy, '*a story that will make you believe in God*' (Martel 2002a, viii). Like *Midnight's Children*, *Life of Pi* contains an internal audience: the writer to whom the adult Pi tells his story, as well as, at the end of the novel, the two Japanese officials who interview the teenaged Pi.

In terms of *Life of Pi*'s magic realism, the novel is 'unwaveringly detailed and empirical', as Pi itemises the boat's contents and meticulously records his survival, but the presence of '[t]he tiger is one sustained element of magic that remains' (Aldea 2011, 79). It is this element that the Japanese officials indicate they do not believe, challenging the veracity of Pi's explanation of his survival. They demand another story, one that excludes animals. Pi's first version of the story, which occupies most of the book, details his upbringing in a Pondicherry zoo, the development of his simultaneous adherence to three religions (Hinduism, Christianity and Islam), his family's decision to migrate to Canada in the midst of the Emergency, and, following the ship's sinking, the initial occupants of the lifeboat: Pi, a hyena, an orang-utan, a zebra with a broken leg, and Richard Parker, a 450-pound Bengal tiger – until the hyena kills the orang-utan and the zebra, only to be killed by the tiger, leaving Pi alone with Richard Parker. The son of a zookeeper, Pi uses his zoological knowledge to train Richard Parker and thereby keep himself alive for 227 days until the lifeboat reaches the coast of Mexico. Pi tells this story to an anonymous writer who interviews him as an adult (now living Toronto) about his experiences many years ago on the lifeboat.

But the novel's final section includes a second version of Pi's shipwreck, embedded in a report, to which the anonymous writer has access. This section appears in the form of a transcript from Pi's interview in a Mexican hospital with Mr Chiba and Mr Okamoto from the Japanese Ministry of Transport, investigating, for insurance purposes, the cause of the ship's sinking. Doubting the veracity of the story that Pi will presumably eventually tell the writer in Toronto, the officials demand another story. After a '[l]ong silence' (334), Pi offers a second story, one that takes up a scant eight pages, rather than the first story's ninety-seven chapters. In the second story that Pi offers to the Japanese officials, the initial lifeboat occupants consist of Pi, his mother, a Taiwanese sailor with a broken leg and the ship's cook, who is French. This second story revolves around horrific violence: the cook, who is described almost immediately as eating flies on the lifeboat, insists the sailor's injured leg must be amputated for the sailor's own good, then admits he has carried out the amputation in order to use the flesh as fishing bait. When the sailor dies, the cook eats some of his body, while Pi and his mother, who are vegetarian when under better circumstances, look on, horrified. Ultimately, the cook murders Pi's mother (who has attacked the cook in retaliation for his having hit Pi); in revenge, Pi kills the cook, and commits acts of cannibalism himself: 'His heart was a struggle – all those tubes that connected it. I managed to get it out. It tasted delicious … I ate his liver. I cut off great pieces of his flesh' (345).

The officials decide between them that the first story, with the tiger, constitutes an allegorical version of this second story: the hyena represents the cannibalistic cook; the zebra with a broken leg represents the sailor; Orange Juice, the orang-utan (whose maternal qualities Pi emphasises in the first story [see 143]) represents Pi's mother; and Richard Parker represents Pi himself. (However, they have no idea what to do with other elements of Pi's first story of his voyage, especially an episode prior to Pi's arrival in Mexico, when he arrives at a carnivorous island populated largely by meerkats: 'what about the island? Who are the meerkats ... Whose teeth were those in the tree?' [346].) Despite their seeming (if partial) 'decoding' of Pi's original story through the second story, the officials concede, when asked by Pi, that the first story, 'the story with animals', is 'the better story' (352), although they do not give reasons why (just as Pi does not give any criteria for the determination of 'the better story'). Conversely, Mr Chiba describes the second story of human violence as 'a horrible story' (345).

I have argued elsewhere (Roberts 2011, 203) that the second story offers a violently failed multiculturalism, given the multiple national and racialised identities of the human occupants of the lifeboat. In the 'better story', violence occurs between animals, rather than humans: the hyena viciously dismembers the zebra and the orang-utan, but the hyena's story does not underscore a deeply unethical relation between humans. The potential for human violence exists in the novel's version of the first story, when Pi, temporarily blinded due to his starvation, encounters another blinded man (who happens to be French, and who is also starving) in another lifeboat. Pi invites the man aboard his boat, but this visitor, immediately attempting to attack Pi in order to eat him, meets a swift death thanks to Richard Parker. In this scene, animal violence pre-empts human violence. It does, however, include an element of cannibalism:

> I will confess that I caught one of his arms with the gaff and used his flesh as bait. I will further confess that, driven by the extremity of my need and the madness to which it pushed me, I ate some of his flesh. I mean small pieces, little strips that I meant for the gaff's hook that, when dried by the sun, looked like ordinary animal flesh. They slipped into my mouth nearly unnoticed. You must understand, my suffering was unremitting and he was already dead. I stopped as soon as I caught a fish. I pray for his soul every day. (284)

The Japanese officials wonder if this blind French man was the ship's cook, which assists in their conflation of Pi with Richard Parker; but there are ways in which this element of the story complicates the neat allegory they try to forge after Pi's second story, given Pi's admission of cannibalism in the first story.

As previously mentioned, the second story appears to the reader through the form of a transcript, the novel ending with Mr Okamoto's final report on the inconclusiveness of how the *Tsimtsum* sank. In Ang Lee's film version, there is also a shift in representation between the first and second story, although the nature of this shift has been adapted for the cinema. Again, the second story is brief, taking up five minutes, a small percentage of the film's overall two-hour running time. In contrast to *Midnight's Children*, Lee's film is striking for its visual effects, not simply the CGI animals that have been constructed as Pi's (Suraj Sharma's) companions but also the rendering of the ocean and the sky in spectacular colour (the more remarkable for the film having been shot in a water tank with bluescreen). The novel emphasises the tedium of Pi's experience onboard the lifeboat: at best, it is a combination of 'boredom and terror' (240): 'Life on a lifeboat isn't much of a life' (241). The film, unsurprisingly, eschews this element of tedium, privileging instead the spectacular elements of narration that can be maximised visually for the audience: for instance, where, in the novel, Pi loses his supplies as a result of a storm ('I noticed the loss of the raft at dawn ... Much of our food was gone, either lost overboard or destroyed by the water that had come in' [253]), the film inserts another, earlier scene, in which an enormous whale breaches next to the lifeboat, upturning the raft and all the supplies Pi has stowed there. This night-time scene is full of bioluminescence, making an additional spectacle out of the loss of supplies where no additional scene exists in the novel. Similarly, Pi's thoughts about his relationship to Richard Parker and his lost family appear in the scene where he hallucinates (for the viewer's benefit), seeing the depths of the ocean through the tiger's eyes, Pi's mother's (Tabu's) face appearing in an explosion of blossoming light. Although the novel includes Pi's observation that 'the sea is a city. Just below me, all around, unsuspected by me, were highways, boulevards, streets and roundabouts bustling with submarine traffic' (194), it does not encompass the more fantastical and hallucinatory elements of this scene in the film, which features zoo animals as well as Pi's mother below the surface.

Given the film's staging (and addition) of spectacular events, it is notable that Pi's second story (told, as in the novel, because of the Japanese official's doubts about the story of Richard Parker) is dramatised for the viewer. Following the hyperreal visuals of the rest of the film in the lifeboat narrative, the sedate visuals in the Mexican hospital present a shocking contrast, perhaps the 'dry, yeastless factuality' (336) that Pi claims the Japanese officials seek. Instead of the human version of the lifeboat narratives, we see Pi in his hospital bed, the camera zooming in on his face while he narrates the second story for the officials, weeping by the time this second story reaches its conclusion. On the one hand, the shift from hyperreal special effects to a realist mode – as manifest in the acting of Suraj Sharma – presents a cinematic adaptation of the shift in register in the novel, between Pi's narration (as recreated by the anonymous author who encounters him) and the interview transcript (see Figure 4.2). On the other hand, the stakes of this cinematic shift are even higher, given that the second story appears in a realist rather than visually fantastic mode.

Ultimately, the film suggests that the second story is more credible than the first, whereas, I would argue, the novel maintains a balance between the credibility of each of the stories.[6] The film omits the narrative of Pi's temporary blindness and encounter with the French man. Instead, at the beginning of the ship's voyage, the film inserts a racist encounter between Pi's family and the ship's cook (Gérard Depardieu). Pi's mother requests a vegetarian meal; this is rudely refused by the cook, who places a tiny bit of parsley on top of the sausages and gravy he has served her. When Pi's father rebukes the cook for his behaviour, the cook insists that he makes food for 'sailors, not curry-eaters'. Thus, the film introduces a failed multiculturalism early on; conversely, the political complexity of Pi's adherence to three religions – Hinduism, Christianity and Islam – in India in the 1970s is all but absent in the film, with no equivalent of the novel's encounter between the pandit, imam and priest with Pi's family (71–7; although, admittedly, Martel's engagement with the politics of religion in India is minimal compared with Rushdie's, covering some of the same period of India's history).

Figure 4.2 Pi tells his second story to the Japanese officials.

In Lee's *Life of Pi*, the Buddhist sailor (Bo-Chieh Wang) – presumably the Taiwanese sailor from the novel – immediately attempts to befriend the Patels after their confrontation with the cook, telling them that gravy is just flavour, perhaps a sign from the film that intercultural encounter need not always be circumscribed by racism. But the film audience may be prepared for the second story in a way that lends it more credibility through having witnessed the actions of the cook prior to the ship's sinking.

Some reviews of the film suggest that, for all 'the studio's seeming willingness to respect the novel's ambiguous ending' (Castelli 2012, 18), the second story is the 'real' story, the factual explanation for the fantastic narrative that has preceded it. Yet the realist acting that delivers the second story may belong not solely to Sharma, but also to the character of Pi himself, for his audience of the two Japanese officials. Just as the teenaged Pi weeps as he relates the details of his mother's death at the hands of the murderous cook, so the adult Pi (Irrfan Khan), years later, concludes his narration to the writer (Rafe Spall), in tears, as he describes Richard Parker's abandonment of him on the Mexican beach, when the tiger leaps into the jungle without turning back to acknowledge him. In the film, the discussion about what constitutes 'the better story' unfolds between Pi and the writer, not Pi and the Japanese officials. In the film, Pi concedes that '[t]he investigators didn't seem to like the [second] story, exactly', but it is the writer whom he asks which story he prefers. The writer replies, 'The one with the tiger. That's the better story.' As in the novel, to the Japanese officials, Pi's response is, 'Thank you. And so it goes with God.' Again, the film includes no criteria from either Pi or the writer for what a 'better story' would contain. The distinction between novel and film in terms of who Pi converses with about which version is 'the better story' makes an important difference, however. The Japanese officials are Pi's first audience following his experiences at sea, and they meet his extensive, detailed narrative of Richard Parker with disbelief. 'The better story' may indeed be better because it is less violent, less upsetting and keeps intact the possibility of ethical human interaction, even amid extreme crisis. Thus, it may be 'the better story' because it is the story the that officials would like to believe about humanity. In contrast, the film, in a way, provides an anachronistic precursor to the novel. In the novel, we get the writer's perspective from the very beginning, framing Pi's narrative by relating how the writer came across Pi's story in the first place. Pi's story is thus always already the writer's version of Pi's story: '*It seemed natural that Mr. Patel's story should be told mostly in the first person, in his voice and through his eyes. But any inaccuracies or mistakes are mine*' (x). Conversely, in the film, we witness the meeting of Pi and the writer, as well as the writer's response to Pi's own narration of his story; thus, that narration is *not* filtered through the writer, who acts as Pi's immediate audience in the film. When the *writer* identifies which is 'the better story' in the film, he means that it is the one that he will go on to write (as confirmed when he says to Pi, 'It's an amazing story. Will you really let me write it?').

To a certain extent, these shifts from novel to film are rather minor, allowing some elements of the novel to be adapted for a different medium. In another sense, however, they have the capacity to reconfigure *Life of Pi* almost completely through their different emphases on veracity and visibility. In adapting a source text that engages with the very notion of the extent to which narrative is trustworthy, the film's ability to stage narrative events for the audience is inevitably powerful in our determination of which version of events is true. But whereas the novel's version of Pi, written by former philosophy student Martel, reminds us (and the Japanese officials) that 'telling about something – using words, English or Japanese – [is] already something of an invention[.] [J]ust looking upon this world [is] already something of an invention' (335), the film introduces no such fundamental gap between representation and reality.

If the film's dialogue does not invoke this gap, the film's production often, in terms of location, substitutes one place for another. A product of 20th Century Fox, *Life of Pi* might be considered American given its financial backing. Unlike *Midnight's Children*, the film was shot in India (the location of much of the novel's – and some of the film's – action towards the beginning of the narrative), as well as in Taiwan, New Zealand, and, in accordance with the novel's external frame, in Canada. As such, we must attend to multiply embordered national production contexts amid global cultural flows, given the scale of both the film's production and the circulation of the source novel.

The adult Pi in the novel lives in Toronto, relocated by the film adaptation in which he lives in another major Canadian city – Montreal – instead.[7] This change from novel to film operates alongside several heightened references to the French language in the film, perhaps ironic given the source text's Québécois author. In the film, the unnamed writer, having encountered Pi's 'mamaji', Francis Adirubasamy (Elie Alouf), in Pondicherry, cites Francis's ostensibly tidy connection between Pi's origins and his ultimate destination: 'So, a Canadian who's come to French India in search of a story. Well, my friend, I know an Indian in French Canada with the most incredible story to tell. It must be fate that the two of you should meet.' The inversions of a Canadian in India, an Indian in Canada, connected through legacies of French imperialism, appear in the film as both neat and destined, while denying Pi the status of Canadian, contradicting the novel's presentation of Pi's self-identification, in the middle of the

Pacific Ocean, as 'INDO-CANADIAN' (183) already. The film's change from Toronto to Montreal also dilutes Martel's interest in radical simultaneity: in the novel, Pi's foster mother is Québécoise, a Toronto resident with a 'French-speaking mind' (54), echoing many of Martel's characters in other texts who experience displacement and apparent disjunctions between their identities and their locations.[8] The film implicitly 'returns' Pi's foster mother (even if she never appears or is mentioned in the film) to a location where French Canadianness constitutes a majority identity.

At the same time, the film includes references to French in the parts of the narrative set in India that do not appear in the Québécois Martel's novel. As a child and teenager, Pi is periodically shot reading a book in French (e.g. *L'Ile mystérieuse*, the French original of Jules Verne's *Mysterious Island*, suggestive of his later encounter with the carnivorous island in the Pacific; and Albert Camus's *L'Étranger*). We also witness Pi announcing his new name to his class in French. Pi indicates French as a pedagogical priority when, following his father's traumatic lesson about animals' capacity for violence, in which Richard Parker kills a tethered goat through the bars of an enclosure,[9] Pi narrates that he has become dissatisfied with life, and that school is 'nothing but facts, fractions, and French'. Pi's parents also speak to the cook aboard the *Tsimtsum* in French. The visible and audible references to the French language not only emphasise the history of French imperialism in India, then, but they also suggest that in Montreal, Pi has found a logical home, regardless of his original destination of Winnipeg. Further, the embedding of French into the film's narrative, even during its Indian and Pacific Ocean settings, implicitly acknowledges and makes visible its Québécois location of production and post-production.

In national, rather than provincial, cross-border terms, the film retains Canada as the destination for the Patels' migration and includes the present-day scenes between Pi and the unnamed writer in Montreal. Conversely, the United States (to which the film ostensibly 'belongs') is absent from the screen. If Martel's novel, which takes place mostly in a lifeboat on the Pacific Ocean, 'could almost be set nowhere' (Payne 2002, 12), according to one British reviewer, perhaps the fact that the film was largely shot in a water tank on blue screen accentuates this placelessness in the adaptation, 'an infrastructural elsewhere' in Charles R. Acland's terms (2018, 156), the water tank standing in for the Pacific Ocean of the narrative prior to the addition of visual effects. But *Life of Pi*'s water tank does not exist outside of geography itself, but rather in Taiwan.

Life of Pi thus chimes with Hamid Naficy's definition of a 'multiplexing', a cinema born of the intersection between 'two movements in the world, one (the post-diasporic) involv[ing] increasing physical displacement and dispersion of people across the globe, the other (the post-digital) … the increasing consolidation and digitization of media' (2010, 13). Regardless of what we do or do not recognise as viewers at the surface level of the text, therefore, the materiality of production introduces multiple border crossings and emphasises the Taiwanese-American director's multiple positionings and cultural ties at the same time as it evidences Naficy's observation that multiplexing accommodates filmmakers' 'returning to their places of origin, where they may stay (or not)' (2010, 13). For Lee, the return is temporary, driven by Hollywood budget considerations, which allows the studio, 20th Century Fox in this case, to 'reac[h] multiple markets and higher profits' (Naficy 2010, 18) as well as the recognition bestowed by the Oscars that indicates he is 'a fully paid-up, albeit flexible, citizen of Hollywood' with 'complete integration into Hollywood-style filmmaking' (Lim 2012, 139). During his acceptance speech for Best Director for *Life of Pi* (his second such honour after *Brokeback Mountain* [2005]), however, Lee took the opportunity to remind (or indeed, inform) viewers that most of the film had been shot in Taiwan, even if most of the film's global audience had no idea while watching it.

If *Life of Pi*'s production encompasses multiple nation-state borders, it also interpolates additional borders through the shift in setting from Toronto to Montreal and through the economics of film production and post-production. *Life of Pi* crosses the provincial border between Ontario and Quebec, the province from which Martel's family hails, but where he himself (now resident in the province of Saskatchewan) has lived for only a small proportion of his life. In this sense, the film of *Life of Pi* might also be said to return Martel (along with Pi's foster mother) to his 'native' province; this 'return' has been prefigured in much press coverage about Martel's winning the Man Booker Prize for *Life of Pi* that was devoted to explaining why Martel writes in English rather than French, as a means of maintaining his connection to Québécois culture (see Bégin 2002, Guy 2002, Lessard 2003). But materially speaking, the tax credits offered by the Quebec government feature prominently in this reconfiguration of *Life of Pi* in its cinematic version.

The Québécois production context for *Life of Pi* coexists with multiple other sites, however, particularly although not exclusively those responsible for visual effects. Martel's novel, describing the storm that sinks the *Tsimtsum*, asserts:

> Nature can put on a thrilling show. The stage is vast, the lighting is dramatic, the extras are innumerable, and the budget for special effects is absolutely unlimited. What I had before me was a spectacle of wind and water, an earthquake of the senses, that even Hollywood couldn't orchestrate. (113)

Translated from the page to cinema, of course, this scene – and count-less others in the effects-laden adaptation – is indeed subject to budget-ary concerns and implicated in the de-territorialising of what 'Hollywood' actually signifies. Rhythm & Hues, one of the visual effects studios that worked on the film of *Life of Pi*, accepted the Oscar for best visual effects – alongside the Montreal unit of Moving Picture Company – just eleven days after the company declared bankruptcy. The documentary *Life after Pi* (Scott Leberecht, 2014) makes clear that the visual effects industry has been colossally undermined through such elements as the fixed bidding scheme. Further, tax incentives offered outside the United States (as in Quebec, for instance) have some transnational implications for labour and the ability of visual effects companies' employees to find permanent work in one place.[10]

Both the novel and the film version of *Life of Pi* acknowledge the eco-nomic considerations embedded in cultural production. Not only does Pondicherry furnish the setting of the beginning of both versions of the narrative but both novel and film also address India's economic posi-tion. The unnamed narrator of Martel's novel – referred by critics as the 'author-narrator' (Cole 2004, 23) or the 'Martel-like narrator' (Stratton 2004, 5) – begins the Author's Note by describing a failed attempt to write a novel with a Portuguese setting in 1939:

> *I flew to Bombay. This is not so illogical if you realize three things: that a stint in India will beat the restlessness out of any living creature; that a little money can go a long way there; and that a novel set in Portugal in 1939 may have very little to do with Portugal in 1939.* (v)

The narrator leaves open the possibility that this (ultimately discarded) novel, ostensibly Portuguese in its subject, might have more to do with India, or at least, that the setting is somehow irrelevant. What *is* relevant for the purposes of cultural production, however, is the fact 'that a little money can go a long way' in India.

In the film adaptation, the unnamed writer articulates some of this information in conversation with the adult Pi in Montreal, disclosing that he meets Pi's honorary uncle Francis while trying to write his novel in India. When Pi assumes that the writer's novel is about India, the writer corrects him with the statement, 'It's cheaper living in India.' Spall speaks this line somewhat sheepishly, as though the writer is embarrassed for hav-ing taken financial advantage of India without attempting to represent it in his novel; the line may also gesture towards 'the imperial framework that grants mobility as the privilege of whiteness' (Wesling 2008, 41), given the (white) writer's ease of travel in contrast to Pi's ordeal of migration.

The film suggests, however, that the writer will redress his financial advantage in India when he writes Pi's story. Sitting in Montreal as he utters this statement, the writer also draws attention to the materiality of cultural production, explicitly in relation to his own (fictional) work, and implicitly in relation to the film itself, which, given the positioning of Canada in general and particularly Quebec in American protests surrounding the VFX industry, perhaps unwittingly features as a kind of meta-apology.

In cross-border provincial terms, the shift in the adult Pi's home from Toronto to Montreal may also be implicitly addressed and excused in this line of dialogue that acknowledges cultural production as cheaper in some locations than others. Canadian cities are no strangers to acting the parts of other cities, particularly 'American "body doubles"' (Elmer and Gasher 2005, 9); the correlation between the filming location and setting in the film, therefore, constitutes somewhat of a rarity for a non-Canadian film (even if Montreal's role in the film amounted to just two days of shooting [Lee 2012, 14]). But if the Montreal setting and location for the Canadian portions of the narrative potentially gesture to Martel's family origins, in fact, 'more than 70 percent of *Life of Pi* was shot in Taiwan' (Lu 2019, 236),[11] aligning with Lee's own personal history but also enabling a 10 per cent cut in the film's budget for 20th Century Fox through Taiwan's lower production costs and subsidies (Lu 2019, 238). Lee's own story of the shift to Taiwan for production invokes a kind of narrative fidelity, observing that if the *Tsimtsum* sinks 'just north of the Mariana Trench', then '[t]he land closest to Pi's journey happens to be Taiwan, the floating island, the "zoo" where I grew up' (2012, 14).[12] Nonetheless, much to the dismay of Taiwanese fans encouraged to identify with the film through 20th Century Fox's promotional activities in their country, ultimately 'film locations in Taiwan were used to stand in for locales in other countries or the diegetic fantasy world, [so] these Taiwanese film locations are conveyed in the film so as to be completely unidentifiable' (Lu 2019, 238); this experience for local Taiwanese viewers echoes the position of Canadian audiences' 'familiar estrangement' (Acland 2018, 133) when viewing runaway productions filmed in their local area and presented to the world as the United States.

If Taiwanese viewers did not feel the benefit of recognition for the part their country plays in the creation of *Life of Pi*'s cinematic world, raw material extracted for a film's budget reduction, Martel himself had already become embroiled in a controversy involving his own perceived failure to acknowledge a source of his own. Just as '[a]daptations are seen as parasitical on literature; they burrow into the body of the source text and steal its vitality' (Stam 2005, 7), so too Martel's *Life of Pi* was cast in a parasitic light when a plagiarism scandal erupted. Accusations that Martel plagiarised Brazilian novelist Moacyr Scliar's novel *Max and the Cats* (1981) suggested Canadian culture operating as a parasite in a hemispheric context, through a very different kind of inter-American cultural exploitation from the dynamic across the 49th parallel that Canadian nationalists would recognise.[13] Scliar's short novel, first published in Portuguese in 1981, tells the story of Max, a Berliner whose father is a furrier with a shop named The Bengal Tiger, featuring a stuffed tiger on the wall. Following a sexual liaison with Frida, a shop employee, Max must flee Germany in order to escape the Nazis, to whom Frida's husband has denounced Max. Embarking on a ship from Hamburg bound for Brazil, Max soon finds himself a castaway in a dinghy, the ship having been sabotaged, with a jaguar for company. Max arrives unscathed in Porto Alegre twenty pages later, and the rest of the novel's action takes place in Brazil, focusing on Max's suspicions about a neighbour's Nazi affiliations.

The plagiarism controversy – which died down relatively quickly – was contextualised in the Canadian media through economic tensions, 'political rows[,] and diplomatic wrangles' between Canada and Brazil, stemming from disputes over corned beef, aircraft companies and a high-profile kidnapping of a Brazilian businessman by a group that included two Canadians (Vincent 2002, A1). Ultimately, the dispute surrounding *Life of Pi* did not escalate into a lawsuit. Martel's novel includes a reference to Scliar in the Author's Note – and it did so even prior to the plagiarism controversy – where Martel and/or the unnamed narrator declares that he owes the novel's 'spark of life' to the Brazilian writer, as though the novel of *Life of Pi* is itself a kind of adaptation. The intertextual relationship between *Life of Pi* and *Max and the Cats* is clear, therefore, and even made visible within Martel's text itself (whereas, in contrast, intertextual gestures to Edgar Allan Poe's *Narrative of Arthur Gordon Pym* are not highlighted as such).[14] Tellingly, after the plagiarism controversy, a new edition of *Max and the Cats* was published, which emblazons the phrase 'the spark of life' on the back cover, recruiting Martel and his success for the purposes of marketing the earlier Brazilian text, presumably on the expectation that Martel's acknowledgement – now read as an endorsement – would extend *Max and the Cats'* afterlife and generate further profits, a reversal of the parasitic relationship between the two novels. Thus, both *Life of Pi*'s own afterlife, in the form of the film adaptation, and the novel's most visible antecedent demonstrate a plethora of transnational cultural flows.

How are nations made visible in cinema, and what does transnationalism look like on screen? The adaptation pairings of *Midnight's Children* and *Life of Pi* encompass narratives (both fictional and, for their creators, biographical) of the diasporic and the cosmopolitan: the text of *Midnight's Children* does not leave the subcontinent, but it was written by Rushdie as a British Indian and filmed by the Indo-Canadian Mehta. Martel, the only author or filmmaker in this chapter to reside in the country of his parents' birth, is nonetheless a cosmopolitan figure (see Roberts 2011, 4), having been born in Spain and grown up all over the world, the child of diplomatic Québécois parents. The career of the Taiwanese-American Lee, 'the most successful Asian director in terms of box office receipts and Oscar statuettes', has been understood by some as 'the apotheosis of Taiwanese cosmopolitan strivings' (Coe 2014, 21, 26). The experiences of Taiwanese audiences watching *Life of Pi* demonstrate that the traces of production in transnational cinema are not universally visible – intentionally so, given the economic imperative for a film with *Life of Pi*'s budget to be legible to as large – as global – an audience as possible. Mehta's *Midnight's Children* seeks to represent India at its birth as a postcolonial independent nation, but none of the film was shot there; the Pondicherry Zoo in *Life of Pi* is largely played by the Taipei Zoo (Castelli 2012, 62). Cultural power may be claimed or sought by different audiences detecting themselves, their territory, their culture on screen, but the de- and/or reterritorialising of transnational production will remain submerged for most viewers.

Stam's argument that cinema may itself be inherently magic realist encompasses these contradictions between the real and the apparent, accentuated by these two adaptations' relationships to transnational and diasporic production, on the one hand, and magic realism, on the other. The film of *Life of Pi* accentuates the visual signification of the 'magic' in magic realism in ways that the film of *Midnight's Children* does not – and the diverging contexts of production and their financial implications contribute to this sharp contrast, given *Life of Pi*'s 20th Century Fox financing and *Midnight's Children*'s status as a small Canadian film. In some ways, however, the film of *Life of Pi* separates out the magic from the realism, given the special effects deployed not just to construct the tiger, but also to film the lifeboat scenes in their entirety, in contrast to the psychological realism of the delivery of the second story. Conversely, despite the relative absence of visual signification of magic, *Midnight's Children* sustains magic realism throughout its narrative, even if in a largely verbal capacity. In terms of cinema, and the fantastic elements of both narratives, much is at stake in what the audience witness, how they are invited to suspend their disbelief. And indeed, perhaps curiously for a film, *Life of Pi* leads us to believe in a version of events to which we have the least visual access, and the least opportunity to witness.

CHAPTER 5

Cultural Appropriation:
The Chant of Jimmie Blacksmith,
Black Robe and *Dance Me Outside*

In 2017, Hal Niedzviecki, editor of the Writers' Union of Canada's publication *Write*, published an editorial in which he suggested there should
be an 'Appropriation Prize'. As an introduction to an issue of the publication that featured several Indigenous writers, Niedzviecki's editorial
attracted both support (and funding for an actual such prize), largely from
white Canadian journalists, and outrage (some of which was directed to
funding the Indigenous Voices Awards in response). The second decade
of the twentieth century was not the first time that cultural appropriation was hotly contested in Canada and beyond. The early 1990s saw a
number of Indigenous writers demand that white artists, in the words of
Lenore Keeshig-Tobias (Anishinaabe), 'stop stealing [Indigenous] stories'
(1990, 7). In 1994, an Australian legal case (*Milpurrurru et al. v. Indofurn
Pty Ltd et al.*) addressed Indigenous copyright in patterned carpets; the
ruling stipulated that '[t]he right to create paintings and other artworks
depicting creation and dreaming stories, and to use pre-existing designs
and well recognized totems of the clan, resides in the traditional owners
(or custodians) of the stories or images' (qtd in Ziff and Rao 1997b, 16).
Yet cultural appropriation – and its defenders – despite the work of the
1990s contesting it – has persisted: white US author Lionel Shriver at
the Brisbane Writers' Festival in 2016, the year before Niedzviecki's editorial, had equated cultural appropriation with '*try[ing] on other people's
hats*' (qtd in Convery 2016), dismissing and deflating concerns about cultural representation, particularly when those in the position of doing the
representing belong to the white mainstream and those being represented
do not. As Bruce Ziff and Pratima V. Rao write, however, 'When white
writers appropriate the images of [non-white people], a political event has
occurred' (1997b, 5). White artists who cry foul at accusations of cultural
appropriation use art as a defence against politics, as though art is always
already exempt from the political.

This chapter examines three film adaptations in the context of cultural appropriation, specifically the appropriation of Indigenous cultures in the settler-colonial contexts of Australia and Canada: *The Chant of Jimmie Blacksmith* (1978), directed by the white Australian director Fred Schepisi from the novel of the same title, published in 1972 and written by white Australian novelist Thomas Keneally; *Black Robe* (1991), an Australia–Canada co-production directed by the Australian director Bruce Beresford from the novel of the same title, published in 1985 by white Northern Irish-Canadian novelist Brian Moore; and *Dance Me Outside* (1995), directed by white Canadian director Bruce McDonald from the short story collection of the same title, published in 1977, by white Canadian author W. P. Kinsella. *The Chant of Jimmie Blacksmith* and *Black Robe* are both historical fictions, looking back to early twentieth-century Australia and seventeenth-century New France, respectively, that draw on the colonial archive of Australia and Canada; in contrast, *Dance Me Outside* is set contemporaneously to the moment of its production.

In seeking to represent Indigenous peoples in Australia and Canada, all three adaptations are concerned with voice and point of view in their literary and cinematic iterations, concerns that highlight – if unintentionally – the fraught politics of white representation of Indigenous cultures. If *The Chant of Jimmie Blacksmith* and *Black Robe* adaptations reach into the colonial past, to the archive beyond their literary sources, McDonald's *Dance Me Outside* had multiple afterlives that attempted to exceed the Kinsella provenance, with a graphic novel adaptation of the film's screenplay by Nick Craine (1994) and a CBC television spin-off, *The Rez* (1995–8). This chapter treats the adaptations in chronological order of the films' release, although this order includes some doubling back in the timeline of the literary texts' publication, with Kinsella's collection published eight years prior to Moore's novel. The chronological order is not intended to suggest that, with each subsequent adaptation, the cultural appropriation has become less severe or more palatable; indeed, in many ways, *The Chant of Jimmie Blacksmith* is most critical of settler-colonial history than the later case studies addressed here. But *Dance Me Outside*'s adaptation trajectory demonstrates both the possibilities of exceeding and critiquing the source text and the limitations of extrapolating from a white-authored text focusing on Indigenous communities.

The Chant of Jimmie Blacksmith

Thomas Keneally based his novel, *The Chant of Jimmie Blacksmith* (1972), on the true story of Jimmy Governor, an Indigenous man in New South

Wales who exacted revenge on his white employers for the racist injustice done to him, a narrative told by the historian Frank Clune in his 1959 book *Jimmy Governor*. Set just before Australian federation at the turn of the twentieth century, Keneally's book was written in the wake of the 1967 referendum in which Australians voted in favour of a constitutional amendment to include Indigenous people. The timing of the novel's composition is crucial to understanding the stakes of representation of Indigenous people in Australia. As Henry Reynolds notes, the referendum campaign 'was a highly successful exercise in consciousness-raising, the massive majority for the . . . changes to the constitution indicating the great weight of opinion seeking a new relationship between white and black' (2008, 3). Published following a land rights case in the Northern Territory in 1971 and the establishment of the Tent Embassy by Indigenous people in front of the Australian Parliament House in Canberra in early 1972, Keneally's novel 'was launched at a moment when the community was on the eve of significant political change, when Aboriginal issues were more prominent than ever before and when racism was a focus of both national and international attention' (Reynolds 2008, 3). That Keneally should reflect on events coinciding with the advent of Australian federation in 1900 overlies two historic moments of self-definition for the Australian settler-colonial nation-state.

By the time of the adaptation of *The Chant of Jimmie Blacksmith* (1978), written and directed by Fred Schepisi, this film offered 'a thrice-told tale' (qtd in Reynolds 2008, 5), given Keneally's drawing heavily from Clune's book about the historic figure of Jimmy Governor. Perhaps unsurprisingly for a historian, Reynolds's analysis of both Keneally's novel and Schepisi's adaptation concerns itself substantially with the fictionalising of a historical narrative. Keneally stated in 1975 that his novel's historical content represented an attempt 'to tell a parable about the present by using the past', with *The Chant of Jimmie Blacksmith*'s representation of the past constituting 'the present merely rendered fabulous' (27, 29). Reynolds corroborates Keneally's declaration to a certain extent, arguing that both novel and film are 'characteristic products of the 1970s' (2008, 3) in their concern with settler-colonial Australia's understanding of both itself and its relationship to Indigenous peoples. At the same time, Reynolds's critique of both Keneally's novel and Schepisi's film is based on their claims to history: 'both Schepisi and Keneally rest the validity, cogency and immediate relevance of their work on its relationship with the known and recorded past' (2008, 6), and yet as might be expected of novelists and filmmakers, they diverge from recorded history in their representation of Jimmy Governor via Jimmie Blacksmith's fictional story. However, in an earlier analysis, Reynolds argues that Keneally's novel's assumptions about race approximate the discourse current at the time of the novel's setting at the turn of the twentieth century, rather than the 1970s (1979, 22). Further, Schepisi, unlike Keneally, consistently invokes the turn of the twentieth century as the point of view his film attempts to replicate: 'in telling a story you've got to tell it from the point of view of the people at that time, not as we know them to be now. Otherwise, you're distorting the whole thing' (2008). Thus, between the novelist, director and the historian, there is no consensus as to whether the present or the past is – or should be – the governing perspective of the narrative. As I have argued elsewhere in this book, however, it is impossible not to project present-day concerns on to representations of the past; the way in which the past *is* represented tells us a good deal about the ideological concerns of the present.

At the same time, Keneally's novel features a 'polyphony of oppositional and mutually negating discourses' (Wynne-Davies 1999, 67). Like its source text, Clune's historical biography *Jimmy Governor*, Keneally's novel follows Jimmie's trajectory of ambition to succeed on white Australian society's terms, working for white employers (mostly, although not exclusively, building fences), suffering continual mistreatment (repeatedly cheated out of fair pay), and marrying Gilda, a white woman (as part of his assimilationist ambitions) only to find they both suffer the racist insults of his white employer's household, the Newbys and their lodger, the schoolteacher Miss Graf, who express their 'horror' (Keneally 1972, 61) at miscegenation and seek to divide Jimmie and Gilda from each other. These attempts to rescue Gilda from Jimmie escalate following the birth of her son, who (unlike in the historical source material) has been sired not by Jimmie but rather by an English cook working, as Jimmie does for a time, for a shearer. When the Newbys renege on their agreement to buy groceries for the Blacksmiths, despite Jimmie's having to provide for a child as well as himself and his wife, the Newbys cite the arrival of some of Jimmie's relatives and an alleged drop in Jimmie's productivity. Jimmie's confrontation with the Newby women while the men are absent results in his killing the members of the household who are present: namely, the women and children. Jimmie and his brother, Mort, then proceed to revisit former employers against whom Jimmie has a grudge, committing more murders (much to Mort's dismay).

The Chant of Jimmie Blacksmith is written in the third person. The narration constantly shifts its alignment with individual characters within individual scenes. Because Jimmie's work is peripatetic, and the second half of the novel following the Newby murders consists of a fictionalised version of what Clune calls 'the biggest manhunt in Australian history'

(1959, 147), there are several characters who are present only fleetingly in the text, but whose perspectives are replicated nonetheless. Despite the 'diversity of situations and characters' (Daniel 1978, 26) that confronts Jimmie, the host of white characters Jimmie encounters is 'representative of this society' (26), a settler-colonial one that relentlessly undermines the cultures and claims of Indigenous peoples, displaying the divergences between Indigenous and white colonial perspectives and the systemic racism that affects every aspect of Indigenous lives. Settler-colonial rhetoric further appears in the novel through the inclusion of letters and newspaper articles, the latter articulating public versions of settler-colonial circumscription of Indigenous identity as they follow the story of 'the black desperadoes' (Keneally 1972, 125).[1]

Both Clune's and Keneally's texts foreground miscegenation, beginning with responses to Jimmy/ie's interracial marriage. Where Clune's narrative starts *in medias res*, with the insult that prompts the massacre, Miss Kerz (the antecedent for Keneally's Miss Graf) proclaiming, 'Pooh, you black rubbish, you should be shot for marrying a white woman' (Clune 1959, 11), Keneally begins his novel with, 'In June of 1900 Jimmie Blacksmith's material uncle Tabidgi – Jackie Smolders to the white world – was disturbed to get news that Jimmie had married a white girl in the Methodist church at Wallah' (Keneally 1972, 1). Both texts, therefore, open with opposition to miscegenation, Clune from a white perspective, and Keneally from an Indigenous perspective.

As Reynolds notes of the historical context surrounding the Governors' marriage, although

> [s]exual relations of one sort or another between Aboriginal women and European men had been commonplace from the earliest years of settlement . . ., sexual contact between Aboriginal men and white women – let alone marriage – was another matter altogether. It both broke through powerful taboos and touched on deep and abiding fears about black men's lust for white flesh which had to be vigilantly guarded against and severely punished wherever and whenever it was manifested. (2008, 12–13)

Tabidgi's concerns about Jimmie's marriage will drive him to seek out Jimmie, returning the tooth extracted from his nephew during his initiation ceremony to 'lay a tribal claim on Jimmie' (Keneally 1972, 1). Tabidgi's arrival with Mort and Peter exacerbates Jimmie's relationship with the Newbys, giving his employer an excuse not to pay him on the grounds that 'yer aren't working as good as yer did before them others came' (77). Yet despite events apparently beginning, according to the structure of the novel, with Indigenous opposition to Jimmie's interracial marriage, it is white racist responses to Jimmie and Gilda's marriage that

precipitate the massacre and subsequent murders perpetrated by Jimmie
and his accomplices.

The focus on miscegenation operates alongside a dwelling in Clune's
and Keneally's texts on Jimmy/ie's mixed-race status. Clune returns to the
quantum of Jimmy's racialised identity almost obsessively. For Clune, 'He
was a half-caste who refused to accept the status of an outcast' (1959, 3).
One of the reasons Clune appears to return constantly to Jimmy's mixed-
race identity is that '[t]he fact that Jimmy Governor was half white [*sic*]
was considered irrelevant. In all newspaper reports he was described as
"a blackfellow"' (86). Keen to point out how, historically, instances of
Indigenous people murdering white people in Australia are vastly outnum-
bered by the deaths of Indigenous people as part of the Australian genocidal project – 'Many more murders have been committed by whites than
by blacks in Australia's recorded history since 1788' (1959, 12–13) – in this
case Clune appears to emphasise Jimmy's parentage strategically, in order
to highlight the hypocrisy of the white press.

Nonetheless, Clune replicates an essentialist view of identity, as in the
following description of Jimmy's education:

> He was a proficient scholar, and learned to read and white [*sic*] well. That was some-
> thing from his white heritage. From his dark heritage he learned the lore of the
> bush – how to hunt possums, find wild bees' nests, and track game. (16)

Perhaps fittingly, Clune's typographical error presumably substitutes
'write' for 'white', which brings to mind Homi Bhabha's notion of mim-
icry – '*almost the same, but not quite*' / '*[a]lmost the same but not white*' (2004,
122, 128) – fitting for the frustrations of Governor's dis-interpellation from
Blackness and his assimilationist ambitions. Further, of Jimmy's brother,
Joe (Mort in Keneally's novel), Clune writes, 'Joe was neither as intelligent, nor as well-educated as Jimmy. He was a throwback to the aboriginal
side, rather than to the white' (44). Although Clune takes white Australia
to task for the demonisation of Indigenous peoples, his initial attempt to
contextualise Jimmy's violence in relation to the injustices he suffers at the
hands of settler-colonial society lapses into increasing animalistic portray-
als of Jimmy and his brother, as the Darwinism of 'throwback' implies. For
Clune, Joe is a 'half savage simpleto[n]' (93), and he describes the brothers
during the manhunt as 'two wild animals in human form' (107), 'two wild
beasts who were being hunted . . . like feral quadrupeds' (125). Whether
Clune intends to invoke the actual, genocidal hunting of Indigenous
people here is unclear, but given this escalating racist depiction of the
brothers, it seems unlikely.

For his part, Keneally describes Jimmie as:

> a hybrid. If he had been a tribal man, love would have been written into the order of his day. All his acts would have been acts of solemn and ritual preference. Love would have been in their fibre.
>
> But having chosen to grub and build as whites do, he knew that love was a special fire that came down from God. . . .
>
> Suspended between the loving tribal life and the European rapture from on high called falling in love . . ., Jimmie Blacksmith held himself firm and soundly despised as many people as he could. . . .
>
> In fact, Jimmie was surprised to find that he loved his half-brother Morton, who was innocent and loyal. (1972, 27)

If Jimmie has 'alien ambitions [that make] him a drinker of moderation' (20), Mort, in contrast, is 'less complex' (30). Mort serves as Jimmie's conscience; he himself only kills one woman, and by accident. Of Jimmie's body count, Mort protests, screaming at his brother, 'But it's woman-blood . . . and it's child-blood' (101).

Later, McCreadie, the schoolteacher whom the brothers take hostage, urges Jimmie to leave him and Mort behind on the grounds that

> [t]he boy isn't really your brother. He's an aborigine, Jimmie. Not like you. There's too much Christian in you, Jimmie, and it'll only bugger him up. Like it's buggered you. . . .
>
> Don't ask him. He'll stay with you because he's an aborigine, and loyalty's in it. (151)

It is to McCreadie's advantage to separate the brothers from each other, and he intuits he will be safer with the placid Mort than the volatile Jimmie. Yet it is telling that McCreadie's strategy not only acts as 'a vivid, if unconscious, metaphor for the whole policy of child removal' suffered by the Stolen Generations in Australia, who were separated from their families as part of the state's assimilationist and genocidal agenda, but it also 'betrays . . . a whole set of conventional ideas about the perils of miscegenation – the mestizo is by nature dangerous, dysfunctional and confused' (Reynolds 2008, 48–9), undermining McCreadie's claim to understand the Blacksmiths where the rest of settler-colonial society does not.

McCreadie is the most sympathetic white character in Keneally's novel. Admittedly, there is no real competition for this distinction given the despicable, overt racism exhibited by the representatives of white settler-colonial society. McCreadie, rare amongst the novel's white characters, does not cheat the Blacksmiths financially, and he acknowledges the irony of the uproar over the murders they perpetrate in contrast to the genocide of Indigenous people in Australia, saying,

> [H]ow many whites really ever got killed by aborigines? No one knows. I bet it wasn't more than four or five thousand. If that. Then, you might ask, how many aborigines did the whites kill? The answer is a quarter of a million. Two hundred and seventy thousand have gone. I can understand your being angry. (143)

Indeed, some critics identify McCreadie, a product of Keneally's 'authorial self-awareness' (Wynne-Davies 1999, 66), as Keneally's mouthpiece in the novel (see McFarlane 1983, 100; Reynolds 2008, 48); his comparison of the murders perpetrated by white and Indigenous people also echoes Clune's point on this matter cited above.

If McCreadie's status 'as an enlightened go-between who is knowledgeable about Aboriginal culture' (Ryan-Fazilleau 2002, 37) represents Keneally, however, the fictional character's knowledge of Indigenous culture via the writing of Scottish anthropologist Andrew Lang (Keneally 1972, 144) is both telling and troubling. Mort's response to McCreadie's invocation of Lang gestures towards the epistemic violence of white knowledge about, and the white gaze at, Indigenous peoples: 'Mort was frightened and angry about Andrew Lang's writing. God knew what secrecies of his heritage were written down for whites to read' (144). For McCreadie, other white people – even those who do not live in Australia – are the experts on Indigenous people. For Reynolds, the addition of McCreadie to the Governors' story enables a white man 'to articulate the cause of the Aborigines more effectively than the brothers themselves. They need a white spokesman' (2008, 48). In this sense, McCreadie appears – if unintentionally – to illustrate the limits of 'the liberal white man who is horrified by the history of violent dispossession' (48), who presumes to be in a better position to speak for subjugated peoples. In this capacity in particular, McCreadie might be said to stand in for Keneally who, like McCreadie, 'appointed himself spokesman for the Aboriginal cause' (Ryan-Fazilleau 2002, 38), and who, along with Schepisi, sought to bequeath to Indigenous people in Australia a 'modern legend' in Jimmy Governor's fictionalised story in an 'unsolicited gift' (Reynolds 2008, 26); Yet as with Lang's anthropological work, 'written down for whites to read', Keneally's novel, based in a settler-colonial epistemology that replicates assumptions about blood quantum (despite its acknowledgement of dispossession and sympathy for some of its Indigenous characters), primarily addresses itself to a non-Indigenous readership. Just as McCreadie can be considered a proxy for Keneally, so too this character lays bare some of the clearest evidence of the appropriative status of the project of *The Chant of Jimmie Blacksmith*.

In the film version, however, Keneally makes a cameo appearance not as McCreadie (Peter Carroll) but as the white shearer's cook with whom Jimmie's wife (Angela Punch) has an affair before she meets Jimmie (Tommy Lewis). The film was released with high expectations that were not ultimately met. Although the film was entered into Official Competition at the Cannes Film Festival in 1978, it did not win the Palme d'Or. With a budget of 1.2 million Australian dollars, *The Chant of Jimmie Blacksmith* was, at that point, the most expensive film in Australian cinema history (Schepisi 2008). The relatively large investment in the film was coupled with substantial promotion. Although *The Chant of Jimmie Blacksmith* was generally, if not universally, well received in the Australian press, it was a disappointment at the box office (see Donnar 2011). Tellingly, as Glen Donnar observes, (presumably white) critics seemed most likely to praise Freddie Reynolds' representation of Mort (2011, para. 4), who 'is essentially and wholly a victim . . . not being in any crucial sense an agent' (McFarlane 1983, 98), a characterisation later identified by critics as adhering to stereotype in a manner that is not 'unfaithful to the textual sources' (Couzens 2015, 53).

Schepisi's comments on the making of *The Chant of Jimmie Blacksmith* present a contradictory approach to the representation of Indigenous and settler-colonial culture, one very much in evidence in the text of the film itself. Reflecting on the film's production thirty years after its release, Schepisi recalls that he 'started the film trying to give an impression of . . . Aboriginal life . . . particularly contrasted with the people who have arrived there . . . believing that bringing religion to the Aborigines was their mission and goal in life' (2008). At the same time as he seeks to 'respect Aboriginal traditions', citing by way of example a shot of a boy whirring a bullroarer where the bullroarer itself does not appear onscreen because women in that Indigenous nation are not permitted to see it, Schepisi also concedes that 'we probably did the wrong thing in relation to other areas. It's a complex issue' (2008).

Further, Schepisi indicates,

> We tried to do everything in the film from the white point of view, not from the perspective now but from the perspective of the time, where they came from, what they were used to, what their mores were and the difficulties they would have been going through. (2008)

The film bears out Schepisi's intention to contrast Indigenous and settler-colonial lifeways and relationship to landscape, with 'white people at odds with the landscape in contrast to the Aboriginals' (2008). The film creates this juxtaposition through close-up shots of Australian flora and fauna as well as bird's eye view shots of Indigenous communities. Whereas Indigenous people are filmed outdoors, and often barefoot, white settlers such as the Nevilles appear within confined indoor spaces. Near the beginning of the film, Jimmie, encouraged by the Reverend Neville (Jack Thompson) and his wife (Julie Dawson), expresses his desire to acquire property and marry 'a nice girl', immediately translated by Mrs Neville as a white girl: 'Then your children would be only quarter-caste; and your grandchildren one-eighth caste.' The three characters sit at the Nevilles' dining table, with the camera tracking back out of the room so they are framed by the doorway, their enclosure a visible contrast to the Indigenous community's representation.

Despite the stark contrast between Indigenous and settler, however, Schepisi's ambition 'to show . . . that the Aborigines are part of the landscape' (2008) unwittingly echoes white supremacist assumptions about Indigenous peoples. As Graeme Turner argues,

> Aborigines have been, and continue to be seen as metonyms for an Australian landscape; like kangaroos and Ayers Rock, they are among the natural attributes of the continent. This is dehumanizing, and has served to legitimate white settlers' treatment of the Aborigines as pests well into the twentieth century. (1988, 140)

Further, Schepisi and his DoP Ian Baker's desire to emulate white Australian landscape painters whose 'pictorial tradition . . . ran parallel with the historical writing of the late nineteenth century and early twentieth century with its emphasis on the struggle to conquer the land' (Reynolds 2008, 66) underscores that *The Chant of Jimmie Blacksmith*'s landscape shots always already replicate the settler-colonial gaze. On the one hand, the film's opening shot of an Indigenous community, which turns out to be a point-of-view shot from the perspective of a white character (Reverend Neville), perhaps demonstrates the problem of a non-Indigenous filmmaker seeking to represent Indigenous people. On the other hand, this opening framing suggests the audience cannot escape this governing perspective on the people the film seeks to represent and, perhaps, for whom it attempts to advocate.

If the immediate source material of the film – Keneally's novel – flits in and out of different characters' perspectives, this change in point of view is mostly absent from the film. Schepisi (2008) explains that the first murder scene alternates between an objective camera and subjective viewpoints of the killers, both Jimmie and his uncle, Tabidgi/Jackie Smolders (Steve Dodds).[2] But it is only at the film's very end that a clear, coherent view from Jimmie's perspective is offered: captured at the convent where he has gone to sleep, nursing a gunshot wound to his face, Jimmie is carried away by the white men who have been pursuing him. At this point, 'the camera adopts Jimmie's gaze' (Wynne-Davies 1999, 69): a series of point-of-view shots from Jimmie's perspective show low-angled shots, looking up at the white men who carry Jimmie to a wagon, and others who threaten him with violence, on his way to having to reckon with the settler-colonial legal system (see Figure 5.1). These shots are striking and disruptive in their clear and sudden shift in camerawork and editing. They are also striking in their status as the few brief moments that seek to represent clearly Jimmie Blacksmith's perspective, reminding us (probably unintentionally) that the rest of the film, based on the novel of white author in the position of 'voyeur' (Ryan-Fazilleau 2002, 37) in relation to Indigenous people, has replicated the settler-colonial gaze with which the film begins.

As Reynolds points out, the historical Jimmy Governor was exceedingly vocal during his final days, giving an account of himself that was 'recorded after his capture by journalists, jailers and court reporters' (2008, 51). In contrast, Schepisi's Jimmie has nothing to say for himself: 'It's as though Keneally and Schepisi didn't want him to talk. It's their story – not his' (Reynolds 2008, 51). Indeed, the film delivers its last shot of a silent Jimmie through the keyhole to his prison cell from the perspective of the hangman, fusing our gaze with that of the white executioner before the film

Figure 5.1 Jimmie's view of white Australian male violence.

cuts to an extreme long shot of the landscape and birds in flight, implicitly tying Jimmie once again to the Australian landscape beyond the confines of his cell. If the film opens with Indigenous people who turn out to be the objects of Reverend Neville's gaze, the ending suggests an attempt to exceed the settler-colonial gaze by adding the landscape shot after the hangman's keyhole assessment of Jimmie. Yet given the pictorial tradition to which Schepisi and Baker seek to gesture, we are unable to escape the settler-colonial gaze after all.

Despite its numerous weaknesses of representation, *The Chant of Jimmie Blacksmith* does appear interested in addressing racial injustice, more so than the other two case studies in this chapter, as it displays both on the page and on the screen the litany of racist humiliations to which Jimmie is subject, attempting a 'full-throated . . . note of protest' (McFarlane 1983, 103). Yet if, as Janet Wilson notes, the novel of *The Chant of Jimmie Blacksmith* has been considered 'a minor classic [with] . . . an important statement on race relations in Australia' (2007, 193) it is significant that Keneally acknowledges in a 2001 preface to a new edition that if writing his novel now, he would do so using a white perspective, gesturing towards the appropriative limits of attempting to represent Indigenous culture – limits that are evident both in the novel and its screen adaptation. However sympathetic the liberal Keneally and Schepisi may be to Indigenous peoples – Jimmy Governor/ Jimmie Blacksmith in particular – ultimately their literary and cinematic narratives are embedded in settler-colonial epistemology and aesthetics as they attempt to represent a story that is not theirs to tell.

Black Robe

Like *The Chant of Jimmie Blacksmith*, *Black Robe* is derived not just from a literary text of the same title, but also from a larger colonial archival history. Brian Moore's preface to his novel begins with an acknowledgement of his source material: the Jesuit *Relations*, led to him by Francis Parkman's *Jesuits in North America* (1867). Moore praises the veracity and authenticity of the *Relations*, particularly concerning their representation of Indigenous people, which, Moore claims, 'bear little relationship to the "Red Indians" of fiction and folklore' (1984a, ix). In contrast, Moore states,

> The Huron, Iroquois, and Alongkin [*sic*] were a handsome, brave, incredibly cruel people who, at that early stage, were in no way dependent on the white man and, in fact, judged him to be their physical and mental inferior. They were warlike; they practiced ritual cannibalism and, for reasons of religion, subjected their enemies to prolonged and unbearable tortures. (ix)

Of course, Moore's impression of Indigenous people in the seventeenth century emerges from what he claims is 'the only real record of the early Indians of North America' (viii): that produced by the colonial archive in the form of the Jesuit *Relations*.

Moore acknowledges that in the seventeenth century, the Indigenous peoples 'were not known to the French as "Indians," but by the names of their tribal confederacies, and were referred to collectively as "Les Sauvages" (the Savages)' (viii). *Black Robe* tends to emulate the French more often in the latter than in the former practice, with the word 'savages' littering the text. Further, Moore's introduction singularises 'the Huron, Iroquois, and Alongkin' as 'a' people (there is no sense in the novel of the Haudenosaunee confederacy[3] and its individual constituent nations). Although Moore's introduction professes an interest in Indigenous people's contempt for Europeans and the clash between Indigenous and European cultural, religious and familial priorities, that Hallvard Dahlie identifies *Black Robe* 'as Moore's obligatory response to the Canada he first became acquainted with as a new immigrant . . ., a land he saw as essentially empty and wild . . . where one could literally get lost mere moments away from any habitation' (1988, 89) is telling.

The invocation of *terra nullius* in Moore's perspective on Canada is deeply troubling in its implications for *Black Robe*'s representation of Indigenous peoples and the colonial encounter. Fittingly, Dahlie views *Black Robe* as 'a "Conradian" tale of a journey upriver. A journey into the darkness of a continent, and into the darkness of one's heart' (1988, 88). In addition to the similarities between *Black Robe* and *Heart of Darkness*, Moore's own acknowledged source texts – both the *Relations* and what Moore considers 'Parkman's great work' (viii) – demand further consideration. As Catharine Randall writes of the *Relations*, the Jesuits 'become the translators for those otherwise silenced native voices': 'The natives are not present in any immediate way, but rather are mediated to us. . . . The Jesuits become the medium through which native voices can speak again' (2010, 2, 3). For Randall, this mediation of Indigenous voices is

> better than nothing, and often the Jesuits' recollections of the natives' statements are, as best as we can discern, faithfully and compellingly articulated . . . We experience the native mind-set, as it were, in a form of palimpsest: like a watermark on fine paper, their perspective lies beneath the surface of the Jesuits' words. (3)

But how can we discern a 'faithful' articulation by Jesuits of Indigenous people? How can we possibly 'experience the native mind-set' through a radically discontinuous epistemology? Are the Indigenous peoples in the

Relations mediated by the Jesuits or are they ventriloquised by them? As Randall acknowledges, the *Relations* was deployed 'in fund-raising propaganda campaigns intended to secure the success of the missions to Canada' (2010, 9). The history of the Jesuit order unfolded in tandem with the colonisation of North America, with its founding by the Basque Ignatius of Loyola occurring the same year as Jacques Cartier's claiming North American territory for the king of France (1534). The establishment of the Jesuits six years later in France enabled a dovetailing of Jesuit and imperial interests (Randall 2010, 10).

For Randall, the *Relations* demonstrates 'the epic drama of colonization and "soul saving" during the early years of the settlement of *la nouvelle France*' (2010, 10). But this spiritual drama operated in tandem with – and cannot be separated from – the concomitant imperial resource extraction and transfer of wealth from the colonies to the imperial centre. As David Leahy argues, 'In *Black Robe* . . . the Jesuits' *mission civilisatrice* is dissociated from the economic imperatives of the French fur trade. This flies in the face of their vital political-economic function as the vanguard of French colonial ideology among the natives' (1988, 312); for indeed, as Patrick Hicks notes, 'if the so-called Savages were "civilised," violent opposition to the exportation of their fur would be reduced' (2004, 416). In privileging the Jesuits' spiritual mission and the cultural antagonisms between European colonisers and Indigenous nations, Moore's text elides 'the economic and geographic abuse of such meetings' and exempts the Jesuits from the status of 'agents of financial affairs' (Hicks 2004, 417). Thus, Moore's appeal to the colonial archive to justify his representation of Indigenous people is deeply problematic, taking the Jesuits at their word even as his novel attempts to reflect on the epistemological chasm between coloniser and colonised. Furthermore, Moore's introduction to the *Relations* via Parkman is rather apt, given the racism of 'Parkman's ugly fables' (Churchill 2007, 129).[4] These historical sources merit attention here because of Moore's own emphasis on them in the preface to his book, part of his framing the narrative and justifying his choices of representation. More specifically, Randall's notion of the *Relations* mediating Indigenous voices has implications for this chapter's concern with cultural appropriation and the construction of Indigenous voice by non-Indigenous authors, especially for the purposes of entertaining non-Indigenous audiences.

The main Jesuit character of Moore's novel, Father Laforgue, based on 'Noel Chabanel, a Jesuit who hated his life among the Indians in Canada' (Flood 1990, 40), volunteers to go to New France for the possibility of martyrdom, on the expectation that his efforts to save Indigenous souls will come to a violent end. The novel follows Laforgue's journey with a group of Algonquin, at the behest of the French explorer Samuel de Champlain, to the Jesuit mission at Ihonitiria in Huron territory. Laforgue struggles in his attempts to convert the Algonquin and with his distaste for Indigenous lifeways, in contrast to his protégé, Daniel Davost, whose earlier ambition to join the priesthood falls by the wayside when, in an example of colonial desire, he becomes sexually active in New France (with three Algonquin women, including Annuka, daughter of Chomina, whom he wants to marry). If Laforgue responds to the Algonquin with nausea (Moore 1985a, 37, 42), Daniel both 'paddl[es] skilfully as a Savage' and 'squat[s] in the Savage fashion, contentedly calling out in the Algonkian [*sic*] tongue to those near him' (29, 38).[5] On the journey to the Huron mission, the Algonquin party is divided about whether to continue accompanying Laforgue. The smaller party that results, consisting of Chomina and his family, Laforgue, and Daniel, are intercepted by the Iroquois, who kill Chomina's wife and son and torture the men. After Chomina, his daughter and the two French men escape, Chomina dies before they reach the Huron mission. When Laforgue reaches Ihonitiria, he finds the mission rife with disease.

If Moore himself, according to Dahlie, viewed Canada as 'a land where one could literally get lost mere moments away from any habitation', Laforgue does actually get lost as soon as he takes a few steps away from his Algonquin travelling companions on their way to the Huron mission: 'The woods were dangerous. . . . [I]f you did not track your path exactly you could become lost as in a maze. . . . On every side, the forest was the same' (Moore 1985a, 72). Laforgue's constitutes the primary European perspective in the novel, supplemented by that of Daniel with his very different priorities in New France. Both Laforgue and Daniel have been renamed by the Algonquin: Laforgue as 'Nicanis',[6] Daniel as 'Iwanchou'. This renaming of Laforgue and Daniel, along with the reference to Black Robes (which the Indigenous characters use to refer to the Jesuits), acts as a cue to the reader to signal shifts in the novel's perspective insofar as sections featuring these names for the European characters are from the perspective of the Algonquin characters. For example:

> 'The other Norman is now awake,' Chomina said.
> Neehatin, who had just told his dream to the senior men, looked up and saw the boy Iwanchou come across the clearing. Unlike the Blackrobe, this boy had keen ears. . . . Neehatin pointed downriver. 'Nicanis is awake and went down there. Find him and tell him we are ready.' (44)

Thus, the novel's third-person narration shifts between European and Indigenous focalisers, with 'Savages' appearing in Europeans' (especially

Laforgue's) sections as part of the narration (not just in dialogue), as well as phrases that can be explanatory and/or judgemental, as in the reference to, in Laforgue's terms, 'the foul corn gruel called sagamité [being] cooked over an open fire' (48). As Dahlie notes of the novel's structure, 'Moore sets up successive sections with parallel beginnings – "Neehatin woke" and "Laforgue woke"' (1988, 91) – in order to juxtapose Indigenous and European perspectives directly.

Despite this juxtaposition and the undermining of Laforgue's perspective on Indigenous spirituality (which he associates with the devil), however, the novel is framed as Laforgue's story, with the narration beginning with him in the first chapter, when he awaits news of when his journey to the Huron mission, guided by the Algonquin, will begin, and ending with him in the final chapter amongst the Huron. Thus, even the Indigenous characters' perspectives that run counter to Laforgue's serve the purpose of telling his story, of his ultimately feeling love for 'these Savages' (the Hurons, by this point) among whom 'he would spend his life' (246). The novel's resolution therefore unfolds within the framework of imperial Catholicism. Notably, Laforgue is not in this moment among the Iroquois, who are clearly beyond the pale, practising (according to the novel) a gleeful cannibalism, in which they kill the Algonquin Chomina's child and eat him in front of him (and of course, cannibalism is mentioned several times in the Jesuit *Relations*).

The representation of the Iroquois as particularly bloodthirsty and merciless is especially notable in relation to the adaptation of Moore's novel, given the release date of Beresford's film: 1991, the year after the standoff between the Mohawk and the Quebec police, followed by the Canadian army, at Kanehsatake, when plans were announced to extend a golf course into Mohawk territory, and 'a peaceful blockade on a snow covered dirt road' (Ladner and Simpson 2010, 2) attracted the repressive state apparatus; the blockade lasted nearly three months. As Mohawk anthropologist Audra Simpson writes, what came to be known as the Oka Crisis (after the Québécois town where the golf course in question was located) 'is the most recent act of "domestic warfare" in Indian-settler relations to date. The incident received massive coverage; it was spectacular, an event of seemingly epic proportions' (2014, 148). Given that the standoff's representation 'in the media reinforced Manichean stereotypes of violent Natives versus besieged settlers, while eliding the historical roots of the conflict' (McCall 2011, 77), the timing of *Black Robe*'s release reinforces settler-colonial depictions of Indigenous peoples – particularly the Haudenosaunee via the Mohawk – soon after a major flashpoint in Canadian and Indigenous relations. Further, *Black Robe* was much celebrated both in the Canadian media and the Canadian film industry. Released the same year as Kevin Costner's *Dances with Wolves*, *Black Robe* was considered the superior, more authentic film north of the border, portraying Indigenous people, as one reviewer claimed, with 'sensitivity, sympathy, and some ethnographic accuracy' (qtd in Gittings 2002, 199).[7] Yet as Métis critic Marilyn Dumont observes, the film (much like the novel) portrays Indigenous people as 'brutal, treacherous and cold. The Indians in fact . . . become the manifestation of the devil himself as they fornicate openly and delight in the torture of their enemies' (qtd in Gittings 2002, 199). In this sense, the Indigenous characters of the film of *Black Robe* – although the film eschews the novel's cannibalism – appear to replicate Laforgue's view, with no real challenge from Indigenous perspectives (in contrast to the novel).

Whereas the novel attempts to offer an Indigenous perspective on European culture, signalled by the names given to Laforgue and Daniel by the Algonquin, the names 'Nicanis' and 'Iwanchou' do not appear in the film.[8] The film does adapt some of the novel's parallel narration, its alternation of scenes from European and Indigenous perspectives, namely in the juxtaposition of Champlain (Jean Brousseau) and Chomina's (August Schellenberg) preparations to negotiate with each other: the film cuts back and forth between Champlain being dressed for the meeting and Chomina applying face paint and also being dressed. This juxtaposition may also serve to endorse the statement of Tallevant, one of the Frenchmen, who claims that Champlain, adorned in a fur cloak, is 'dressed like a savage chieftain. We're not colonising the Indians – they're colonising us.'[9] Yet this assertion mistakes syncretism for power, creating a false equivalence between European and Indigenous influence on each other. Further juxtapositions include the cutting between a low-angle shot of tree tops and the 'massive verticals' of Rouen Cathedral (Scott 2012, 137), although both these shots are ostensibly from Laforgue's (Lothaire Bluteau) point of view, the latter a flashback. In this example, then, the film illustrates a contrast between the cultures of New France and France.

But just as the novel embeds Laforgue in its framing, ultimately aligning itself with a European perspective with its 'noticeably white orientation' (Leahy 1988, 313), so too the film frames the narrative in colonial terms. The opening credits feature maps of New France and Renaissance-era illustrations, including a compass, a crown, a settlement and naked people with bows and arrows facing off against one clothed person armed with a rifle. The first live-action shot of the film is of Laforgue's back (his black robe), while the film ends with a cluster of Huron individuals near the cross mounted outside the church before a low setting sun. If, as James F. Scott argues, the film reveals Chomina as 'a true visionary', while

'Laforgue's spirituality is almost entirely a function of memory' (2012, 137) and a desperation to convert souls despite the motivations of the Huron, the revelation to the viewer of the She Manitou, whom Chomina awaits to herald his impending death, is ultimately enfolded within a resolutely European visual context. Prior to the final credits, the following titles appear: 'Fifteen years later, the Hurons, having accepted Christianity, were routed and killed by their enemies, the Iroquois. The Jesuit mission to the Hurons was abandoned and the Jesuits returned to Quebec.' After the final title, the frame has emptied of Huron figures, with only the cross remaining (see Figure 5.2). Thus, the cartographic introduction to the film in the initial credits is bookended by European political – via spiritual – domination, the Huron having requested baptism as an anticipated cure for the epidemic brought by the French imperial project. As in the novel, there is no sense of the imperial economics that have shaped the rivalry between Haudenosaunee nations and the Huron (see Leahy 1988, 313).

In addition to the film's visual framing of the narrative through Euro-colonial imagery and iconography, the aural frame also prioritises European cultural references. Both the opening and closing credits roll accompanied by Renaissance-era music. The film juxtaposes Indigenous and European

Figure 5.2 The end of *Black Robe*, emptied of Huron people.

music in the scene where Champlain and Chomina prepare to negotiate, with (purportedly) Algonquin singing and French instruments heard sometimes simultaneously, sometimes sequentially; after their capture by the Iroquois, when they are made to sing during their torture, Chomina sings a (purportedly) Algonquin song while Laforgue and Daniel sing 'Ave Maria'. For the most part, however, it is European music that dominates the film, particularly on the non-diegetic soundtrack. The fact that the film's non-diegetic music is so clearly (and audibly) aligned with Europe – the seventeenth century in particular – clarifies the film's positioning, with the soundtrack both accompanying (as in the extreme long shots from a high angle of the canoe journey to Huron territory, lending 'a grandeur of epic proportions to the mission' [Flood 1990, 123]), and operating as a sonic equivalent to, the camera's eye.

Black Robe, this seemingly 'authentic' version of Indigenous peoples was awarded six Genie Awards in Canada, including Best Picture. Yet despite the film's effort 'to present historical detail with absolutely meticulous accuracy' (Freebury 1992, 122) in visual terms, there are major problems with the film's 'authenticity', and not just because of its source material derived from the colonial archive. Two Algonquin characters in the film are played by non-Indigenous actors, in examples of what Ella Shohat and Robert Stam call casting 'substitutable others' (1994, 189): not only does Harrison Liu play Awondoie, but Sandrine Holt also plays Annuka. (Indeed, the casting of Holt, 'a runway model of French and Chinese heritage with no acting experience', prompted Cree-Métis actor Tantoo Cardinal, who plays Chomina's wife in the film, to 'voic[e] her consternation to a producer: "We've got actresses who can do that"' [Johnson 2019]). Further, the Algonquin characters (and French characters, on occasion) speak not Algonquin but Cree, 'a language spoken by *none* of the peoples portrayed' in the film (Churchill 2007, 133); ironically, this is even the case when characters discuss the speaking of Algonquin. When the Algonquin, in the company of Laforgue and Daniel (Aden Young), meet the Montagnais in the film, a Montagnais tells the Algonquin that Laforgue 'can't speak properly'. As in the novel, the Algonquin and Montagnais are presented as somehow speaking the same language, since they are mutually intelligible.[10]

Curiously, although the credits thank Alex Stead for providing an 'Ojibway travelling song', presumably for scenes involving the Algonquin travelling, they also thank the Alberta Cree for providing traditional songs, thousands of kilometres away from traditional Algonquin and Huron territories. Although the screenplay was written by Moore himself, the film eschews the novel's simplistic 'Savagespeak' and its 'reduc[tion]' of Indigenous languages 'to a flurry of obscenities' (Hicks 2004, 418) worthy of 'the most linguistically debased contemporary anglophones' (McSweeney 1987, 116) in the English representation of Indigenous characters speaking as well as the novel's consistent use of the word 'Savages'.[11] Yet the film's substitution of one Algonkian language for another indicates an interchangeability of Indigenous nations and cultures on the part of the filmmakers, who even misspell 'Mohawk' in the credits.

This final error likely reflects the film's status as the first Canada–Australia co-production: not only was the film 'directed by an Australian, photographed, designed and edited by Australians' (Freebury 1992, 120), but post-production also took place in Australia, rather than in Canada, the site of most shooting as well as the setting. As Jane Freebury observes, 'the events which take place in the film occurred when Australia was a large southern land mass only just taking shape under the European cartographer's hand' (120), and the film does not engage with Australia's own settler-colonial history. Nonetheless, the film's errors regarding Indigenous languages are amongst many signals that *Black Robe* is directed at an uninformed settler-colonial audience. Further, the fact that Chomina, the film's most positively portrayed Indigenous character, is also the one who speaks the most English (presumably French according to the diegesis), suggests that settler-colonial viewer sympathies are limited by linguistic intelligibility (and a relative lack of subtitles). The Iroquois, in contrast, often speak in Mohawk with no subtitles offered at all, emphasising audience disidentification; tellingly, the first appearance of subtitled Iroquois characters' dialogue is when their chief says to the captured men, 'Today was but the first caress. You will die slowly. We will peel all the skin from you and you will still be alive', a clear indication that the viewers should be afraid of and revolted by the Iroquois.

Crucially, then, Chomina (along with the 'dusky maiden' portrayal of his daughter, Annuka, whose desiring gaze at Daniel is also a gaze at the camera and, by extension, the viewer) is the most sympathetic and the most legible Indigenous character for a non-Indigenous audience. When he protests that the Algonquin party must make good on their promise to Champlain to bring Laforgue to the Huron, Chomina insists, 'But we accepted their gifts! We have come to need them. That is our undoing – and it will be our ending.'[12] This sort of prophecy aligns with the 'doomed Indian' trope of settler-colonial history, insisting upon an Indigenous disappearance that is belied in the continuing presence of Indigenous nations today, nations that actively resisted the settler-colonial repressive apparatus at Kanehsatake the year before the film was released.

Although Moore's novel attempts to offer an opposition between Indigenous and European settler-colonial worldviews that 'show[s] that each of [their] beliefs inspired in the other fear, hostility, and despair' (1985a, ix), this purported even-handedness never transpires. Like the Jesuits in his source material, Moore ventriloquises Indigenous voices to offer a counterpoint to the European perspective of Laforgue that never fundamentally destabilises Western epistemology. If *Black Robe* writes towards, even if it is not dramatised, 'the destruction and abandonment of the Jesuit mission, and the conquest of the Huron people by the Iroquois, their deadly enemy' (ix), this narrative is not fundamentally interested in troubling colonial historiography. The film, scripted by Moore and closely following the novel's narrative arc, attempts even less structural counter-point between Indigenous and European perspectives. Although Laforgue is dramatised as a figure of fun by Indigenous children, a burden by the Algonquin charged with delivering him to the Huron, a cautionary tale of austere Christian life for Daniel, *Black Robe* is, nevertheless, ultimately his story. The Algonquin characters tasked with accompanying him have either abandoned him or died in the attempt to honour their promise. If, as Scott contends, the film reveals the Jesuit mission working 'to publicly enact the legitimacy of European dominion in the Canadian wilderness, in effect, to stage the cultural supremacy of Europe' (2012, 128), the film's own framing of this narrative reinscribes this notion of cultural supremacy, suggesting the Huron were a nation doomed to fade into history without any sense of the imperial project that put this history in motion. Although the 1990 Kanehsatake standoff has been partly responsible for 'ignit[ing a] cultural renaissance' (McCall 2011, 77) of Indigenous-authored work, sig-nalling the essential need for Indigenous self-representation, it is all the more revealing that, released the year following the standoff, *Black Robe*'s adaptation clings to the imperial gaze, tired stereotypes about Indigenous people worthy of 'the diegetic world of the western' (Freebury 1992, 122) and blatant errors regarding Indigenous histories, cultures and languages.

Dance Me Outside

Although the film *Dance Me Outside* (1995), directed by Bruce McDonald, was released four years after *Black Robe*, its source material was published prior to Moore's novel. White Canadian writer W. P. Kinsella published several collections of short stories about the Ermineskin Reserve near Hobbema, Alberta, between 1977 and 1992, beginning with *Dance Me Outside*. This collection – the title story in particular – has prompted sev-eral different adaptations, including McDonald's film; the graphic novel adaptation of the screenplay, by Nick Craine, the film's storyboard artist (published in 1994); and the CBC TV series *The Rez* (its first episodes airing in 1995; revived in 1997 and then cancelled in 1998). If, as Linda Hutcheon argues, 'the act of adaptation always involves both (re-)interpretation and then (re-)creation; this has been called both appropriation and salvaging, depending on your perspective' (2013, 8), Hutcheon's use of appropriation here does not necessarily invoke cultural appropriation; however, to a certain extent, the adaptations of Kinsella's *Dance Me Outside* might be said to attempt to 'salvage' the work of this writer in the 1990s, given the political contexts of standoffs at Kanehsatake, Ipperwash (1995) and Gustafsen Lake (1995), the failed Meech Lake Accord (1990) and the Charlottetown Agreement (1992) and the Royal Commission on Aboriginal Peoples (1991–6),[13] as well as the very public demands by Indigenous artists that white artists cease the theft of Indigenous stories.

Kinsella's stories about the Ermineskin Reserve both provide a clear example of cultural appropriation and, at times, even address the issue of cultural appropriation in order to undermine it as a legitimate critique of cultural representation. Kinsella's stories are told in the first person, from the point of view of Silas Ermineskin, who is eighteen years old in the first collection. Not only did Kinsella reportedly use the real names of people living on the reserve in his stories, as well as some of their own stories (Ziff and Rao 1997b, 2), but there is also clearly an appropriation of voice, given that his white perspective on Indigenous people is articulated through the narration of an Indigenous character. Silas begins writing as part of an assignment at a technical college, where he has an appreciative instructor, Mr Nichols, who is 'the guy who is fix up the spelling in my stories' (1994, 83). Silas explains:

> He corrects my spellings and puts in those commas and stuff, but he say he leave the syntax like it is. He explain syntax to me once but I didn't understand much. I just glad Mr. Nichols like it enough to leave it alone. (133)

The intermittent references to Mr Nichols are suggestive of Kinsella's own position, as though he is a white editor of an Indigenous author, in a familiar told-to paradigm (see Chapter 6) – yet Silas is Kinsella's creation as well as his mouthpiece.

Kinsella's Cree narrator becomes a mouthpiece for white commentary on Indigenous culture and politics. Although the stories frequently point out white racism targeted at Indigenous people, they also position Indigenous activism as both ineffectual and corrupt:

> I never been involved in this business of aboriginal rights and land claims and all that stuff, and neither have my friends. I don't understand the issues. And I'm pretty sure most of the guys involved, especially the ones who yell the loudest, don't either. (1986, 78)

One of the key failings of any Indigenous activist, according to Silas's (and Kinsella's) worldview, is the lack of a sense of humour. In the story 'Truth', in *The Fencepost Chronicles* (1986), we learn the local hockey team is called 'the Hobbema Wagonburners': 'Some people complain the team name is bad for our Indian image, but they ain't got no sense of humour' (3). Kinsella also uses Silas to attack his critics about cultural appropriation. As Silas declares in 'Turbulence', from *Brother Frank's Gospel Hour* (1996),

> I'm what's known as a white-knuckle flyer, even though some whiney Indians would say I was downplaying my Indianness by claiming to have white knuckles. Those are the same Indians who think just because they're Indians they should get published, no matter how bad a storyteller they are. . . . Story writing is story writing no matter the color of your skin. (71, 72)

Thus, Kinsella ventriloquises an Indigenous voice to object to criticisms of cultural appropriation, giving himself licence to make such proclamations as 'it seem like the smaller the minority the louder they whine' (164).

In the film adaptation of *Dance Me Outside*, directed by Bruce McDonald, Silas's voice-over narration is articulated in standard English, and some characters' names have been changed (Silas Ermineskin becomes Silas Crow [Ryan Black]; his girlfriend, Sadie One-wound becomes Sadie Maracle [Jennifer Podemski]). The location and Indigenous nations shift, too, from Cree territory in Alberta to Anishinaabe territory in Ontario on the fictional Kidiabinessee reserve. Although Cree playwright Tomson Highway wrote a version of this screenplay, it was deemed 'too expensive' to produce (McDonald and Van Denzen 2008); the ultimate screenplay was written by McDonald, Don McKellar and John Frizzell.

The appearance of Indigenous actors and the sound of Silas through his voice-over attempt to represent the film of *Dance Me Outside* as an Indigenous-authored story, as we see and hear the voice-over originating from the Anishinaabe character. The film is framed, both visually and aurally, through Anishinaabe artists: at the beginning, a painting of four crows by Duke Redbird dissolves into an actual crow on the road (see Figure 5.3), to which Silas attempts to offer a cigarette (Redbird was also an associate producer on the film); over the final credits plays the song 'NDN KARS' by Keith Secola (which also features earlier in the film), suggesting an attempt to situate the narrative as an Anishinaabe narrative. As Christopher Gittings writes, 'Clearly McDonald sought to create a progressive film about life on a reserve that would negotiate racial tensions and represent Natives with dignity' (2002, 212). Further, 'the film's vaunted authenticity and perceived success in avoiding malicious stereotypes is all the more remarkable given its freighted source text' (213).

Figure 5.3 Dissolve from Redbird's image to a live crow in *Dance Me Outside*.

And yet as Gittings concedes, the film 'remains a white vision of Aboriginal life in Canada' (215); and indeed, ultimately, the Anishinaabe narrator of the film recites lines written by non-Indigenous scriptwriters.

Although Steve Van Denzen, a Cree crew member on the film who also played the small role of 'the mean cop', attests to the film's popularity in 'every reserve across Canada', he also concedes that he received 'negative feedback' (McDonald and Van Denzen 2008) about *Dance Me Outside*'s portrayal of reserves from some community members. Indeed, Terry Lusty declared in *Windspeaker*,

> There is hardly a scene throughout the entire 87-minute run of this flick which does not set apart Indians and their home-land as drinking, cheating, poverty-stricken, pool-playing, fist-fighting and racist people who have nothing better to do than tear about in old beat-up clunkers. (1994, 18)

Additionally, one of the Anishinaabe characters, Poppy, is played by Sandrine Holt, the non-Indigenous actor who also played the Algonquin Annuka in *Black Robe* (the two films, unsurprisingly, had the same casting director; as Nancy Wang Yuen notes, '[c]asting directors can play a big role in reproducing racism' [2017, 44]). Ironically, the casting of non-Indigenous actors to play Indigenous roles in films is something Kinsella himself derides in the short story 'The Managers' in *The Fencepost Chronicles*.

Cree actor Michael Greyeyes, who plays the character of Gooch in *Dance Me Outside*, has said that '[t]he film isn't culturally specific, meaning it's not written with . . . Native people in mind, in that it could be set anywhere else' (qtd in Fatzinger 2016, 309). The eschewing of Highway's screenplay by the filmmakers represents a lost opportunity to restore Cree authorship to Kinsella's narratives about a Cree community. Perhaps surprisingly, much of Highway's dialogue in his draft screenplays is taken from the Kinsella stories, probably more than the ultimate shooting script is. Like McDonald's film, Highway's screenplay – both drafts of it (composed in 1991 and 1992, respectively) – is largely structured around the title story, 'Dance Me Outside', which is, in fact, only seven pages long. McDonald's film also adapts 'Illianna Comes Home' and 'The Inaugural Meeting'. The murder of Little Margaret and the community's women avenging her death, the subject of 'Dance Me Outside', more or less book-end the rest of the events in both Highway's screenplay and McDonald's film, although Highway's first draft also adapted 'The McGuffin', in which Silas and Frank travel from the reserve to Edmonton to visit Silas's older sister and misplace her baby while out on the town; 'Linda Star', in which Silas studies at the Northern Alberta Institute of Technology and gets involved with the troubled eponymous character; and 'Lark Song', in which Joseph, Silas's elder and disabled brother – 'He just got a tiny kid's mind in a big man's body' (Kinsella 1994, 114) – is removed from the family by white officials. Highway's second screenplay draft dropped the content from 'The McGuffin'.

Although Highway's drafts engage with more of Kinsella's content than McDonald's film ultimately does, one major shift from Kinsella's stories to Highway's screenplay concerns the character of Silas. Kinsella's conception of Silas as a writer is retained by McDonald et al., and Silas's writing becomes his ticket off the reserve (as well as Frank's and Sadie's): he is supposed to write a story to get into technical college, which he does successfully (and ghost-writes Frank's as well). The final shot of McDonald's film shows Silas on the back of Sadie's motorbike as she drives them away from their community. In contrast, not only does Highway translate Silas's ambitions from writing to a determination to open his own garage in order to make an economic contribution to his community and to remove its dependence on white, off-reserve business, but Highway's draft screenplays also focus more on the women of the community. Highway's narrative resolution entails not Silas's and Sadie's departure from the community but rather an image of the community (playing baseball) that still includes Silas and Sadie.[14] Further, Highway's screenplay includes a significant amount of dialogue in Cree, with the screenplay's second draft beginning with Sadie telling a story in Cree about the Great Spirit dangling a baby boy.

Film studio personnel and industry professionals advised Highway to enhance Silas's importance, with McDonald suggesting, 'Silas needs two or three scenes by himself as the once and future king. He doesn't know it, but we the audience begin to see that he is the *chosen* one who will eventually lead his people' ([1991], [3]) and asking, '[D]oes Silas have the potential to be a spiritual dude – a visionary?' ([1991], [4]) as well as what is in the film for 'the white suburban punk who listen's [*sic*] to thrash metal' ([1991], [1])?[15] Highway's eschewing of male heroism in favour of the role of Indigenous women and community diverges from McDonald's choices and their implications for an expanded audience.

Nick Craine adapts McDonald et al.'s screenplay into a graphic novel that seeks to problematise the white male perspective on the story that *Dance Me Outside* tells; indeed, 'Craine took the opportunity to critique the racial politics of both Kinsella's Indian stories and McDonald's handling of the texts' (Betts 2003, 103). Craine does this most explicitly in his 'Artist's Note' at the end of his text, in which he confesses, 'I used to be somewhat of a McVey [Silas's white brother-in-law]. We all have a little of brother Bob in our hearts; a bit arrogant, very ignorant – all in all, self-serving. And we white people so easily accept the past with this apathetic "I wasn't even born back then" kind of attitude. But our Canadian history will make fools of us all if we ignore it' (1994, [101]). On his relationship to, in Gittings's words, the 'freighted source text', Craine writes,

> I saw this as an opportunity to inject my own voice into the story, to recognize and examine that I am a white guy telling this story. I am a white guy telling a story based on another white guy's screenplay, which is in turn based on another white guy's book of short stories based on his own interpretation of life on an Alberta First Nations reserve. Now if that isn't screwed up, I don't know what is. ([101])

We might argue that this is not a story that needs another white guy's own voice, that the recognition of appropriation would be more fruitfully resolved by making space for other voices. But in terms of the representational strategies Craine deploys, the Artist's Note presents a concluding frame (analogous to the framing of the film through Anishinaabe cultural production), one that finds a counterpart in an early panel that reminds the reader, by way of a road sign: 'YOU ARE NOW ENTERING OJIBWAY TERRITORY' (6). At the same time, however, Craine himself enters Anishinaabe territory, 'inject[ing his] own voice' into the story, as Kinsella does, via the character of Silas.

Craine's text diverges from both the film and the Kinsella material through a sequence involving Jacques Cartier and a critique of Canadian history textbooks that peddle justifications for settler-colonialism. That the textbook material, read by Silas in the graphic novel, is juxtaposed to the announcement that Clarence Gaskell has been released from prison implicitly ties the settler-colonial project to Missing and Murdered Indigenous Women, especially given one of the final quotations from the textbook: 'To the Indian women [Cartier] gave for instance, some tin bells; and so enraptured were some of the dusky beauties of the tribe with these presents, that they fell on his neck and smothered him . . . with kisses' (1994, 74). As Bart Beaty argues, 'Craine's insertions into the text have a tendency to repoliticize and recontextualize the events that the film minimizes' (2004, 28–9). The graphic novel creates a palimpsest of images of New France and the Kidiabinessee reserve, with Silas reading this version of Canadian history in the foreground, suggesting that, as Audra Simpson argues, 'Canada requires the death and so called "disappearance" of Indigenous women in order to secure its sovereignty' (2016), hardwired into the settler-colonial project.

The title of 'Dance Me Outside' (the story, the book, and the film and its screenplay adaptation) refers to the narrative of Little Margaret's murder by the white Clarence Gaskell (though the phrase is used differently in the story and in the film). The title story furnishes the film with the bulk of its narrative alongside the first story in the collection, 'Illianna Comes Home', in which Silas's older sister brings her white husband home to the reserve for the first time. Focusing on the murder of Little Margaret (Tamara Podemski) by the white Gaskell (Hugh Dillon) and its fallout, the film foregrounds the issue of Missing and Murdered Indigenous Women at a time prior to its becoming as widespread a public concern in Canada as it has since. As in the story, Gaskell gets off lightly: he is found guilty only of manslaughter, though his sentence is longer in the film than it is in the story, one year as opposed to ninety days in Kinsella's version.

The discrepancy in Gaskell's sentence from story to film protracts the narrative: in the story, Silas's narration of Gaskell's release occurs a paragraph after his sentencing; in the film, other stories from the *Dance Me Outside* collection intervene between Gaskell's arrest and his release, including the narrative within 'Illianna Comes Home' of her impregnation by her ex-boyfriend (Eathen Firstrider in the story, called 'Gooch' in the film – the name of a different character in Kinsella's collection). In the film, Sadie breaks up with Silas at the dance at which Little Margaret is murdered, and during the ensuing year becomes politically active as a result of Gaskell's scandalously short sentence. The film incorporates the story 'The Inaugural Meeting', in which Kinsella writes scathingly about the American Indian Movement (AIM), and the event of Silas and his best friend Frank Fencepost (Adam Beach) trashing the car of Hobart Thunder, an AIM activist, rather than that of the federal officers who have him under surveillance. In the film, Sadie has invited Thunder to speak, and Silas and Frank's mistake works to justify her having ended her relationship with Silas. The politicising of Sadie marks a striking contrast between the source material and the film. Kinsella's Silas describes his girlfriend as 'nice, but she ain't pretty to anyone but me' (Kinsella 1989, 16), and 'always been real shy' (165), a far cry from Jennifer Podemski's Sadie (in both *Dance Me Outside* and *The Rez*). Sadie's shift in character-isation appears to incorporate Kinsella's character of Bedelia Coyote, a friend of Silas actively involved in many causes: 'Sometimes I worry about Bedelia. She is so political and socially conscious she getting to sound like a politician' (Kinsella 1986, 158). Despite the addition of political activism to Sadie's character on screen, however, the resolution of the story 'Dance Me Outside', in which Sadie and her female friends are revealed to be responsible for the death of Gaskell, differs from the film version insofar as the latter becomes about Sadie's sacrifice for her man: Silas, Frank and other men have been intending to kill Gaskell upon his release. In the film, Sadie, covered in blood, weeps as she explains to Silas that the women had to kill Gaskell themselves in order to keep Silas and his friends out of jail. This sacrifice paves the way for Sadie and Silas's reconciliation and the renewal of their relationship.

Sadie's politicising continues in the CBC series *The Rez*, in which she works as an assistant to Chief Tom (Gary Farmer), often critiquing her boss for his nepotistic favours and failure to act in their community's best interests. The shift from McDonald's film to the CBC series is marked by the acknowledgement in the film's opening credits that the film is 'based on the book by W. P. Kinsella', in contrast to *The Rez*'s credits, which state, 'based on characters created by W. P. Kinsella'. Such a shift might implicitly distance the series from the 'freighted source text' in an attempt to salvage it. Some episodes, such as 'The Lark' (an adaptation of 'Lark Song' in the *Dance Me Outside* collection), are clearly based on individual Kinsella stories, suggesting more connection between Kinsella and the TV programme than the credits concede. As Mary Jane Miller points out, however, some episodes of *The Rez*, unlike its cinematic coun-terpart, were 'written by Aboriginal writers, including Jordan Wheeler' (2003, 71), making the programme (in this capacity as least) arguably the most Indigenous-authored of any of the incarnations of Kinsella's work. Further, the adaptation of 'Lark Song', in which Joseph is removed from his family, includes a reference to Indian Residential Schools as a kind of analogy for Joseph's removal by the white establishment, a context that Kinsella's original story does not invoke. Sadie's activism is prominent in *The Rez*, encompassing land claims, as in the episode 'Golf and Politics' (2009), in which she tapes a border down the middle of the marina bar run by the white (and suggestively named) Ellen Nanabush. It also features resistance to cultural appropriation, as in 'Poster Girl', when Sadie refuses to wear an Iroquois headdress while modelling jeans for a white photographer, and 'Like Father, Like Son', in which Sadie castigates Frank and Chief Tom for Frank's attempt to sell stereotypically 'Indian' dolls to tourists.

Sadie's politics often put her at odds with others on the reserve, including the chief's son, Charlie (Adam Beach, who plays Frank in the film). When Sadie says she wants to apply for funds for 'a daycare centre for teenaged mothers', Charlie replies, 'What, reward babies for having babies?' Sadie retorts, 'You know, you should join the Reform Party', to which Charlie responds, 'They take Indians?' This acknowledgement of the Reform Party's (1986–2000) racism constitutes one of the clearest examples of salvaging Kinsella, given that the author actually campaigned for the Reform Party (Todd 2016), treated here with scorn by Sadie.[16] At the same time, however, *The Rez*, described by Podemski (2009) as designed to be 'funny and lighthearted', demonstrates the limitations of its state broadcasting origins, as well as its immediate source material in McDonald's film, 'a light comedy about serious social injustices' (Beaty 2004, 30). The conclusion of the programme, in which Sadie, having broken up with Silas, attends an Aboriginal Youth Council in Toronto, includes the following pronouncement by the conference facilitator, who advocates 'staying involved in the process of government: Standoffs and blockades are fun and exciting, but, in the long term . . .'. The rest of his dialogue is obscured, but not many years removed from the standoff at Kanehsatake, and even fewer from Ipperwash and Gustafsen Lake, the dismissive characterisations of resistance as 'fun', here articulated by an Indigenous character, reinscribes a settler-colonial broadcasting framework.

The two-part final episode, 'No Reservations', constitutes the only example in the TV programme where we see the main characters leaving the rez for an urban location. The issue of Missing and Murdered Indigenous Women resurfaces here, for Lucy has left the rez for Toronto to try to begin an acting career. Her failure to stay in touch with Sadie has the latter worried, and prompts Sadie's trip to Toronto even more than her political ambitions do. She looks for Lucy every night on the streets of Toronto, with no success. Silas and Frank (Lucy's on-again, off-again boyfriend, played by Darrell Dennis in the TV series) are also in Toronto while Silas attends a creative writing workshop. Frank is certain he has seen Lucy getting into a car, convinced that she is involved in prostitution (and perhaps viewers of *Dance Me Outside* sense an intratextual threat to Lucy, given she is played by Tamara Podemski, the same actor who played Little Margaret in the film). Frank ultimately bursts in on Lucy in a strange man's bedroom, only to discover a film crew is present: Lucy is acting, not, as he fears, engaged in sex work. While looking for Lucy, Sadie encounters a woman from the rez, Barbara, who *is* working on the street in Toronto, an example, seemingly, of Kinsella's assertion that 'so many Indian girls . . . go bad; the unluckiest go to the cities alone, end up drinking too much and selling themselves on the street' (1989, 115), the onus placed here on the so-called 'Indian girls' who fail to prevent themselves from being 'unlucky' or 'going bad'. Sadie is shaken up by her encounter with Barbara, and yet the issue of Missing and Murdered Indigenous Women seems ultimately to resolve comically, given the resolution of Lucy's whereabouts (and, additionally, another reconciliation between Sadie and Silas at the end of the episode, and indeed, the programme as a whole).

In many ways, therefore, *The Rez* and its characters have come a long way from Kinsella's Ermineskin Reserve, geographically, politically, culturally and personally. With each visual incarnation, the 'freighted source text' gets left further behind. But despite the increasing Indigenous visibility (and, in some episodes of *The Rez*, Indigenous authorship) with each incarnation of the source material, it is difficult to conclude that the material, so weighed down with cultural appropriation, has been salvaged to the point where it has been translated into Indigenous representational sovereignty. Each incarnation of *Dance Me Outside* addresses racism and the ongoing crisis of Missing and Murdered Indigenous Women, far more prominent now in the Canadian settler-colonial nation-state's consciousness than at the time of *Dance Me Outside*'s iterations. McDonald indicated to Tomson Highway that Little Margaret's murder is 'very resonant' ([1991], [4]) – which is even more the case today. However, these versions of *Dance Me Outside* remain limited by their settler-colonial origins and the cultural industries from which they emerge. In viewing Kinsella's characters on the large and small screen, in the context of Indigenous resistance of the 1990s, settler audiences could, perhaps, be reassured by this version of Indigeneity, thus salvaging their own claims to belong in the territory claimed by Canada.

In the shift from literary to cinematic incarnations of *The Chant of Jimmie Blacksmith*, *Black Robe* and *Dance Me Outside*, the content moves from the imagined world of white writers to dramatised versions on screen, versions that feature Indigenous actors. Given the collaborative nature of film as a medium, there is an extent to which Indigenous actors become co-creators of the content. Yuen, in her study of Hollywood racism's impact on actors in particular, argues:

> the idea that white writers can never write authentic stories about people of color is problematic. It falsely assumes that people of color are defined only by their race and glosses over national, ethnic, and geographic diversity within racial groups. (2017, 58)

Yuen challenges Hollywood to 'stop showing the false white world of [her] youth' (160), one imagined by a film industry where white people are overrepresented in positions of power. Although Yuen's argument rightly seeks to critique Hollywood's projection of whiteness, and studies of actors such as Yiman Wang's analysis of Anna May Wong reveal how racialised actors can demonstrate an agency bound up in ironising and challenging stereotypical roles (2005, 175, 177), cultural appropriation, particularly the telling of Indigenous stories by non-Indigenous artists, detracts from the representation of Indigenous people and can even abrogate Indigenous knowledge protocols.

The trajectory of Kinsella's *Dance Me Outside* to *The Rez*, particularly through the character of Sadie as played by Jennifer Podemski, demonstrates a tension between the white provenance of the original material and the more activist Sadie becomes the further she gets from Kinsella. At the same time, Podemski, now with two decades of directing and producing experience, has said of her work on Canada's Aboriginal Peoples Television Network's (APTN) series *Future History*, a non-fiction series dedicated to telling the stories of Indigenous peoples across Canada, 'There is so much space to fill. There has been a void for so long and we are all storytellers doing this work today, all perspectives, and indigenous perspectives are filling the hole' (2019). If *The Chant of Jimmie Blacksmith*, *Black Robe* and *Dance Me Outside* each sought to dramatise the perspective of Indigenous people in Australia nd Canada, respectively, as authored by white artists, their adaptations particularly have accorded Indigenous actors space on the screen. Yet as Podemski suggests, such works have never 'filled the hole' of Indigenous perspectives in mainstream settler-colonial cultures; white-authored stories about Indigenous people are not to be equated with Indigenous stories. And indeed, had the film of *Dance Me Outside* used

Highway's rather than McDonald et al.'s screenplay, the translation of Kinsella's material into something more meaningful would have occurred much sooner. If *Dance Me Outside* represents a missed opportunity for greater Indigenous authorship in jettisoning Highway's screenplay, the final two chapters of this book examine Indigenous stories as they are adapted both by non-Indigenous filmmakers and by Indigenous filmmakers themselves.

Told-to Adaptations: *Rabbit-Proof Fence*, *Whale Rider* and *The Lesser Blessed*

This chapter examines three films adapted from Indigenous source material by non-Indigenous directors: *Rabbit-Proof Fence* (2002), adapted from Mardudjara writer Doris Pilkington/Nugi Garimara's *Follow the Rabbit-Proof Fence* (1996) and directed by white Australian Phillip Noyce; *Whale Rider* (2002), adapted from Māori writer Witi Ihimaera's novel *The Whale Rider* (1987) by Pākehā Niki Caro; and *The Lesser Blessed* (2012), adapted from Tłı̨chǫ (Dogrib) writer Richard Van Camp's 1996 novel of the same title by Ukrainian-Canadian filmmaker Anita Doron. Films made by a non-Indigenous director adapting an Indigenous text, I argue, can be considered 'told-to' adaptations, in the manner of 'told-to' literary texts in which Indigenous narratives are shepherded through publication by a white co-author. If told-to texts are typically Indigenous authors' narratives that are collected or edited by non-Indigenous people, films made by white filmmakers adapting Indigenous material can be conceptualised as 'told-to adaptations', as they replicate many features of told-to texts, which include, according to Sophie McCall, the forging of 'a variety of contact zones', 'debates over cultural property' and the potential for cross-cultural collaboration in 'a meeting ground for multiple voices' (2011, 2–3, 4, 5).[1] Although the capacity for these adaptations to represent Indigenous culture is certainly much greater than those discussed in the previous chapter, given the provenance of the source material, particular issues arise within the contexts of production in each example and the ways in which the filmmakers choose to orient their adaptation to as large (implicitly white) an audience as possible: namely, these Indigenous stories undergo alterations for the sake of their translation for the cinema designed to appeal to mainstream audiences.

One key concern with told-to narratives is 'the unequal power relationship traditionally at play in the production of the text' (Rymhs 2006, 92). This imbalance of power undermines terms such as 'collaboration' that suggest a more level playing field between narrator and collector. The term 'composite' has also been used to represent the process of telling and circulating these narratives (Sands 1997, 39). In the context of cinema, the collaborative venture of filmmaking itself furnishes an example of 'composite' authorship, inflecting the collaborative capacity of told-to adaptations in particular industrial ways. Granted, there are some key differences between told-to narratives in the more traditional sense and the film adaptations examined in this chapter. Told-to narratives often involve the interviewing of an Indigenous person by a non-Indigenous authoritative figure (e.g. an anthropologist or writer), who then presents the material in a format more likely to lend itself to a non-Indigenous audience. As Deena Rymhs notes, 'These collaborations typically involve a transaction involving a narrating subject who does not have access to literary or publishing institutions and an editor who is representative of a more powerful social class' (2006, 92). Clearly, the examples discussed here diverge from this model insofar as all three films are adapted from published work.

At the same time, all three adaptations in this chapter are based on source material that incorporates oral culture to varying degrees. Although *Rabbit-Proof Fence* has its roots in oral testimony given that *Follow the Rabbit-Proof Fence* tells the story of its author's mother and aunt, Pilkington/Garimara's version is itself a written text. Witi Ihimaera's *Whale Rider* is partly based on a Māori Traditional Story, but this narrative is enclosed within a late-twentieth-century novel. *The Lesser Blessed*'s narrator and protagonist, Larry Sole, according to the novel's author, is 'a traditional storyteller' (qtd in Saltman interview 2003), one who tells stories not only to the reader but also to other characters. Like *The Whale Rider*, however, Van Camp's *Lesser Blessed* is readily legible as a novel.

These adaptations also diverge from traditional told-to narratives through the processes of filmmaking itself: feature filmmaking is inevitably a collaborative form, even when it does not involve the adaptation of a prior work. Hundreds of people contribute to the production of a film, complicating the *auteurist* equation of the director with the author. At the same time, the director is placed in a privileged position, and despite the many other artists involved in making a film, is often understood as producing the overall artistic vision for the project. Even the opening credits of a film, following the acknowledgements of the studio(s) and producer(s), will tend to state 'a [insert director's name] film' before the film's title appears. Although this structuring of film credits is conventional, in the case of the adaptations in question it risks replicating the appropriative tendencies of told-to narratives that sometimes 'bear the name of the collector, not the narrator, as sole author' (Sands 1997, 41). Of the film adaptations discussed in this chapter, only *The Lesser Blessed* adopts this model in the credits: both *Rabbit-Proof Fence* and *Whale Rider* delay the

director's name until the end of the film, but they also delay their acknowledgements of the Indigenous source material until the end (with the director's name in both cases appearing before the source text and its author);
The Lesser Blessed is framed as 'an Anita Doron film' in the opening credits, but Van Camp's text goes unacknowledged until the final credits. In all
three films, the earlier (sometimes much earlier) attribution of the film to
the non-Indigenous director masks both the Indigenous source material
and, in some cases, the contribution of the Indigenous community to the
film production process itself. Deferral of this acknowledgement to the
final credits also risks the audience missing this information.

Whereas the conventional told-to narrative is collected by a figure
deemed culturally authoritative by the non-Indigenous mainstream, there
are varying degrees of cultural authority attached to the directors of the
three adaptations examined here. Phillip Noyce, director of *Rabbit-Proof
Fence*, had considerable experience of both Australian and Hollywood
filmmaking prior to his making of this adaptation. Conversely, Niki Caro
and Anita Doron were much less well known at the time of *Whale Rider*'s
and *The Lesser Blessed*'s respective releases. And while cultural differences
form the central focus of this chapter regarding the authors of the source
material and the directors (who are also the screenwriters in the case of
Whale Rider and *The Lesser Blessed*), each of these adaptations also features
a gender reversal from literary author to adaptation director, with Noyce's
film adapting the work of a Mardudjara woman and Caro's and Doron's
films adapting the work of a Māori man and a Tłıchǫ man, respectively.
Given concerns about the 'level of dominance [that] occurs when a male
collector works with a female Native narrator' (Sands 1997, 42), the case of
Rabbit-Proof Fence in particular invites further scrutiny of gender dynamics through the told-to narrative analogy.

Rabbit-Proof Fence

Although the career of white Australian director Phillip Noyce began
in Australian cinema, he had been working on Hollywood films, particularly in the 'action-thriller genre' (Villella 2002, para. 1), for several
years prior to the production of *Rabbit-Proof Fence*; thus, the adaptation
of Pilkington/Garimara's text 'was the antithesis of the type of film he
had been making in Hollywood for the past decade' (Petzke 2007, 233).[2]
Pilkington/Garimara's text tells the story of her mother, Molly, a member of the Stolen Generations – mixed-race children who were separated
by the state from their families, 'remov[ed] to special reserve locations at
great distances' (Renes 2013, 178) – who was abducted from her home in

Jigalong, Western Australia, along with her sister, Daisy, and their cousin, Gracie. They were taken to the Moore River Native Settlement, from whence they escaped and walked a thousand miles home to Jigalong by following the eponymous fence.

The genre of *Follow the Rabbit-Proof Fence* is complicated in its representation of the author's mother's life story, albeit with material that exceeds that story. For Marie Lovrod, *Follow the Rabbit-Proof Fence* is an example of 'mirror talk', a term coined by Susanna Egan to 'refe[r] to "dialogic" or "polyphonic" autobiographies with a doubling of voice that establishes authenticity', while the life-writing 'presents the life stories of others in relation to the writers' own experiences' (Lovrod 2005, 44). As Dorothee Klein emphasises, in the life-writing of Pilkington/Garimara, and a feature of Indigenous life-writing more generally, 'the focus is . . . communal rather than private, presenting the self as part of the community and the personal story as part of a larger narrative' (2016, 591). For Pilkington/Garimara, the telling of her mother's story as part of the Stolen Generations includes the history of colonialism. If Indigenous life-writing 'is inherently political and didactic in that it challenges and corrects non-Indigenous assumptions about Aboriginal identity' (Klein 2016, 591), Pilkington/Garimara includes four chapters detailing the history of Australia from an Indigenous perspective before arriving at the point of her mother's birth as 'the first half-caste child to be born amongst the Jigalong people' (Pilkington/Garimara 2002a, 38). Pilkington/Garimara contextualises Molly's birth by first relating the arrival of white settlers in Australia, described as 'ruthless white pirates, desperados and escaped convicts' (4). Violence against Indigenous women particularly appears early in this history, fusing the colonial project with femicide: 'Those cruel and murderous men came ashore and stole Aboriginal women and kept them on board their ships as sexual slaves, then murdered them and tossed their bodies into the ocean when their services were no longer required' (4). Pilkington/Garimara thereby pre-empts the colonial perspective on Indigenous peoples as uncivilised by offering evidence of settler-colonial violence perpetrated by 'the white invaders' (15).

The history that leads up to Molly's birth also includes the colonial cartography that brings the rabbit-proof fence into being, first through the introduction by Europeans of rabbits on a continent where they had no natural predators, and then the mechanism installed by the colonial state in order to manage the exploded rabbit population: the rabbit-proof fence. However, as Pilkington/Garimara explains, if the fence was intended to 'halt the invasion of rabbits into Western Australia from the eastern states', it proved unsuccessful: 'there were more rabbits on the Western Australian side of the fence than there were on the South Australian side' (32). Fences were also detrimental to Indigenous peoples whose hunting trails were disrupted by them. Pilkington/Garimara contrasts this deprivation through dispossession to settler attempts to import European hunting culture: settlers 'were advised to "keep up their Englishness" at all costs. This meant having picnics, fox hunts and balls' (13). The colonial project's cartography and Indigenous dispossession resulted in the birth of Pilkington/Garimara's mother: not only was Jigalong depot 'founded for the purpose of the construction of the fence' (Ralph 2014, 5), but Molly's father, an Englishman named Thomas Craig, was also an inspector of the fence and therefore both a European himself and a representative of the colonial state hired to maintain its demarcations.

Given the origins of Pilkington/Garimara's text, *Rabbit-Proof Fence* is a kind of 'twice-told' adaptation, first told to Pilkington/Garimara by her mother and aunt, then adapted by Noyce from documentary filmmaker Christine Olsen's screenplay. If in told-to publications, the non-Indigenous author/collaborator tends to be an established, authoritative literary figure, of all the directors examined in this chapter, Noyce is arguably the most 'authoritative' in terms of his prior filmmaking experience and exposure. Yet *Rabbit-Proof Fence* constituted a considerable departure from the work he had been engaged in in the years leading up to the making of this film. Noyce has described his Hollywood career as 'making sausages' and himself as a 'migrant worker in this Hollywood system' (qtd in Collins and Davis 2004, 134), positioning his return to Australia to make *Rabbit-Proof Fence* as re-establishing his status as both an artist and an Australian at home (via, it must be said, an Indigenous narrative). At the same time, however, not only did he have 'to overcome the peculiar alienation of the expatriate' (Collins and Davis 2004, 134), but he also brought many aspects of the Hollywood machinery with him to the production of *Rabbit-Proof Fence* from his experience of 'making sausages', including his sense of the narrative as 'a marvellous adventure story and a thriller' (qtd in Petzke 2007, 233) and a 'star-making' (Collins and Davis 2004, 137) strategy to turn the actors playing the three girls into celebrities (see also Villella 2002, para. 4).

Rabbit-Proof Fence is simultaneously a film based on Indigenous experience in Australia, particularly the history of the Stolen Generations, and widely recognised as a mainstream film. Indeed, Noyce has explicitly articulated his determination that the film be firmly located within the mainstream:

> The idea of making a story where the heroine is the Aboriginal girl and you are presenting that as a normal, everyday part of popular culture, and selling it aggressively in cinema multiplexes in the suburbs, made the whole project worthwhile. (qtd in Petzke 2007, 238)

Noyce was clearly determined that *Rabbit-Proof Fence* should be a commercial success: 'I did not want to marginalize the movie by using subtitles – I did not want it to become an arthouse movie' (qtd in Chan 2008,
124).[3] If we take Noyce as an authoritative figure in this told-to adaptation,
he inhabits this role not just (or perhaps, not particularly) on aesthetic
grounds, but also on commercial grounds; that is, it is not so much his
cultural capital that he brings to the adaptation but rather the promise of
capital itself in terms of the film's box office success as he shifts concerns
about marginalisation from Indigenous people to commercial viability.

Part of the strategy to make *Rabbit-Proof Fence* a commercial success
involved the recruitment of other male authoritative figures in cinema,
namely Kenneth Branagh, who plays Western Australia's Chief Protector
of the Aborigines, A. O. Neville, and David Gulpilil, who plays Moodoo, a
tracker based at the Moore River Settlement (and whose daughter is one
of the inmates) who follows the escaped girls in an attempt to effect their
recapture. Neville appears periodically in Pilkington/Garimara's text,
largely through archival material in the form of correspondence relating to
attempts to recapture the girls. Moodoo, in contrast, is a fictional addition
to the narrative. Branagh and Gulpilil, 'the quintessential Aboriginal character actor in Australian cinema', fulfil the roles of 'recognisable star[s]' to
help bolster the film's marketability (Petzke 2007, 234). Given the film's
structuring of scenes that alternate between the girls' experiences of their
return home and scenes of the men who seek them (Neville from his office
in Perth, Moodoo on horseback in pursuit of the girls), the film inevitably
lends more weight to these male figures than Pilkington/Garimara's text
does. The publicity images for the film that feature Branagh's face taking
up the bulk of the frame, looming over small images of the three girls
walking, both gesture to the power that Branagh's character, Neville, had
over Indigenous peoples in Western Australia, and reinscribe a hierarchy
of celebrity that has been harnessed to facilitate box office returns.

Nonetheless, the film clearly identifies Neville as its chief representative of empire, responsible for the violence perpetrated against Indigenous
peoples in Western Australia. The children incarcerated at Moore River
Native Settlement consistently refer to him as 'the Devil' in a refrain that
rhymes with his surname. Tony Hughes D'aeth reads Branagh's performance as one of 'distancing Britishness' (2002, para. 18), suggesting either
a lack of warmth on the part of Neville's characterisation or an attempt
to displace genocidal policies away from Australian figures by attaching
them instead to representatives of the imperial centre (although Neville
was in fact born in England). But if *Rabbit-Proof Fence*'s Neville appears
to be 'relatively benign' (Morrissey 2007, para. 7), and 'not just a racist

caricature' (Petzke 2007, 238), he is also consistently presented as alienating, and framed in 'his methodical and bleak office' (Frieze 2012, 124) in such a way as to convey his ideology as distortion.[4] The scenes in Neville's office in Perth use obtrusive camera angles to undermine Neville's position. Shots of Neville himself are frequently medium close-ups shot from a low angle to include the ceiling behind and above him, literally exposing his institutional framing. Such shots tend to be juxtaposed to shots of his secretary, Miss Thomas (Lorna Leslie), usually in a canted frame, emphasising the racist ideology of these characters' discourse through the visual disturbance.

The first scene that takes place in the office bears out the claim of one of the film's introductory titles, which reads, 'the Aborigines Act . . . controls their lives in every detail'. Thus, the office location becomes a staging ground for the white supremacist settler-colonial state's genocidal policies. Miss Thomas enters Neville's office with a stack of files, the contents of which she summarises for Neville. The cases include applications for permission to marry, to visit children who have been abducted from their families by the state and to purchase new shoes. To this last request, Neville mutters, 'She had a new pair a year ago', while his hand stamps a form in close-up. Thus, our introduction to Neville's character establishes the extreme regulation of Indigenous people's lives by the white supremacist state. On more than one occasion, high-angle shots through the office window onto the street reveal a queue of Indigenous people (see Figure 6.1), waiting to be seen, although the film never shows them inside the building or in conversation with Neville. The Indigenous people are 'look[ed] down on and thus dehumanize[d]' (Frieze 2012, 126), captured by the high-angle shot that replicates the perspective of white representatives of the settler-colonial state.

Neville explicates his eugenicist and genocidal ideology at a meeting of the Perth Women's Service Guild, in which he articulates both an anxiety about 'ever-increasing numbers' of mixed-race children who constitute 'an unwanted third race' and his proposed solution: diluting Indigenous descent from one generation to the next until 'white blood finally stamps out the black colour . . . The Aboriginal has simply been . . . bred out.' As Donna-Lee Frieze observes, Neville in this scene appears from the perspective of an Indigenous servant (2012, 125), returning the white surveillant gaze and formally undermining him. Neville includes a slide show in his presentation, featuring an image of three generations of a mixed-race family, looking increasingly phenotypically white. This image and some lines of dialogue in this scene appear in the historical A. O. Neville's book *Australia's Coloured Minority: Its Place in the Community* (1948; see 58–9, 80), suggesting that

Figure 6.1 The queue outside Neville's office.

Noyce's film also adapts Neville's text, enveloping it within the adaptation of Pilkington/Garimara's.

Yet Neville inevitably has more presence in the film through his representation by Branagh and the structuring of the film's narrative, alternating between the state and the girls, in a way that diverges from Pilkington/Garimara's text including yet subordinating 'the colonialist documents that chart her mother's progress' (Lovrod 2015, 78). Significantly, in *Follow the Rabbit-Proof Fence*, the register and status of those documents present considerable differences from the narrative of the girls' escape and return home; in contrast, Noyce's film dramatises both the girls' narrative and Neville's. Although the use of obtrusive camera angles and framing of Neville attempt to distinguish his representation from the girls', and his cinematic representation effectively conveys his 'obsessive determination' (Pilkington/Garimara 2002b, 61) to capture the girls, he nevertheless takes up narrative space in the film that has no real antecedent in Pilkington/Garimara's text.

The scene of the girls' abduction presents one of the clearest contrasts between the written text and the film adaptation, as many critics have addressed. The use of handheld, low-angle camera shots, the suspenseful musical score, the physical resistance of the girls (especially Molly [Everlyn Sampi]) and their mothers contribute to the film's 'exploit[ation of] the removal scene . . . for its shock value' (Hosking 2011, 230). As Rosanne Kennedy points out, the film's representation of this scene differs markedly from the text's, in which 'the response to removal is neither individualised nor gendered' (2008, 168). When Constable Riggs announces, 'I've come to take Molly, Gracie and Daisy, the three half-caste girls, with me to go to school at the Moore River Native Settlement', the community responds through grief:

> The old man nodded to show that he understood what Riggs was saying. The rest of the family just hung their heads refusing to face the man who was taking their daughters away from them. Silent tears welled in their eyes and trickled down their cheeks. (44)

On the one hand, the film's 'spectacularisation of ethnocide' (qtd in Morrissey 2007, para. 5), most clearly exemplified in the abduction scene, allows the film to dramatise genocide, particularly through the juxtaposition of Molly's hunting the goanna prior to her abduction and the suggestion that Riggs, in abducting the three girls, is also 'legally engaged in hunting' (Frieze 2012, 130), as emphasised by the literal chasing of the girls in the film in an extended pursuit sequence. Although Frieze argues that the film neither depicts nor implies genocide through 'mass murder' (2012, 130) but rather through Neville's 'biological absorption plan' (122), I suggest the hunting correlation does, in fact, gesture towards Australia's genocidal history and the hunting of Indigenous people by settlers.

On the other hand, the construction of suspense around the adaptation of the abduction scene is ethically dubious when considered in the context of Noyce's generic understanding and promotion of this film: his sense of the narrative as a 'marvellous adventure story and a thriller'. The scene heightens the suspense and anxiety around the girls' abduction, and certainly stages it *as* an abduction, albeit legally sanctioned. Riggs's repeated invocation of the piece of paper that attests to his orders to remove the children dramatises the violence of settler-colonial law. But viewing this scene in the context of Noyce's categorisation of the film as a 'thriller' also suggests that the audience should be *excited* by this scene. As Queenie Monica Chan writes, 'the film had to negotiate a complex and difficult relationship between Indigenous and non-Indigenous Australians, while also entertaining international audiences' (2008, 124). Thus, in heightening the drama of this scene in its translation from written text to cinema, the film inevitably seeks to thrill and entertain its audience through a traumatic, genocidal encounter.

As a filmmaker with experience in both Australian and Hollywood filmmaking contexts, Noyce explicitly intended the film to circulate internationally, which it did. As many critics have identified, one strategy to enhance the film's global success was the film's articulation of 'politics at a universal level' (Chan 2008, 124). The specificity of Indigenous experience therefore clashes with the filmmaker's aspirations towards universal resonance in overseas markets. In addition to his generic positioning of the film, Noyce has also made comments that clearly invoke the universal:

> *Rabbit-Proof Fence* is . . . a story of any outsider who exceeds their own expectations of themselves and the limitations other people place on them. It's about any underdog who overcomes the odds. And essentially it's not about the uniqueness of Aboriginal culture, but the ways in which we're all the same. (qtd in Petzke 2007, 238–9)

From this perspective, the girls' experience of being captured by and eluding the infrastructure of the white supremacist Australian state can be substituted with anyone in any position. Further, Noyce's comment on the casting of the film that he 'wanted kids who people all over the world would want to adopt as their own children' (2011) dovetails with the American publicity for the film, featuring the poster tagline, 'What if the government kidnapped your daughter?' (qtd in Hughes D'aeth 2002, para. 5). This marketing strategy invites the potential viewer to identify with the mothers of the girls, as if such an act could easily happen to anyone, rather than members of a dispossessed community targeted by a white supremacist state. At the same time, the appeal to audience members to want to adopt these Indigenous children also unwittingly chimes with Indigenous child removal policies of settler-colonial states.

The discourse of universality harnessed to facilitate the film's international circulation operates simultaneously with narratives of collaboration surrounding the film's production. Pilkington/Garimara is listed in the film's credits as Script Consultant, and she has praised Noyce as 'excellent. He'd bring unfinished versions of particular scenes for me to view. There were two scenes that I objected to very, very strongly in the early drafts of script. So he asked me why and I told him' (Pilkington 2007, 145). Rachel Maza, the Indigenous acting coach for the child actors Sampi, Tianna Sansbury (Daisy) and Laura Monaghan (Gracie), also lauded Noyce's efforts to include the community: 'As far as white people go . . . Phillip's got integrity. He's asking all the right people, getting the right permission, taking the time it needs to take – and that doesn't always happen' (qtd in Chan 2008, 125). These references to dialogue and collaboration underpin a film adaptation version of told-to exchange that included representatives from Jigalong, who, Noyce recounts, were on 'set whenever we were depicting their country and people, to advise us on cultural matters' (qtd in Petzke 2007, 235). Although such collaboration is reassuring given the power dynamic of a white Australian male director adapting an Indigenous female writer's text, it is 'hard to assess and ensure Indigenous Australian output' (Chan 2008, 128) and 'impossible to know how equitable the negotiations actually were' (Thorner 2007, 142), filtered as they are largely through the film's publicity machinery. Further, significant elements of cultural specificity were altered in the film. Although the adult Molly's voice-over is spoken in Mardu, 'the Aboriginal language employed elsewhere in the film narrative is . . . Wangkatjunka' (Thorner 2007, 142) to accommodate the language spoken by Ningali and Myarn Lawford, the actors who play Molly's mother and grandmother, respectively. Most audience members, of course, will assume it is the same language spoken in the voice-over and in the scenes featuring these characters.

Additionally, much of the film was shot in South Australia rather than Western Australia as per the historical events and their detailing in Pilkington/Garimara's text, a decision justified by Noyce on the grounds that

> [t]he topography of Western Australia remains quite similar over vast distances . . . it would have been quite impractical to keep moving the cast and crew every couple of days to find a new kind of landscape that would help us to describe the enormity of the journey undertaken by these kids. (qtd in Thorner 2007, 142)

Unsurprisingly, the South Australian Film Corporation contributed to the film's funding. Although Western Australia and South Australia are adjacent states, the territory traversed by Molly, Daisy and Gracie is approximately 1,000 kilometres from the border between them. Given the importance of 'Indigenous place-based practices and associated forms of knowledge' (Coulthard and Simpson 2016, 254), or, as Leslie Marmon Silko (Laguna Pueblo) puts it, the fact that '[t]he stories cannot be separated from geographical locations, from actual physical places within the land' (qtd in Basso 1996, 64), such a geographical shift disrupts their story's connection to the land.

If the change of Indigenous language and the discrepancy between the setting and the location of filming compromise the adaptation's authenticity, the real-life footage of the elderly Molly and Daisy at the end of the film arguably partially restores that authenticity; it also underscores the historical facts of the Stolen Generations and the girls' escape. Given that right-wing commentators in Australia attempted to deny the veracity of the Stolen Generations (see Petzke 2007, 236; Collins and Davis 2004, 135–7), it appears that for some viewers, this emphasis on historical fact was necessary; if *Rabbit-Proof Fence* is 'the film that made Australia cry' (Elder 2016, 113), not all settler viewers were moved. Yet 'therapeutic weeping' (Hosking 2011, 232) has its limits, as Hughes D'aeth illustrates in his critique of the film's harnessing of 'the empathetic imperative of Hollywood film' (2002, para. 20). For empathy, as Kennedy contends, 'when it leads to an unexamined identification with the victim, may distract Australians from recognising our own positions as participants in and beneficiaries of colonisation' (2008, 163). If *Rabbit-Proof Fence* produced 'a wave of national non-Indigenous catharsis' (Elder 2016, 114), perhaps considered a good moral return on the state funds that supported it in excess of half the film's budget (see Chan 2008, 124), it enabled the processing of settler-colonial guilt and shame, not restitution for Indigenous dispossession.

The film does find ways to gesture towards 'the passive complicity of ordinary Australians in Indigenous child removal' (Kennedy 2008, 169). Kennedy reads the fence worker who witnesses the abduction of the three girls from Jigalong as representative of ordinary white Australians who witness 'uncomfortably at the margins' (2008, 169) without intervening. Another example arises later in the film through the white farmer's wife who helps the girls after their absconding from Moore River, giving them food and jackets for their journey. Yet she also informs the authorities that she has seen them, thus not only upholding and trusting in the white supremacist state structures that regulate Indigenous life but also doing so duplicitously by withholding this intention from the girls. She is not the ally she appears to be. The film illustrates this formally by presenting the farmhouse within a canted frame (recalling shots of Neville's office), indicating that the white woman's offer is suspect, as well as potentially underscoring the ideological foundations of Indigenous dispossession: she has caught Molly attempting to steal eggs, and scolded her, 'You want something to eat, you ask for it', bolstering white settler ownership and construing Molly as the intruder on stolen Indigenous land. But if the film highlights the apparently helpful white woman as problematic at best, the film's chief interest in producing empathy for the girls minimises the white audience's opportunity to 'reflec[t] critically on the compromised positions of the white characters' (Kennedy 2008, 169). The film's invitation to the audience 'to not just identify with Molly and the experience of being stolen, or having one's own child taken away, but to actually *be* her, seeing what she sees and feeling what she feels' (Potter and Schaffer 2004, para. 8), detracts from critical self-reflection in terms of ongoing settler-colonial dispossession of Indigenous peoples.

Granted, white Australians did not constitute the only audience for this film, as indeed was the intention of its producers. As 'one of the few Stolen Generations narratives to circulate internationally' (Kennedy 2008, 167), *Rabbit-Proof Fence* wields tremendous representational power in the global cultural marketplace. If the film is a 'produce[r] of what it means to be Aboriginal in Australia' (Thorner 2007, 147), it inevitably bears a responsibility of representation, particularly given that it was not made by an Indigenous filmmaker. Pilkington/Garimara refers positively to the film at the end of *Under the Wintamarra Tree*, which details her own experiences of being separated from her mother following Molly's reincarceration by the state: of *Rabbit-Proof Fence*, Pilkington/Garimara writes,

> That story was a privilege given to me by Auntie Daisy and my mother, to be shared with everybody all throughout this country and indeed the world. The film of their story has highlighted the issue of the Stolen Generation and has encouraged other people to take the step forward on the journey of healing as the film goes around nationally and internationally. Non-Indigenous people will be aware of what we are saying, of what the Stolen Generation means to Aboriginal people. (2002b, 206–7)[5]

Yet although the film brought the history of the Stolen Generations to an international audience, most of which would be unfamiliar with it, it was nevertheless made at the expense of local histories: 'Mum says that's not my story' (qtd in Thorner 2007, 142), Pilkington/Garimara reports of her mother's response to the film. Of course, in dramatising the girls' escape from Moore River and successful return home for Molly and Daisy, 'the extra-diegetic ending', which appears through subtitles, is 'without resolution or reconciliation' (Kennedy 2008, 171), given Molly's recapture after the birth of her two daughters. Although the footage of the elderly Molly and Daisy at Jigalong at the end of the film testifies to 'the ongoing-ness of their lives' (Potter and Schaffer 2004, para. 19), it also unwittingly demonstrates how a mainstream film positions itself as speaking for them: they are clearly speaking in the footage, but we do not hear what they are saying, as they are spoken over, and for, by the told-to adaptation.

Whale Rider

Whale Rider (2002), the film adaptation of Māori writer Witi Ihimaera's novel *The Whale Rider* (1987), was directed by Pākehā (i.e. white New Zealander) filmmaker Niki Caro. Like *Rabbit-Proof Fence*, this widely circulated adaptation features an Indigenous child, although Caro's film retains more focus on its source material's Indigenous protagonist than Noyce's does. Narratives surrounding the production of *Whale Rider* emphasise a collaboration between the director and Ngāti Konohi, the *hapū* (or clan) at Whangara, where the picture was shot on location, adding another layer of told-to discourse. Nonetheless, this adaptation, enormously successful in the global cultural marketplace, ultimately exhibits the cultural pitfalls of adapting an Indigenous text for global consumption, retrenching both Western aesthetic practices and epistemologies for profit.

Ihimaera's novel, *The Whale Rider*, retells a Traditional Story of Ngāti Porou (a Māori *iwi*, or people, of which Ngāti Konohi is a part):[6] the story of Paikea, first named Kahutia Te Rangi, who travelled to Aotearoa on the back of a whale (and who is the original whale rider). Ihimaera's novel focuses on a female descendant of Paikea, destined to be chief despite her great-grandfather Koro Apirana's objections because of her gender. Koro insists that the lineage of chiefs must pass from first-born son to first-born son. But his grandson, Porourangi, and his wife, Rehua, have a girl, whom they name after the mythic whale rider, Kahu. Koro is angered both by the fact that Kahu is female, breaking the male line, and the fact that her parents have named her as such, with encouragement from his wife, Nani Flowers, who is from another *iwi*, and whose own prominent ancestor was a powerful female chief, Muriwai. Koro is determined that Kahu is of no use to him, but she is fixated on him from her infancy, and gradually shows her leadership skills, her affinity with Māori culture and her 'kinship with the sea' (Ihimaera 1987, 80) – whales especially – over the course of her childhood. Meanwhile, Koro gives instruction to male members of the community to pass on their 'history and . . . customs. Just the men . . . because men were sacred. . . . [T]he purpose would be . . . to keep the Maori language going, and to increase the strength of the tribe' (Ihimaera 1987, 27). In conducting this teaching, Koro also hopes to identify 'a young boy . . . to pull the sword out of the stone' (55), that is, to be the prospective chief in his great-granddaughter's generation. Ultimately, however, no boy comes to fulfil this role; instead, it is Kahu who completes the ultimate challenge Koro sets for the boys (retrieving a carved stone from the depths of the sea), and who, amid a crisis involving stranded whales on the beach in their community at Whangara, becomes the new incarnation of the whale rider, leading the bull whale back to sea, and finally becoming recognised by Koro as the chief presumptive of her generation.

The novel is narrated by Kahu's uncle, Rawiri, the younger brother of Porourangi. Thus, Kahu is represented through her uncle's gaze, and at times at great geographical remove, as he spends some years away from

Whangara in Australia and Papua New Guinea before returning home. In Caro's film, the voice-over belongs to the protagonist, Pai (Keisha Castle-Hughes), whose name has been changed from Kahu in the adaptation, taking the whale rider's second name of Paikea instead. Other changes in the film include a downgrading of Rawiri's (Grant Roa's) significance, now that he is no longer narrator, and a removal of his experiences outside of Aotearoa New Zealand; indeed, there are no scenes outside of Aotearoa New Zealand, or even much beyond Whangara, in the film. In the novel, Porourangi is developing into the chief of his generation, while his father's generation goes entirely uncommented on; in the film, Porourangi (Cliff Curtis), now the son rather than grandson of Koro (Rawiri Paratene), explicitly refuses to take on the responsibility of chief. In both novel and film, Rehua (Elizabeth Skeen), his wife, dies after giving birth to their daughter. In the novel, Kahu is raised for her first six years by her maternal grandparents, before Porourangi moves back to Whangara and Kahu with him; he has another daughter with his second wife, Ana, exacerbating Koro's frustration with the interruption of the male line. In the film, Porourangi is an artist who has been working in Europe while his parents raise Pai. Now based in Germany, he returns home with the news that his new partner, a German woman named Anne (Jane O'Kane), is pregnant. Although he asks Pai to come stay with him in Germany after an argument between him and his father, she feels unable to leave due to her attachment to Whangara and Koro. As in the novel, she displays leadership skills, besting the boys Koro teaches at challenges he sets for them, and ultimately leading the bull amongst the stranded whales back to sea. For his part, Porourangi is shown as (probably temporarily) reabsorbed into the community at the end of the film, returned to complete the *waka* (war canoe) he had been carving but abandoned; the film ends with the *waka* being launched at sea, Pai and Koro sat together in the chiefs' position (Figure 6.2).

The film has been both celebrated and heavily criticised for its representation of Māori culture. Unlike *Rabbit-Proof Fence* and *The Lesser Blessed*, filmed at vast distances from the Indigenous territories where the stories take place, *Whale Rider* was shot on location at Whangara, and much has been made in both promotional materials and some criticism of the engagement with Ngāti Konohi and their involvement in the production. Virginia Pitts, based on her interviews with Caro, Ihimaera and Hone Taumaunu, the film's liaison with Ngāti Konohi, declares the film to be 'a genuinely dialogic intercultural encounter' (Pitts 2013, 60). Caro learned to speak Māori in preparation for making the film and clearly consulted with Ngāti Konohi during the filmmaking process; journalistic accounts and promotional materials emphasise the positive experience of both

Figure 6.2 Pai and Koro in the *waka* at the end of *Whale Rider*.

filmmaker and the community represented in the film (with many locals appearing on screen). Taumaunu has said of Caro, 'The fact she spoke Maori opened all the doors, and her humility grabbed our people, with her desire not to offend' (qtd in Shepheard 2003, 84). This dialogue and the opportunity for Ihimaera to comment on Caro's versions of the script suggest one of the more positive elements of the told-to paradigm outlined by McCall, that of 'a meeting ground for multiple voices' (5).

But there are also problems with identifying *Whale Rider* as 'a collaboration between [a] white director . . . and a local tribe' (Wilson 2011, 199). And indeed, the focus on the relationship between Ngāti Konohi and Caro echoes the discourse of told-to narratives in publishing: as McCall writes, 'Avowals of friendship, trust, mutual responsibility, shared agendas . . . are common' in the prefaces of told-to narratives (7). In briefing notes prepared to pre-empt criticism of the film based on its not having a Māori director, Ihimaera cautions, 'Don't hierarchise the director so much' (2001, [1]). Yet most of *Whale Rider*'s crew were Pākehā, not just its director. This fact contradicts the film's having been 'defined by many as a Māori film' (Leotta 2012, 108).[7] Stuart Murray argues that the film of *Whale Rider* is an example of using 'Indigenous narratives as "story material" for a wider commercial cinema that lacks an appropriate knowledge of the issues such films raise' (2008, 28). Indeed, *Whale Rider* has prompted debates over cultural property (McCall 2011, 4) that tend to accompany told-to narratives. A very public debate took place through a series of pieces in *Onfilm: New Zealand's Film, TV & Video Magazine* after an interview with the film's Pākehā producer, John Barnett, in which he describes his response to reading Ihimaera's novel:

> I was immediately in love with it because, for me, it was absolutely an international story – I never had a moment's doubt. It was absolutely specifically set here, it was absolutely a part of NZ, of Maori, of Ngati Porou, of Whangara, but I could think of 50 societies where the same issues were being debated and fought over. (2)

Barnett's framing of *The Whale Rider* as an international story intersects with Murray's concern about the use of Indigenous narratives as raw material for commercial cinema.

Māori filmmaker Barry Barclay criticised Barnett in the first of several open letters in *Onfilm* debating not just the authorship of *Whale Rider* but also the status of Māori filmmakers in Aotearoa New Zealand. In response to Barnett, Barclay declared,

> Many stories may be 'absolutely international' but, unless the rights are cleared, nobody can use them commercially. You're at pains to tell how you obtained the commercial (copyright) rights but, whatever you may have declared to Mäori in Whangara, whether you honourably cleared with Ngati Porou rights relevant under Mäori Custom Law may remain, for some Mäori at least, an open question. (2003b, 11)

There is therefore tension between the celebrated relationship of the filmmakers with Ngāti Konohi and the potential of the larger *iwi* to raise objections, as well as the responsibility of representing Māori culture more generally, particularly in an internationally circulated and celebrated film.

Further, for Barclay, *Whale Rider*'s Pākehā director must be contextualised by the fact that, at that point, at least ten years had elapsed since the last Māori-directed feature film funded by the New Zealand Film Commission (NZFC) that treated Māori culture as its subject (i.e. Lee Tamahori's *Once Were Warriors*).[8] Indeed, much was made of the fact that *Whale Rider* was funded in part by the New Zealand Film Production Fund (NZFPF), which was

> established in 2000 . . . to operate as an autonomous public–private partnership, partially funding one major feature per year (to ten times the average level of NZFC support) provided it (1) drew at least 40 percent of its funding from offshore sources; (2) was commercially viable; and (3) had 'significant' New Zealand content. (Werry 2011, 210)

Thus, the fund gave more money than usual to the production of this Pāhekā-directed film of a Māori story, at a time when Māori feature films, as Barclay points out, were not receiving support. At the same time 'a typically "third way" initiative' (Werry 2011, 210), NZFPF funding was contingent on financial support from and viability within overseas markets.

For his part, Ihimaera, author of the original novel and of many screenplay drafts before Caro's involvement, has spoken positively about the adaptation. His own discourse echoes Barnett's when he states, 'Although its [sic] based in Aotearoa, it tells a universal story that everybody in the world can relate to' (qtd in 'South Pacific Pictures' 2011, 12). Nevertheless, material in the archive points to Ihimaera's own concern with Māori cultural property in an exchange with Barnett. In response to an April 1998 draft of the screenplay attributed to Nancy Greystone, Ian Mune and himself, 'based on the novel by Witi Ihimaera', Ihimaera wrote a note on the cover letter sent by Barnett, stipulating: 'Tell John that I <u>must</u> be listed as <u>first</u> script writer, as this plus other versions is really the result of my <u>script</u> work. It's important that I protect my interest, and the <u>Maori</u> kaupapa of the project' (1998). As Te Ahukaramū Charles Royal explains, 'Kaupapa Māori' can

> refer to any particular plan of action created by Māori, expressing Māori aspirations and certain Māori values and principles. . . . [I]t is generally held that the design of the proposed action is created by Māori, reflecting Māori aspirations, ideals, values, and perspectives. (2017)

Thus, at this point in the adaptation process, Ihimaera expresses concern not only for his own but also collective cultural property.

Later, once Caro was on board, Ihimaera would write in the aforementioned briefing notes, 'I told John Barnett I would remove myself from scripting and trust to Niki's vision. In all this I retained my Associate Producer position' (2001, [3]). A comparison of scripts annotated by Ihimaera with later scripts (as well as the final film) indicates that Caro did adopt some of Ihimaera's minor changes (the occasional Māori word substituted for an English one, for instance, or the omission of some suggestive jokes).[9] However, it is notable that Ihimaera suggested more dialogue in Māori, which was not adopted. Over the course of Caro's drafts, the screenplay contains less Māori linguistic and cultural content with each iteration. (For instance, even Caro's first draft – drawing on Ihimaera's earlier versions – begins with the figure of Paikea himself, who is eliminated before the shooting script.) The final screenplay that is annotated by Ihimaera, dated 18 October 2001, indicates very few moments where he finds the screenplay offensive or otherwise inappropriate for the Māori community: a boy dressed as a whale farting in the meeting house; a joke about cigarette-smoking vaginas; and the use of a crane to lift the *waka* at the end of the film. All these elements were retained in the final version. Although ultimately Taumaunu and Ihimaera 'granted their approval' (Pitts 2013, 51) of the film's final cut, *Whale Rider*'s status as 'a contemporary exemplar of bicultural creative practice' (Murdoch 2003, 98) masks the fact that Ihimaera expressed his displeasure with some of these elements in more than one version of the screenplay, but Caro did not make the requested alterations.

Part of the shift away from Māori cultural content in the film includes a recasting of the narrative through a lens of what Tānia Ka'ai refers to as 'Eurocentric feminisms' that Caro 'enlists . . . as the basis of her writing and film directing' (2005, 2). Pai appears more oppositional than in the novel in her challenging of her patriarchal grandfather in ways that are more legible to Western feminism, or 'the non-Maori theme of "girl power"' (Fatzinger 2016, 314). For instance, she sits next to the men in front of the meeting house on the marae where custom dictates that she should not (and she is thrown off the marae by her grandfather as a result). Caro herself has admitted, 'When you watch this film with a Maori audience, and she sits, and she sits *there*, in the front, with the men, you can hear an audible gasp: it is so transgressive what she does' (2008). Caro sounds triumphant when she articulates this transgression, as though she herself has liberated Pai from a homogeneous patriarchy that Caro's film has constructed in the first place.[10] In contrast to the suggestion of *Whale Rider*'s narrative, 'seen through Pākehā eyes, and not without a degree of condescension' (Fox 2017, 158), Ka'ai points out that Ngāti Porou is particularly renowned for 'women . . . assum[ing] key leadership roles in the *iwi*' (2005, 5). Māori women's roles on the marae, as Kathie Irwin argues, are particularly misunderstood by Western feminism, which has no way of acknowledging how women speak on the marae or the significance of 'highly valued Māori oral arts' (1993, 12).[11] Radhika Mohanram argues that a Western conception of identity politics constructs an 'additive model', in which 'indigenous women in Aotearoa New Zealand, led by their Pākehā counterparts, discover their identity as oppressed women *prior to* their awareness of their identity as oppressed Maori women' (1996, 60). This model is certainly in evidence in the film's rendering of Pai: oppressed as female while her racialised identity as Māori seemingly has no impact on her life.

Curiously, given Ihimaera's original text (as well as screenplay drafts), the film all but erases Pai's powerful female ancestry. At the beginning of Kahu's story, Koro complains to his wife that her 'female side [is] too strong' (1987, 10), holding Nani Flowers responsible for the fact that Kahu is female. Early in the novel, Nani Flowers invokes her own ancestor: 'I'm a descendant of old Muriwai, and *she* was the greatest chief of my tribe' (13). As Ka'ai points out, the film's focus is limited 'solely to one ancestor, Paikea' (2005, 3). Muriwai is diminished to a brief mention from Nanny [*sic*] Flowers (Vicky Haughton) to Pai while they talk in the unfinished *waka* after Koro explodes in anger at Pai's use of the *taiaha* on the marae: 'You've got the blood of Muriwai in your veins, girl.' Caro's August 2001 script included a longer explanation of Muriwai's significance in this scene (58), but as Caro later indicated,

> It's actually an amazing legend, but one of those situations where it sort of . . . made the scene drag a little bit. And it was enough just for Nanny to be there, and her very kind of strong, gentle self urging Pai to totally disobey her grandfather. (2008)

Thus, the audience has no context for Muriwai's significance, or the fact that she saved a canoe full of members of her community by '*mak[ing] [her]self a man*' (Ihimaera 1987, 15) and paddling them to safety.[12] Just as Caro's Eurocentric feminism frames Pai's narrative as a struggle against a patriarchal culture, with even the filming of Pai constructed so that 'her interactions with her elders are in opposition' (Joyce 2009, 247), so too Caro's sense of Western film aesthetics trumps the significance of Pai's female ancestor, allowing the protagonist's lineage to appear completely dominated by Paikea.

Whale Rider provides an example of how 'Māori culture is thrown into the global market where it functions like any other commodity' (Leotta 2012, 120). In fact, the film itself gestures towards the global commodification of Māori culture, through Porourangi's career as a sculptor. In the film, Koro and Porourangi clash after a slide show of the latter's art, interrupted by images of his new – and pregnant – German partner, Anne, thus giving way to arguments about his future and his relationship to his family and community. Porourangi's sculpture, which we only see through the mediation of the slide show projected on a sheet suspended in his parents' living room, 'may be influenced by traditional Maori carving but bears little resemblance to it' (Heffelfinger and Wright 2011, 91). During the argument with his father, Porourangi says, 'I'm not here shovelling shit, but Dad, I'm doing my share. . . . Did you even see my work? Did you . . . even look at it?' Koro replies, 'You call it work. It's not work. It's souvenirs.' Koro obviously deflates the significance of Porourangi's art in both aesthetic and labour terms. For Chris Prentice, this line 'is an ambivalent moment', given the undermining of Koro's perspective through his treatment of Pai, on the one hand, and Koro's 'evo[cation of] a problem that remains unarticulated: the disappearance of culture's symbolic dimension in favour of its objectification' (2006, 264, 265), on the other.

If Māori critic Brendan Hokowhitu reads this moment as a way of critiquing Caro's film itself – 'Just as Koro chastises Porourangi for selling sculptures to Europeans by invalidating his son's art as "not work" but "souvenirs", I chastise the filmmakers for creating a simplistic and possibly dangerous depiction' (2008, 133) – an earlier version (July 2000) of Caro's screenplay, with Bill Gavin, presents a slightly different inflection of this scene, one that arguably (and still unwittingly) undermines the film. In this version, Porourangi returns to Whangara with the express purpose of taking Pai back with him to Germany.[13] His exchange with Koro about his daughter and his work unfolds as follows:

> POROURANGI: There's a whole world out there, Koro. She deserves to see it.
> KORO: Like you've seen it?
> POROURANGI: Why not?
> KORO: Nice way to see the world, riding on the back of your culture. . . .
> POROURANGI: So I'm not back here shoveling shit, but I'm serving our people.
> KORO: That what you call it?
> POROURANGI: That's what it is. I'm taking the Maori culture out into the world.
> KORO: No, boy. It's taking you. (Caro and Gavin 2000, 28–9)

I suggest that, ironically, this scene having been scripted by Caro, this notion of Māori culture being the vehicle for an outsider's artistic and commercial success characterises the dynamic at play in and around *Whale Rider*.

If many specificities of Māori culture have been flattened out in Caro's adaptation, the film also, significantly, removes all the novel's white characters. Consequently, although on the one hand the excision of white characters enables a near-exclusive focus on a Māori community, on the other hand, the film also 'remove[s] the backdrop of the colonial reality and, in so doing, purge[s] Pākehā and other Westerners of any responsibility for the oppression of indigenous peoples' (Hokowhitu 2008, 128). In implying 'the suppression of [Māori] people by their own primitive traditions' (Hokowhitu 2007, 58) rather than by colonialism, the film therefore diverges sharply from the novel. In *The Whale Rider*, Rawiri refers to participating in the Springbok protests of 1981 (Ihimaera 1987, 30), where Māori especially objected to the New Zealand government's welcome of apartheid South Africa's all-white rugby team, and he details the racism he both witnesses and is personally subject to when staying with his white friend Jeff's family in Papua New Guinea, where he travels to work on the family's plantation. Meeting Jeff's mother, Rawiri recounts, 'Although Jeff had told her I was a Maori it was obvious that I was still too dark' (53); further, when Jeff accidentally hits one of his Indigenous employees with his car, his mother convinces him to drive away: 'His tribe could be on us any second. Payback, it could be payback for us. It's only a native' (58), much to Rawiri's disgust. Closer to home, the novel (as well as earlier drafts of the screenplay authored by Ihimaera) also points to Māori political engagement with the settler-colonial state. In the novel's first instance of whale stranding (there are two, as opposed to the single incident at Whangara in the film), Koro and Porourangi are on the South Island for a land dispute (88). If the novel, as Werry notes, 'takes place against the broad sweep of global postcolonial activism', the interpenetration of 'indigenous rights, ecological justice, and antiracist causes' (2011, 215) finds no equivalent in the film.

In addition to the told-to premise of Caro's adaptation, *Whale Rider* is a New Zealand–Germany co-production, with implications for the narrative.[14] The only white character in the film is Anne, in a non-speaking role, Porourangi's German partner (the Māori woman Ana in the novel). Europe figures as a space in which Pai's father can be truly appreciated for his work, and the film shows no negative portrayal of white people, unlike the novel's exploration of the racism faced by Rawiri. Porourangi, played sympathetically by Cliff Curtis, is properly appreciated within a European art institutional context, the film suggests, and discarded by his own people as represented in the figure of his father. Partly reliant on German funds for its very existence, the film's gesture towards the superior taste of a discerning European audience presents a troubling imbalance of cultural power between Māori and non-Indigenous cultures.

In his open letter to John Barnett in *Onfilm*, Barry Barclay writes, 'There will be a Mäori opinion . . . on whether we have in *Whale Rider* true pounamu [i.e. a treasure or something of value] or true plastic. That opinion may be decades in the coming' (2003b, 14). Two decades now after the film's release, it seems there are some divisions in Māori views of the adaptation, given the discrepancy between Ihimaera's and Ngāti Konohi's celebration of the film and objections raised by Māori filmmakers and critics. Part of the issue concerns the scale and the stakes of representativeness: as Janet Wilson notes, *Whale Rider* 'implies that the Māori are a single, homogeneous people, while the specific Māori genealogical story, which is true of only one or two tribes, is introduced as though it is generally relevant' (2011, 208). Certainly, *Whale Rider* is a long way from the Fourth Cinema theorised and advocated by Barclay himself, given the funding structure that underpins Caro's film that dictates it was always already oriented to the global market, rather than for a Māori audience.

Indeed, the public–private funds that birthed *Whale Rider* set limits on the 'specific form . . . Māori personhood and property have to take to be legible, valuable, and trafficable in the global culturescape' (Werry 2011, 212). As Hokowhitu writes, 'The market logic . . . privileges the western gaze as the perspective that has to be satiated' (2007, 54). The elimination of a historical frame of colonialism caters precisely to that gaze and its satiation, given how 'the "western" world would so much like to be convinced that indigenous populations can recover from European settlement' (Rauwerda 2004, para. 7) as a means of absolution. For Pākehā critic Claire Murdoch, *Whale Rider* ultimately 'give[s] the jaded contemporary film-festival consumer access to an easy poetic "they", an ethnic exotic, a ready-coded "meaningful" that is too easily misunderstood' (104) as part of an '"indigenous-yet-accessible" recipe' (105). I would particularly argue that is the case given the increasing erosion of Māori culture over the course of the film's scriptwriting, especially once the Pākehā director becomes involved. If *Whale Rider* was hailed as an immense international success, this told-to adaptation nevertheless demonstrates the ambivalences of representing and circulating Indigeneity in the global cultural marketplace.

The Lesser Blessed

Richard Van Camp's novel *The Lesser Blessed* (1996) was the first book by a Tłįchǫ (Dogrib) author to be published. The film adaptation, written and directed by Ukrainian-Canadian filmmaker Anita Doron, was released in 2012. Although this film features a young protagonist in the teenager Larry Sole, it does not provide an 'uplifting' story of an Indigenous child as *Rabbit-Proof Fence* or *Whale Rider*, and did not have the same exposure as these two prior films, as it was released only in Canada. However, it is a significant adaptation insofar as the narrative of the source text rests on the intergenerational violence of Indian Residential Schools, and the film was made during the period of Canada's Truth and Reconciliation Commission (TRC, 2008–15) to address the state-sanctioned violence towards Indigenous children for more than a century during the operation of the schools. Although the adaptation is timely, the excision of some essential cultural specificities of the narrative operates to universalise the film at the same time as, implicitly, the film addresses an insider audience in the form of the novel's readers through a strategy of selective translation. The film offers, in many ways, a sensitive reading of Van Camp's novel, yet it removes the residential school context that underpins the source text, vacating the narrative of a framework through which to understand the violence within the family of its protagonist.

There are many close resemblances between the film and Van Camp's novel, despite some simplification (multiple antagonists at Larry's school in the novel version, for instance, are combined in the film in the character of Darcy McMannus). The film's overarching narrative matches the novel's, focusing on Larry's relationships to a new student at school, Johnny Beck, and his girlfriend, Juliet Hope (also the object of Larry's affection), as well as to his mother and her on-again, off-again boyfriend, Jed. Some details regarding Indigenous identities are changed in the film version: in the novel, Johnny is Métis; in the film, his nation is not disclosed. In the novel, Jed is Slavey; the film leaves his nation unspecified (although, as in the novel, he wears a Denendeh: One Land One People T-shirt, which encompasses both Slavey and Tłı̨chǫ/Dogrib, as well as Chipewyan, Yellowknives and Sahtu). In terms of representing Indigenous territories, although Joel Nathan Evans, who plays Larry, is from Fort Smith, NWT (Richard Van Camp's home-town and the model for the fictionalised Fort Simmer in the novel), location shooting took place not in the Northwest Territories, where the book is set, but in Sudbury. This geographical move is even greater than that between *Rabbit-Proof Fence*'s Western Australian journey and South Australian film-ing, as Sudbury is in Atikameksheng Anishnawbek territory, some sixteen latitudes and 4,000 kilometres to the south of Fort Smith. What is presented to the audience as the Northwest Territories is, in fact, Ontario, a reflection, no doubt, of the film's funding in part by the Northern Ontario Heritage Fund Corporation and Ontario Media Development Corporation.

On the one hand, 'Fort Simmer' is itself a fictional place, albeit based on Fort Smith: as Van Camp explains,

> If I had done this story in Fort Smith it might trigger people from Fort Smith with things that have happened in our history that people still don't want to talk about. I think when you create a fictional community in a way you're creating a safe place for people to read and not be triggered, in a way you're being a ninja yourself as the author by giving a community that doesn't exist on paper but can really be anywhere. It can be Fort Smith, it can be Hay River, it can be the ghost of Pine Point, it can be a little bit of Inuvik, it can be a suburb of Yellowknife. (Qtd in Wilson 2008)

For Van Camp, then, 'Fort Simmer' allows a malleability that not only pro-tects residents of Fort Smith but also enables him (and, presumably, read-ers) to draw connections with other northern communities. Significantly, however, all of Van Camp's examples of other locations are in the Northwest Territories. Although Sudbury is far from Ontario's centre of political and economic power in the southern part of the province, it is still a great deal closer to it than any of the locations in Van Camp's Northwest Territories litany. The economics of film production have immense implications, not just for the way in which texts are produced but also for the texts themselves that are produced, what is rendered visible, what representation looks like – whether it does, in fact, represent.

Just as the Northwest Territories themselves are absent from the film, so too is the history that underpins how Larry came to live in Fort Simmer, away from Dogrib territory. In both the novel and the film, Larry bears scars on his body from being badly burned (see Figure 6.3), and his past traumatic experiences appear through 'fragmentary flashbacks [as] we put together Larry's horrific history' (Fagan 2009, 212), one that includes sexual abuse by his father, the witnessing of his father's sexual violence towards his mother and aunt, and the death of his father by 'smoke inhalation and contusions to his skull' (Van Camp 1996, 1), for which, the novel hints, Larry is responsible. The novel begins with a brief section, 'Me', in which Larry obsesses about the word 'NO':

> I scratch with a knife the word NO a hundred million times on the back of all the mirrors in our house, so my mother sees that I say NO to her, so my mother sees that I say NO to my father, so my mother sees that I say NO to the world, and to the acts unforgivable. (1)

Larry's clear opposition to his parents here is juxtaposed to the following section, 'Them', which consists of the newspaper report of an unnamed Dogrib man dying in a fire in Fort Rae (1), whom we understand to be Larry's father. In the film, we see Larry start the fire that kills his father, a reaction to his father's abusive behaviour (the sexual abuse only hinted at in the film, whereas the novel is more explicit). In both the novel and the film, his mother has also suffered violence from his father, to the point where '[t]he tear duct my father had destroyed would never work again, so even though she made the sounds of crying, nothing came' (82). But in the novel Larry's mother is complicit in both his abuse and, it is suggested, the rape of her sister by her husband.

The novel contextualises this violence in relation to residential schools. As Lauren Vedal observes, Larry's recollection that his father would speak French when he drank 'gestures to the culturally genocidal mission' of the residential school system (2013, 112). In one flashback, Larry's father speaks French before raping his unconscious wife with a broomstick: 'My mom was passed out on the couch. . . . This was back when she used to drink. She had gone to the residential schools, too' (58). There is no narrative of what happened at residential schools to either Larry's father

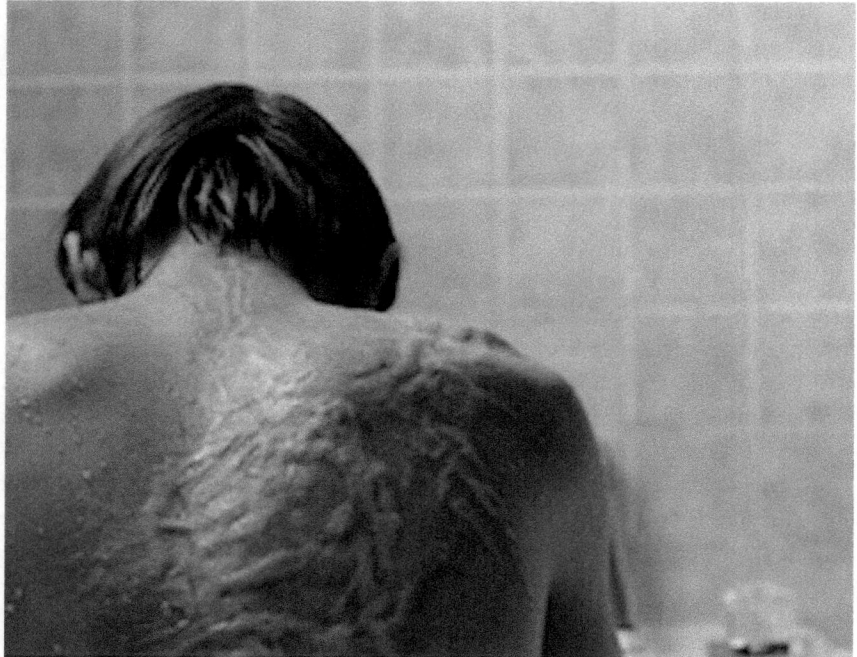

Figure 6.3 Shot of Larry's scars in *The Lesser Blessed*.

or his mother, and the novel's invocation of residential schools is fleeting. Nevertheless, as Vedal points out, 'Larry's father serves a figurative role, embodying the continued impact of violence long after the event' (2013, 113) – the event that we, as readers, must infer. These references, and this inference, constitute the colonial context for the violence of Larry's father in the novel (as well as his mother's complicity prior to her recovery from alcoholism). In the film, there is no sense of Larry's mother having been complicit in the violence (only that she herself was also a victim); but neither is there any reference to residential schools to provide context for that violence as 'the potential aftermath of genocidal practice' (McKegney 2009, 212). Whereas, in the novel, '[b]oth Larry's mother and father pass on the violence of the schools, demonstrating how the schools left psychic scarring not just in the immediate victims but in their descendants as well' (Vedal 2013, 113), the film positions Larry's father as the site of that violence's origin, thus implicitly absolving the Canadian state as the film eschews a systemic, colonial context in its framing.

The removal of the Indian Residential Schools context from the narrative dovetails with some of the comments made by Doron, the director, about the making of this film. Addressing her position as a non-Indigenous filmmaker adapting an Indigenous text, Doron focuses on the 'many shared experiences' between people:

> I can understand the specifics, but the general, the experience of being a teenager in a small community, being different than the people around you, being a headbanger – those basic things I understand, from a different angle but it's the same experience . . . I never felt like I cannot be telling this story because I am not Native. Larry happens to be Native. It doesn't matter if he's Native, Jewish from [the] Soviet Union – we share experiences and that's enough to tell an authentic story. (2013)

Doron demonstrates a concern, then, with the authenticity of her told-to adaptation, and rests her claim to authenticity on a universalising of adolescent experience, one that presumably cannot accommodate the historical and socio-cultural contexts of residential schools. Doron continues,

> You watch a story about a kid in the Northwest Territories and you realize that 'I know how that feels' and 'I have those moments,' and you fill in the nooks in yourself with the parallels you have with the character, and then the different becomes familiar, and we feel all a bit more like a family, and I think that's what good films can do – we just erase borders, erase differences, erase all the things that make us hate each other and fear each other and fight with each other – and make us feel a bit more closer. (2013)

For Doron, then, the purpose of the film is to reflect back on the viewer, reminding them of themselves – their own experience and their own cultural context. As such, Larry's narrative (which, for Doron, just 'happens to be Native') is something always already to be translated by a non-Indigenous audience to reinforce their own worldview.

Comments by cast members echo Doron's perspective in varying ways: Benjamin Bratt, who plays Jed, Larry's step-father figure, considers the film to offer a 'universal . . . depiction of [a] teenager in crisis' (2013). Tamara Podemski, who plays Verna, Larry's mother, links the film more closely to contemporary Indigenous experience, gesturing towards the 'rising demographic of [Indigenous] youth', for instance (2013). Although Podemski talks of the film's 'messages of family, the messages of overcoming trauma, the messages of the loner in high school' (2013) that intersect with the universalising discourse of Doron and Bratt, she returns these 'messages' to the experiences of Indigenous youth in her commentary. Yet Podemski also makes a crucial observation that implicates a non-Indigenous audience, praising Doron's 'sensitivity to convey it [the narrative] in a way that won't scare people' (2013). Podemski does not specify what might be considered particularly 'scary' about the source text – Larry's abuse by his father? the references to residential schools? – but her complimenting of Doron for her sensitivity invokes a white fragility on the part of the anticipated audience, one that is particularly perplexing given the work of the TRC that was ongoing at the time of the film's production.

Doron's desire to 'erase borders' through film also indicates an ambition to reach a large international audience, something the novel's author and executive producer of the film, Van Camp, echoes: 'I think the international community will be drawn to this' (2013). As Van Camp suggests, the casting of the film is designed to attract a non-Canadian audience (one that did not ultimately materialise in cinematic release). Although Podemski is familiar to Canadian audiences (known for her roles in the film *Dance Me Outside* and the CBC TV series spin-off *The Rez*; see Chapter 5), Larry is played by first-time film actor Joel Nathan Evans. The other key Indigenous roles in the film, Jed and Johnny, are played by Hollywood actors Bratt (of *Law and Order* fame) and Kiowa Gordon (best known for *Twilight*). Van Camp speaks of an *American* audience being particularly attracted to the film 'because of Benjamin Bratt . . . they want to see what he's up to – he has many, many fans', as does Gordon.[15] Bratt's mother is a Quechua activist, originally from Peru; Gordon, despite his birth in Berlin, is a member of the Hualapai, whose territory is in northern Arizona. In the film's casting, therefore, a hemispheric Indigeneity stands in for the specificities of Indigenous identities in the novel, at the same time as this hemispheric Indigeneity circulates into Canadian cinema – the film of *The Lesser Blessed* – via Hollywood.

If Indigenous identities are translated into other Indigenous identities (and indeed, Podemski may be from north of the 49th parallel, but she is Anishinaabe, not Tłįchǫ), and Doron's discourse about the film rests on a translation of Indigenous histories and narratives into non-Indigenous experience, the film does make a particular use of language that both incorporates and diverges from the novel in its *lack* of translation. In the novel, Larry speaks 'Raven Talk', which he explains for the reader, as in the following exchange with Johnny:

> 'You bet!' I called out. '. . . Sol later.' 'Sol later' is Raven Talk. It's 'see you later' said really fast. The correct response is 'Sol' but Johnny didn't say it. (14)

Johnny is a newcomer in Fort Simmer at this stage (and most readers of the novel could be considered 'newcomers' as well). In the film, although Larry greets Johnny in Dogrib, then explains that that means 'How are you', there is no translation given for the exchanges between Larry and Jed and Larry and Donny, Johnny's younger brother, in Raven Talk. Just as Raven Talk identifies who is 'in the know' (qtd in Vranckx 2011, 295), so too the film's lack of translation creates insiders within the audience (those familiar with Raven Talk, the novel's readers) as it excludes those who cannot provide the translation themselves. This decision on the part of the filmmakers contrasts with the universalising impulse behind the film.

Van Camp's enthusiasm for the film adaptation of his novel echoes the universalising discourse of Doron in many ways, identifying *The Lesser Blessed* as a 'coming of age story', a 'love story', a 'story of redemption', 'a celebration of the resiliency of the human spirit' and a 'story of forgiveness' (2013), all narratives that would presumably appeal to an audience beyond both Canada and the novel's readership. The invocation of forgiveness here, in the context of a novel that identifies residential schools as the point of origin of violence in Larry's family, suggests the discourse of reconciliation, one that has become fused with Indian Residential Schools through the TRC's work (which began after the novel's publication in 1996 but was in progress at the time of the film's production). It may be that the role of forgiveness in the film is meant to stand in for the absent context of residential schools; yet forgiveness arises in the adaptation primarily through Larry and his mother. In a sequence that is not in the novel, Larry runs away from home after Darcy tells other students at the school about Larry having burned his father to death. When Jed ultimately finds Larry in the wilderness and brings him home, his mother says, 'I'm sorry, Larry. Forgive me?' The film does not include elements of Larry's family history, such as his father's raping his mother or his aunt, and his mother's denial of her husband's rape of her sister. As such, in the film, Verna implicitly seeks her son's forgiveness for staying with his father despite his abuse of them both, for not preventing Larry's need to murder his father in order to save them.

In terms of the larger context of the TRC, then, although the novel identifies residential schools as the origin of violence within Larry's family, in the film forgiveness needs to happen within the Indigenous family unit, with no external colonial structure to explain what has led to that violence. Thus, as in Glen Coulthard's (Yellowknives Dene) critique of settler-colonial states' politics of reconciliation, 'state-sanctioned approaches to reconciliation must . . . purposely disentangle processes of reconciliation from questions of settler-coloniality as such' (2014, 108). As far as the film is concerned, a white audience need not feel implicated in the destructiveness of the Indigenous family unit: forgiveness is for Verna to ask and Larry to bestow. If, as Audra Simpson (Mohawk) observes, 'The settler state is asking to forgive and to forget, with no land back, no justice and no peace' (2016), the interpersonal forgiveness of Larry and his mother ignores the state altogether, and the spectre of restitution need not even arise for the white viewer.

Tellingly, Van Camp claims, 'I think this is our *Atanarjuat*, I think this is our *Rabbit-Proof Fence*, I think this is our *Whale Rider*' (2013). Besides Zacharias Kunuk's *Atanarjuat*, produced within the context of Isuma's community production ethos (see Chapter 7), Van Camp invokes other told-to adaptations as models, those adaptation pairings discussed earlier in this chapter. Despite the pitfalls of *Rabbit-Proof Fence* and *Whale Rider* in terms of the adaptation of Indigenous texts by non-Indigenous film-makers, Van Camp likely invokes them here because of the success represented by their global circulation, one that *The Lesser Blessed* would not ultimately match (despite a positive review in *The Hollywood Reporter*, which praised it as a 'coming-of-age film that weaves its cultural themes into the narrative without coming off like it's trying to teach you something', one that 'offer[s] some stylish visual flourishes without interfering with the picture's convincing hinterlands atmosphere' ['Lesser Blessed' 2013]). If told-to adaptations generate contact zones between Indigenous and non-Indigenous artists, from the point of view of those involved in the making of *The Lesser Blessed*, the objective appears to be a proliferation of contact zones through enhanced circulation of the film, but one that is perhaps effected through a flattening of cultural context and a universalism that was designed to travel (even if it failed in travelling) unimpeded across the globe.

Just as 'told-to narratives [are] tightly bound up in [a] history of dispossession' (McCall 2011, 27), so too all three adaptations examined in this chapter raise questions about cultural property, exchange and authorship. Each Indigenous author adapted in the films discussed has spoken positively about the result of the adaptation process, and indicated a desire for or a sense of gratification about the ability of their narrative to travel beyond the borders of the territories where these stories were produced. But just as in told-to narratives, non-Indigenous brokers may consider themselves to be '"giv[ing] voice" to marginalized Aboriginal groups' while 'sometimes overlook[ing] their own role as mediators in cross-cultural dialogues and exchanges' (McCall 2011, 13), so too do film adaptations of Indigenous-authored works circulate the content of their source material more widely while also mediating and modulating it in the interests of a non-Indigenous, international audience. Thus, while the 'voice' of the source material may be heard by a greater number of viewers, that 'voice' is invariably inflected by the economics of a global cultural marketplace that privileges the entertainment of a non-Indigenous audience.

CHAPTER 7

Indigenous Representational Sovereignty:
Once Were Warriors and *Atanarjuat: The Fast Runner*

Once Were Warriors (1994), directed by Lee Tamahori, and *Atanarjuat: The Fast Runner* (2001), directed by Zacharias Kunuk, are both Indigenous films adapted from Indigenous source materials: Alan Duff's novel *Once Were Warriors* (1990), and an Inuit Traditional Story, respectively. These films were made a world away from each other, at the bottom of the southern hemisphere in Aotearoa New Zealand and the top of the northern hemisphere in Nunavut, and they present starkly different worlds: an impoverished and dispossessed Māori community in late-twentieth-century Auckland; and a sixteenth-century Inuit community in Igloolik and beyond. The pairing of these two adaptations demonstrates a range of Indigenous narratives and filmmaking practices.

Despite the vast differences in geography, territory, narrative and language, however, *Once Were Warriors* and *Atanarjuat: The Fast Runner* share key features of production, circulation and reception. Both films were made with a large proportion of Indigenous crew members: 'half the crew' of *Once Were Warriors* were Māori, according to its director (Tamahori 1995, 27); and all but the director of photography for *Atanarjuat: The Fast Runner* were Inuit. Both films were landmarks of the cinemas of the respective settler-colonial nation-states that claim them: *Once Were Warriors* was the highest-grossing film of Aotearoa New Zealand at that point; *Atanarjuat: The Fast Runner*, the first feature film entirely in Inuktitut, was the highest-grossing Canadian film in 2002. That both films also found success on the international festival and art-house circuit further testifies to their dual audiences at home and abroad, although 'at home' audiences do not simply encompass the nation-state. Pākehā viewers in Aotearoa New Zealand and 'Southern' viewers in Canada are not insider audiences for these films. Both films either minimise or eschew the presence of white people: for *Once Were Warriors*, this near-excision runs counter to the source text of Duff's novel; for *Atanarjuat: The Fast Runner*, the historical narrative dictates this absence. Both films also alter their source material, most significantly in the narratives' respective endings. Questions of fidelity in relation to film adaptation are internal rather than external to the Indigenous communities relevant to these projects, in contrast to the adaptations examined in the previous chapter: changes are not imposed by non-Indigenous screenwriters and filmmakers. Yet in each case, they do have implications that may particularly affect – and attract – an international, non-Indigenous audience.

I position both these adaptations as examples of Indigenous representational sovereignty, understanding that sovereignty as a starting point, rather than suggesting it is an end goal that erases complexities of representation and production choices. As Brendan Hokowhitu (Māori) writes, 'Indigenous sovereignty refers to the way Indigenous peoples choose to represent their worlds' (2013, 119). Further, in comparing Indigenous films across the globe from each other, it is essential to bear in mind the different valences of sovereignty for the Inuit and the Māori. Māori filmmaker Barry Barclay's seminal theorisation of Fourth Cinema provides a crucial context for the discussion of these two films. But as *Once Were Warriors* and *Atanarjuat* are both adaptations, I use the term Indigenous representational sovereignty to encapsulate both the Indigenous-produced source material, the film incarnation and the relationship between them. Randolph Lewis's conception of representational sovereignty encompasses the connections between 'cultural and political self-determination' and 'representational self-determination' (2006, xxiii). Further, he argues that

> the cinema of sovereignty is about authority, autonomy, and accountability in the representational process. . . . [I]t is the embodiment of an insider's perspective, one that is attuned to cultural subtleties in the process of imagemaking [*sic*] as well as in the final image itself. (2006, 180)

As Linda Tuhiwai Smith (Māori) writes, 'Indigenous peoples want to tell our own stories, write our own versions, in our own ways, for our own purposes' (2012, 72). If these narratives are to remain Indigenous people's 'own stories', their cinema of sovereignty cannot be made by non-Indigenous filmmakers, in contrast to the examples of the previous chapters. In Barclay's own notion of 'image sovereignty', community is paramount: 'the sovereign community is ultimately what the Indigenous image expresses' (Turner 2013, 222).

Representational sovereignty underscores both the cultural and political significance of Indigenous peoples telling their own stories. The form that political sovereignty takes may differ between Indigenous peoples. Stephen Turner writes of Māori notions of sovereignty,

> not . . . in the sense of nationhood, which has never been a collective ambition of Maori, nor in the sense of a politics of identity or simple 'struggle for recognition.' For the primary struggle is . . . to recognize themselves, to understand who they are in a way they take to be appropriate or adequate to where they are from (at once a place and a history). (2002, 80)

The concept of sovereignty 'imperfectly translates what would appear the Maori equivalent, *tino rangatiratanga*, which combines chieftainship with the domain or territory of chiefly kin. Sovereignty is commonly expressed in the form of a kinship grouping' (80). For Turner, most relevant to discussion of Māori narratives, questions 'inseparable from sovereignty' include '"whose is the claim to know" or "who are you that claims to know?"' (81), questions that intersect with Lewis's view of the cinema of sovereignty.

Although Barclay viewed Fourth Cinema as able to 'contain the multiple forms of Indigenous cinema as it operates on an international level' (Murray 2008, 2), given common experiences of Indigenous peoples across the world of being '[d]ispossessed by colonisation and the practices of the nation state, and further threatened by the forces of globalisation in the contemporary era' (11), local nation–state formations have had a particular impact on the shape that state-sanctioned Indigenous rights and sovereignties take, with concomitant effects for culture in both broad and specific terms. In Aotearoa New Zealand, the Treaty of Waitangi (1840) and the Waitangi Tribunal (1975) and their legacies have produced divisions between 'pan-Maori organizations, particularly urban Maori groupings' and 'a significant strand of Maori-dom [that] dispute[s] that there is any such whole and maintain tribal allegiance as the primary source of identification. This split is . . . is in fact constitutive of Maori-ness and any notion of Maori sovereignty' (Turner 2002, 85). In a Canadian context, with Indigenous groups consisting of the Inuit, the Métis and the First Nations, the latter encompassing a multitude of Indigenous nations with numerous language groups, it is the First Nations particularly that have been subject to the Indian Act (1976), although the Inuit and Métis have also been profoundly dispossessed by the nation-state. The Inuit are especially politically distinct through the formation of Nunavut as Canada's third territory in 1999. As a territory of Canada, Nunavut is governed by the Government of Nunavut through parliamentary politics, as is non-Indigenous politics in the rest of Canada. The Nunavut settlement is not a template for other Indigenous nations in Canada, and conceptions of sovereignty are not uniform between different Indigenous peoples in Canada.[1] Another crucial element shared by Indigenous filmmakers in Aotearoa New Zealand and Canada, as is the case for *Once Were Warriors* and *Atanarjuat: The Fast Runner*, is the funding from the settler-colonial nation-state that underpins these productions, even as, as Barclay has written, 'Indigenous cultures "are outside the national outlook *by definition*"' (qtd in Murray 2008, 16). Thus, in many cases, expressions of Indigenous representational sovereignty are nonetheless bound up in the funding structures of the nation-state.[2]

Both Aotearoa New Zealand and Canada are settler-colonial nation-states officially committed to 'ethnic recognition . . . [as] a defining mandate' (Werry 2011, 192), Aotearoa New Zealand under the aegis of biculturalism and Canada through multiculturalism. Whereas Aotearoa New Zealand's biculturalism 'implies coexistence between Māori and Pākehā' (Johnston 2014, 8), Canada's official multiculturalism in fact sidesteps both Indigenous peoples and, curiously, Canadians of British and French descent, its policy focused on non-Indigenous ethnic-minority groups.[3] If Aotearoa New Zealand's biculturalism functions as 'a smokescreen over white supremacy, the still-beating heart of colonization' (Johnston 2014, 9), the same critique has been levelled at Canadian multiculturalism, given its propensity to 'recognize ethnic differences, but only in a contained fashion, in order to manage them' (Kamboureli 2000, 82). These nation-state attempts to recognise difference are not divorced from commodification: in Aotearoa New Zealand, 'a liberal biculturalism . . . has become increasingly market-oriented' (Murray 2008, 4); in Canada, multiculturalism has been accused of being mere 'sanctioned exoticism' (Kamboureli 2000, 107), one that renders it 'a kind of cultural shopping centre' (Godbout 1990, 357). As Margaret Werry observes, 'As the nation negotiates its uncertain position in the new global division of cultural labor, film makes visible such collisions and collusions between sovereignties: national sovereignty, cultural sovereignty, sovereign individualism, and the sovereignty of capital' (2011, 192). The successful circulation of films such as *Once Were Warriors* and *Atanarjuat: The Fast Runner* in the global cultural marketplace raises important questions about commodification, audience and sovereignty in relation to Indigenous filmmaking in settler-colonial nation-states, particularly as they pertain to the remaking of Indigenous stories for the cinema.

Once Were Warriors

Questions of fidelity have surrounded adaptation studies since its inception. As the previous chapter demonstrated, issues pertaining to fidelity are particularly charged in adaptations of works by Indigenous writers, especially those directed by non-Indigenous filmmakers. Fidelity also takes on additional urgency in Indigenous filmmaking: 'All Indigenous film-makers have to negotiate the difficult boundary between achieving a fidelity of the culture being represented and the demands of funding authorities and majority audiences' (Murray 2008, 28). *Once Were Warriors* presents a case in which even the source material's fidelity to Māori culture was under scrutiny in the response to the novel by Alan Duff, a 'highly visible neo-conservative Maori polemicist' (Waller 1998, 337). *Once Were Warriors* became further embroiled in debates about fidelity through changes to the narrative by Māori playwright Riwia Brown, tasked with rewriting Duff's own screenplay, and the film's director Lee Tamahori. With a substantially Māori crew, *Once Were Warriors* can be comfortably identified as an Indigenous film, but its imbrication in commercial cinema suggests it does not adhere to Barclay's notion of Fourth Cinema. That said, the film, in its national and international circulation, addressed different audiences in diverse ways, not merely in a dual capacity: the Māori audience was itself divided, particularly although not exclusively according to gender. Both narrative and formal changes from Duff's unconventional, polyphonic novel to the film also have implications for the film's representation of Māori identity and articulation (or, for some, lack thereof) of the contexts for Māori dispossession in contemporary Aotearoa New Zealand.

Duff's novel tells the story of the Heke family – Jake, Beth and their six children, of whom Nig, the eldest son, Mark (known as Boogie), the third son and Grace, the eldest daughter, are most prominent in the narrative. The Hekes live in state housing in the Pine Block estate in Two Lakes, a fictionalised version of Rotorua (Oder 1996, 137), on welfare payments following Jake's dismissal from his job at the quarry, where he has worked for fourteen years (Duff 1995, 20). Jake and Beth and their friends are characterised by their alcohol consumption, and Jake additionally by his sometimes violent behaviour towards Beth. They and their community have little to no contact with traditional Māori culture, Beth alienated from her family for her having married 'beneath' her (Jake will reveal that he is descended from enslaved people [102]). Over the course of the novel, Nig seeks out alternative community with the gang the Brown Fists. Meanwhile, Boogie is taken into state custody following an appearance in court from which his parents are absent, Jake having beaten up Beth badly the night before; only Grace takes on the responsibility to accompany him. Grace, whose best friend Toot is a street kid who lives in a wrecked car, consistently compares her environment to that of the Pākehā Trambert family whose land and wealth are juxtaposed to the nearby Pine Block.

Devastated by Boogie's removal from the family, Beth quits drinking in order to save up money to rent a car in order to visit him at the Boys Home. Prior to the scheduled visit, Grace is raped in the family home during a party, and is uncertain who her attacker is, wondering if it might be her father. The much-anticipated visit to Boogie does not transpire, as Jake, after driving the car through an affluent neighbourhood and past Beth's village, decides to go to the pub instead. Grace hangs herself from a tree on the Tramberts' property. Her funeral takes place at her mother's village, but Jake refuses to attend. Neither does Nig, initiated into the Brown Fists on the same day. Grace has left her mother a suicide note, telling of the rape and her speculation that it might have been Jake. Beth throws him out, and he becomes homeless, his only community a street kid he begins to look after. Meanwhile, Boogie has been rehabilitated at the Boys Home, where he has gained an understanding of traditional Māori culture, as Beth first witnesses at Grace's funeral: 'how proud, how ramrod-straight this teaching had made her boy. And thinking of how he yet belonged to the state, was still a ward of Them, and yet looked so . . . so *free*' (132). For her part, Beth becomes a community leader in Pine Block, blending self-help with the facilitation of traditional Māori teachings. Trambert donates land for a rugby field. Nig dies, set up by the leader of the Brown Fists. Thus, the novel concludes with a sense of both tragedy for Beth, having lost two of her children, and hope, given her work revitalising her community.

But the novel is not just focused on Beth, although it begins with her point of view, albeit articulated through the third person as she gazes at the Trambert property: 'Bastard, she'd think, look out her back kitchen window. Lucky white bastard, at that glimpse of two-storey house through its oh so secure greater surround of rolling green pastureland' (Duff 1995, 7). Subsequent chapters deliver not just Beth's but also Jake's, Nig's, Grace's and Boogie's perspectives as Duff alternates focalisers. Throughout the novel, no quotation marks appear to indicate speech, producing 'a stream-of-consciousness and second-person direct-address technique' (Renes 2011, 91). The narrative voice sometimes slides into free indirect discourse, and is sometimes replaced with the thoughts and implied speech of characters. At times, characters' voices interrupt the narrative voice through parenthetical interjections; at other times, parentheses are absent. For instance, in the chapter 'They Who Have History', which recounts Boogie's court appearance largely through Grace's perspective, Grace examines the physical and aesthetic trappings of the settler-colonial repressive state apparatus: 'Those pictures: great big things in fancy frames and every one ofem a grey-haired white man. Hah, imagine a Maori in one ofem.

Some chance. Only Maoris in here get to sit where we are, I bet' (32). Later in the chapter, Grace responds thus to Pākehā authority:

> Then magistrate (God) spoke from his on high position of slightly higher elevation. Made Grace's heart jump. An inner panic that for some extraordinary reason he was speaking to her. (Oh I'd just *die* if he spoke to *me*.) (33)

Thus, Duff's novel presents not only a range of experiences from within the Heke family but also a range of voices that weave in and out of the narrative voice itself, with concomitant shifts in register.

Duff, considered to be removed from 'the [Māori] people's struggle for emancipation and social advancement' (qtd in Lawn 2011, 89), is a controversial figure, and this novel 'is commonly, but somewhat unfairly read as merely a transparent literary vehicle for [his] anti-welfare, self-help philosophy' (89). As a result, Tamahori has acknowledged he anticipated resistance to the film from audiences:

> I was expecting a backlash when I made this movie. I thought that no matter how sophisticated we were, whatever story we told, Maori them-selves [*sic*] would not go to see it – it being such a potentially negative view of their own society. (1995, 27)

The film retains much of the novel's plot, with some key changes. Whereas minor adjustments include reducing the number of Heke children from six to five (excising Abe, whose presence in the novel is minimal, from the film), more significant alterations have greater implications: the absence of the Tramberts (resulting in Grace hanging herself in her own back yard); the fact that Nig does not die (just one example of how the gang – now Toa Aotearoa – is portrayed more positively in the film); the identification of Grace's rapist ('Uncle' Bully, a friend of Jake's), for the audience, Grace herself, and, following her death, for her family when Beth discovers the truth in Grace's journal; and the film ending shortly after Jake violently beats Bully in the bar, hearing from Beth that his friend raped his daughter, and is discarded by Beth and their remaining children as they return home without him. The film also changes the narrative location from the fictionalised Rotorua to Auckland, Aotearoa New Zealand's capital and largest city.

Although Duff wrote a screenplay for the adaptation, Riwia Brown was then hired to write the script, one acknowledged to be more interested in the character of Beth than of Jake, much to Duff's displeasure (Adah 2001, 54). That Tamahori believed Duff was too close to his own material 'to make the changes to keep people in their seats' (qtd in Renes 2011, 89) indicates a concern with pleasing the audience and concomitant financial implications. Indeed, for some critics, Tamahori's pre-*Once Were Warriors*

career as a director of commercials, and the status of the film's production company, Communicado, at the time as 'New Zealand's premier
advertising agency' (Thornley 2001, 26), always already compromises this
film adaptation on commercial and political grounds, and undermines its
relationship to Fourth Cinema. As Davinia Thornley asserts, '*Once Were
Warriors* was made to make money, and make money it did' (2001, 28).
But the film did not only make money: it also did certain kinds of cultural
work. It initiated conversations about Māori warriorhood and masculinity
in the late twentieth century, and about domestic violence with references
to 'warriors [*sic*] problem[s]', in the discourse of the press, 'the government, social agencies and personal confessionals'; the dramatisation of
Beth's experience of violence at the hands of her husband prompted 'a
surge in admissions [to women's refuges]' while 'police noted a rise in the
reports of domestic violence' (Thompson 2003, 233). The fact that 'Jake
the Muss', so-called for his muscles, was also upheld by some Māori viewers for emulation 'as an antisocial hero' (Thompson 2003, 234) demonstrates the proliferation of Māori audiences. But clearly, with one in three
New Zealanders seeing the film, it made a tremendous impact that cannot
be reduced solely to economics.

That said, the loss – many of them largely inevitable – of some elements
of the novel in the translation to screen resulted in a flatter exploration of
urban Māori communities. Beth ruminates at length in the novel about the
disenfranchisement of her people, thinking about the Māori – ironically,
within the pages of Duff's novel – as 'a bookless society' (1995, 10), about
addiction to alcohol and cigarettes (40; 100–1), and about the lack of connection in her Pine Block community to traditional Māori culture. The
most graphic beating Beth endures from Jake in the film, 'one of the most
horrific episodes of spousal violence ever depicted on screen' (Fox 2017,
124), occurs during a party at their house: in the film (with no precedent
in the novel), Beth attempts drunkenly to converse with Nig, asking him to
have a drink with her. Nig dismisses her – 'You're drunk' – and she slaps
him. Horrified with herself, she angrily refuses to cook Jake's friend some
eggs, which Jake responds to excessively violently, beating as well as, it is
suggested when he throws her on their bed, raping her. In the novel, Grace
(from whose perspective the scene is narrated) overhears Beth castigate
the room of party-goers, prior to Jake's beating:

> Maoris, eh? Can any of us in this room speak the language? No reply. What do we
> know of our culture? . . . She told them the Maori of old had a culture, and he had
> pride, and he had warriorhood, not this bullying, man-hitting-woman shet, you call
> that manhood? It's not manhood, and it sure as hell ain't Maori warriorhood. So ask
> yourselves what you are. (28)

Beth undergoes Jake's wrath after her refusal to apologise to 'the men[, who] weren't listening' (28), and although Grace 'wonder[s] *why* does she bring it on herself half the time' the scene knits together an absence of connection to Māori culture with violence. The novel also includes Beth's internal response to Jake's disclosure that his ancestors were enslaved: '(You never *told* me, Jake. You never told me . . . Oh, poor Jake. I never dreamed . . . How dare they bring my husband up believing he was a slave)' (103). In the film, Beth remains silent and unresponsive after Jake's recounting of his family history, depriving the audience of Beth's perspective.

The removal of Nig's death from the film's narrative, in addition to minimising the story's tragedy for the audience, perhaps also compensates somewhat for the loss of the novel's polyphony. Nig's survival – and particularly his reincorporation into the family unit, coinciding with Jake's expulsion from it – suggests an endorsement from the film of his version of Māori masculinity, alongside that of his brother, Boogie and his training by Bennett, the 'social worker cum youth advocate cum teacher and embodiment of *taha Maori*' (Waller 1998, 344), at the Boys Home. As Gregory A. Waller observes, Nig and Boogie 'do not literally share the same screen space until late in the film when they carry Grace's casket at her *tangi*' (1998, 344), where they are both reincorporated into the family: Boogie, because he has been at the Boys Home for most of the film; and Nig, because he has opted for Toa Aotearoa as his site of belonging, rather than the abusive nuclear family unit. Part of Nig's gang's difference in the film compared to the novel is that not only is he permitted to attend Grace's *tangi* in the adaptation (and is denied the opportunity by the Brown Fists' leader in the novel [138]), but also, in fact, his fellow Toa Aotearoa members attend Grace's *tangi* as well: 'Your mates did you proud today', Beth tells her eldest, gathered with her children and Toot at the Heke home, thereby dissolving the boundaries between family and gang belonging.

Part of Nig's belonging in Toa Aotearoa is signified by his *moko*, half his face covered in a tattoo.[4] During dinner after Grace's *tangi*, Boogie and his older brother have the following exchange about Nig's *moko*:

BOOGIE: Good look, bro.
NIG: Would you like one, bro.
BOOGIE: No thanks, man. I wear mine on the inside.

Boogie echoes Bennett's discourse of inner strength and mental training. When Boogie, newly arrived at the Boys Home, uses a *taiaha* to smash windows in the gymnasium, Bennett tells him, 'You think your fist is your weapon? When I have taught you, your mind will be. You'll carry your *taiaha* inside you.' Boogie's response to Nig demonstrates both his assimilation of Bennett's teachings and that the separate trajectories of the two brothers (visually and diegetically) have nonetheless ultimately brought them into family unity at the same time as they are both valorised by the film as legitimate 'express[ions of] contemporary Maori identity' (Treagus 2008, 188), and more specifically Māori masculinity. If the film suggests that 'Warriorness . . . exists in potential in all Maori' (Waller 1998: 348) – and indeed, Michaela Moura-Koçoğlu argues that the film's suggestion of Boogie and Beth taking on warrior status demonstrates its commitment to the most disregarded figures in the community, 'a woman . . . and a boy, rejected by his father Jake for not being able to fight' (2012, 377) – it is particularly crucial that the film addresses masculinity. In the novel, Nig, it seems, has learned from his father, when he slaps Tania, whom he has just slept with, having 'felt like giving her one. A backhander. Teacher to talk to him, a man (or near enough) like that' (Duff 1995, 151). In the film, 'Nig's Girlfriend' is a non-speaking role, and Fran Viveaere, the actor who plays her, only appears behind him, amongst Toa Aotearoa members, in a few brief scenes; there is no suggestion of a violent relationship. Thus, the recuperation of Nig is key to the film's representation of Māori masculinity and different possibilities that diverge from Jake the Muss as viable alternatives.

This recuperation of Māori masculinity operates alongside Beth's self-assertion and her separation from her violent husband. Yet for many, the film's focus on 'gender empowerment' means it is 'less concerned with race and class inscription', and the film becomes 'more conventiona[l] as a universal family drama' (Renes 2011: 97, 99). Further, some critics argue that the film 'actually did a disservice to race relations in New Zealand by providing graphic violence at the expense of wider social analysis, particularly recognition of the impact of colonization and systematic degradation on the Maori race' (Thornley 2001, 28). To what extent do viewers read the Heke family and their community through the lens of colonial dispossession? If these are 'the root causes of the Heke family's dysfunction' (Joyce 2007, 162), how visible are these roots, and how visible can they be when the film is virtually devoid of white people? It may be that with 'no non-Maori characters' the film refuses 'to provide inroads for the non-Maori audience' (Fatzinger 2016, 314); at the same time, however, without the immediate juxtaposition of the affluent Trambert family, the film provides no contrast that contextualises the racialisation of poverty (Lawn 2011, 89) in Aotearoa New Zealand.

Where the novel reveals Grace's internal response to attending court with Boogie, the film aligns the power of the repressive settler-colonial status apparatus with whiteness, through not only the court figures (with exception of the Māori Bennett) but also the police who bring Boogie home when he is caught at the scene of a theft. Beth's response is instructive:

POLICE OFFICER: Been keeping bad company.
BETH: Was that before or after you picked him up?

Absent from Boogie's court date the morning after a vicious beating from Jake, Beth only appears in the company of a white character here and makes clear her distrust of the state and its policing of Māori. If state custody is implicitly 'part and parcel of the genocidal mechanism of colonization that has severed Māori ties to one another' (Johnston 2014, 11), the 'masterful double agent' (Lawn 2011, 92) of Bennett recuperates it for the teachings of *Maoritanga* that he confers on the inmates of the Boys Home. Tamahori admits that the limiting of white actors to roles within the settler–colonial repressive state apparatus was deliberate: 'Like any postcolonialist structure, and especially with a dominant white Anglo-Saxon culture, the administration of justice and the enforcement arms of the law have always been white' (1995, 26). Beth's mistrust of law enforcement underscores from the outset that there is no expectation of justice for Māori from the settler–colonial legal system. Further, if the novel provides more context through the Tramberts and the ruminations of its dispossessed characters on the fate of their community, settler–colonial power surfaces as an explanation only to be minimised in its relevance to Māori advancement: Te Tupaea exhorts his audience at Pine Block at the end of the novel to 'stop blamin the Pakeha for their woes even if it *was* the Pakeha much to blame' (182), consistent with Beth's turn to self-help.

If Tamahori's film eschews the presence of the Tramberts, it does provide a stark contrast at the outset of the film that exposes the disjunction between settler–colonial New Zealand and urban Māori life. Much discussed by critics, the 'billboard hoax' (Wilson 2011, 204) sets up an expectation of pastoral notions of New Zealand's landscape, only to tilt down to reveal the reality of South Auckland (see Figure 7.1): a busy motorway, urban decay and, across the road, Grace Heke, in the family's back yard, reading to her younger siblings her retelling of a story of a *taniwha*, 'a creature who looks after everyone'. She reads to Polly and Huata under the tree that will be the site of her suicide. The first image is, in fact, an advertisement for EnZpower, a fictionalised corporation that presumably sells energy and promises to 'brin[g] New Zealand a brighter future', one that apparently is unavailable to the Heke children, likely to be dis-interpellated by the advert despite – or indeed because of – living across the motorway from it.

Figure 7.1 Juxtaposition of the billboard and motorway in *Once Were Warriors*.

As Werry argues, this sequence does its work '[w]ith pitiless efficiency
. . . expos[ing] the ironic, and tourist, synchrony of colonialism and neo-
colonialism, liberal state making and neoliberal post-nationhood, and
their racial costs' (2011, 213–14). The pastoral utopia that the billboard
promises harks back to nineteenth-century colonial settlement (Joyce
2009, 241), and the film's opening shot insists that that pastoral landscape
was never empty, and the assumption that it was ready for the settler-
colonial taking has produced the conditions of the Māori family living across the road from and walking beneath the billboard. Moreover,
Tamahori has explained that the opening shot was intended as 'a play on
New Zealand films' (1995, 27). Thus, *Once Were Warriors* levels its critique
not only at settler-colonial utopian visions of a pastoral paradise and the
assumptions that underpin them but also at New Zealand cinema's imbrication in this version of the nation. Given *Once Were Warriors*' support
from the New Zealand Film Commission, this 'filming back', as it were,
critiques the structures that underpin the film itself. At the same time,
criticism of Tamahori's slick aesthetics and commercial training and ambitions find a counter-attack in this shot: if the billboard satirises previous
New Zealand films, and promotes a (fictional) energy company, then New

Zealand cinema itself, a product of the settler-colonial state, has always already been an advertisement for the country, one punctured by Tamahori even before the opening credits. Through the combination of law enforcement casting and the billboard, then, Tamahori's film presents a whiteness at odds with urban Māori reality, regardless of Trambert's absence.

Once Were Warriors does not just adapt Alan Duff's novel of the same title: it also intervenes in dominant settler-colonial fantasies of New Zealand and their manifestation in cinema. If a key component of countering these fantasies is its juxtaposing them to South Auckland Māori life, Turner points out that the film

> seriously distorts the physical environment of Auckland in an effort to make the city look something like south-central Los Angeles. . . . Characters in the film criss-cross the city on foot in impossible ways in order to get more . . . insignia of the urban ghetto with its attendant poverty and violence. . . . All this to make the film fit the conventionalized gang genre of American cinema and to make it appealing to a broader audience. (2002, 86)

The attempt to present 'the most honest and accurate presentation of Maori ever put on film in New Zealand' (Tamahori 1995, 27) thus also appeals in stylistic terms to US cinema genres and their fans worldwide, which makes *Once Were Warriors* somewhat of an awkward fit for Fourth Cinema. On the one hand, Tamahori does not hesitate to identify a wider (i.e. non-Māori) audience as a key objective for the film; on the other, Tamahori declares this 'bleak vision . . . our vision. It's not the only one, but it is one' (27), and indeed, one that resonated with a substantial Māori audience, if for different reasons within that audience. The adaptation of not only Duff's novel but also the geography of Auckland would not be surpassed in popularity within New Zealand until Niki Caro's *Whale Rider* seven years later (see Chapter 6); and it would not be surpassed by the Jake-focused sequel, *What Becomes of the Broken Hearted* (1999), adapted from Duff's sequel with a screenplay by Duff himself and directed by the Pākehā Ian Mune, killing off Nig as the novel of *Once Were Warriors* intended, and focusing on Jake's story as Duff preferred. Leonie Pihama (Māori) points out the weight that cinematic representations of Māori have for non-Māori audiences with no other context for Māori history (qtd in Columpar 2007, 464). For Barclay, key to Fourth Cinema is the community audience and priorities other than financial profit (2003a, 11). *Once Were Warriors* clearly found a large Māori audience as well as an international one, in addition to unprecedented financial success. In terms of Indigenous representational sovereignty, we might also ask what its limits are when the settler-colonial nation-state provides financial support, the case not only for *Once Were Warriors* in Aotearoa New Zealand, but also for *Atanarjuat: The Fast Runner* in Canada.

Atanarjuat: The Fast Runner

Atanarjuat: The Fast Runner is based on an Inuit Traditional Story, adapted for the screen by the Igloolik Isuma Productions collective. Directed by Zacharias Kunuk, the film was made by a majority Inuit crew. Isuma's core members at the time of *Atanarjuat*'s production were Kunuk; Paul Apak Angilirq,[5] who wrote the screenplay in Inuktitut; Pauloosie Qulitalik, an Inuit elder and actor (who appears in *Atanarjuat*); and the white American videographer Norman Cohn, director of photography on *Atanarjuat*. *Atanarjuat*'s production coincided with the coming into being of Nunavut, Canada's third territory.[6] In contrast to *Once Were Warriors*, where, in Duff's novel, Beth decries the dearth of Māori speaking their language, which is only spoken briefly in Tamahori's film, *Atanarjuat* was the first feature-length film in Inuktituk. A remarkable success story, both in Canada and internationally, *Atanarjuat* won the Caméra d'Or prize for best first feature film at the Cannes Film Festival, and six Genie Awards in Canada, including Best Picture; by modest Canadian standards, it was also a commercial success, grossing 6.2 million dollars worldwide, the highest of any Canadian film in 2002 (Seguin 2005, 43). An unconventionally lengthy film, with a running time of 2 hours and 48 minutes, with every word of dialogue in a language most audience members would never have heard, *Atanarjuat* seems an unlikely candidate for a '[c]rossover dramatic blockbuster' (Bessire 2003, 835). Reviews and even some academic responses account for the film's success through attributions of both universality and exoticism. Much depends, however, on the position of multiple audiences: Inuit – especially those local to Igloolik – and Southerner.

   Atanarjuat: The Fast Runner diverges from the other case studies in this book insofar as it is not based on a singular prose text, but rather on a Traditional Story with multiple variants. In constructing the narrative for the film, Paul Apak consulted 'eight to ten elders' (Apak Angilirq 2002, 17), and there are other extant versions, including those collected by Knud Rasmussen and Franz Boas in the early twentieth century, part of the ethnographic archive.[7] Although the film, in one sense, constitutes another telling of the Traditional Story, it is also significant that this telling operates in a different medium; further, its major distinctions from the variants are more significant than those between the variants. As an example of Indigenous representational sovereignty that recreates a Traditional Story for the cinema, *Atanarjuat: The Fast Runner* pushes our understanding of adaptation in light of Inuit storytelling practices. In using modern technology to film *Atanarjuat* but choosing not to resituate this Traditional Story in a modern setting, the members of Isuma raise questions about the audiences they seek out and the role of authenticity in representational sovereignty. The production outtakes that accompany the final credits invite a Southern audience to reflect on their assumptions about Inuit life, and indeed the making of this film. Finally, in a territory where Isuma's productions have made major contributions to the local economy through employment, the role of *Atanarjuat* as, itself, a commodity for global extraction places demands on Southern viewers in terms of ethical spectatorship and the use of 'raw material' in film adaptation.

In the annotated screenplay of *Atanarjuat: The Fast Runner*, co-published by Isuma Publishing and the independent, Toronto-based Coach House Press, anthropologist Bernard Saladin d'Anglure offers 'An Ethnographic Commentary' on the Traditional Story that forms the basis of the film and the lifeways of the Inuit, including the practice of shamanism. This commentary is located after the screenplay, which is itself printed in both syllabics, on the verso side, and in English, on the recto side. Further, informative sidebars appear throughout the screenplay itself, also in syllabic and English versions. In his commentary, Saladin d'Anglure explains:

> In 1972, I collected the second Inuit-language version of the legend at Igloolik while interviewing Michel Kupaaq, who was born in the mid-1920s. Other versions are told by Michel Kupaaq in 1987, 1990 and 1991. These four versions, rounded out by a version by Kupaaq's younger brother, Hervé Paniaq; his cousin, Émile Imaroitok; Guy Makkik; Elizabeth Nutarakittuq; and elders George Kappianaq and François Quassa were the main sources for the film. (Saladin d'Anglure 2002, 199)

Saladin d'Anglure offers a composite narrative in his supplementary materials in the *Atanarjuat* published screenplay, sketching out the 'main elements' (199) of the story. In this composite version, an Igloolik hunter, father to two sons (Aamarjuaq and Atanarjuat), is badly treated in his community. The sons, as adults, become known for their strength and speed, respectively. Successful hunters, they provide for their family, attracting jealousy from some in their community who attempt to steal their dogs and sled, but are caught by the brothers. Each brother has two wives; one wife of each brother is related to those who tried to steal the brothers' dogs and sled. These wives conspire with their relatives to kill Aamarjuaq and Atanarjuat, leaving 'their husbands' caribou stockings and lay[ing] them to dry on the tent's outer surface to mark the spot where their husbands were sleeping' (201). Although Aamarjuaq is killed, Atanarjuat escapes, running naked over twenty miles of ice to evade his would-be killers.

He finds refuge and hospitality with an elderly couple and their child on Siuraq; this family hides Atanarjuat when his assailants arrive, and they help him to heal. Atanarjuat leaves Siuraq to hunt during the summer and autumn, before returning to Siuraq – where the couple presents him with new clothes for his innocent wife – and thence to Igloolik. His wife who had no part in the attempt to kill him is now 'destitute': 'When he saw her so poorly dressed, he tore her clothes apart and offered her new ones' (201, 203). For the wife who has betrayed him, he tears her clothes but gives her 'only a raw caribou hide and sen[ds] her back to her kinfolk' (203). As the Igloolik community is short of meat and caribou hide, Atanarjuat invites them as his guests. In his igloo, after attaching crampons to his boots, Atanarjuat 'club[s] to death all those who had attacked him and killed his brother' (203), thus concluding the narrative.

Other versions of Michel Kupaaq's contain additional details. In his monograph *Isuma: Inuit Video Art*, Michael Robert Evans includes one of Kupaaq's variants from 1990, which mentions that Atanarjuat's wife, who conspired with her family to kill him, has taken another husband prior to Atanarjuat's return (2008, 79) and that, having taken revenge on his brother's killers, Atanarjuat then proceeds to take care of the widowed women and their sons (80). Kupaaq, in an interview excerpt, indicates he has heard another version of the narrative on the radio in which the couple at Siuraq 'were actually his [Atanarjuat's] parents' (qtd in Evans 2008, 82). Evans also includes a second variant from 1990 from Hervé Paniaq, who is credited as an additional writer of the *Atanarjuat* script. Paniaq's variant includes the detail of Aamarjuaq, while under attack, 'carr[ying] the tent with men on top of it stabbing him' (qtd in Evans 2008, 85); further, in this version, Atanaarjuat [*sic*] finds shelter with 'two old couples living there with their grandchild', on 'Siuqat' [*sic*] (85). Evans also includes a third variant, collected by Knud Rasmussen and told to him by Inugpasugjuk. In this variant, the brothers' names are reversed (as Aumarzuat, the survivor of the attempted murder, and Atanârzuat, the brother who dies). There is no mention of their wives being complicit in the attack or the heroic run across the ice, and Aumarzuat hides in his parents' house. When Aumarzuat wreaks vengeance on his enemies, he subsequently takes their wives and kills another man en route to his parents' house: 'He had, as it were, got into the way of killing' (qtd in Evans 2008, 88). Unsurprisingly, perhaps, this version told to Rasmussen in the early twentieth century differs more widely from the other variants than those told by Kupaaq and Paniaq in 1990.

Atanarjuat: The Fast Runner's running time diverges more sharply from any of the Traditional Story variants, in these textual forms, than any other case study in this book. The text of the version told to Rasmussen, for instance, is scarcely longer than a single printed page (Evans 2008, 87–8). Cohn writes of the process of expanding the Traditional Story into a feature-length narrative film,

> These Inuit legends are like riddles or poems, with a few key details but not much character development. To make *Atanarjuat* into a believable movie, as if real people had lived through these events, Apak had to imagine characters, emotions and motivations that were not in the original legend. (Cohn 2002, 25)

In this respect, *Atanarjuat* differs substantially from *Once Were Warriors*, with the film's movement away from the novel's frequent interior thoughts of characters interrupting the narrative voice. *Atanarjuat*'s major changes to and additions from the Traditional Story variants include the introduction of shamanism – absent, as Arnold Krupat notes, from all extant versions of the story (2007: 614). Saladin d'Anglure surmises that this absence rests on the fact that 'this system was so well woven into traditional life that the legend says nothing about it' (2002, 203). Cohn gestures towards the shamanism as part of the attempt to expand the Traditional Story for Isuma's cinematic version: 'When Apak tried to imagine these events happening, he realized it must have been a love story, a triangle of jealousy and revenge, with some evil shamanic force behind it, so that's the story he wrote' (2002, 25). At the outset of the film's narrative, when Atanarjuat and Amaqjuat are children, an evil, powerful stranger, Tuurngarjuaq, arrives in the community, besting and killing Kumaglak, husband of Panikpak. Following Kumaglak's death, Panikpak's brother, Qulitalik, leaves the community with Kumaglak's rabbit foot, given to him by Panikpak. Kumaglak and Panikpak's son, Sauri, becomes leader.

In the film, moving ahead chronologically to when the next generation has become adults, Sauri's son, Oki, is promised to marry Atuat, but she prefers Atanarjuat, who wins her in a fight against Oki. Unlike the variants of the Traditional Story, Atanarjuat and Amaqjuat only have one wife each, until Puja, daughter of Sauri and sister of Oki, seduces Atanarjuat, becoming his second wife. Puja is caught committing adultery with Amaqjuat, then flees to her father and brother, claiming Atanarjuat has tried to kill her. She returns to her husband and is forgiven by Amaqjuat's wife, Ulluriaq, claiming she wants to be of more help to her and Atuat (who has had a son, named Kumaglak, after Panikpak's husband). When Ulluriaq and Atuat are looking for eggs, their husbands asleep in their tent, Puja places Atanarjuat's caribou socks outside the tent to indicate the position the men are sleeping within. Oki arrives with his friends, one of whom sees '*the evil shaman Tuurngarjuaq's head instead on Uqi's broad shoulders*' (Cohn 103).[8] Amaqjuat dies, but Atanarjuat escapes, running across the ice naked to evade Oki and his comrades. He arrives at Sioraq [sic] where he is protected and tended by Qulitalik and his wife. While Atanarjuat is on Sioraq, Oki, still coveting Atuat, kills his father, Sauri, who insists he cannot take Atuat; Oki then rapes Atuat. Eventually, Atanarjuat returns, fully healed, with Qulitalik and his family. He gives Atuat new clothing, cutting her old garment from her. He cuts open Puja's clothing but gives her nothing. Atanarjuat invites Oki and his friends Pakak and Pittiulaq to his igloo to feast, and with crampons on his feet to steady himself on the ice, he appears about to attack the three other men. Oki lunges at him and they wrestle. Atanarjuat raises his club, but instead of striking Oki, the club lands on the ice beside Oki's head. 'The killing will stop. It ends here,' Atanarjuat declares (187). Later, at a community council, Tuurngarjuaq arrives, clashing with Qulitalik, who bests the evil stranger. Panikpak utters while weeping, 'I wish in my heart you can forgive yourself as I forgive you, to find a better life somewhere else' (191), banishing her grandchildren Oki and Puja as well as Oki's friends Pakak and Pittiulaq.

In addition to the shamanism, therefore, major alterations from the variants include the conflict over whom Atuat will marry, Puja's infidelity with her brother-in-law, Oki's rape of Atuat and murder of his own father, and the absence of revenge killings from the narrative's conclusion. Although some have read the change to the ending as a reflection of the encroachment of Christian ideology on Inuit culture through a privileging of forgiveness (see Shubow 2003; Saladin d'Anglure 2002, 203), Evans reports that

> Apak, Kunuk, Cohn, and the others at Isuma decided on a positive ending because they wanted to emphasize the importance of harmony and working together, a vital Inuit value honed over millennia of cooperation in small bands immersed in a harsh environment. (2008, 94)

Ian J. Macrae and Samantha Mackinnon, who read *Atanarjuat: The Fast Runner* through the lenses of legal pluralism and performative jurisprudence, argue that the changed ending testifies to 'Inuit legal systems in practice, as flexible and capable of being updated' (2017, 566). They focus on the practice and purpose of Inuit storytelling:

> the film itself, like the story that it retells, speaks less to manslaughter and violence than it does to the method and intention of Inuit oral traditions. The Inuit storytelling tradition, like traditions of song and story the world over, may serve a diagnostic and transformative function, and operate as an apotropaic device, warning what *could* happen if a community veers out of balance. (552)

To those who would claim that the altered ending is inauthentic – 'a crucial lie', claims Justin Shubow (2003) – Macrae and Mackinnon counter that the Traditional Story of Atanarjuat functions as a kind of cautionary tale rather than a matter of record, as suggested by Kunuk: 'We . . . knew that they used to just send people away instead of killing them and that was a better ending so we chose that' (qtd in Macrae and Mackinnon 2017, 552). Kunuk has also indicated that Paul Apak consulted the elders about the changed ending: 'I remember one of the elders answering him, 'We are storytellers' (qtd in Krupat 2007, 614). If Kunuk is 'a video storyteller' (Evans 2008, 117), *Atanarjuat's* narrative – and its altered ending – may serve the same purpose as the oral variants, but in a different medium, by different means.

One key difference, of course, is the composition of the audience for the Traditional Story as it has been told orally for generations and for the film. Isuma core members have said both that '[o]ur first audience is always Inuit' (Kunuk, qtd in Krupat 2007, 608, n8) and that *Atanarjuat's* audience is 'anybody, no matter who they are and where they are from' (Apak Angilirq 2002, 21). The duality of *Atanarjuat's* audience – Inuit and non-Inuit – underpins the altered ending, given that non-Inuit viewers unaccustomed to Inuit storytelling have no context for interpreting the Traditional Story as it has been told orally, with the warning about revenge killing at the narrative conclusion. In the case of *Atanarjuat*, casual references in film adaptation discourse to being 'faithful' to the 'spirit of the text', often claimed by filmmakers making dramatic changes to the source text (to advocate for 'the necessity of *in*fidelity to its letter or form' [Elliott 2003, 139]), are perhaps more fruitfully borne out in this film. Kamilla Elliott critiques claims about 'the spirit of the text' in adaptation as a 'psychic concept of adaptation', in which '[t]he spirit of a text is commonly equated with the spirit or personality of the author' (2003, 136). This equation 'posits a process of psychic connection in which the spirit of a text passes from author to novel to reader-filmmaker to film to viewer' (137).

Elliott's schematic depends upon individual transmissions of meaning, from singular author to text to singular filmmaker to film to singular viewer. In contrast, *Atanarjuat: The Fast Runner* presents us with a collective model in historical context: Isuma, itself a collective endeavour, adapts the Traditional Story of Atanarjuat by consulting multiple elders; the altered ending of the narrative, diverging from the variants, nevertheless operates according to the practice and purpose of Inuit storytelling, enabling the 'affirming [of] Inuit value systems' as well as the 'revitalizing [of] Inuit oral traditions through their selective transformation' (McCall 2011, 194). Further, not only have 'the filmmakers . . . subtly embedded the present in their representation of the past' (McCall 2011, 194), but they have also, through the altered ending, made legible the Traditional Story to a non-Inuit audience.

The question of the interpellation of a non-Inuit audience is crucial to the consideration of *Atanarjuat: The Fast Runner* as an example of Indigenous representational sovereignty. Scholars have debated the extent to which the film privileges the non-Inuit audience. One key issue in this debate is the temporal setting of the narrative. Shari Huhndorf claims that *Atanarjuat* 'is set in an atemporal realm unaffected by the historical events that have transformed Inuit life over the last century' (2003, 824). Cohn argues that 'Inuit historical fiction is possible because the traditional history is so close in time to contemporary life, [so] there are still people who can live their traditional history as actors' (qtd in Soukup 2006, 241); elsewhere, he identifies the events of *Atanarjuat* as happening to '[a] community in the sixteenth century' (qtd in Evans 2008, 94). Regardless, the pre-contact setting of *Atanarjuat* has drawn criticism: Monika Siebert contends that the film 'shed[s] the trappings of modernity with its settler presence' while 'refus[ing] to narrate the obliteration of the traditional way of life. Instead, it indulges in the fantasy of a world not yet destroyed by colonization' (2006, 534–5). Of course, the existence of the film itself, retelling the Traditional Story of Atanarjuat, already indicates that this Inuit knowledge and culture have not been destroyed, implicitly pointing to a key purpose of the work carried out by Isuma. Other scholars perpetuate a 'widespread allegorical reading' of the film's battle between good and evil as 'a moral tale about the evils of colonialism' (Horton 2012) on the grounds of the stranger, Tuurngarjuaq, who arrives in the community: 'We never knew what he was . . . Or why it happened. Evil came to us like death. It just happened . . . and we had to live with it,' Panikpak narrates.[9] For Jessica L. Horton, reading *Atanarjuat* as a colonial allegory 'has too often functioned as a kind of one-liner' (2012); and indeed, perhaps it is too simple and straightforward to assume, from a twenty-first-century perspective, that the film addresses colonialism. At the same time, for critics like Siebert, the absence of an overt colonial presence, for a twenty-first-century film, suggests *Atanarjuat* is a fantasy (see also Krupat 2007, 611).

Cohn's assertion of Inuit traditional history's proximity to contemporary life perhaps finds an unwitting echo in some critical responses. Lúcia Nagib, for instance, describes *Atanarjuat*'s narrative as 'a story, which supposedly occurred over a thousand years ago, [that] looks like a documentary of Inuit life today', one that 'merge[s] past and present into a timeless physical real' (2011, 41). Such a claim reveals an extraordinary ignorance about contemporary Inuit life, or perhaps a projection of non-Inuit viewers' misconceptions, as indicated by reviewers' refrains of the film as 'timeless' (Bessire 2003, 834). The sense of an ossified Inuit history, unchanging in the present, suggests a Southern, ethnographic gaze. This perspective on Inuit culture in general and *Atanarjuat* particularly ignores the dynamic continuation of culture that makes the narrative present. For instance, the published screenplay includes a photograph of a stone near Igloolik where Atanarjuat is meant to have sat (Saladin d'Anglure 2002, 199). Evans explains of this bench, 'referred to in the legend variants', that '[n]early everyone on the island knows this stone and its significance' (2008, 93). Michel Kupaaq mentions the bench in his variant (Evans 2008, 76, 81), and his discussions of the Traditional Story shift tenses in a manner that demonstrates the continued lived relevance of Atanarjuat. In discussing Atanarjuat's run across the ice, for example, Kupaaq says,

> In the spring there is always an open lead that runs across to Siuraq which is wide. He managed to cross this lead which made the pursuers to turn back as they could not cross this lead. I heard that he had landed at Siuraq. (Qtd in Evans 2008, 82–3)

In addition to the continued presence of the bench, then, features of the landscape also persist into the present, and are integral to the narrative; at the same time, Kupaaq acknowledges the shifts in the landscape over time: '[O]ne must realize the fact that the beach was much closer to those rises than it is today . . . During the spring tide you can see the dampness of the hole in between the raised beaches' (qtd in Evans 2008, 83). Further, Kupaaq's having 'heard that [Atanarjuat] had landed at Siuraq' gives the impression of the narrative circulating through his community. Thus, the local audience brings not just knowledge of the Traditional Story to their viewing of *Atanarjuat* but also a knowledge of the land from which the narrative emerges and the territory in which it continues to circulate.

Like *Once Were Warriors*, *Atanarjuat* was a global success story, emerging from a particular marginalised place made visible to an international audience. Tom Crosbie suggests that *Atanarjuat* can be viewed as an example of 'Fourth World cinema [sic]', despite the role played by the non-Inuit D. P. Cohn (2007, 150, n4). As Michelle H. Raheja (Seneca) observes, Barry Barclay himself includes Kunuk as a 'practitione[r] of Fourth Cinema' (2007, 1167); indeed, Kunuk's emphasis that Isuma's first audience is Inuit resonates with Fourth Cinema films 'crucially speak[ing] to the people they represent' (qtd in Murray 2008, 25). Yet 'Isuma's work is not solely a vehicle aimed at either an internal or an external audience' (Raheja 2007, 1168), and this dual audience, for some scholars, compromises the political potential of *Atanarjuat: The Fast Runner*. For Russell Meeuf, the film is unable to reconcile its two orientations, 'fail[ing] to create a kind of resistant localism that accounts for its own participation in the global marketplace', given it 'relies too heavily on a notion of localism concerned with cultural authenticity and ignores its relationship to globalising processes' (2007, 737). In Siebert's view, *Atanarjuat* 'perform[s] cultural difference' and is ultimately co-opted by the state, given that the film's success has been claimed by the Canadian film industry and thus become 'complicit in Canada's nation-building and global self-promotion' (2006, 548, 544), despite the creation of Nunavut that coincided with the film's production. Even though this lengthy Inuktitut-language film may be said to be 'uncompromising in its refusal to accommodate the South' (Krupat 2007, 609), cultural authenticity – and its international celebration and success – thus becomes a pitfall of co-optation as the film appeals to non-Inuit viewers with little to no knowledge of Inuit culture.

An important element in Isuma's self-positioning – and indeed the position of the local community in Igloolik – in *Atanarjuat* arises through the outtakes that accompany the film's final credits. Like the billboard that opens *Once Were Warriors*, the outtakes present a key moment of self-reflexivity about filmmaking and the expectations of an international, non-Indigenous audience, although in *Atanarjuat* this self-reflexivity focuses on the act of production rather than the canon of representation that precedes the film. *Atanarjuat*'s outtakes demonstrate the late-twentieth-century Inuit community producing the film itself, making use of snowmobiles, but also sleds, containing a cameraperson while the sled is pushed by men to produce a tracking shot (see Figure 7.2). We see a woman in traditional dress holding a fish near a body of water; we see Natar Ungalaaq, who plays Atanarjuat, warming up with a blanket in his flight across the ice scene; we see Peter Henry Arnatsiaq, the actor who plays Oki, wearing a leather jacket and listening to headphones.

Meeuf dismisses these outtakes as 'participat[ing] in the "behind the scenes" discourses of Hollywood's popular insiderism in which a film's production provides another media text that creates a context for the film's consumption rather than a context for politically engaged interpretations' (2007, 743). Similarly, Siebert minimises the credits as 'sixty seconds of explosive self-reflexivity' (2006, 536). Yet the work done in those sixty seconds is vital; and the outtakes are not relegated to bonus features of a DVD but rather part of the film itself, visible not just to DVD owners (and viewers) but also to those who saw the film in the cinema. As Raheja notes, the outtakes that accompany the final credits 'forc[e] the viewer . . . to imagine *Atanarjuat* as a narrative film produced by a vibrant contemporary Inuit community, not a documentary on the mythic past or footage from

Figure 7.2 Tracking shot in *Atanarjuat: The Fast Runner*.

a bygone era' (2007, 1179). The 'explosiveness' that Siebert attributes to this self-reflexivity powerfully rebuts non-Inuit viewer's assumptions of a static Inuit culture. If Meeuf finds the film lacking for a failure to address its own global circulation, such an accusation both expects the film itself to anticipate its ultimate global reach at the point of its own production and, curiously, lays the responsibility for an 'ethical cosmopolitanism [that] entails responsible reading practices' (2007, 743) at the feet of the film-makers rather than the audience. Granted, some scholars and reviewers appear to have collapsed contemporary and traditional Inuit cultures, as comments about the narrative's timelessness indicate. Surely the outtakes in the credits situate, precisely, the temporality of the production, if these viewers care to pay attention.

The disjunction between the temporal setting of *Atanarjuat*'s narrative and the outtakes that accompany the credits has some precedent in previous Isuma productions. For instance, the 1989 video *Qaggiq*, part of a series of films detailed 1930s Inuit life, depicts a time 'after the whalers and missionaries arrived in the Arctic but before the Canadian government's relocation effort forced Inuit into permanent settlements' (Evans 2008, 109).

Evans notes that *Qaggiq* has its own temporal disjunction insofar as '[t]he video's careful indicators of early postcontact life are violated by a few anachronistic glimpses that indicate a videomaking philosophy' (111). These anachronisms, including a watch and a plastic jar, constitute 'evidence of Kunuk's philosophy' and testify to *Qaggiq*'s attempt not to 'show families in the early postcontact Arctic' but rather to 'sho[w] modern families portraying families in the early postcontact Arctic' (111), including children laughing at the camera. Where Nagib reads Isuma's earlier videos about Inuit life 'as separate elements of training that would later coalesce in *Atanarjuat*' (2011, 35), as though these videos are a warm-up to the main act of the feature film, we might alternatively read *Atanarjuat* as carrying on the work of those previous videos, which, in Cohn's view, operate not merely to 'archiv[e] knowledge' but rather to enable it to be 'active and perpetuated' (qtd in Evans 2008, 27).

Part of disseminating knowledge is Isuma's commitment to training. *Atanarjuat*'s credits not only display a temporal disjunction consistent with the anachronism of some of Isuma's earlier video work, but also testify to the company's production practices and principles. As such, the credits' significance encompasses the repetition of names, as individuals take on multiple roles in the making of this film: Pakak Innuksuk, who plays Amaqjuat, is second assistant director; Atuat Akkitirq both plays Sauri's wife and is one of the cooks supporting the production. There are multiple instances of actors fulfilling additional roles as part of the production team. Not only do the credits, in conjunction with the outtakes, 'reveal the collaborative process of making the film' (McCall 2011, 194), but crucially, this collaboration takes place within the community. Isuma 'accomplishes collective social justice off-screen by providing job training' (Raheja 2007, 1166), significant in a region where the unemployment rate can be as high as 60 per cent.

Isuma members explicitly address the larger capitalist and extractivist context in which Nunavut is located, with Cohn and Kunuk criticising the government of Nunavut for prioritising diamond mining over support for filmmaking. As Kunuk observes, 'They're going to be digging for diamonds from the land, and we're sure not going to end up with diamond rings' (qtd in Seguin 2005), acknowledging the environmental destruction of Indigenous territories that lines the pockets of corporations without real benefit to Indigenous communities. As Denis Seguin writes, despite *Atanarjuat*'s critical and financial success, 'In the eyes of the Government of Nunavut, Isuma might as well be a shiny penny compared with a glittering mound of diamonds' (2005). For Cohn, extractivism operates as a metaphor for Isuma's fortunes, in the context of the company having 'been deprived of $600,000–$700,000 of their international revenue' by their international sales agent:

> Being ripped off in the film industry is equal opportunity exploitation. All we are is another diamond mine in an industry where people are not any more culturally sensitive than in the diamond industry. These are the same forces that has operated for centuries, and are not aimed at us exclusively. (Qtd in Ginsburg 2003, 829)

Elsewhere, Cohn invokes resource extraction outside the diamond industry:

> We are fighting a guerrilla battle over a process of production that we think is politically much more progressive than the conventional process of production. Either in conventional filmmaking, which is extremely hard – as military as the military – or conventional television, which is as corporate-controlled as is Wall Street, or the pharmaceutical of the chemical industry. So our 'process competitors' are essentially the military and the oil and gas industry. We see ourselves as a third process alternative for how film and television can actually be made, and it happens to be a quirk of fate that this is occurring in an Inuit community. (qtd in Evans 2008, 73)

Cohn utters these statements out of concern for the sustainability of the kind of community video production that his career has prioritised, which, for him, is 'a much larger constituency than just Inuit' (qtd in Evans 2008, 74). But while he makes his point as a critique of capitalism, again, the comparison to resource extraction is particularly apt in the context of Nunavut.

Further, *Atanarjuat*, given its international success, is part of 'Inuit intellectual property', which has opened up to and circulated within 'a global market':

> The Inuit legend is processed by Inuit artists (the filmmaking team), and in this way it is turned into a modernized Inuit intellectual property. It may be accessed by the Western world, but even more so will be 'used' by the Inuit community and returned as 'their intellectual property.' (Knopf 2008, 318–19)

Fears of co-optation of *Atanarjuat* within the global cultural marketplace resonate with Stuart Murray's concern about using 'Indigenous narratives as "story material" for a wider commercial cinema that lacks an appropriate knowledge of the issues such films raise' (2008, 28). In the case of *Atanarjuat*, however, its makers are also almost all Indigenous themselves. But Isuma's adaptation of the Traditional Story of Atanarjuat, rooted in *Inuit Qaujimajatuqangit* (or 'an Inuit way of doing things' [McCall 2011, 198]) uses 'story' or 'raw' material that means different things to the film's disparate audiences. This is not to condemn the use Isuma makes of the Atanarjuat narrative, but rather to acknowledge that in relation to different audiences, the adaptation may be taken as extractive (particularly

Southern audiences who do not reverse their misconceptions about con-temporary Inuit culture through the credit outtakes) or, conversely, as a dynamic, twenty-first-century perpetuation of a Traditional Story. In this sense, *Atanarjuat* encounters a similar problem to *Once Were Warriors* in its dual audience: for a Māori audience it may turn a spotlight on import-ant issues within the community; for a non-Māori audience it may become a kind of template representation of Māori people.

Film adaptation has been attached to 'a rich constellation of terms and tropes' (Stam 2005, 4). Two most relevant to *Atanarjuat: The Fast Runner* are retelling and translation, but these take on particular resonance for this film in its provenance and its production. Based on a number of variants of the Traditional Story, *Atanarjuat* has no single textual source. Rather, it forms part of and contributes to an ongoing oral storytelling tradition, one that is distant from most viewers of the film but intimately connected to its own community, which, crucially produced the film. According to the terminology of adaptation studies, we might say that *Atanarjuat* consti-tutes a 'translation' from Inuit storytelling to the screen. At the same time, translation itself is embedded in the film through its subtitling for most of the audience. McCall argues that 'the song that Kumaglak refuses to sing in the opening scene of the film', the song that can only be sung to one who understands, 'is sung three times in the film but is never translated into English' (2011, 189). As such, McCall suggests that the film engages in 'strategies of incomplete translation' that acknowledge 'the uneven relations of address both within Inuit audiences and between Inuit and non-Inuit audiences' (McCall 2011, 189). Yet Keavy Martin observes that the film's opening line belongs to the stranger, Tuurngarjuaq, and refers to a different song: 'While Inuit songs are shared according to specific proto-cols and along the lines of particular relationships, this does, on occasion, involve sharing songs with outsiders' (2012, 93). This sharing (and trans-lation) of songs and stories means that despite being 'geared largely toward local, Inuktitut-speaking viewers, [Isuma's] work also functions . . . as a medium for Inuit stories and songs to reach a global audience' (2012, 96).

Isuma followed *Atanarjuat* with *The Journals of Knud Rasmussen* (2006), a Canadian-Danish co-production that did not achieve the popular success of its predecessor. The economic precariousness of Indigenous filmmaking is clear in Isuma's filing for receivership in 2011. Isuma has been subse-quently active in other ways, however, with its most recent feature, *One Day in the Life of Noah Piugattuk* (Kunuk, 2019) at the 2019 Venice Biennale as well as Toronto International and Vancouver International Film Festivals. Further, the isuma.tv website, launched in 2008, hosts Indigenous com-munity videos, not just in Inuktitut but rather in eighty-four languages

(IsumaTV n.d.) in 'a generous distribution' (K. Martin 2012, 96). The website's map of the world with the Indigenous languages it represents stretches from Alaska to Aotearoa New Zealand, testifying to a desire to support Indigenous communities far beyond Igloolik. The website also details the ways in which it attempts to reach communities with poor Internet infrastructure, a long way from the art-house cinemas in which *Atanarjuat* found much of its global audience.

Clearly, as with the aftermath of *Once Were Warriors*, the success of *Atanarjuat* in the last twenty years has not ushered in a rush of Indigenous-made feature films (*Once Were Warriors*' sequel, notably, being directed by a Pākehā filmmaker, and its landmark success in Aotearoa New Zealand cinema being eclipsed by the Pākehā-directed *Whale Rider*). Kunuk has achieved an Oscar nomination for the short animated film *Angakusajaujuq: The Shaman's Apprentice* (2021), another adaptation of a Traditional Story, this one 'primarily aimed at children' (Leiser 2021). The nomination draws global attention to Kunuk's work, yet it is significant that this most recent film is not a feature, and *One Day in the Life of Noah Piugattuk* has not achieved the circulation of *Atanarjuat*. If Indigenous representational sovereignty is to continue on the scale of these *Once Were Warriors* and *Atanarjuat*, if Indigenous narratives are to be more than raw material for non-Indigenous filmmakers, much more support for Indigenous artists is necessary. And yet scale is precisely a key question surrounding both *Once Were Warriors* and *Atanarjuat*, especially in their circulation and audiences (and, as a result, their box office success): just as *Atanarjuat* has been declared by Lucas Bessire to be a '[c]rossover dramatic blockbuster' (2003, 835), so Kirsten Moana Thompson identifies *Once Were Warriors* as 'New Zealand's first indigenous blockbuster' (2003). Blockbusters are ostensibly at odds with Barclay's notion of Fourth Cinema, with profit in opposition to 'ancient core values' (2003, 11); the changes to both source narratives have probably facilitated both films' remarkable circulation and box office returns. But both these films tell Indigenous stories – and indeed, retell them. The Māori storyteller that Grace becomes in Tamahori's film comes from a community with broken connections to traditional Māori culture. 'My people', Beth says, in a famous line of dialogue, 'once were warriors', harking back to a pre-colonial past, articulated in English. For its part, *Atanarjuat* stages an Inuit pre-colonial past in an act of storytelling for a larger audience, even in Inuktitut. If *Atanarjuat* fits more comfortably within Fourth Cinema, its production embedded so firmly within the community of Igloolik, it nevertheless shares with *Once Were Warriors* both the pitfalls and the possibilities of Indigenous storytelling for the community and far beyond.

Conclusion

This book has examined a range of 'raw material' and its film adaptation, from nineteenth-century novels to late-twentieth-century prose fiction to an Inuit Traditional Story. Film adaptation demonstrates the desire on the part of both those who tell stories and their audiences to return to the same material, reimagining it. Who reimagines it, how and for whom, have been key questions throughout this study. Some of these reimaginings, as we have seen, have been pointedly politicised; others have downplayed the political implications of the texts they have adapted. At least part of an adaptation's audience is unlikely to be familiar with the source material in the first place; the adaptation may guide viewers to the source, but equally, it may not.

Some of the examples of adaptations in this book involve a temporal gap of more than a century between the source text and the film. But contemporary publishing functions rather differently. Simone Murray's study of the adaptation industry observes how, so imbricated has publishing become in film adaptation, that adaptation 'is now factored in and avidly pursued from the earliest phases of book production' (2012, 13). The novel *Caging Skies* by Christine Leunens (2019), the source material for Taika Waititi's *Jojo Rabbit* (2019), presents a striking example of this phenomenon insofar as the author thanks Waititi in the novel's acknowledgements (Leunens 2019, 297). Further, the film, clearly in production prior to the publication of the novel, presents some considerable differences from its near-simultaneous source text, including the infusion of humour, the dramatisation of Hitler as imagined by Jojo, and the temporal span of the narrative: Jojo takes mere days to confess to Elsa that the war has ended in the film; whereas in the novel, his ruse continues for years, and he even smuggles Elsa, unaware of the possibility of her own freedom, out of his house and into another flat under the guise that her life, as a Jewish woman, remains endangered, even in 1949. What may be an understandable and pitiable (because brief) deception on the part of a German boy in the film is monstrous in the novel as Jojo ages, his first-person narration

revealing the extent of his deluded self-deception and justification for continuing to hold Elsa prisoner while insisting on his status as her protector.

Jojo Rabbit is particularly relevant for this book as a reversal of some of the
earlier configurations of adaptation in relation to Indigeneity. *Caging Skies*'
author is a US-born New Zealand (Pākehā)-Belgian woman, the adaptation's screenwriter and director a Jewish Māori filmmaker. Waititi's playing
the role of Hitler in the film, his New Zealand accent often audible, visibly
undermines Hitler's genocidal, white supremacist worldview through the
irony of Waititi's often humorous portrayal, undercutting Hitler's ideology. Moreover, at the 2020 Academy Awards, where Waititi won the award
for Best Adapted Screenplay, Waititi also introduced the honorary Oscars,
including one to actor Wes Studi (Cherokee), and prefaced them with a land
acknowledgement: 'The academy would like to acknowledge that tonight
we have gathered on the ancestral lands of the Tongva, the Tataviam and the
Chumash. We acknowledge them as the first peoples of this land on which
the motion picture community lives and works' (qtd in Srikanth 2020).
Although territorial acknowledgements have come under scrutiny for the
lack of reparation that accompanies them (see âpihtawikosisân 2016), it is
notable that Waititi's was the first such acknowledgement at the Academy
Awards, locating the materiality of the Oscar pageant on Indigenous territory. Thus, both the text of *Jojo Rabbit* itself, through Waititi's portrayal of
Hitler, and Waititi's contribution to the Academy Award ceremony inscribe
and reinscribe Indigeneity through his adaptation of a non-Indigenous
novel and his framing of the Oscars' location.

To *Jojo Rabbit* we might add other adaptations or repurposings of material
that seek to Indigenise such material, such as the Australian film *Ten Canoes*
(2006), co-directed by Dutch-Australian filmmaker Rolf de Heer and Peter
Djigirr (Yolngu). The first Australian feature film in an Indigenous language
(Yolngu),[1] *Ten Canoes* is based on ethnographic photos of the Yolngu people
in the Arnhem Land community of Ramgining by Donald Thomson, recon-
textualising and reframing those images. That said, although the impetus
for the film came from prominent Yolngu actor David Gulpilil, the issue
of Indigenous representational sovereignty in this case is complicated by
the role of the white director de Heer, who both claims, 'I didn't impose,
I served' and insists the Ramgining community he collaborated with 'don't
know what to put in a film' (qtd in Rutherford 2013, 144); further, de Heer
was keen for the film to 'work in a Western storytelling tradition' (qtd in
Davis 2007, 7) and 'insist[ed] upon complete nudity' from the actors despite
'contradiction with the photographic evidence' (Renes 2014, 858).

If *Ten Canoes* 'uses the codes of ethnographic film and photography'
(Rutherford 2013, 139), a 2015 series of short films entitled *Souvenir*

made by Indigenous filmmakers in Canada repurposes footage, mostly of Indigenous people by settler Canadian filmmakers, in the National Film Board's (NFB) documentary archive. Jeff Barnaby's (Mi'gmaq) *Etlinisgu'niet (Bleed Down)*, Kent Monkman's (Cree) *Sisters and Brothers*, and Caroline Monnet's (Algonquin) *Mobilize* deploy NFB footage to castigate the Canadian settler-state for its residential school programme and its poisonous extractivism, in the case of Barnaby's and Monkman's films, and to insist upon Indigenous mobility and resurgence, as in Monnet's film. Monnet's focus on the figure of Janice Lawrence (Okanagan), an Indigenous 'hostess' at Montreal's Expo 67 who was selected from her rural British Columbian home to tour visitors around the Indian Pavilion in Montreal, implicitly insists on the bodily sovereignty of Indigenous women at a time when the then Canadian government, led by Stephen Harper (Conservative), refused to launch an inquiry into Missing and Murdered Indigenous Women, stating the crisis was not 'high on our radar' (qtd in Kappo 2014).[2] Although these examples of adaptations and repurposings differ significantly, they all reverse the relationship of 'raw material' to adaptation where Indigeneity is concerned, and particularly in the case of the repurposed NFB images constitute a reclamation of the gaze and the assertion of representational sovereignty.

The *Souvenir* series constitutes a very different mode of adaptation than those considered elsewhere in this book, given the documentary provenance of the films, the fact that they are shorts, and their contexts of exhibition: first at the Aboriginal Pavilion at the Pan Am Games in Toronto in 2015, and now available on the NFB website, they circulate very differently from the feature films with which this book has been concerned. Concerns of circulation affect not only the higher-stakes feature filmmaking but also the reach of the 'original' text, repackaged in the wake of the adaptation for what a publisher hopes will be a newly expanded audience. For both the text and the film, financial considerations are inseparable from the scope of circulation.

Although circulation is full of financial implications, however, it is not completely reducible to them. Not all texts or their adaptations circulate in the same way or with the same reach within and across the global cultural marketplace. If, as Alexa Alice Joubin writes, 'Shakespeare remains alive today in large part because the canon has become a self-validating, self-regenerating commodity in the global cultural marketplace' (2017), not all film versions of Shakespeare will reach a sizeable audience; indeed, 'some of the best adaptations of Shakespeare on screen are not easy to obtain' (Cartmell 2000, x). In terms of this book's focus, one key example is Don Selwyn's *Maori Merchant of Venice* (2002), in the Māori language (*te reo*), which, as Mark Thornton Burnett writes, was well received at scholarly meetings and film festivals, but 'did not move much beyond a circumscribed cultural circle. A long-awaited DVD edition has failed to materialize' (2013, 234). If this film's 'fleeting visibility' and 'relative anonymity … suggests fundamental variations in the universal cultural imprimatur with which Shakespeare is invariably associated' (Burnett 2013, 234), such is not the exclusive fate of some Shakespeare adaptations. *Monkey Beach*, the 2000 novel by Haisla author Eden Robinson that was nominated for several major literary prizes in Canada, was adapted by Métis filmmaker L. Sarah Todd and released in 2019, but at the time of writing this film has yet to be released overseas (and to date I have only seen the film not in the more usually anticipated location of an art-house cinema, but rather on an Air Canada flight home). Widely read and taught in Canada, Robinson's novel might be considered part of the contemporary Canadian literary canon, yet its considerable accolades have not (yet) enabled a circulation of its adaptation in the global cultural marketplace.

In examining how race, nation and cultural power operate in and through film adaptation in the global cultural marketplace, this book has identified a number of patterns in modes of adaptation. These are by no means the only modes of interest in relation to these areas of investigation: this conclusion has gestured to just two others in Indigenous adaptations of non-Indigenous source material and what we might consider inter-Indigenous adaptations along the lines of *Monkey Beach* as well as the much earlier *Smoke Signals* (1998), directed by Arapaho/Cheyenne filmmaker Chris Eyre from Spokane/Coeur d'Alene author Sherman Alexie's screenplay based on his collection of short stories *The Lone Ranger and Tonto Fistfight in Heaven* (1993), which so far has fared better than *Monkey Beach* in the global cultural marketplace. One irony, of course, is that we rely on the global cultural marketplace for most texts and their adaptations to reach us; it is one major means by which we become more acquainted with other nations and cultures. As such, it is even more pressing to examine the representations that circulate so widely, that reach us in the first place, to determine whether they offer critique of dominant narratives that demand further scrutiny, whether they uphold those narratives, intentionally or otherwise, or present radical alternatives to the stories we already know. Adaptation is not going to go away, and we will keep seeing films that tell stories we've heard before, just as we will keep being introduced to pre-existing stories via their adaptations. When these stories reach us from across and via the global cultural marketplace, it is our responsibility not just to take pleasure in them, or take them at face value, but also to consider other versions of these stories, who has told them and for whom.

Notes

Introduction

1. Indeed, Elliott notes that Lewis Melville first 'declare[d] the impossibility of complete fidelity in literature to film adaptation' in 1912 (Elliott 2013, 26).
2. Similarly, Laura U. Marks's study of 'intercultural cinema' focuses on experimental film and video (1999).
3. Richard Van Camp's (and his protagonist's) nation is now known as Tłı̨chǫ. When discussing *The Lesser Blessed* specifically, I use the earlier name 'Dogrib' instead, as do the novel and the film.

Chapter 1

1. There has been a good deal of controversy over Campion's representation of Māori characters in *The Piano* (1992). Although such characters, incidental to the plot, present both implicit and explicit critiques of the exploitative settler Stewart (Sam Neill), they are also portrayed as naïve and childish. See Cooper 2009, 298; Moine 2009, 200; Leotta 2012, 128.
2. Following Gregory Younging's *Elements of Indigenous Style* (2018, 78), I capitalise Indigenous when referring to actual Indigenous people. I use the lower case when referring to processes of indigenisation on the part of settlers.
3. When Campion adapts this scene, only Goodwood's line 'I hate to lose sight of you' gestures to this line of conversation; it also appears in the novel (210).
4. As Roger Luckhurst notes, the serialisation of *The Portrait of a Lady* in 1880–1 coincided with the debating of the Married Woman's Property Act, which ultimately passed in 1882: 'Hitherto, a woman's wealth and property moved from her father to her husband on marriage . . . For English [*sic*] readers, Isabel's choices were being transformed in the year the serialization unfolded' (2009, xxiii).
5. Tellingly – and, in some sense, proleptically – Patricia Crick's notes for the 1984 Penguin edition of *The Portrait of a Lady* connect James's narrative to *Les Liaisons Dangereuses*, Pierre Choderlos de Laclos's eighteenth-century novel, which was adapted as a play by Christopher Hampton (1985), of which

Frears's film is itself an adaptation. Crick argues that Madame Merle's name 'calls to mind the name of the Marquise de Merteuil' (645, n2), Valmont's former lover.

6. For instance, Rustom Bharucha considers Nair's *Salaam Bombay!* to be 'nice, voyeuristic entertainment', a film 'that merely disguises commercial stereotypes in a somewhat unfamiliar idiom': it 'demonstrate[s] how skilfully the "reality" of third world poverty can be commodified in ways that appear to reject the system, but which merely reinforce the premises of our established culture' in an effort 'not to offend her audience too much' (1989, 1275, 1277).

7. For an extended discussion of the film's alterations in Becky's mothering, see Moya 2010.

8. The screenplay, written by Matthew Faulk, Mark Skeet and Julian Fellowes, included in Universal Studios' book *Vanity Fair: Bringing Thackeray's Timeless Novel to the Screen* (2004), gives Biju two lines of dialogue: one muttered in Hindi under his breath, regarding Jos and Becky, translated into English as 'He's harder to land than he looks' (95); the other in response to Becky's question about what his name means in India ('Just Biju' [96]). Neither of these lines appears in the final film.

9. In contrast, the BBC adaptation only mention's Pitt's pamphlet on malt.

10. The DVD bonus material includes a slightly longer version of this scene, in which two men, local to the island, joke about how long Rawdon will last ('He'll be dead in three [years]', one wagers). This version of the scene includes a shot of the Union flag trailing in the dirt behind the procession, an implicit commentary on the fate of the British Empire cut from the final version.

11. If heritage cinema in the 1980s and 1990s was roundly criticised for its conservatism at the same time as it offered 'visual, literary and performative period pleasures', Claire Monk suggests that later films evincing 'a deep self-consciousness about how the past is represented' might be considered 'post-heritage' in their 'implied reaction' to heritage cinema (2001 [1995], 7).

Chapter 2

1. Mrs Norris's very name is a clue to her reprehensible character, as Corinne Fowler observes, for it 'almost certainly alludes to the brutal slave captain, John Norris, condemned by the abolitionist Thomas Clarkson, who was favoured by Austen' (2020, 149).

2. See Perry 1994, 101; Kirkham 2000, 117; Landry 2000, 60.

3. The representation of slavery in Sterne's text, however, is by no means straightforward. Although Laura Brown contends that 'the imprisonment of the starling is a "disguise" for the institution of slavery, and the bird itself . . . is an African slave in the new world' (2001, 253), Ramesh Mallipeddi argues that Sterne invokes slavery in order to refer 'not to the literal enslavement of people of African descent but to the figural captivity of Englishmen' who in the context of Yorick's travels in 'absolutist France' in *A Sentimental Journey*

are 'not literally slaves but religious minorities, victims not of colonial slavery but of Catholic persecution' (2016, 87).

4. Rozema has claimed the reference to tobacco is an attempt not to 'tie things up quite so sweetly', and for the plot resolution offer only 'a partial redemption' (2004, 259).

5. According to Nicholas Draper, 'the universe of absentee slave-owners gives overwhelming evidence that slave-ownership permeated the elites in mid-nineteenth-century Britain'; further, throughout nineteenth-century Britain, 'the total proportion of wealth attributed to slavery fluctuated . . . between 15 and 20 per cent' (2014, 65, 49).

6. Although the novel was published after the abolition of both the slave trade (1807) and slavery (1833) throughout the British Empire, Lockwood's narration begins in 1801 (Brontë 2003, 3); Meyer calculates that Earnshaw finds Heathcliff in 1769 (1996: 98).

7. For other iterations of this argument, see Gérin 1971, 225–27; Eagleton 1995, chapter 1; and Beaumont 2004.

8. See von Sneidern (1995) for a discussion of Isabella's re-racialisation as non-white following her marriage to Heathcliff (182).

9. Initially, however, Arnold 'sought a Romani actor for the part' (Colón Semenza and Hasenfratz 2015, 375). The director also contemplated casting a woman in role of Heathcliff (see Hazette 2015, 297).

10. As Michael D. Friedman notes, however, there is an incoherence in Taymor's film insofar as its Hawaiian location means it 'thereby ahistorically re-defines Hawaii as the site where Caliban is finally set free and slavery ends, despite the fact that African slaves were never actually kept on the Hawaiian islands' (2013, 431).

11. See McClintock 1995, chapter 5, for a discussion of racist soap advertisements in the nineteenth century. Although these began to appear in the mid-nineteenth century, after the publication of Brontë's novel, obviously they predate Arnold's film adaptation.

12. For example, Peter Kosminsky's 1992 film adaptation and ITV's 2009 adaptation directed by Cody Giedroyc both include the second generation of Earnshaws, Lintons, and Heathcliffs, unlike William Wyler's 1939 film version.

13. In contrast, Hazette reads 'Arnold's Cathy [as] a natural political activist' who is 'Heathcliff's liberator' (2015, 301).

14. As Catherine Hall, Nicholas Draper and Keith McClelland note, 'Women slave-owners are currently beginning to attract attention after the long-sustained assumption that all slave-ownership was a masculine prerogative' (2014, 21). In addition to the need to avoid collapsing gendered oppression with slavery, the notion of Brontë's *Wuthering Heights* depicting 'forms of domestic (or internal) colonization' such as 'the colonization of Britain's rural peripheries by an educated elite' (Tsao 2014, 97) miscasts class and regional disparities by overwriting them with racialised (anti)imperial struggles. This

is not to dispute the possibility of 'local culture [being] eradicated' (98), nor to minimise the power imbalances between metropolitan elite and the rural margins, but rather to place this violence in a more appropriate contextual framework. After all, as Heywood's work (1987) tells us, the 'rural periphery' of Yorkshire contained within it slaveholding practices.

15. Since the release of Arnold's film and this song by Mumford & Sons, Winston Marshall, formerly the band's lead guitarist, has been associated with right-wing politics, having publicly praised the work of Andy Ngo (see Richards 2021).

16. For instance, Caryl Phillips's novel *The Lost Child* (2015) includes a partial reimagining of *Wuthering Heights*, in which Earnshaw's journey to Liverpool more explicitly connects him to slavery-related business: 'Please, must you go, Father? Your ship is in Antigua, isn't it? Are there problems at your sugar-works?' (243). Further, Phillips posits that Heathcliff is the child of Earnshaw and a formerly enslaved woman, 'branded with the initials of another man' (251). Critics of Brontë's novel have also speculated that Heathcliff might be Earnshaw's son (see Eagleton 2005, 106; Pybus 2011, 16). Arnold's film raises the possibility of Earnshaw having fathered Heathcliff through rumours that Hindley has heard, but this suggestion is not pursued any further (perhaps because Cathy's notion of Heathcliff as her brother in an affiliative sense is already challenging for the love story between the two protagonists). See also Corinne Fowler's (2017) study of twenty-first-century postcolonial literary responses to *Mansfield Park*.

Chapter 3

1. 'So Much Water So Close to Home' was originally published in Carver's collection *What We Talk about When We Talk about Love*, published in 1981. However, it was one of the stories severely truncated by Carver's editor, Gordon Lish. The full (original) version of the story was published in the 1988 collection, *Where I'm Calling From*. This chapter discusses the full version of the story.

2. The term 'Bollywood' itself is often misapplied. In use predominantly from the late 1990s, 'Bollywood' is often deployed in such a way that 'demonstrates a complete ignorance that feature films are produced in over twenty languages in India every year' (Ganti 2012, 13) and that Bombay/Mumbai is by no means the only site of production of Indian cinema: 'Bollywood' thus 'conceals the hegemonizing hold of Hindi commercial cinema, produced in Mumbai, over other production centres in Chennai, Kolkata, and Hyderabad which are as old, if not as big, as Mumbai' (Gera Roy and Beng Huat 2012, ix). Thus, the use of 'Bollywood' in reference 'to all filmmaking both past and present within India' (Ganti 2012, 13), and indeed, to filmmaking by members of the Indian diaspora who set their work in India, collapses numerous regional, national and linguistic filmmaking contexts. Nonetheless, I retain

the use of 'Bollywood' in this chapter as a reflection of its use by both critics and *Bride and Prejudice*'s filmmakers (see Chadha and Mareyda Berges
2005), and argue that Chadha's film is influenced by, but not a product of,
Bollywood.

3. Namrata Shirodkar, who plays Jaya/Jane, is also a former beauty queen
   (Miss India, 1993).

4. As Andrew Hassam points out, a variety of 'exotic' locations have been
   deployed in Indian films in recent decades: 'The mountains of Kashmir as
   a romantic destination for the hero and heroine were replaced by the Swiss
   Alps in the 1980s, which were themselves supplemented by the mountains of
   New Zealand and Scotland in the 1990s; but the increase in overseas locations
   has also seen an increase in urban settings, with New York and London the
   pre-eminent choice due to a combination of their iconicity, blatant consumer-
   ism, and financial incentives' (2012, 265). Other locations, Hassam continues,
   include Sydney, Toronto, Cape Town, Rome, Paris (the latter two 'due to their
   romantic connotations'), Dubai, Seoul, Singapore, and Bangkok (2012, 265).

5. It is worth noting with reference to Lalita's anti-imperial statements that the
   Bakshis live at 7 Udham Singh Road in Amritsar, named for the Punjabi revo-
   lutionary figure who assassinated a former Lieutenant Governor of Punjab to
   take revenge for the Amritsar Massacre of 1919 and who was involved in the
   movement for Indian independence (Chadha and Mayeda Berges 2005). The
   close-up on the Bakshi house's address prior to the film's introduction of
   the family emphasises this historical reference.

6. In a scene cut from the film but included as part of the DVD's bonus material,
   Kiran also speaks derisively during the Goa trip about NRIs in Southall, the
   location of the Bakshis' UK-based relatives: 'Southall's just so first-gener-
   ation . . . I thought anyone who'd made it moved out ages ago.' After Jaya
   leaves the group following this comment, with Balraj going after her, it is
   Darcy who criticises Kiran for her insulting remarks. This scene was retained
   in the core narrative of the film's Hindi version, *Balle Balle! Amritsar to LA*.

7. Chandra's emphasis on the hotel's size, however, rather than Elizabeth's
   appeal to Darcy's 'beautiful grounds at Pemberley' (Austen 2004, 286), suggests a phallic reference on Chandra's part.

8. However, the market scenes set in Amritsar were, in fact, filmed on a
   purpose-built set in Mumbai (Chadha and Mayeda Berges 2005).

9. *Mabo* refers to the 1992 High Court decision in the *Mabo v. Queensland* case
   that 'overturned the nation's founding doctrine of *terra nullius*' and 'force[d]
   Australians to rethink "race relations"' and 'the story of the nation's origin'
   (Collins and Davis 2004, 3, 4).

10. Note that Carver's 'Stuart' becomes 'Stewart' in *Jindabyne*.

11. Juchau, for instance, claims that Claire's 'longing look suggests much is for-
    given' (2006, para. 7), but Claire's pained expression is by no means unam-
    biguously 'longing'.

12. Although an imperfect tool for gauging the national mood, *Jindabyne*'s failure to win any Australian Film Institute awards, despite being nominated in nine categories, and in particularly losing in the Best Picture category to *Ten Canoes*, which focuses on Indigenous people and is co-directed by Rolf de Heer and Indigenous actor Peter Djigirr, perhaps underscores the limitations of exploring the relationship between Indigenous and non-Indigenous communities while prioritising settler experience. See, however, the Conclusion.

Chapter 4

1. As Simone Murray observes, even novels shortlisted for the Booker Prize have been disproportionately adapted, noting that in the first forty years of the prize's existence, 'an astounding 21 per cent of shortlisted novels have resulted in produced films or television adaptations' (2012, 110).
2. There are some critical detractors from the view that *Midnight's Children* is a magic realist text, of course. For instance, Edward Barnaby argues that the novel 'is more holistically understood as a realist satire of the neuroses of an Indian man who becomes convinced by the competing imagery and rhetoric of the spectacles of imperialism and nationalism that the events of his life mirror the historical narrative of modern India' (2005, 3). Although Barnaby draws partly on Rushdie's account of his attempt to convince Ken Taylor, a prospective scriptwriter for the failed BBC adaptation, that the narrative of *Midnight's Children* featured 'apparently "magical" moments [that] had naturalistic explanations', Barnaby does not include Rushdie's confession in the same essay that 'I now think it was quite wrong of me to "sell" Ken this naturalistic version of my book. I suppose I thought it would allow him to pull the dramatic structure of the serial into shape, and if the scripts needed an injection of "unnaturalism", that could be added later. Things turned out to be more complicated' (Rushdie 2002, 79).
3. Similarly, as Ananya Jahanara Kabir notes, Nadir Khan, Saleem's mother's first husband, has an 'uncomplimentary portrayal from the start of the novel'; his representation by Zaib Shaikh in the film is a far cry from '[p]hysically unattractive, lank-haired, soft-paunched' literary counterpart (2002, 257).
4. *Cracking India* was originally published in the UK under the title *Ice-Candy-Man* in 1988; the new title accompanied the novel's US publication in 1991.
5. *Midnight's Children* was filmed in Sri Lanka (that country described as a 'drip from [Saleem's] nose' in Rushdie's novel [232]) under 'the subterfuge of a false title' (Malamud 2012). Mehta's 2005 film, *Water*, was also partly filmed there, after protests in Varanasi, where the film was initially shot in India. Moreover, initial plans to adapt *Midnight's Children* into a BBC series also included filming in Sri Lanka when permission to film in India was denied; however, the Sri Lankan government rescinded their permission in 1998 after pressure from Iran, nine years after the issuing of the *fatwa*. Mehta's film

production was also halted due to pressure on Sri Lanka from Iran once news of the film was leaked, but the president, Mahinda Rajapaksa, permitted the production to continue (see BBC 2011).

6. For his part, Martel states that when asked which version of the story is correct, 'I never g[i]ve ... a definitive answer' (2012, 9).

7. Similarly, Anthony Minghella's 1996 film adaptation of Michael Ondaatje's novel Booker Prize-winning *The English Patient* (1992) also featured a switch in the protagonist's hometown from Toronto to Montreal, in this case to accommodate the French accent of Juliette Binoche, who plays the character of Hana (although Binoche's accent is clearly not Québécois; see Roberts 2002, 210).

8. See Roberts 2011, 186–98.

9. In the novel, however, the tiger in this scene is not Richard Parker but Mahisha (Martel 2002, 38).

10. As Charles R. Acland emphasises, however, the counter-narrative presented by *Life after Pi* is partial in its discussion of labour, mainly through its effacement of Rhythm & Hues' *Canadian* employees, leaving the documentary to suggest that the company – and indeed, the VFX industry as a whole – has responsibilities only to its American workers, wedging the Canada–US border between different nation-states' members of the VFX workforce. Thus, aspects of the film's afterlife, including the VFX protests at the Oscar ceremony, the truncation of Rhythm & Hues employee Bill Westenhofer's acceptance speech once he began to address the company's bankruptcy on air, and *Life after Pi*, feed the narrative that subsidy-offering countries such as Canada operate as 'vulture nations' (2018, 149).

11. Ang Lee places this figure at 80 per cent for 'the bulk of the pre-production and production [... taking] place in an abandoned airport in Taichung, Taiwan's third-largest city, along with brief side trips to the Taipei Zoo and the beaches of Kenting' (2012, 14).

12. The filmmakers 'shifted the spot where the *Tsimtsum* sinks to the northern Marianas Trench' in the interest of plausibility, although even with such a change, had Pi's journey occurred in real life, 'he would be going against the wind and currents no matter where he was, never making it to Mexico at all' (Castelli 2012, 72).

13. Martel claimed in an essay written for the Powell's Books website that he had read a review of Scliar's novel by John Updike in *The New York Times*. Intrigued by the description of a novel that Updike seemed to have found 'forgettable', Martel 'didn't really want to read the book. Why put up with the gall? Why put up with a brilliant premise ruined by a lesser writer. Worse, what if Updike had been wrong? What if not only the premise but also its rendition were perfect?' (2002c). It later transpired that Updike never reviewed *Max and the Cats*, and that *The New York Times* never printed a review of the novel at all. Later, in a Q&A session with readers on *The Guardian*'s website,

Martel stated, 'Clearly I got some of my facts wrong' (2002b) and maintained it was still the case that he had not yet read *Max and the Cats* itself.

14. Both the name 'Richard Parker' and the scenes of cannibalism in *Life of Pi* have antecedents in Poe's narrative. See Ketterer 2009 for a further exploration of the links between these texts.

Chapter 5

1. Keneally notes that in the writing of historical fiction, 'the newspapers of the day are beyond value' (1975, 28).

2. Jacky Porter, 'known to the Governor brothers as "Uncle"', is Tabidgi's antecedent in Clune's text (1959, 46).

3. The term 'Iroquois' has been supplanted by 'Haudenosaunee'. At the time of the French imperial project in North America, the Haudenosaunee consisted of five nations: the Cayuga, the Mohawk, the Seneca, the Onondaga and the Oneida. A sixth nation, the Tuscarora, joined the confederacy in 1722.

4. For instance, Parkman's racism is evident when he declares, 'the mind of the Indian . . . was and is almost hopelessly stagnant. The very traits that raise him above the servile races are hostile to the kind and degree of civilization which those races so easily attain. His intractable spirit of independence, and the pride which forbids him to be an imitator, reinforce but too strongly that savage lethargy of mind from which it is so hard to rouse him. No race, perhaps, ever offered greater difficulties to those laboring for its improvement' (1900 [1867]), 87).

5. 'Algonkian' is not the language of the Algonquin. Algonquian is, rather, a language group, to which Algonquin does belong. Moore spells Algonquin as 'Algonkin' throughout the novel. His first draft of the screenplay mostly uses 'Algonquin', with occasional retention of 'Algonkian' (see Moore 1985b, 6, 153).

6. Jeanne A. Flood notes that 'Nicanis' was the name given to the Jesuit Paul Je Jeune, and was taken to mean 'friend' (1990, 50n21).

7. This comparison between *Dances with Wolves* and *Black Robe* was particularly visible in the latter's marketing, with posters and DVD covers featuring such review excerpts as 'Forget "Dances with Wolves", this is the real thing' (*Daily Express*) and 'Packs twice the punch as *Dances with Wolves*' (John Anderson, *Newsday*).

8. The first draft of Moore's screenplay initially uses 'Nicanis' to refer to Laforgue in dialogue uttered by Algonquin characters, and occasionally by Laforgue referring to himself. These references are deleted in the annotations, with 'Nicanis' replaced with 'Blackrobe' when Algonquin characters speak, and with 'Laforgue' when he refers to himself (see Moore 1985b, 35, 41). Daniel is never referred to as 'Iwanchou' even in the first draft of the screenplay.

9. In the novel, Tallevant asks, 'Why is the Commandant dressed like a Savage?' (Moore 1985a, 20), but it is Doumergue who states, 'We're not colonizing the Savages. They're colonizing us' (22).

10. Moore's preface acknowledges, 'I am aware that I have taken a novelist's license in the question of Algonkian understanding of Iroquoian speech' (1985a, viii) and presumably extends this same license to the Montagnais' speech.

11. The first draft of Moore's screenplay similarly has Indigenous characters speaking largely in obscenities. The film also replaces 'Savages' with 'Indians', and refers to the French, rather than the Normans, replicating twentieth-century nomenclature. The first draft of the screenplay, by Moore, retains both 'Savages' (in both directions and dialogue) and 'Normans'; however, 'Normans' is replaced in annotations by 'French' (e.g. Moore 1985b, 17). In the film, 'Savages' is uttered by the French priest Laforgue meets at Rouen Cathedral, who is missing an ear after his journey to New France, claiming Indigenous people are 'uncivilised' and 'live in utter darkness'; in a later scene, Laforgue asks, 'Lord, I beg you, show your mercy to these savage people', and Father Jerome at the Huron mission tells Laforgue, 'Who knows what the savages will do. Who knows what they think.' That 'savages' should first be uttered by the priest missing an ear, however, appears to attest to the veracity of this noun, even if 'Indian' dominates the dialogue, departing from the original script. As critics of the novel have noted, Laforgue's own ailments are symbolic, his deafness representing 'his incapacity not just to hear but to understand anything of the Savages' [sic] language or of their culture or beliefs' (O'Donoghue 1993, 133). Yet this reading does not account for the fact that Laforgue's deafness ultimately clears, some hundred pages before the end of the novel: 'His ears, which a few days ago had been dulled by infection, now seemed to him like the ears of a Savage in their ability to detect the merest sound' (Moore 1985a, 151). If Laforgue's deafness has been symbolic, this logic suggests that Laforgue comes to understand the Indigenous nations he attempts to convert, indeed, in an appropriative claiming of Indigenous people's posited superior hearing.

12. A version of this line appears in the novel (127).

13. Both the Meech Lake Accord and the Charlottetown Agreement were attempts by the federal government in Canada to bring Quebec into the Constitution (which it has still not signed). Meech Lake failed when Elijah Harper, Oji-Cree Member of the Legislative Assembly of Manitoba, refused his consent on the grounds that the Accord failed to address Indigenous people's concerns ahead of Quebec's. Charlottetown was subject to a national referendum in the wake of Meech Lake's failure, but it did not have sufficient votes to pass. The Royal Commission on Aboriginal Peoples, tasked with 'mak[ing] recommendations promoting reconciliation between aboriginal peoples and Canadian society as a whole' (qtd in McCall 2011, 109), was launched in response to both the 'Oka Crisis' and the demise of Meech Lake. Most of its recommendations were not implemented.

14. The baseball game at the end of the Highway's screenplay appears to be a nod to Kinsella, who, in addition to authoring many short story collections about the Ermineskin reserve, also wrote several books about baseball, most famously *Shoeless Joe* (1982), which was adapted into the film *Field of Dreams*, directed by Phil Alden Robinson (1989).

15. Further items housed in the University of Guelph's Tomson Highway Script Collection offering similar, Silas-centred advice include story edit notes by Allan Magee for Yorktown Productions and by script editor Walter Donohue.

16. At its inception, the Reform Party was designed to represent Western Canadian disaffection from central Canada, where federal political power, as well as financial power, is based. This right-wing party came to be associated with such issues as opposition to immigration, official bilingualism, gun control and support for reinstating capital punishment in Canada. The Reform Party, rebranded as the Canadian Alliance in 2000, in turn merged with the Progressive Conservatives in order to put a stop to a division of Canada's right-wing vote, and to form the Conservative Party of Canada in 2003.

Chapter 6

1. In a somewhat different formulation, Michelle Raheja (Seneca) conceives of some works by white filmmakers representing Indigenous cultures, such as Edward Curtis's *In the Land of War Canoes: A Dream of Kwakiutl Life in the Northwest* (1914; first titled *In the Land of the Head Hunters*), as 'to some extent, collaborative, similar to the "as told to" autobiographies of indigenous people who worked with white amanuenses' (2007, 1182 n13).

2. Prior to making *Rabbit-Proof Fence*, Noyce's films included Hollywood productions such as *Clear and Present Danger* (1993), *Patriot Games* (1993), *The Bone Collector* (1999) and *The Saint* (1997). As Ingo Petzke explains, Noyce decided to make *Rabbit-Proof Fence* when 'he was working on the script of The Sum of All Fears [*sic*], the third of his adaptations of Tom Clancy novels starring Harrison Ford, but the actor refused to commit to the film' (2007, 233).

3. There are, in fact, a few subtitles in *Rabbit-Proof Fence*, but most of the dialogue is in English.

4. The screenplay originally showed Neville in a more sympathetic light by including details of his family, particularly his son, who is the same age as Daisy (Olsen 2002, 68).

5. For a discussion of the implications of circulating Stolen Generations testimony – including 'across a wide and international readership' (198) – see Whitlock 2001.

6. Although the terms *iwi* and *hapū* have often been translated into English as tribe and sub-tribe, as Angela Ballara observes, such translations ascribe 'a hierarchical and static model' that does not reflect Māori kinship; hence 'peoples' and 'clans [. . .] would be better glosses' (1998, 19, 17).

7. Jennifer L. Gauthier includes *Whale Rider* as an 'indigenous feature film' (2004, 64), along with *Atanarjuat* and – just as problematically as *Whale Rider* – *Rabbit-Proof Fence*. Ihimaera has also indicated that he considers *Whale Rider* to be a Māori film (qtd in Hokowhitu 2007, 66), although John Barnett has explicitly said, 'it's set in a Maori village, but it's not a Maori film' ('Behind the Scenes Featurette' 2008). For Brendan Hokowhitu, *Whale Rider* constitutes a 'pseudo-indigenous film' (2007, 54).

8. As Pitts notes, 'By the time *Whale Rider* was released in 2003, only four of the 92 dramatic feature films financed by the NZFC were directed by Māori' (2013, 47). Margaret Werry further explains, 'no dedicated production company existed for Māori film, a situation for which some held the NZFC largely responsible' (2011, 212).

9. Such changes are in evidence in the comparison of Ihimaera's annotations on Caro's 9 August 2001 draft (2001a) and the white revisions dated 18 October 2001 (2001b).

10. See Hokowhitu 2008 for an in-depth analysis of the construction of Māori patriarchy in *Whale Rider*.

11. See Ka'ai (2005, 8) for a discussion of *Whale Rider*'s inappropriate use of Pai during the *karanga* on the marae.

12. In contrast, Ihimaera's third draft screenplay, with Ian Mune (undated), amplifies Nani Flowers's and her female ancestors' significance, even beyond the novel.

13. Porourangi is also characterised in this draft of the screenplay as a kind of celebrity of the art world, and at the end of the film somewhat of a villain, as he takes a chainsaw to carve up the carcass of a stranded dead whale, much to his brother Rawiri's horror.

14. The film's post-production was also carried out in Germany.

15. Van Camp has also discussed the publication of his children's books by American presses in the context of greater exposure: 'Had [they] gone to a Canadian publisher or an Aboriginal publisher, I'm worried [they] wouldn't have gotten the publicity that [they] did' (qtd in Saltman 2003).

Chapter 7

1. See, for instance, Taiaiake Alfred's (Mohawk) critique of sovereignty: 'For people committed to transcending the imperialism of state sovereignty, the challenge is to de-think the concept of sovereignty and replace it with a notion of power that has at its root a more appropriate premise' (2005, 47). Further, the Government of Nunavut is not synonymous with self-government, as Nunavut Tunngavik Incorporated (NTI), which represents Inuit under the Nunavut Land Claims Agreement (1993), passed a resolution in November 2021 to pursue self-government, arguing that 'the full and effective implementation of critical articles of the Nunavut Agreement' had not taken place: as NTI president Aluki Kotierk writes, 'It has now been twenty-two years since

the public government was created. Our expectations for Nunavut have not matched our reality. Instead, we see that Inuit lives have largely not improved', given Nunavut's 'housing crisis, with crumbling and inadequate infrastructure, grave food insecurity, and no real measures to protect our language' (2021).

2. These structural funding issues are commonplace. Although Monika Siebert takes issue with *Atanarjuat* because of its financial support by the Canadian government via the National Film Board, she also praises the work of Abenaki filmmaker Alanis Obomsawin, who makes films for the NFB (2006, 541–2).

3. The Canadian Multiculturalism Act (1988) only includes Indigenous peoples insofar as they are mentioned as follows in the preamble: 'AND WHEREAS the Constitution of Canada recognizes rights of the aboriginal peoples' (369). Further, as Rinaldo Walcott observes, 'embedded in the Act is a double move whereby the *Official Languages Act* places English and French Canada outside the *Multiculturalism Act*. Thus, English and French Canada's heritage begins and ends in Canada' (2003, 136–7). The underlying assumption of the Act is that English and French Canadianness constitute originary, core Canadianness, to which other ethnic groups can only supplement their difference. Conversely, New Zealand's biculturalism 'excludes all those people who are not Māori nor descendants of European settlers' (Hokowhitu and Devadas 2013b, xx).

4. Duff's version is far more cynical about Nig's tattoo, given that it is done by a Pākehā tattooist who is 'cop[ying] out of a book from a photograph of a real tattooed Maori head' (181). For more examination of the role of *moko* in *Once Were Warriors*, see Treagus 2008.

5. Paul Apak Angilirq, commonly known as Paul Apak, died in 1999 prior to the shooting of *Atanarjuat*. Also credited as additional writers on the film are Cohn, Kunuk and the elder Hervé Paniaq. Cohn wrote the English screenplay for the sake of Southern funders in Canada, 'since no one in the Canadian film industry could read Inuktitut or think like Inuit' (Cohn 2002, 25).

6. Prior to the creation of Nunavut in 1999, Canada had ten provinces and two territories, the latter being the Yukon and the Northwest Territories. Following the Nunavut Land Claims Agreement, Nunavut was created in 1999 out of land previously belonging to the Northwest Territories. Although Inuit people also in live in Alaska, Greenland and Siberia, Nunavut's population is majority Inuit (Saladin d'Anglure 2002, 205).

7. Boas's version is presumed to have come from Captain George Comer (Saladin d'Anglure 2002, 207).

8. The spelling of some characters' names differs between the film's subtitles and the published screenplay due to the difference in standardised and simplified spelling of Inuktitut. As Kerstin Knopf notes, 'The script . . . uses the standard spelling, whereas the subtitles . . . use the simplified spelling' (2008, 316, n153). I use the simplified spelling when discussing the film but the standardised spelling of the screenplay when quoting from this text.

9. We are told in the film that Tuurngarjuaq is an 'up-north stranger', which does not map neatly onto the colonial narrative.

Conclusion

1. There is an English voice-over narration, however, delivered by David Gulpilil.
2. Harper's successor as Prime Minister of Canada, the Liberal Justin Trudeau, did launch an inquiry into Missing and Murdered Indigenous Women and Girls, which began in September 2016 and concluded in June 2019.

Bibliography

Acland, Charles R. 2018. 'An Empire of Pixels: Canadian Cultural Enterprise in the Digital Effects Industry.' In *Reading between the Borderlines: Cultural Production and Consumption across the 49th Parallel*, edited by Gillian Roberts, 143–70. Montreal and Kingston: McGill-Queen's University Press.

Adah, Anthony. 2001. 'Post- and Re-Colonizing Aotearoa Screen: Violence and Identity in *Once Were Warriors* and *What Becomes of the Broken Hearted?*' *Film Criticism* 25, no. 3: 46–58.

Aldama, Frederick Luis. 2003. *Postethnic Narrative Criticism: Magicorealism in Oscar 'Zeta' Acosta, Anna Castillo, Julie Dash, Hanif Kureishi, and Salman Rushdie*. Austin: University of Texas Press.

Aldea, Eva. 2011. *Magical Realism and Deleuze: The Indiscernibility of Difference in Postcolonial Literature*. London: Continuum.

Alfred, Taiaiake. 2005. *Wasáse: Indigenous Pathways of Action and Freedom*. Toronto: University of Toronto Press.

Alleva, Richard. 2004. 'Mythmaking: *Hero* & *Vanity Fair*.' *Commonweal* 22: 22–3.

Almond, Ian. 2003. 'Mullahs, Mystics, Moderates and Moghuls: The Many Islams of Salman Rushdie.' *ELH* 70, no. 4: 1137–51.

Andrew, Dudley. 1984. *Concepts in Film Theory*. Oxford: Oxford University Press.

Andrews, Baroness. 2013. 'Foreword.' In *Slavery and the British Country House*, edited by Madge Dresser and Andrew Hann, vi. Swindon: English Heritage.

Apak Angilirq, Paul. 2002. Interview with Nancy Wachowich. In Apak Angilirq, Cohn and Saladin d'Anglure 2002, 16–21.

Apak Angilirq, Paul, Norman Cohn and Bernard Saladin d'Anglure. 2002. *Atanarjuat: The Fast Runner*. Toronto and Igloolik: Coach House Books and Isuma Publishing.

âpihtawikosisân [Chelsea Vowel]. 2016. 'Beyond Territorial Acknowledgments.' 23 September. http://apihtawikosisan.com/2016/09/beyond-territorial-acknow ledgments/.

Aragay, Mireia. 2003. 'Possessing Jane Austen: Fidelity, Authorship, and Patricia Rozema's *Mansfield Park* (1999).' *Literature/Film Quarterly* 31, no. 3: 177–85.

Armstrong, Nancy. 1992. 'Emily's Ghost: The Cultural Politics of Victorian Fiction, Folklore, and Photography.' *NOVEL* 25, no. 3: 245–67.

Ashcroft, Bill. 2012. 'Bollywood, Postcolonial Transformation, and Modernity.' In *Travels of Bollywood Cinema: From Bombay to LA*, edited by Anjali Gera Roy and Chua Beng Huat, 1–18. Delhi: Oxford University Press.

Ashcroft, Bill, Gareth Griffiths and Helen Tiffin. 1998. *Key Concepts in Post-Colonial Studies*. London: Routledge.

Atanarjuat: The Fast Runner, directed by Zacharias Kunuk. 2009 (2001). London: ICA Films, DVD.

Austen, Jane. 2003 (1814). *Mansfield Park*, edited by Kathryn Sutherland. London: Penguin.

Austen, Jane. 2004 (1813). *Pride and Prejudice*. Oxford: Oxford University Press.

Ballara, Angela. 1998. *Iwi: The Dynamics of Māori Tribal Organisation from c. 1769 to c. 1945*. Wellington: Victoria University Press.

Balle Balle! Amritsar to LA, directed by Gurinder Chadha. 2005. Mumbai: Sony Digital Home Entertainment, DVD.

Bangert, Axel, Paul Cooke and Rob Stone. 2016. 'Introduction.' In *Screening European Heritage: Creating and Consuming History on Film*, edited by Paul Cooke and Rob Stone, xvii–xxxiv. Basingstoke: Palgrave Macmillan.

Barclay, Barry. 2003a. 'Celebrating Fourth Cinema.' *Illusions* 35: 7–11.

Barclay, Barry. 2003b. 'An Open Letter to John Barnett from Barry Barclay.' *Onfilm: New Zealand's Film, TV & Video Magazine* 20, no. 2: 11, 14.

Barczewski, Stephanie. 2014. *Country Houses and the British Empire, 1700–1930*. Manchester: Manchester University Press.

Barnaby, Edward. 2005. 'Airbrushed History: Photography, Realism, and Rushdie's *Midnight's Children*.' *Mosaic* 38, no. 1: 1–16.

Bassi, Shaul. 1999. 'Salman Rushdie's Special Effects.' In *Coterminous Worlds: Magical Realism and Contemporary Post-Colonial Literature in English*, edited by Elsa Linguanti, Francesco Casotti and Carmen Concilio, 47–60. Amsterdam: Brill/Rodopi.

Basso, Keith H. 1996. *Wisdom Sits in Places: Landscape and Languages among the Western Apache*. Albuquerque: University of New Mexico Press.

Batty, Nancy E. 1999 (1987). 'The Art of Suspense: Rushdie's 1001 (Mid-) Nights.' In Mukherjee 1999, 95–111.

Bauer, Dale M. 1997. 'Jane Campion's Symbolic Portrait.' *Henry James Review* 18, no. 2. Literature Online.

Bavidge, Jenny. 2016. 'Brontë Soundscapes: The Role of Soundtracks in Adaptations of *Wuthering Heights* in Brontë Heritage Discourse.' In *English Topographies in Literature and Culture: Space, Place, and Identity*, edited by Ina Habermann and Daniela Keller 2016, 116–33. Amsterdam: Rodopi.

BBC. 2005. 'BNP Sees Increase in Total Votes.' *BBC News*, 6 May. http://news.bbc.co.uk/1/hi/uk_politics/vote_2005/frontpage/4519347.stm.

BBC. 2011. 'Rushdie's Midnight's Children Filmed in Sri Lanka.' *BBC News*, 19 May 2011. https://www.bbc.co.uk/news/world-south-asia-13460108.

Beaty, Bart. 2004. 'Imagining the Written Word: Adaptation in the Work of Bruce McDonald and Nick Craine.' *Canadian Journal of Film Studies* 13, no. 2: 22–44.

Beaumont, Matthew. 2004. 'Heathcliff's Great Hunger: The Cannibal Other in *Wuthering Heights*.' *Journal of Victorian Culture* 9, no. 2: 137–63.

Bégin, Jean-François. 2002. 'Yann Martel remporte le Booker Prize.' *La Presse*, 23 October: A1.

'Behind the Scenes Featurette.' 2008. *Whale Rider*. London: Icon Films, DVD.

Bentley, Nancy. 2002. 'Conscious Observation: Jane Campion's *Portrait of a Lady*.' In *Henry James Goes to the Movies*, edited by Susan M. Griffin, 127–46. Lexington: University Press of Kentucky.

Bessière, Irène. 2009. 'Portraits of a Woman: Jane Campion and Henry James.' In Radner, Fox and Bessière 2009, 125–36.

Bessire, Lucas. 2003. 'Talking Back to Primitivism: Divided Audiences, Collective Desires.' *American Anthropologist* 105, no. 4: 832–8.

Betts, Gregory. 2003. 'Dialogic Phantasy in Bruce McDonald's Adaptive Narratives.' In *Double-Takes: Intersections between Canadian Literature and Film*, edited by David R. Jarraway, 95–109. Ottawa: University of Ottawa Press.

Bhabha, Homi K. 2004 (1994). *The Location of Culture*. London: Routledge.

Bharucha, Rustom. 1989. 'Haraam Bombay!' *Economic and Political Weekly*, 10 June. 1275–9. JSTOR.

Black Robe, directed by Bruce Beresford. 2008 (1991). Santa Monica: Lions Gate Entertainment, DVD.

Bluestone, George. 2003 (1957). *Novels into Film*. Baltimore: Johns Hopkins University Press.

Boudreau, Kristin. 2000. '*Is* the World Then So Narrow? Feminist Cinematic Adaptations of Hawthorne and James.' *Henry James Review* 21: 43–53.

Boulokos, George E. 2006. 'The Politics of Silence: "Mansfield Park" and the Amelioration of Slavery.' *NOVEL* 39, no. 3: 361–83.

Brantlinger, Patrick. 1990. *Rule of Darkness: British Literature and Imperialism, 1830–1914*. Ithaca: Cornell University Press.

Bratt, Benjamin. 2013. Interview with Benjamin Bratt. *The Lesser Blessed* [DVD]. Prompton Plains, NJ: Monterey Media.

Brennan, Timothy. 1989. *Salman Rushdie and the Third World: Myths of the Nation*. London: Palgrave Macmillan.

Bride and Prejudice, directed by Gurinder Chadha. 2005 (2004). London: Pathé Distribution International, DVD.

Brontë, Emily. 2003 (1847). *Wuthering Heights*, edited by Pauline Nestor. London: Penguin.

Brown, Laura. 2001. *Fables of Modernity: Literature and Culture in the English Eighteenth Century*. Ithaca: Cornell University Press.

Brydon, Diana. 2013. '"Difficult Forms of Knowing": Enquiry, Injury, and Translocated Relations of Postcolonial Responsibility.' In *Postcolonial Translocations: Cultural Representation and Critical Spatial Thinking*, edited by Marga Munkeit, Markus Schmitz, Mark Stein and Silke Stroh, 3–28. Amsterdam: Rodopi.

Buchanan, Ian. 2012. 'February 13, 2008, and the Baleful Enchantments of an Apology.' *Cultural Politics* 8, no. 1: 45–60.

Bunting, Madeleine. 2005. 'Blame It on the Asians.' *The Guardian*, 14 February. https://www.theguardian.com/politics/2005/feb/14/immigration. immigrationandpublicservices.

Burnett, Mark Thornton. 2007. *Filming Shakespeare in the Global Marketplace*. Basingstoke: Palgrave Macmillan.

Burnett, Mark Thornton. 2013. *Shakespeare and World Cinema*. Cambridge: Cambridge University Press.

Cantwell, Nancy Marck. 2015. 'Waist Not, Want Not: The Corseted Body and Empire in *Vanity Fair*.' *Nineteenth-Century Gender Studies* 11, no. 2. www.ncgs-journal.com/issue112/cantwell.html. 21 paras.

Capitani, Diane. 2002. 'Moral Neutrality in Jane Austen's *Mansfield Park*.' *Persuasions On-line* 23, no. 1: 1–6. www.jasna.org/persuasions/on-line/vol23no1/capitani.html.

Caro, Niki. 2001a. 'The Whale Rider.' Final Draft. South Pacific Pictures: 9 August. Victoria University Wellington Library archives A2003/26/02.

Caro, Niki. 2001b. 'Whale Rider' White Revisions. South Pacific Pictures: 18 October. Victoria University Wellington Library archives A2003/26/02.

Caro, Niki. 2008. DVD commentary. *Whale Rider*. London: Icon Films.

Caro, Niki and Bill Gavin. 2000. 'The Whale Rider.' 3rd Draft Polish. South Pacific Pictures: 6 July. Victoria University Wellington Library archives A2003/26/02.

Cartmell, Deborah. 2000. *Interpreting Shakespeare on Screen*. Basingstoke: Macmillan.

Cartmell, Deborah. 2010. *Jane Austen's* Pride and Prejudice: *The Relationship between Text and Film*. London: Methuen Drama.

Cartmell, Deborah and Imelda Welehan. 2010. *Screen Adaptation: Impure Cinema*. Basingstoke: Palgrave Macmillan.

Carver, Raymond. 1993 (1988). 'So Much Water So Close to Home.' In *Short Cuts*, 69–92. London: Harvill.

Castelli, Jean-Christophe. 2012. *The Making of Life of Pi: A Film, A Journey*. New York: HarperCollins.

Chadha, Gurinder and Paul Mayeda Berges. 2005. DVD commentary. *Bride and Prejudice*. London: Pathé Distribution International.

Chan, Queenie Monica. 2008. 'Reconstructing Images of History: Christopher Doyle, *Rabbit-Proof Fence* and Postcolonial Collage.' *Studies in Australasian Cinema* 2, no. 2: 121–40.

Chandler, Karen Michele. 1997. 'Agency and Social Constraint in Jane Campion's *The Portrait of a Lady*.' *Henry James Review* 18, no. 2. Literature Online.

The Chant of Jimmie Blacksmith, directed by Fred Schepisi. 2008 (1978). Kew, Victoria: Umbrella Entertainment, DVD.

Chordiya, Deepa P. 2007. '"Taking on the Tone of a Bombay Talkie": The Function of Bombay Cinema in Salman Rushdie's *Midnight's Children*.' *ARIEL* 38, no. 4: 97–121.

Churchill, Ward. 2007. 'Reasserting "Consensus": A Somewhat Bitterly Amused Response to Kristof Haavik's "In Defense of *Black Robe.*"' *American Indian Culture and Research Journal* 31, no. 4: 121–43.

Clarke, Micael M. 2008. 'Celluloid Satire, or the Moviemaker as Moralist: Mira Nair's Adaptation of Thackeray's *Vanity Fair.*' In *In/Fidelity: Essays on Film Adaptation*, edited by David L. Kranz and Nancy C. Mellerski, 38–51. Newcastle: Cambridge Scholars Press.

Clune, Frank. 1959. *Jimmy Governor*. Sydney: Horwitz.

Coe, Jason. 2014. 'Competing Narratives: Choosing the Tiger in Ang Lee's *Life of Pi.*' *American Journal of Chinese Studies* 21, no. 1: 21–9.

Cohn, Norman. 2002. 'The Art of Community-Based Filmmaking.' In Apak Angilirq, Cohn and Saladin d'Anglure 2002, 24–7.

Cole, Stewart. 2004. 'Believing in Tigers: Anthropomorphism and Incredulity in Yann Martel's *Life of Pi.*' *Studies in Canadian Literature* 29, no. 2: 22–36.

Collins, Felicity and Therese Davis. 2004. *Australian Cinema after Mabo*. Cambridge: Cambridge University Press.

Colón Semenza, Greg M. and Bob Hasenfratz. 2015. *The History of British Literature on Film, 1895–2015*. New York: Bloomsbury Academic.

Columpar, Corinn. 2007. '"Taking Care of Her Green Stone Wall": The Experience of Space in *Once Were Warriors.*' *Quarterly Review of Film and Video* 24, no. 5: 463–74.

Connor, J. D. 2007. 'The Persistence of Fidelity: Adaptation Theory Today.' *M/C Journal* 10, no. 2. https://journal.media-culture.org.au/mcjournal/article/view/2652.

Convery, Stephanie. 2016. 'We Need to Talk about Cultural Appropriation.' *The Guardian*, 15 September. https://www.theguardian.com/books/2016/sep/15/we-need-to-talk-about-cultural-appropriation-why-lionel-shrivers-speech-touched-a-nerve.

Cooper, Annabel. 2008. '"I Am Isabel, You Know?": The Antipodean Framing of Jane Campion's *Portrait of a Lady.*' *M/C Journal* 5. http://journal.media-culture.org.au/index.php/mcjournal/article/view/99.

Cooper, Annabel. 2009. 'On Viewing Jane Campion as an Antipodean.' In Radner, Fox and Bessière 2009, 279–304.

Corse, Sarah M. 1997. *Nationalism and Literature: The Politics of Culture in Canada and the United States*. Cambridge: Cambridge University Press.

Coulthard, Glen. 2014. *Red Skin, White Masks: Rejecting the Colonial Politics of Recognition*. Minneapolis: Minnesota.

Coulthard, Glen and Leanne Betasamosake Simpson. 2016. 'Grounded Normativity/Place-Based Solidarity.' *American Quarterly* 68, no. 2: 249–55.

Couzens, Andrew James. 2015. 'Recalling Romance and Revision in the Film Adaptations of *Robbery Under Arms* and *The Chant of Jimmie Blacksmith.*' *Adaptation* 9, no. 1: 46–57.

Craine, Nick. 1994. *Dance Me Outside: The Illustrated Screenplay*. Cambridge, ON: Black Eye.

Crosbie, Tom. 2007. 'Critical Historiography in *Atanarjuat The Fast Runner* [*sic*] and *Ten Canoes.*' *Journal of New Zealand Literature* 24, no. 2: 135–52.

Dahlie, Hallvard. 1988. 'Moore's "Conradian" Tale and the Quest for Self.' *Irish University Review* 18, no. 1: 88–95.

Dance Me Outside, directed by Bruce McDonald. 2008 (1995). Toronto: Video Service Corp., DVD.

Daniel, Helen. 1978. 'Purpose and the Racial Outsider: *Burn* and *The Chant of Jimmie Blacksmith.*' *Southerly* 38: 25–43.

Davis, Therese. 2007. 'Remembering Our Ancestors: Cross-Cultural Collaboration and the Mediation of Aboriginal Culture and History in *Ten Canoes* (Rolf de Heer, 2006).' *Studies in Australasian Cinema* 1, no. 1: 5–14.

Derrida, Jacques. 2000. *Of Hospitality: Anne Dufourmantelle Invites Jacques Derrida to Respond*. Translated by Rachel Bowlby. Stanford: Stanford University Press.

Desai, Jigna. 2004. *Beyond Bollywood: The Cultural Politics of South Asian Diasporic Film*. New York and London: Routledge.

De Vos, Laura M. 2020. *Spirals of Transformation: Turtle Island Indigenous Social Movements and Literatures*. University of Washington. https://digital.lib.washington.edu/researchworks/bitstream/handle/1773/45983/DeVos_washington_0250E_21748.pdf?sequence=1&isAllowed=y.

De Zwaan, Victoria. 2015. 'Experimental Fiction, Film Adaptation, and the Case of *Midnight's Children*: In Defense of Fidelity.' *Literature/Film Quarterly* 43, no. 4: 246–62.

Dicecco, Nino. 2015. 'State of the Conversation: The Obscene Underside of Fidelity.' *Adaptation* 8, no. 2: 161–75.

Donahue, Peter. 1997. 'Collecting as Ethos and Technique in *The Portrait of a Lady.*' *Studies in American Fiction* 25, no. 1: 41–56.

Donnar, Glenn. 2011. 'ReViewing *Jimmie*: The Critical Reception of *The Chant of Jimmie Blacksmith.*' *Senses of Cinema* 60. http://sensesofcinema.com/2011/schepisi-dossier/reviewing-jimmie-the-critical-reception-of-the-chant-of-jimmie-blacksmith/.

Doron, Anita. 2013. Interview with Anita Doron. *The Lesser Blessed* [DVD]. Prompton Plains, NJ: Monterey Media.

Draper, Nicholas. 2014. 'Possessing People: Absentee Slave-Owners within British Society.' In Hall, Draper and McClelland 2014a, 34–77. Cambridge: Cambridge University Press.

Duff, Alan. 1995 [1990]. *Once Were Warriors*. London: Vintage.

During, Simon. 1985. 'Postmodernism or Postcolonialism?' *Landfall* 39, no. 3: 366–80.

Durix, Jean-Pierre. 1998. *Mimesis, Genres, and Post-colonial Discourse: Deconstructing Magic Realism*. Basingstoke: Palgrave Macmillan.

Dwyer, Rachel and Divia Patel. 2002. *Cinema India: The Visual Culture of Hindi Film*. London: Reaktion Books.

Dyer, Richard. 1998 (1979). *Stars*. 2nd edn. London: British Film Institute.

Eagleton, Terry. 1995. *Heathcliff and the Great Hunger: Studies in Irish Culture*. London: Verso.

Eagleton, Terry. 2005 (1975). *Myths of Power: A Marxist Study of the Brontës*. 2nd edn. Basingstoke: Palgrave Macmillan.

Elder, Catriona. 2016. 'Watching *Bran Nue Dae* in Japan.' *Journal of Australian Studies* 40, no. 1: 109–17.

Elliott, Kamilla. 2003. *Rethinking the Novel / Film Debate*. Cambridge: Cambridge University Press.

Elliott, Kamilla. 2013. 'Theorizing Adaptations / Adapting Theories.' In *Adaptation Studies: New Challenges, New Directions*, edited by Jørgen Bruhn, Anne Gjelsvik and Eirik Frisvold Hanssen, 19–45. London: Bloomsbury Academic.

Elmer, Greg and Mike Gasher. 2005. "Introduction: Catching Up to Runaway Productions." In *Contracting Out Hollywood: Runaway Productions and Foreign Location Shooting*, edited by Greg Elmer and Mike Gasher, 1–18. Lanham, MD: Rowman & Littlefield.

'The English Patient.' 1997. *Seinfeld*, Episode 17, Season 8. NBC: 13 March.

Evans, Michael Robert. 2008. *Isuma: Inuit Video Art*. Montreal and Kingston: McGill-Queen's University Press.

Fagan, Kristina. 2009. 'Weesageechak Meets the Weetigo: Storytelling, Humour, and Trauma in the Fiction of Richard Van Camp, Tomson Highway and Eden Robinson.' *Studies in Canadian Literature* 34, no. 1: 204–26.

Fatzinger, Amy S. 2016. '*Winter in the Blood*: A Case for Maintaining Cultural Content in Adaptations of Indigenous Stories.' *Adaptation* 9, no. 3: 307–27.

Fergus, Jan. 2003. 'Two *Mansfield Parks*: Purist and Postmodern.' In MacDonald and MacDonald 2003, 69–89.

Ferguson, Moira. 1991. '*Mansfield Park*: Slavery, Colonialism, and Gender.' *Oxford Literary Review* 13: 118–39.

Fermi, Sarah. 2015. 'A Question of Colour.' *Brontë Studies* 40, no. 4: 334–42.

Fleishman, Avrom. 1970 (1967). *A Reading of Mansfield Park: An Essay in Critical Synthesis*. Baltimore: Johns Hopkins University Press.

Flood, Jeanne. 1990. '*Black Robe*: Brian Moore's Appropriation of History.' *Eire-Ireland: A Journal of Irish Studies* 25, no. 4: 40–55.

Fowler, Corinne. 2017. 'Revisiting Mansfield Park: The Critical and Literary Legacies of Edward W. Said's Essay "Jane Austen and Empire" in *Culture and Imperialism* (1993).' *Cambridge Journal of Postcolonial Literary Inquiry*: 1–20.

Fowler, Corinne. 2020. *Green Unpleasant Land: Creative Responses to Rural England's Colonial Connections*. Leeds: Peepal Tree.

Fox, Alistair. 2011. *Jane Campion: Authorship and Personal Cinema*. Bloomington: Indiana University Press.

Fox, Alistair. 2017. *Coming-of-Age-Cinema in New Zealand*. Edinburgh: Edinburgh University Press.

Fraiman, Susan. 1995. 'Jane Austen and Edward Said: Gender, Culture, and Imperialism.' *Critical Inquiry* 21, no. 4: 805–21.

Francke, Lizzie. 2001 (1996). 'On the Brink.' In Vincendeau 2001, 81– 5.

Freebury, Jane. 1992. 'Black Robe: Ideological Cloak and Dagger?' *Australian-Canadian Studies* 10, no. 1: 119–26.

Friedman, Michael D. 2013. 'Where Was He Born? Speak! Tell Me!: Julie Taymor's *Tempest*, Hawaiian Slavery, and Birther Controversy.' *Shakespeare Bulletin* 31, no. 3: 431–52.

Frieze, Donna-Lee. 2012. 'The Other in Genocide: Responsibility and Benevolence in *Rabbit-Proof Fence*.' In *Film and Genocide*, edited by Kristi M. Wilson, 122–32. Madison: University of Wisconsin Press.

Ganti, Tejaswini. 2012. *Producing Bollywood: Inside the Contemporary Hindi Film Industry*. Durham, NC: Duke University Press.

Gauthier, Jennifer L. 2004. 'Indigenous Feature Films: A New Hope for National Cinemas?' *Cineaction* 64: 63–71.

Gay, Penny. 2004. 'Rozema's Fanny Price: Wild Colonial Girl.' In *Re-Drawing Austen: Picturesque Travels in Austenland*, edited by Beatrice Battaglia and Diego Saglia, 387–94. Naples: Liguori Editore.

Gentry, Ric. 1997. 'Painterly Touches.' *American Cinematographer*, January: 50–7.

Gera Roy, Anjali and Chua Beng Huat. 2012. 'The Bollywood Turn in South Asian Cinema: National, Transnational, or Global?' In *Travels of Bollywood Cinema: From Bombay to LA*, edited by Anjali Gera Roy and Chua Beng Huat, ix–xxxi. Delhi: Oxford University Press.

Geracht, Maurice A. 2016. 'Race in W. M. Thackeray's *Vanity Fair* and *The Virginians*.' *Image & Narrative* 17, no. 1: 43–54.

Gérin, Winifred. 1971. *Emily Brontë: A Biography*. Oxford: Clarendon.

Gilbert, Sandra M. and Susan Gubar. 1980. *The Madwoman in the Attic: The Woman Writer and the Nineteenth-Century Literary Imagination*. New Haven: Yale University Press.

Ginsburg, Faye. 2003. '*Atanarjuat* Off-Screen: From "Media Reservations" to the World Stage.' *American Anthropologist* 105, no. 4: 827–31.

Gittings, Christopher E. 2002. *Canadian National Cinema: Ideology, Difference and Representation*. London: Routledge.

Godbout, Jacques. 1990. Interview with Sherry Simon. In *Other Solitudes: Canadian Multicultural Fictions*, edited by Linda Hutcheon and Marion Richmond, 356–60. Toronto: Oxford University Press.

'Golf and Politics.' 2009 (1996). *The Rez*, Episode 2, Season 1. CBC Television; Toronto: Video Service Corp., DVD.

Gordon, Rebecca M. 2002. 'Portraits Perversely Framed: Jane Campion and Henry James.' *Film Quarterly* 56, no. 2: 14–24.

Gregory, Melissa Valiska. 2004. 'From Melodrama to Monology: Henry James and Domestic Terror.' *Henry James Review* 25: 146–67.

Griffin, Hollis. 2014. 'Songs from Nowhere: Integrating Music, Diaspora, and Gender in Gurinder Chadha's *Bride & Prejudice*.' *Quarterly Review of Film and Video* 31, no. 6: 531–41.

Groenendyk, Kathi. 2004. 'Modernizing *Mansfield Park*: Patricia Rozema's Spin on Jane Austen.' *Persuasions On-line* 25 no. 1: 1–6. http://jasna.org/persuasions/on-line/vol25no1/groenendyk.html?.

Gruß, Susanna. 2009. 'Negotiating Bollywood, Hollywood and Heritage Aesthetics in *Bride and Prejudice*.' *Zeitschrift für Anglistik and Americanistik* 57: 47–57.

Gunew, Sneja. 2004. *Haunted Nations: The Colonial Dimensions of Multiculturalisms*. London: Routledge.

Guy, Chantal. 2002. 'Les hauts et les bas de l'année littéraire 2002.' *La Presse*, 29 December: F2.

Hall, Catherine, Nicholas Draper and Keith McClelland. 2014a. *Legacies of British Slave-Ownership*. Cambridge: Cambridge University Press.

Hall, Catherine, Nicholas Draper and Keith McClelland. 2014b. 'Introduction.' In Hall, Draper and McClelland 2014a, 1–33.

Han, Jane. 2012. 'Behind the Scenes.' In *Midnight's Children*, DVD. London: Entertainment One UK.

Harris, Jocelyn. 2003. '"Such a transformation!": Translation, Imitation and Intertextuality in Jane Austen on Screen.' In MacDonald and MacDonald 2003, 44–68.

Hassam, Andrew. 2012. '"It Was Filmed in My Home Town": Diasporic Audiences and Foreign Locations in Indian Popular Cinema.' In *Travels of Bollywood Cinema: From Bombay to LA*, edited by Anjali Gera Roy and Chua Beng Huat, 260–78. Delhi: Oxford University Press.

Hateley, Erica. 2009. '"Everything's Turning to White": Palimpsestuous Revelations Made in the Journey from Jindabyne to *Jindabyne*.' *Antipodes* 23, no. 2: 141–6.

Hazette, Valérie V. 2015. *Wuthering Heights on Film & Television: A Journey across Time and Cultures*. Bristol: Intellect.

Heffelfinger, Elizabeth and Laura Wright. 2011. *Visual Difference: Postcolonial Studies and Intercultural Cinema*. New York: Peter Lang.

Heinen, Sandra. 2009. 'Gurinder Chadha's "Commodified Hybrid Utopia": The Programmatic Transculturalism and Culture-Specific Audience Address of *Bride and Prejudice*.' *Zeitschrift für Anglistik und Americanistik* 57: 59–70.

Hermansson, Casie. 2015. 'Flogging Fidelity: In Defense of the (Un)Dead Horse.' *Adaptation* 8, no. 2: 147–60.

Heywood, Christopher. 1987. 'Yorkshire Slavery in *Wuthering Heights*.' *Review of English Studies* 38 (150): 184–98.

Hicks, Patrick. 2004. 'The Languages of the Tribes in Brian Moore's *Black Robe*.' *Studies: An Irish Quarterly Review* 93: 415–26.

Higbee, Will and Song Hwee Lim. 2010. 'Concepts of Transnational Cinema: Towards a Critical Transnationalism in Film Studies.' *Transnational Cinemas* 1, no. 1: 7–21.

Higson, Andrew. 2003. *English Heritage, English Cinema: Costume Drama Since 1980*. Oxford: Oxford University Press.

Hokowhitu, Brendan. 2007. 'Understanding Whangara: *Whale Rider* as Simulacrum.' *New Zealand Journal of Media Studies* 10, no. 2: 53–70.

Hokowhitu, Brendan. 2008. 'The Death of Koro Paka: "Traditional" Māori Patriarchy.' *Contemporary Pacific* 20, no. 1: 115–41.

Hokowhitu, Brendan. 2013. 'Theorizing Indigenous Media.' In Hokowhitu and Devadas 2013a, 101–23.

Hokowhitu, Brendan and Vijay Devadas, eds. 2013a. *The Fourth Eye: Māori Media in New Zealand*. Minneapolis: University of Minnesota Press.

Hokowhitu, Brendan and Vijay Devadas. 2013b. 'Introduction: Fourth Eye. The Indigenous Mediascape in Aotearoa New Zealand.' In Hokowhitu and Devadas 2013a, xv–1.

Hollyfield, Jerod Ra'Del. 2018. *Framing Empire: Postcolonial Adaptations of Victorian Literature in Hollywood*. Edinburgh: Edinburgh University Press.

Hopkins, Lisa. 2009. *Relocating Shakespeare and Austen on Screen*. Basingstoke: Palgrave Macmillan.

Horne, Philip. 2001 (1998). In Vincendeau 2001, 85–91.

Horton, Jennifer L. 2012. 'Alone on the Snow, Alone on the Beach: "A Global Sense of Place" in *Atanarjuat* and *Fountain*.' *Journal of Transnational American Studies* 4, no. 1. https://escholarship.org/uc/item/54p2f9pq.

Hosking, Susan. 2011. 'Water, Soap and Sanitation: Assimilationist Whitewash and Stolen Generations Narratives in South-West Australia.' *Landscape, Place and Culture: Linkages between Australia and India*, edited by Deb N. Bandyopadhyay, Paul Brown and Christopher Conti, 218–36. Newcastle: Cambridge Scholars.

Huggan, Graham. 2001. *The Post-Colonial Exotic: Marketing the Margins*. London: Routledge.

Hughes D'aeth, Tony. 2002. 'Which Rabbit-Proof Fence? Empathy, Assimilation, Hollywood.' *Australian Humanities Review* 27. http://australianhumanitiesreview.org/2002/09/01/which-rabbit-proof-fence-empathy-assimilation-hollywood/.

Huhndorf, Shari. 2003. '*Atanarjuat, The Fast Runner*: Culture, History, and Politics in Inuit Media.' *American Anthropologist* 105, no. 4: 822–6.

Hussey, Miciah. 2016. 'Eyeing the Beholder: Henry James's Immaterial Portrait of a Lady.' *Henry James Review* 37: 174–90.

Hutcheon, Linda. 2013 (2006). *A Theory of Adaptation*. New York: Routledge.

Ihimaera, Witi. 1987. *The Whale Rider*. Harlow: Heinemann.

Ihimaera, Witi. 1998. Annotations to letter from John Barnett to Witi Ihimaera, 28 April. Victoria University Wellington library Accession 2002/39 Box 1/1.

Ihimaera, Witi. 2001. Briefing notes addressed to Andrew Shaw, 12 December. Victoria University Wellington library Accession A2003/026/02 Box 2/4.

Ihimaera, Witi and Ian Mune. [undated]. 'The Whale Rider.' 3rd draft. Victoria University Wellington Library Accession A2206/24 Box 1/1.

Iordanova, Dina, David Martin-Jones and Belén Vidal. 2010. 'Introduction: A Peripheral View of World Cinema.' In *Cinema at the Periphery*, edited by Dina Iordanova, David Martin-Jones and Belén Vidal, 1–19. Detroit: Wayne State University Press.

Irwin, Kathie. 1993. 'Towards Theories of Māori Feminisms.' In *Feminist Voices: Women's Studies Texts for Aotearoa/New Zealand*, edited by Rosemary DuPlessis, 1–21. Auckland: Oxford University Press.

Isuma TV. n.d. http://www.isuma.tv.

James, Henry. 1984 (1880–1; 1908). *The Portrait of a Lady*, edited by Geoffrey Moore. Harmondsworth: Penguin.

Jindabyne, directed by Ray Lawrence. 2007 (2006). London: Revolver Entertainment, DVD.

Johnson, Brian D. 1997. 'The Canadian Patient (Why Can't Canada Make Its Own Hit Movies).' *Maclean's*, 24 March: 42–6.

Johnson, Brian D. 2019. 'Tantoo Cardinal Finally Gets the Recognition She Deserves.' *Maclean's*, 3 January. https://www.macleans.ca/culture/movies/tantoo-cardinal-finally-gets-the-recognition-she-deserves/?fbclid=IwAR2jJneRn-PfjhPHRIuBnl SbFEcB94odNBd76zitrFcQr0y5vsWeLw78mUDA.

Johnson, Claudia L. 1988. *Jane Austen: Women, Politics, and the Novel*. Chicago: University of Chicago Press.

Johnson, Claudia L. 2000. 'Introduction.' In *Mansfield Park: Final Shooting Script*, by Patricia Rozema, 1–10. New York: Talk Miramax.

Johnson, Claudia L. 2012. *Jane Austen's Cults and Cultures*. Chicago: University of Chicago Press.

Johnson, Patricia E. 1997. 'The Gendered Politics of the Gaze: Henry James and George Eliot.' *Mosaic* 30, no. 1: 39–54.

Johnston, Emily R. 2014. 'Trauma Theory as Activist Pedagogy: Engaging Students as Reader-Witnesses of Colonial Trauma in *Once Were Warriors*.' *Antipodes* 28, no. 1: 5–17.

Jones, Gail. 2004. 'Sorry-in-the-Sky.' In *Imagining Australia*, edited by Judith Ryan and Chris Wallace-Crabbe, 159–71. Cambridge, MA: Harvard University Press.

Jones, Laura. 1997 (1996). *The Portrait of a Lady: The Screenplay Based on the Novel by Henry James*. London: Penguin.

Jordan, Elaine. 2000. 'Jane Austen Goes to the Seaside: *Sanditon*, English Identity and the "West Indian" Schoolgirl.' In Park and Rajan 2000, 29–55.

Joubin, Alexa Alice. 2017. 'Global Shakespeares in World Markets and Archives: An Introduction to the Special Issue.' *Borrowers and Lenders: The Journal of Shakespeare and Appropriation* 9, no. 1: 1–11. Proquest.

Joyce, Hester. 2007. 'Once Were Warriors.' In *The Cinema of Australia and New Zealand*, edited by Geoff Mayer and Keith Beattie, 157–64. London: Wallflower.

Joyce, Hester. 2009. 'Out from Nowhere: *Pakeha* Anxieties in *Ngati* (Barclay, 1987), *Once Were Warriors* (Tamahori, 1994) and *Whale Rider* (Caro, 2002).' *Studies in Australasian Cinema* 3, no. 3: 239–50.

Juchau, Mireille. 2006. 'Below the Surface.' Realtime 76. https://www.realtime.org.au/below-the-surface/.

Ka'ai, Tānia M. 2005. '*Te Kaue Mārō o Muri-ranga-whenua* (The Jawbone of Muri-ranga-whenua): Globalising Local Indigenous Culture – Māori Leadership, Gender and Cultural Knowledge Transmission as Represented in the Film *Whale Rider*.' *Portal Journal of Multidisciplinary International Studies* 2, no. 2: 1–15.

Kabir, Ananya Jahanara. 2002. 'Subjectivities, Memories, Loss of Pigskin Bags, Silver Spittoons and the Partition of India.' *Interventions* 4, no. 2: 245–64.

Kamboureli, Smaro. 2000. *Scandalous Bodies: Diasporic Literature in English Canada*. Don Mills, ON: Oxford University Press.

Kaplan, E. Ann. 2004. 'Traumatic Contact Zones and Embodied Translators: With Reference to Select Australian Texts.' In Kaplan and Wang 2004a, 45–63.

Kaplan, E. Ann and Ban Wang. 2004a, ed. *Trauma and Cinema: Cross-Cultural Explorations*. Aberdeen and Hong Kong: Hong Kong University Press.

Kaplan, E. Ann and Ban Wang. 2004b. 'Introduction: From Traumatic Paralysis to the Force Field of Modernity.' In Kaplan and Wang 2004a, 1–22.

Kappo, Tanya. 2014. 'Stephen Harper's Comments on Missing, Murdered Aboriginal Women Show "Lack of Respect".' *CBC News*, 19 December. https://www.cbc.ca/news/indigenous/stephen-harper-s-comments-on-missing-murdered-aboriginal-women-show-lack-of-respect-1.2879154.

Karan, Kavita and David J. Schaefer. 2012. 'Marketing, Hybridity, and Media Industries: Globalization and Expanding Audiences for Popular Hindi Cinema.' In *Bollywood and Globalization: Indian Popular Cinema, Nation, and Diaspora*, edited by Anjali Gera Roy and Chua Beng Huat, 78–97. Delhi: Oxford University Press.

Keeshig-Tobias, Lenore. 1990. 'Stop Stealing Native Stories.' In Ziff and Rao 1997a, 71–3.

Keneally, Thomas. 1972. *The Chant of Jimmie Blacksmith*. Harmondsworth: Penguin.

Keneally, Thomas. 1975. 'Doing Research for Historical Novels.' *Australian Author* 7.1: 27–9.

Kennedy, Rosanne. 2008. 'Vulnerable Children, Disposable Mothers: Holocaust and Stolen Generations Memoirs of Childhood.' *Life Writing* 5, no. 2: 161–84.

Ketterer, David. 2009. 'Yann Martel's *Life of Pi* and Poe's *Pym* (and "Berenice").' *Poe Studies: History, Theory, Interpretation* 42: 80–6.

Kinsella, W. P. 1994 (1977). *Dance Me Outside: More Tales from the Ermineskin Reserve*. Boston: Nonpareil.

Kinsella, W. P. 1986. *The Fencepost Chronicles*. Don Mills: Totem.

Kinsella, W. P. 1989. *The Miss Hobbema Pageant*. Toronto: Harper & Collins.

Kinsella, W. P. 1996 (1992). *Brother Frank's Gospel Hour*. Dallas: Southern Methodist University Press.

Kirkham, Margaret. 2000. *Jane Austen, Feminism and Fiction*. 2nd edn. London: Bloomsbury.

Klein, Dorothee. 2016. 'Narrating a Different (Hi)Story: The Affective Work of Counter-Discourse in Doris Pilkington's *Follow the Rabbit-Proof Fence*.' *Interventions* 18, no. 4: 588–604.

Klein, Michael. 1981. 'Introduction: Film and Literature.' In *The English Novel and the Movies*, edited by Michael Klein and Gillian Parker, 1–13. New York: Frederick Ungar.

Kluwick, Ursula. *Exploring Magic Realism in Salman Rushdie's Fiction*. New York: Routledge, 2011.

Knopf, Kerstin. 2008. *Decolonizing the Lens of Power: Indigenous Films in North America*. Amsterdam: Rodopi.

Kotierk, Aluki. 2021. "A New Conversation on Inuit Self-Government in Nunavut." Policy Brief. *Yellowhead Institute* 109, November. https://yellow-headinstitute.org/wp-content/uploads/2022/02/inuit-self-govt-nov-2021-kotierk.pdf.

Kramer, Lawrence. 2002. 'Recognizing Schubert: Musical Subjectivity, Cultural Change, and Jane Campion's *The Portrait of a Lady*.' *Critical Inquiry* 29, no. 1: 25–52.

Krupat, Arnold. 2007. '*Atanarjuat: The Fast Runner* and Its Audiences.' *Critical Inquiry* 33, no. 3: 606–31.

Kuwahara, Kuldip Kaur. 1995. 'Jane Austen's *Mansfield Park*, Property, and the British Empire.' *Persuasions* 17: 106–10.

Ladner, Kiera L. and Leanne Simpson. 2010. 'This Is an Honour Song.' In *This Is an Honour Song: Twenty Years Since the Blockades*, edited by Leanne Simpson and Kiera Ladner, 1–9. Winnipeg: Arbeiter Ring.

Lamm, Kimberly. 2011. 'A Future for Isabel Archer: Jamesian Feminism, Leo Bersani and Aesthetic Subjectivity.' *Henry James Review* 32: 249–58.

Landry, Donna. 2000. 'Learning to Ride at Mansfield Park.' In Park and Rajan 2000, 56–73.

'The Lark.' 2009 (1996). *The Rez*, Episode 5, Season 1. CBC Television; Toronto: Video Service Corp., DVD.

Lawn, Jennifer. 2011. 'Neoliberalism and the Politics of Indigenous Community in the Fiction of Alan Duff and Witi Ihimaera.' *Social Semiotics* 21, no. 1: 85–99.

Lawrence, Michael. 2016. 'Nature and the Non-human in Andrea Arnold's *Wuthering Heights*.' *Journal of British Cinema and Television* 13, no. 1: 177–94.

Leahy, David. 1988. 'History: Its Contradiction and Absence in Brian Moore's *The Revolution Script* and *Black Robe*.' *World Literature Written in English* 28, no. 2: 308–17.

Leberecht, Scott, dir. 2014. *Life after Pi*. Hollywood Ending Movie.

LeCouteur, Amanda. 2001. 'On Saying "Sorry": Repertoires of Apology to Australia's Stolen Generations.' In *How to Analyse Talk in Institutional Settings: A Casebook of Methods*, edited by Alec McHoul and Mark Rapley, 146–58. London: Continuum.

Lee, Ang. 2012. 'Introduction: Another Dimension: Some Thoughts on *Life of Pi*.' In Castelli 2012, 12–15.

Leiser, Mathiew. 2021. 'Inuit Short Film Makes the Oscars Short List.' *Eye on the Arctic*, 21 December. https://www.rcinet.ca/eye-on-the-arctic/2021/12/22/inuit-short-film-oscars-shaman/.

Leotta, Alfio. 2012. Touring the Screen: Tourism and New Zealand Film Geographies. Bristol: Intellect.

Lessard, Valérie. 2002. 'L'histoire de Yann.' *Le Droit*, 23 August: A2.

The Lesser Blessed, directed by Anita Doron. 2013 (2012). Prompton Plains, NJ: Monterey Media, DVD.

'The Lesser Blessed: Film Review.' 2013. *Hollywood Reporter*, 12 June. https://www.hollywoodreporter.com/movies/movie-reviews/lesser-blessed-film-review-567607/#!

Leunens, Christine. 2019. *Caging Skies*. London: John Murray.

Lewis, Randolph. 2006. *Alanis Obomsawin: The Vision of a Native Filmmaker*. Lincoln: University Nebraska Press.

Life of Pi, directed by Ang Lee. 2013 (2012). London: Twentieth-Century Fox Home Entertainment, DVD.

'Like Father, Like Son.' 2009 (1997). *The Rez*, Episode 4, Season 2. CBC Television; Toronto: Video Service Corp., DVD.

Lim, Song Hwee. 2012. 'Speaking in Tongues: Ang Lee, Accented Cinema, Hollywood.' In *Theorizing World Cinema*, edited by Lúcia Nagib, Chris Perriam and Rajinder Dudrah, 129–44. London: I. B. Tauris.

Loh, Lucienne. 2013. *The Postcolonial Country in Contemporary Literature*. Basingstoke: Palgrave Macmillan.

Lovrod, Marie. 2005. 'Shifting Contexts, Shaping Experiences: Child Abuse Survivor Narratives and Educating for Empire.' *Meridians* 5, no. 2: 30–56.

Lovrod, Marie. 2015. 'Narrow Escapes: Gendered Adolescent Resistance to Intergenerational Neo/Colonial Violence across Time and Space.' *Rocky Mountain Review* 69, no. 1: 68–86.

Lu, Wan-Jun. 2019. 'Made in Taiwan: Paratexts of *Life of Pi* and a Dynamic Sense of Place.' *Critical Studies in Media Communication* 36, no. 3: 235–48.

Luckhurst, Roger. 2009. 'Introduction.' In *The Portrait of a Lady* by Henry James, edited by Roger Luckhurst, vii–xxvi. Oxford: Oxford University Press.

Lusty, Terry. 1994. 'Dance Me Outside Maintains Stereotypes.' *Windspeaker* 12, no. 1: 18.

McCall, Sophie. 2011. *First Person Plural: Aboriginal Storytelling and the Ethics of Collaborative Authorship*. Vancouver: UBC Press.

McClintock, Anne. 1995. *Imperial Leather: Race, Gender, and Sexuality in the Colonial Contest*. New York: Routledge.

MacDonald, Andrew, and Gina MacDonald, eds. 2003. *Jane Austen on Screen*. Cambridge: Cambridge University Press.

McDonald, Bruce. [1991]. Fax to Tomson Highway. Tomson Highway Script Collection. University of Guelph library archives XZ1MSA889007, Box 1, File 5.

McDonald, Bruce and Steve Van Denzen. 2008. DVD commentary. *Dance Me Outside*. Toronto: Video Service Corp.

McFarlane, Brian. 1983. *Words and Images: Australian Novels into Film*. Richmond: Heinemann.

McFarlane, Brian. 1996. *Novel to Film: An Introduction to the Theory of Adaptation*. Oxford: Clarendon.

McGrath, Ann. 2010. '"Bad" History, Good Intentions and Australia's National Apology.' In *Antipodean Childhoods: Growing up in Australia and New Zealand*, edited by Helga Ramsey-Kurtz and Ulla Ratheiser, 47–67. Newcastle: Cambridge Scholars Press.

Machalias, Helen. 2011. 'Enraptured with Every Scent and Flavour of the East'? Mira Nair's *Vanity Fair* as a Contrapuntal Film Adaptation.' In *Pockets of Change: Adaptation and Cultural Transition*, edited by Jane Stadler, Peta Mitchell, Adam Atkinson and Tricia Hopton, 43–56. Lanham: Lexington.

McHugh, Kathleen A. 2007. *Jane Campion*. Urbana and Chicago: University of Illinois Press.

McHugh, Kathleen A. 2009. 'Jane Campion: Adaptation, Signature, Autobiography.' In Radner, Fox and Bessière 2009, 139–54.

McKegney, Sam. 2009. '"Beautiful Hunters with Strong Medicine": Indigenous Masculinity and Kinship in Richard Van Camp's *The Lesser Blessed*.' *Canadian Journal of Native Studies* 29, nos 1–2: 203–27.

Macrae, Ian J. and Samantha Mackinnon. 2017. 'The Sense of a Better Ending: Legal Pluralism and Performative Jurisprudence in *Atanarjuat the Fast Runner* [*sic*].' *Journal of Canadian Studies* 51, no. 3: 547–70.

McSweeney, Kerry. 'Sorceries.' Rev. of *Black Robe*. *Essays on Canadian Writing* 34: 111-118.

Malamud, Randy. 2012. '"Midnight's Children" Flourishes in Screen Adaptation.' *Chronicle of Higher Edu*cation, 8 October. https://www.chronicle.com/article/Midnights-Children/134832/.

Mallipeddi, Ramesh. 2016. *Spectacular Suffering: Witnessing Slavery in the Eighteenth-Century British Atlantic*. Charlottesville: University of Virginia Press.

Malone, Maggie. 1993. 'Patriarchy and Slavery and the Problem of Fanny in *Mansfield Park*.' *Essays in Poetics* 18, no. 2: 28–41.

Mansfield Park, directed by Patricia Rozema. 2000 (1997). London: Buena Vista Home Entertainment, DVD.

Mardorossian, Carine M. 2006. 'Geometries of Race, Class, and Gender: Identity Crossing in *Wuthering Heights*.' In *Approaches to Teaching Emily Brontë's Wuthering Heights*, edited by Sue Lonoff de Cuevas and Terri A. Hasseler, 44–50. New York: Modern Language Association of America.

Marks, Laura U. 1999. *The Skin of the Film: Intercultural Cinema, Embodiment, and the Senses*. Durham, NC: Duke University Press.

Martel, Yann. 2002a (2001). *Life of Pi*. Toronto: Vintage.

Martel, Yann. 2002b. 'May Richard Parker Be Always at Your Side.' *Guardian*, 26 November. https://www.theguardian.com/books/2002/nov/26/fiction.

Martel, Yann. 2002c. '*How I Wrote Life of Pi*.' Powells.com. www.powells.com/fromtheauthor/martel.html.

Martel, Yann. 2012. 'Foreword.' In Castelli 2012, 8–9.

Martin, Amy. 2012. 'A Battle on Two Fronts: *Wuthering Heights* and Adapting the Adaptation.' In *Film Remakes, Adaptations and Fan Productions*, edited by Kathleen Loock and Constantine Verevis, 67–86. Basingstoke: Palgrave Macmillan.

Martin, Keavy. 2012. *Stories in a New Skin: Approaches to Inuit Literature*. Winnipeg: University of Manitoba Press.

Mathur, Suchitra. 2007. 'From British "Pride" to Indian "Bride": Mapping the Contours of a Globalised (Post?)Colonialism.' *M/C Journal* 10, no. 2: 1–5.

Mee, Jon. 2000. 'Austen's Treacherous Ivory: Female Patriotism, Domestic Ideology, and Empire.' In Park and Rajan 2000, 74–92.

Meeuf, Russell. 2007 'Critical Localism, Ethical Cosmopolitanism and *Atanarjuat*.' *Third Text* 21, no. 6: 733–44.

Mehta, Rini Bhattacharya. 2010. 'Bollywood, Nation, Globalization: An Incomplete Introduction.' In *Bollywood and Globalization: Indian Popular Cinema, Nation, and Diaspora*, edited by Rini Bhattacharya Mehta and Rajeshwari V. Pandharipande, 1–14. London: Anthem.

Mendes, Ana Cristina and Joel Kuortti. 2017. 'Padma or No Padma: Audience in the Adaptations of *Midnight's Children*.' *Journal of Commonwealth Literature* 52, no. 3: 501–18.

Mercer, Kobena. 1994. *Welcome to the Jungle: New Positions in Black Cultural Studies*. Abingdon: Routledge.

Meyer, Susan. 1996. *Imperialism at Home: Race and Victorian Women's Fiction*. Ithaca: Cornell University Press.

Michie, Elsie. 1992. 'From Simianized Irish to Oriental Despots: Heathcliff, Rochester and Racial Difference.' *NOVEL* 25, no. 2: 125–40.

Midnight's Children, directed by Deepa Mehta. 2013 (2012). London: Entertainment One UK, DVD.

Miller, J. Hillis. 2005. *Literature as Conduct: Speech Acts in Henry James*. New York: Fordham University Press.

Miller, Mary Jane. 2003. 'The CBC and its Presentation of the Native Peoples of Canada in Television Drama.' In *Screening Culture: Constructing Image and Identity*, edited by Heather Norris Nicholson, 59–76. Lanham: Lexington.

Miller, Toby, Nitin Govil, John McMurria, Richard Maxwell and Ting Wang, 2005. *Global Hollywood 2*. London: BFI.

Mishra, Vijay. 2002. *Bombay Cinema: Temples of Desire*. New York and London: Routledge.

Mohanram, Radhika. 1996. 'The Construction of Place: Maori Feminism and Nationalism in Aotearoa/New Zealand.' *NWSA Journal* 8, no. 1: 50–69.

Moine, Raphaëlle. 2009. 'From Antipodean Cinema to International Art Cinema.' In Radner, Fox and Bessière 2009, 189–204.

Monaghan, David. 2007. 'Reinventing Fanny Price: Patricia Rozema's Thoroughly Modern *Mansfield Park*.' *Mosaic* 40, no. 2: 85–101.

Monk, Claire. 2001 (1995). 'Sexuality and Heritage.' In Vincendeau 2001, 6–11.

Mooney, Nicola. 2012. 'From Chandigarh to Vancouver: Reimagining Home and Identity in the Films of Harbhajan Mann.' In *Travels of Bollywood Cinema: From Bombay to LA*, edited by Anjali Gera Roy and Chua Beng Huat, 238-259. Delhi: Oxford University Press.

Moore, Brian. 1985a. *Black Robe*. London: Jonathan Cape.

Moore, Brian. 1985b. 'Black Robe.' Original first draft screenplay. International Cinema Corporation: 13 July. Harry Ransom Center Manuscript Collection MS-04867 Box 10, Folder 7.

Morrissey, Philip. 2007. 'Aboriginal Children.' *Australian Humanities Review* 42. http://australianhumanitiesreview.org/2007/08/01/aboriginal-children/.

Mottesheard, Ryan. 2003. 'Girl Power: New Zealand Writer/Director Niki Caro Talks About "Whale Rider."' *Indiewire*, 6 June. https://www.indiewire.com/2003/06/girl-power-new-zealand-writerdirector-niki-caro-talks-about-whale-rider-79678/#!

Moura-Koçoğlu, Michaela. 2012. 'From Noble Savage to Brave New Warrior? Constructions of a Maori Tradition of Warfare.' In *Literature for Our Times: Postcolonial Studies in the Twenty-First Century*, edited by Bill Ashcroft, Ranjini Mendis, Julie McGonegal and Arun Mukherjee, 369–82. Amsterdam: Rodopi.

Moya, Ana. 2010. 'The Politics of Re-Presenting *Vanity Fair*.' *Atlantis* 32, no. 2: 73–87.

Muir, John Kenneth. 2006. *Mercy in Her Eyes: The Films of Mira Nair*. New York: Applause Theatre and Cinema Books.

Mukherjee, Meenakshi, ed. 1999a. *Midnight's Children: A Book of Readings*. Delhi: Pencraft International.

Mukherjee, Meenakshi. 1999b. 'Introduction.' In Mukherjee 1999a, 9–27.

Mulvey, Laura. 1989. *Visual and Other Pleasures*. Bloomington: Indiana University Press.

Murdoch, Claire. 2003. 'Holy Sea-Cow.' *Landfall* 206: 97–105.

Murray, Simone. 2012. *The Adaptation Industry: The Cultural Economy of Contemporary Literary Adaptation*. New York and London: Routledge.

Murray, Stuart. 2008. *Images of Dignity: Barry Barclay and Fourth Cinema*. Wellington: Huia.

Nadel, Alan. 1997. 'The Search for Cinematic Identity and a Good Man: Jane Campion's Appropriation of James's Portrait.' *Henry James Review* 18, no. 2. Literature Online.

Naficy, Hamid. 2001. *An Accented Cinema*: *Exilic and Diasporic Filmmaking*. Princeton: Princeton University Press.

Naficy, Hamid. 2010. 'Multiplicity and Multiplexing in Today's Cinemas: Diasporic Cinema, Art Cinema, and Mainstream Cinema.' *Journal of Media Practice* 11, no. 1: 11–20.

Nagib, Lúcia. 2011. *World Cinema and the Ethics of Realism*. New York: Continuum.

Nair, Mira. 2005. DVD commentary. *Vanity Fair*. London: Universal Pictures.

Neville, A. O. 1948. *Australia's Coloured Minority: Its Place in the Community*. Sydney: Currawong.

'No Reservations.' 2009 (1997). *The Rez*, Episodes 12 and 13, Season 2. CBC Television; Toronto: Video Service Corp., DVD.

Norton, Sandy Morey. 1993. 'The Ex-Collector of Boggley-Wollah: Colonialism in the Empire of *Vanity Fair*.' *Narrative* 1, no. 2: 124–37.

Noyce, Phillip. 2011. DVD commentary. *Rabbit-Proof Fence*. London: StudioCanal.

Oder, Norman. 1996. 'Alan Duff and Once Were Warriors – Ventilating Race in New Zealand.' *Antipodes: A North American Journal of Australian Literature* 10, no. 2: 137–39.

O'Donoghue, Jo. 1993. 'Historical Themes, Missionary Endeavour and Spiritual Colonialism in Brian Moore's *Black Robe*.' *Studies: An Irish Quarterly Review* 82: 131–9.

Oliete Aldea, Elena. 2012. 'Gurinder Chadha's *Bride and Prejudice*: A Transnational Journey through Time and Space.' *International Journal of English Studies* 12, no. 1: 167–82.

Olsen, Christine. 2002. *Rabbit-Proof Fence: The Screenplay*. Sydney: Currency.

Once Were Warriors, directed by Lee Tamahori. 1999 (1994). London: Entertainment in Video, DVD.

O'Regan, Tom. 1996. *Australian National Cinema*. London: Routledge.

Orr, Christopher. 1984. 'The Discourse on Adaptation.' *Wide Angle* 6, no. 2: 72–6.

Orr, Jeffrey. 2013. 'Strangers in Strange Lands: Cultural Translation in Gaétan Soucy's *Vaudeville!*' In *Parallel Encounters: Culture at the Canada–US Border*, edited by Gillian Roberts and David Stirrup, 279–92. Waterloo: Wilfrid Laurier University Press.

Park, You-me and Rajeswari Sunder Rajan, eds. 2000. *The Postcolonial Jane Austen*. London: Routledge.

Parkman, Francis. 1900 (1867). *The Jesuits in North America in the Seventeenth Century*, volume 1. Toronto: George N. Morang.

Parrinder, Patrick. 2006. *Nation and Novel: The English Novel from its Origins to the Present Day*. Oxford: Oxford University Press.

Payne, Tom. 2002. 'The Weird Bunch: This Year's Booker Prize Shortlist Is Full of Strange Books by Non-English Writers.' *Daily Telegraph*, 28 September: 12.

Perry, Ruth. 1994. 'Austen and Empire: A Thinking Woman's Guide to British Imperialism.' *Persuasions* 16: 95–105.

Petzke, Ingo. 2007. 'Rabbit-Proof Fence.' In *The Cinema of Australia and New Zealand*, edited by Geoff Mayer and Keith Beattie, 233–9. London: Wallflower.

Phillips, Caryl. 2015. *The Lost Child*. London: Oneworld.

Pilkington, Doris/Nugi Garimara. 2002a. (1996). *Follow the Rabbit-Proof Fence*. St Lucia: Queensland University Press.

Pilkington, Doris/Nugi Garimara. 2002b. *Under the Wintamarra Tree*. St Lucia: Queensland University Press.

Pilkington, Doris/Nugi Garimara. 2007. 'The Stolen Generations: Rites of Passage: Doris Pilkington Interviewed by Anne Brewster.' *Journal of Commonwealth Literature* 42, no. 1: 143–59.

Pitts, Virginia. 2013. 'Contestations of Intercultural Collaboration: The Case of *Whale Rider*.' In *Impure Cinema: Intermedial and Intercultural Approaches to Film*, edited by Lúcia Nagib and Anne Jerslev, 43–65. London: I. B. Tauris.

Plasa, Carl. 2000. *Textual Politics from Slavery to Postcolonialism: Race and Identification*. Basingstoke: Palgrave Macmillan.

Podemski, Jennifer. 2009. DVD commentary. 'Poster Girl.' *The Rez*. Toronto: Video Service Corp.

Podemski, Jennifer. 2019. 'Jennifer Podemski on APTN's Future History.' Interview with Anne Brodie. *What She Said Radio*, 13 May. www.whatshe-saidradio.com/what-she-said/jennifer-podemski-on-aptns-future-history/.

Podemski, Tamara. 2013. Interview with Tamara Podemski. *The Lesser Blessed* [DVD]. Prompton Plains, NJ: Monterey Media.

Polan, Dana. 2001. *Jane Campion*. London: British Film Institute.

Ponzanesi, Sandra. 2014. *The Postcolonial Cultural Industry: Icons, Markets, Mythologies*. Basingstoke and New York: Palgrave Macmillan.

The Portrait of a Lady, directed by Jane Campion 2001 (1996). London: Universal Pictures UK, DVD.

'Poster Girl.' 2009 (1997). *The Rez*, Episode 3, Season 2. CBC Television; Toronto: Video Service Corp., DVD.

Potter, Emily and Kay Schaffer. 2004. '*Rabbit-Proof Fence*, Relational Ecologies and the Commodification of Indigenous Experience.' *Australian Humanities Review* 31–2. http://australianhumanitiesreview.org/2004/04/01/rabbit-proof-fence-relational-ecologies-and-the-commodification-of-indigenous-experience/.

Prentice, Chris. 2006. 'Riding the Whale? Postcolonialism and Globalization in *Whale Rider*.' In *Global Fissures: Postcolonial Fusions*, edited by Clara A. B. Joseph and Janet Wilson, 247–67. Amsterdam: Rodopi.

Preus, Nicholas. 1995. 'Power Houses and Polite Fiction.' *Persuasions* 17: 167–74.

Pride and Prejudice, directed by Simon Langton. 1995. BBC Television.

Pride and Prejudice, directed by Robert Z. Leonard. 1940. BBC2 Television. Broadcast 17 February 2016. https://learningonscreen.ac.uk/ondemand/index.php/prog/000EBF98?bcast=121073794.

Pucci, Suzanne R. 2003. 'The Return Home.' In *Jane Austen and Co.: Remaking the Past in Contemporary Culture*, edited by Suzanne R. Pucci and James Thompson, 133-55. Albany: State University of New York Press.

Punathambekar, Aswin. 2013. *From Bombay to Bollywood: The Making of a Global Media Industry*. New York: New York University Press.

Pybus, Cassandra. 2011. 'Tense and Tender Ties: Reflections on Lives Recovered from the Intimate Frontier of Empire and Slavery.' *Life Writing* 8, no. 1: 5–17.

Rabbit-Proof Fence, directed by Phillip Noyce. 2011 (2002). London: StudioCanal, DVD.

Radner, Hilary, Alistair Fox and Irène Bessière, eds. 2009. *Jane Campion: Cinema, Nation, Identity*. Detroit: Wayne State University Press.

Raheja, Michelle H. 2007. 'Reading Nanook's Smile: Visual Sovereignty, Indigenous Revisions of Ethnography, and *Atanarjuat (the Fast Runner)*.' *American Quarterly* 59, no. 4: 1159–85.

Ralph, Iris. 2014. 'The Systemic Approach, Biosemiotic Theory, and Ecocide in Australia.' *CLCWeb: Comparative Literature and Culture* 16, no. 4. https://docs.lib.purdue.edu/clcweb/vol16/iss4/7/.

Randall, Catharine. 2010. *Black Robes and Buckskin: A Selection from the Jesuit Relations*. New York: Fordham University Press.

Raphael, Amy. 2011. 'Love Will Tear Us Apart.' *Sight & Sound*, December 2011: 34–6.

Rauwerda, Antje M. 2004. 'Book and Film Review: The Whale Rider.' *Postcolonial Text* 1, no. 1. http://postcolonial.org/index.php/pct/article/view Article/292/779.

Rayner, Jonathan. 2009. 'Adapting Australian Film: Ray Lawrence from *Bliss* to *Jindabyne*.' *Studies in Australasian Cinema* 3, no. 2: 295–308.

Renes, Cornelis Martin. 2011. '*Once Were Warriors*, But How About Maoritanga Now? Novel and Film as a Dialogic Third Space.' *Miscelánea* 44: 87–105.

Renes, Cornelis Martin. 2013. 'Kim Scott's Fiction within Western Australian Life-Writing: Voicing the Violence of Removal and Displacement.' *Coolabah* 10: 177–89.

Renes, Cornelis Martin. 2014. 'Reel Indigeneity: *Ten Canoes* and Its Chronotopical Politics of Ab/Originality.' *Continuum: Journal of Media and Cultural Studies* 28, no. 6: 850-61.

Resnick, Laura. 2005. 'Bride and Prejudice.' In *Flirting with* Pride and Prejudice*: Fresh Perspectives on the Original Chick Lit Masterpiece,* edited by Jennifer Crusie with Glenn Yeffeth, 87–96. Dallas: BenBella.

Reynolds, Henry. 1979. 'Jimmy Governor and Jimmie Blacksmith.' *Australian Literary Studies* 9, no. 1: 14–25.

Reynolds, Henry. 2008. *The Chant of Jimmie Blacksmith*. Sydney: Currency.

Richards, Will. 2021. 'Mumford & Sons' Winston Marshall Praises "Brave" Right-wing Agitator Andy Ngo.' *NME*, 7 March. https://www.nme.com/news/music/mumford-sons-winston-marshall-praises-brave-right-wing-agitator-andy-ngo-2895342.

Roberts, Gillian. 2002. '"Sins of Omission": *The English Patient*, THE ENGLISH PATIENT, and the Critics.' *Essays on Canadian Writing* 76: 195–215.

Roberts, Gillian. 2011. *Prizing Literature: The Celebration and Circulation of National Culture*. Toronto: University of Toronto Press.

Rocha Antunes, Luis. 2015. 'Adapting with the Senses – *Wuthering Heights* as a Perceptual Experience.' *The Victorian* 3, no. 1: 1–12.

Roy, Sohinee. 2016. 'Beyond Crossover films: *Bride and Prejudice* and the Problems of Representing Postcolonial India in a Neoliberal World.' *Journal of Popular Culture* 49, 5: 984–1002.

Royal, Te Ahukaramū Charles. 2017. 'Politics and Knowledge: Kaupapa Māori and Mātauranga Māori.' In *Critical Conversations in Kaupapa Māori*, edited by Te Kawehau Hoskins and Alison Jones. Wellington: Huia.

Rozema, Patricia. 2000. *Mansfield Park: Final Shooting Script*. New York: Hyperion.

Rozema, Patricia. 2004. '*Mansfield Park* and Film.' Interview with Hiba Moussa. *Literature / Film Quarterly* 32, no. 4: 255–60.

Rushdie, Salman. 1995 (1981). *Midnight's Children*. London: Vintage.

Rushdie, Salman. 2002 (1999). 'Adapting *Midnight's Children*.' In *Step Across this Line: Collected Non-Fiction, 1992–2002*. London: Jonathan Cape.

Rushdie, Salman. 2010a (1991). *Imaginary Homelands: Essays and Criticism 1981–1991*. London: Vintage.

Rushdie, Salman. 2010b. (1982). 'Imaginary Homelands.' In Rushdie 2010a, 9–21.

Rushdie, Salman. 2010c. (1987). 'The Riddle of Midnight: India, August 1987.' In Rushdie 2010a, 26–33.

Rutherford, Anne. 2013. '*Ten Canoes* as Inter-Cultural Membrane.' *Studies in Australasian Cinema* 7, no. 2–3: 137–51.

Ryan-Fazilleau, Sue. 2002. 'Thomas Keneally's *The Chant of Jimmie Blacksmith* and the Palimpsest of Jimmy Governor.' *Commonwealth* 25, no. 1: 27–40.

Rymhs, Deena. 2006. 'Auto/biographical Jurisdictions: Collaboration, Self-Representation, and the Law in *Stolen Life: The Journey of a Cree Woman*.' In *Auto/biography in Canada: Critical Directions*, edited by Julie Rak, 89–108. Waterloo, ON: Wilfrid Laurier University Press.

Sadoff, Dianne F. 1998. '"Intimate Disarray": The Henry James Movies.' *Henry James Review* 19, no. 3. Literature Online.

Said, Edward W. 1994 (1993). *Culture and Imperialism*. London: Vintage.

Saladin d'Anglure, Bernard. 2002. 'An Ethnographic Commentary: The Legend of Atanarjuat, Inuit and Shamanism.' In Apak Angilirq, Cohn and Saladin d'Anglure 2002, 196–227.

Sales, Roger. 2004. 'Paying the Price for the Party: Patricia Rozema's 1999 Version of *Mansfield Park*.' In *Re-Drawing Austen: Picturesque Travels in Austenland*, edited by Beatrice Battaglia and Diego Saglia, 177–94. Naples: Liguori Editore.

Saltman, Judi. 2003. Interview with Richard Van Camp. www.hanksville.org/storytellers/VanCamp/JSaltman.html.

Sanders, Julie. 2006. *Adaptation and Appropriation*. London: Routledge.

Sands, Kathleen Mullen. 1997. 'Collaboration or Colonialism: Text and Process in Native American Women's Autobiographies.' *MELUS* 22, no. 4: 39–59.

Schembri, Jim. 2006. 'Ray Lawrence Knows Who You Are.' *The Age*, 28 July: Entertainment Guide 8.

Schepisi, Fred. 2008. DVD commentary. *The Chant of Jimmie Blacksmith*. Kew, Victoria: Umbrella Entertainment.

Scliar, Moacyr. 2003 (1981). *Max and the Cats*. Translated by Eloah F. Giacomelli. New York: Plume.

Scott, James F. 2012. 'Performing Christendom in the Imperial Discourse of *Black Robe*.' *Allegorica* 28: 126–42.

Seeber, Barbara K. 2007. 'A Bennet Utopia: Adapting the Father in *Pride and Prejudice*.' *Persuasions On-line* 27, no. 2: 1–10.

Seguin, Denis. 2005. 'Freeze Frame.' *Canadian Business* 76, no. 17: 43–6.

Shachar, Hila. 2012. *Cultural Afterlives and Screen Adaptations of Classic Literature: Wuthering Heights and Company*. London: Palgrave Macmillan.

Shepheard, Nicola. 2003. 'Niki Caro: Riding the Whale.' *North & South* 203 (February): 80–7.

Shohat, Ella and Robert Stam. 1994. *Unthinking Eurocentrism: Multiculturalism and the Media*. London: Routledge.

Short Cuts, directed by Robert Altman. 2007 (1993). London: Paramount Home Entertainment, DVD.

Shubow, Justin. 2003. 'Cold Comfort.' *The American Prospect*, 28 February 2003. https://prospect.org/article/cold-comfort/.

Siebert, Monika. 2006. '*Atanarjuat* and the Ideological Work of Contemporary Indigenous Filmmaking.' *Public Culture* 18, no. 3: 531–50.

Simpson, Audra. 2014. *Mohawk Interruptus: Political Life across the Borders of the Settler States*. Durham, NC: Duke University Press.

Simpson, Audra. 2016. 'The State is a Man: Theresa Spence, Loretta Saunders and the Gender of Settler Sovereignty.' *Theory & Event* 19 no. 4. http://muse.jhu.edu/article/633280.

Smith, Andrew. 2011. 'C. L. R. James, *Vanity Fair* and the Audience.' *New Formations* 73: 11–25.

Smith, Linda Tuhiwai. 2012. *Decolonizing Methodologies: Research and Indigenous Peoples*. 2nd edn. London: Zed.

Soukup, Katarina. 2006. 'Report: Travelling through Layers: Inuit Artists Appropriate New Technologies.' *Canadian Journal of Communication* 31: 239–46.

'South Pacific Pictures Nets Whale of a Film Project.' 2001. *Onfilm*, October 2001: 12.

Srikanth, Anagha. 2020. 'The Oscars Acknowledged the Indigenosu Land Hollywood Sits On.' *The Hill*, 10 February. https://thehill.com/changing-america/enrichment/arts-culture/482357-the-oscars-acknowledged-the-indigenous-land/.

Stables, Kate. 2013. Rev. of *Midnight's Children*. *Sight and Sound*, January: 103.

Stadtler, Florian. 2012. 'Rushdie's Hero as Audience: Interpreting India through Indian Popular Cinema.' In *Postcolonial Audiences: Readers, Viewers and*

Reception, edited by Bethan Benwell, James Proctor and Gemma Robinson, 115–27. New York: Routledge.

Stadtler, Florian. 2014. *Fiction, Film, and Indian Popular Cinema Salman Rushdie's Novels and the Cinematic Imagination*. New York: Routledge.

Stam, Robert. 2005. *Literature through Film: Realism, Magic, and the Art of Adaptation*. Malden, MA and Oxford: Blackwell.

Stevenson, John Allen. 1988. '"Heathcliff Is Me!": *Wuthering Heights* and the Question of Likeness.' *Nineteenth-Century Literature* 43, no. 1: 60–81.

Stewart, Garrett. 1999. Between Film and Screen: Modernism's Photo Synthesis. Chicago: University of Chicago Press.

Stewart, Maaja A. 1993. *Domestic Realities and Imperial Fictions: Jane Austen's Novels in Eighteenth-Century Contexts*. Athens: University of Georgia Press.

Stoneman, Patsy. 2012. 'Adaptations, Prequels, Sequels, Translations.' In *The Brontës in Context*, edited by Marianne Thormahlen, 207–23. Cambridge: Cambridge University Press.

Stratmann, Gerd. 2009. 'Currying the Victorian Novel: Mira Nair's "Indianised" Version of *Vanity Fair*.' *Zeitschrift fur Anglistik und Amerikanistik* 57, no. 1: 83–91.

Stratton, Florence. 2004. '"Hollow at the Core": Deconstructing Yann Martel's *Life of Pi*.' *Studies in Canadian Literature* 29, no. 2: 5–21.

Stratton, Jon. 2009. 'The Murderous State: The Naturalisation of Violence and Exclusion in the Films of Neoliberal Australia.' *Cultural Studies Review* 15, no. 1: 11–32.

Syed, Mujeebuddin. 1999 (1994). '*Midnight's Children and Its Indian Con-Texts*.' In Mukherjee 1999, 149–64.

Tamahori, Lee. 1995. 'Social Realism with Style: Interview with Lee Tamahori.' Interview with Robert Sklar. *Cinéaste* 21, no. 3: 25–7.

Tankard, Alexandra. 2008. 'Emasculation, Eugenics, and the Consumptive Voyeur in *The Portrait of a Lady* (1881) and *The Story of a Nobody* (1893).' *Critical Survey* 20: 61–78.

Thackeray, William Makepeace. 1983 (1847–8). *Vanity Fair*. Oxford: Oxford University Press.

Thompson, Kirsten Moana. 2003. '*Once Were Warriors*: New Zealand's First Indigenous Blockbuster.' In *Movie Blockbusters*, edited by Julian Stringer, 230–41. London: Routledge.

Thomson, Patricia. 2012. 'Wild Passion: Robbie Ryan, BSC and Director Andrea Arnold Set Their Bold Version of *Wuthering Heights* in a Vivid, Tactile World.' *American Cinematographer*, May: 42–51.

Thorner, Sabra G. 2007. 'Changing the Rules of Engagement: How *Rabbit-Proof Fence* and *Whale Rider* Forge a New Dimension of Ethnographic Media.' *Visual Anthropology Review* 23, no. 2: 137–50.

Thornham, Sue. 2016. '"Not a Country at All": Landscape and *Wuthering Heights*.' *Journal of British Cinema and Television* 13, no. 1: 214–31.

Thornley, Davinia. 2001. 'White, Brown, or "Coffee"? Revisioning Race in Tamahori's *Once Were Warriors*.' *Film Criticism* 25, no. 3: 22–36.

Tincknell, Estella. 2013. *Jane Campion and Adaptation: Angels, Demons and Unsettling Voices*. Basingstoke: Palgrave Macmillan.

Todd, Douglas. 2016 (1994). 'W. P. Kinsella Rejected Religion, Academics and Afterlife.' *Vancouver Sun*, 16 May. https://vancouversun.com/news/staff-blogs/w-p-kinsella-rejected-religion-academics-and-afterlife.

Treagus, Mandy. 2008. 'Representing Pacific Tattoos: Issues in Postcolonial Critical Practice.' *Journal of Postcolonial Writing* 44, no. 2: 183–92.

Troost, Linda and Sayre Greenfield. 2008. 'Appropriating Austen: Localism on the Global Scene.' *Persuasions On-line* 28, no. 2: 1–11. www.jasna.org/persuasions/on-line/vol28no2/troost-greenfield.htm.

Trousdale, Rachel. 2004. '"City of Mongrel Joy": Bombay and the Shiv Sena in *Midnight's Children*.' *Journal of Commonwealth Literature* 39, vol. 2: 95–110.

Trumpener, Katie. 1997. *Bardic Nationalism: The Romantic Novel and the British Empire*. Princeton: Princeton University Press.

Tsao, Tiffany. 2014. 'Postcolonial Life and Death: A Process-Based Comparison of Emily Brontë's *Wuthering Heights* and Auy Utami's *Saman*.' *Comparative Literature* 66, no. 1: 95–112.

Tuck, Eve and K. Wayne Yang. 2012. 'Decolonization Is Not a Metaphor.' *Decolonization: Indigeneity, Education & Society* 1, no 1: 1–40.

Tuite, Clara. 2000. 'Domestic Retrenchment and Imperial Expansion: The Property Plots of *Mansfield Park*.' In Park and Rajan 2000, 93–115.

Turner, Graeme. 1988. 'Breaking the Frame: The Representation of Aborigines in Australian Film.' *Kunapipi* 10, no. 1–2: 135–45.

Turner, Stephen. 2002. 'Sovereignty, or the Art of Being Native.' *Cultural Critique* 51: 74–100.

Turner, Stephen. 2013. 'Reflections on Barry Barclay and Fourth Cinema.' In Hokowhitu and Devadas 2013a, 162–78.

Universal Studios. 2004. *Vanity Fair: Bringing Thackeray's Timeless Novel to the Screen*. New York: Newmarket Press.

Verhoeven, Deb. 2009. *Jane Campion*. London: Routledge.

Van Camp, Richard. 1996. *The Lesser Blessed*. Vancouver: Douglas & MacIntyre.

Van Camp, Richard. 2013. Interview with Richard Van Camp. *The Lesser Blessed* [DVD]. Prompton Plains, NJ: Monterey Media.

Vanity Fair, directed by Marc Munden (1998). BBC Television.

Vanity Fair, directed by Mira Nair. 2005. London: Universal Pictures, DVD.

Vedal, Lauren. 2013. 'Closure or Connections? Healing from Trauma in Richard Van Camp's *The Lesser Blessed*.' *Studies in Canadian Literature* 38, no. 2: 106–25.

Vidal, Belén. 2006. 'Playing in a Minor Key: The Literary Past through the Feminist Imagination.' In *Books in Motion: Adaptation, Intertextuality, Authorship*, edited by Mireia Aragay, 263–84. Amsterdam: Rodopi.

Villella, Fiona. 2002. 'Long Road Home: Phillip Noyce's *Rabbit-Proof Fence*.' *Senses of Cinema* 19. http://sensesofcinema.com/2002/australian-cinema-and-culture/rabbit/.

Vincendeau, Ginette, ed. 2001. *Film/Literature/Heritage*. London: British Film Institute.

Vincent, Isabel. 2002. '"New Chapter in Nation's Rage Toward Canada": Beef, Bombardier, Books.' *National Post*, 7 November: A1. Nexis.

Vine, Steven. 1994. 'The Wuther of the Other in *Wuthering Heights*.' *Nineteenth-Century Literature* 49, no. 2: 339–59.

Von Sneidern, Maja-Lisa. 1995. '*Wuthering Heights* and the Liverpool Slave Trade.' *ELH* 62, no. 1: 171–96.

Vranckx, Sylvie. 2011. 'The Ambivalence of Cultural Syncreticity in Highway's *Kiss of the Fur Queen* and Van Camp's *The Lesser Blessed*.' In *Old Margins and New Centers*, edited by Marc Maufort and Caroline De Wagter, 291–305. Brussels: Peter Lang.

Wagner, Geoffrey. 1975. *The Novel and the Cinema*. Rutherford, NJ: Fairleigh Dickinson University Press.

Walcott, Rinaldo. 2003. *Black Like Who? Writing Black Canada*. 2nd edn. Toronto: Insomniac.

Waller, Gregory A. 1998. 'Embodying the Urban Maori Warrior.' In *Places through the Body*, edited by Heidi J. Nast and Steve Pile, 337–55. London: Routledge.

Walton, Priscilla L. 1997. 'Jane and James Go to the Movies: Post-colonial Portraits of a Lady.' *Henry James Review* 18, no. 2. Literature Online.

Wang, Yiman. 2005. 'The Art of Screen Passing: Anna May Wong's Yellow Yellowface Performance in the Art Deco Era.' *Camera Obscura* 60: 159–92.

Watson, Tim. 2005. 'Improvements and Reparations at Mansfield Park.' In *Literature and Film: A Guide to the Theory and Practice of Film Adaptation*, edited by Robert Stam and Alessandra Raengo, 53–70. Malden, MA; Oxford: Blackwell.

Werry, Margaret. 2011. *Tourist State: Performing Leisure, Liberalism, and Race in New Zealand*. Minneapolis: University of Minnesota Press.

Wesling, Meg. 2008. 'Why Queer Diaspora?' *Feminist Review* 90: 30–47.

Whale Rider, directed by Niki Caro. 2008 (2002). London: Icon Films, DVD.

Wilinsky, Barbara. 2001. *Sure Seaters: The Emergence of Art House Cinema*. Minneapolis: University of Minnesota Press.

Williams, Raymond. 1975 (1973). *The Country and the City*. St Albans: Paladin.

Wilson, Cheryl A. 2006. '*Bride and Prejudice*: A Bollywood Comedy of Manners.' *Literature/Film Quarterly* 34, no. 4: 323–31.

Wilson, Janet. 2007. 'Reconsidering Fred Schepisi's *The Chant of Jimmie Blacksmith* (1978): The Screen Adaptation of Thomas Keneally's Novel (1972).' *Studies in Australasian Cinema* 1, no. 2: 191–207.

Wilson, Janet. 2011. 'Re-presenting Indigeneity: Approaches to History in Some Recent New Zealand and Australian Films.' In *New Zealand Cinema: Interpreting the Past*, edited by Barry Keith, Alistair Fox and Hilary Radner, 197–215. Bristol and Chicago: Intellect.

Wilson, Jordan. 2008. An Interview with Richard Van Camp. http://canlit.ca/an-interview-with-richard-van-camp-december-2008/.

Wiltshire, John. 2003. 'Decolonising *Mansfield Park*.' *Essays in Criticism* 53, no. 4: 303–322.

Whitlock, Gillian. 2001. 'In the Second Person: Narrative Transactions in Stolen Generations Testimony.' *Biography* 24, no. 1: 197–214.

Wuthering Heights, directed by Andrea Arnold. 2012 (2011). London: Artificial Eye, DVD.

Wynne-Davies, Marion. 1999. 'The Rhythm of Difference: Language and Silence in *The Chant of Jimmie Blacksmith* and *The Piano*.' In *Post-Colonial Literatures: Expanding the Canon*, edited by Debora L. Madsen, 58–71. London: Pluto.

Yeazell, Ruth Bernard. 1984. 'The Boundaries of Mansfield Park.' *Representations* 7: 133–52.

Younging, Gregory. 2018. *Elements of Indigenous Style: A Guide for Writing By and About Indigenous Peoples*. Edmonton: Brush Education.

Yuen, Nancy Wang. 2017. *Reel Inequality: Hollywood Actors and Racism*. New Brunswick, NJ: Rutgers University Press.

Zagarell, Sandra A. 2014. '*The Portrait of a Lady*: "No Intention of Deamericanising."' *Henry James Review* 35, no. 1: 23–33.

Ziff, Bruce and Pratima V. Rao, eds. 1997a. *Borrowed Power: Essays on Cultural Appropriation*. New Brunswick, NJ: Rutgers University Press.

Ziff, Bruce and Pratima V. Rao. 1997b. 'Introduction to Cultural Appropriation: A Framework for Analysis.' In Ziff and Rao 1997a, 1–27.

Zoli, Corri. 2007. '"Black Holes" of Calcutta and London: Internal Colonies in *Vanity Fair*.' *Victorian Literature and Culture* 35: 417–49.

Index

Note: *italic* indicates figure; n signifies note